Records Management

SEVENTH EDITION

AUTHORS

Judith Read-Smith
Instructor & Department Chair
Computer Information Systems
Portland Community College
Portland, Oregon

Mary Lea Ginn, Ph.D.
Content Development Consultant
Cincinnati, Ohio

Norman F. Kallaus
Professor Emeritus
University of Iowa
Iowa City, Iowa

CONTRIBUTING AUTHORS

Joyce P. Logan
Associate Professor
College of Education
University of Kentucky
Lexington, Kentucky

Jane Connerton, CRM
Corporate Records Manager
Procter and Gamble
Cincinnati, Ohio

Marti Fischer, CRM
Iron Mountain Consulting Services LLP
San Jose, California

SOUTH-WESTERN
★
THOMSON LEARNING

Australia • Canada • Mexico • Singapore • Spain • United Kingdom • United States

SOUTH-WESTERN
THOMSON LEARNING

Records Management, 7th edition
by Judith Read-Smith, Mary Lea Ginn, and Norman F. Kallaus

Executive Editor:
Karen Schmohe

Developmental Consulting Editor:
Dianne S. Rankin

Permissions Editor:
Linda Ellis

Project Manager:
Marilyn Hornsby

Production Manager:
Jane Congdon

Cover Design:
Lamson Design

Editor:
Martha Conway

Manufacturing Manager:
Carol Chase

Internal Design:
Lamson Design

Channel Coordinator:
Chris McNamee

Art and Design Coordinator:
Darren Wright

Compositor:
Custom Editorial Productions, Inc.

Marketing Coordinator:
Sharon Turner

Photo Researcher:
Fred Middendorf

Printer:
RR Donnelley

For more information, contact
South-Western Educational Publishing
5101 Madison Road
Cincinnati, OH 45227-1490.
Or you can visit our Internet site at
www.swep.com.

For permission to use material from this text or product, contact us by
Phone: 1-800-730-2214
Fax: 1-800-730-2215
www.thomsonrights.com

Library of Congress Cataloging-in-Publication Data
Read-Smith, Judith,
   Records management / Judith Read Smith, Mary Lea Ginn, Norman F. Kallaus; contributing authors, Joyce P. Logan, Jane Connerton, Marti Fischer.7th ed.
         p. cm.
   Includes index.
   ISBN 0-538-96931-8 (alk. paper)
   1. Filing systems.   2. Records--Management.   I. Ginn, Mary L. (Mary Lea)- II. Kallaus, Norman Francis   III. Title.
HF5736 .JC 2002
651.5'3--dc21   00-06793

THE FUTURE OF RECORDS MANAGEMENT!

Records Management 7E is a comprehensive introduction to the increasingly complex field of records management. The text and accompanying material cover filing and management of the records system. South-Western is dedicated to providing you with materials that will prepare you for your future, so join us as we enter an information age that will require a comprehensive knowledge of records management.

Text/Data Disk Package	0-538-72466-8
Study Guide	0-538-72467-6
Practice Set	0-538-72468-4

PREPARE yourself for continued success with these additional office professional resources from South-Western. The information age is here, and South-Western is paving the way with these market-leading texts!

Procedures for the Office Professional

Equip yourself to handle the ever-changing workplace with this comprehensive text for office professionals. Instructions and activities directed toward technology, communication, human relations, and decision-making will lead you toward lifelong learning and improvement.

Text/Data Disk Package	0-538-72212-6
Workbook	0-538-72213-4
Presentation Software	0-538-72214-2

Speech Recognition Series

Explore a unique opportunity to develop the skills needed to excel in the world of speech recognition. You will apply voice skills to real-world tasks, including *hands-off* activities common to corporate offices as well as the legal and medical fields.

L&H Voice Xpress™ for the Office Professional	0-538-72370-X
Dragon NaturallySpeaking® for the Office Professional	0-538-72371-8
IBM® ViaVoice™ for the Office Professional	0-538-72372-6

Quick Skills Series

Quickly sharpen your essential foundation skills for job success and professional development with these targeted guides. This series features career-related scenarios for relevant and real application of skills.

Self-Management and Goal Setting	0-538-69022-4
Speaking and Presenting	0-538-69014-3
Attitude and Self-Esteem	0-538-69026-7
Handling Conflict	0-538-69833-0
Managing Change	0-538-69839-X

Join us on the Internet at www.swep.com

SOUTH-WESTERN
★
™
THOMSON LEARNING

PREFACE

RECORDS MANAGEMENT, Seventh Edition, continues the strong tradition of serving as an introduction to the increasingly comprehensive field of records management. As such, the Seventh Edition emphasizes principles and practices of effective records management for manual and electronic records systems. This approach offers practical information to students, as well as to professionals, at managerial, supervisory, and operating levels.

The experiences and basic philosophies of the authors are presented clearly in this latest revision. Emphasis is placed on the need to understand the record life cycle within which information functions in the organization. Because the operations of all records systems—manual and electronic—rely on basic storage and retrieval rules, the authors offer a blended approach to the study of records management: traditional paper-based and electronic examples with records management practices identified and discussed.

As a text for students in postsecondary institutions, RECORDS MANAGEMENT, Seventh Edition, may be used for short courses or seminars emphasizing filing systems or longer courses such as quarter or semester plans. Basic manual systems concepts are discussed, and the concepts needed for understanding electronic records storage and retrieval methods are introduced.

As a reference book, this latest edition of RECORDS MANAGEMENT serves several purposes. It presents sound principles of records management that include the entire range of records—paper, image records, and electronic media used in computerized systems. Although the key management functions as they relate to records management are introduced, emphasis is placed upon control for ensuring that the records system achieves its stated goals. Professionals who direct the operation of records systems will find this Seventh Edition to be valuable because it includes alphabetic indexing rules that agree with the Simplified Filing Standard Rules of the Association of Records Managers and Administrators, Inc.

Organization of Text

The text consists of 5 parts organized into 12 chapters and 2 Appendixes. Part 1 introduces the student to the expanding area of records and information management. Following this overview, Part 2 focuses on alphabetic storage and retrieval methods for manual and electronic systems. Part 3 presents a detailed description of adaptations of the alphabetic storage and retrieval method; namely, subject, numeric, and geographic storage methods.

Part 4 covers information technology, which includes an update of image systems and the technology that integrates the computer with other automated records systems. This part also stresses the continuing need to understand basic records and information management principles before delving into the complexities of computerized systems. To complete the textbook from a management perspective, Part 5 offers a comprehensive view of the role of control in records systems. In addition, it reviews many practical procedures for controlling paperwork problems in both large and small offices. Appendix A describes career and job descriptions in the records management field; Appendix B describes card and special records commonly used in many offices.

Learning objectives for the student are included at the beginning of each chapter. Important terms are printed in bold type throughout each chapter and are listed alphabetically at the end of each chapter for easy review. In the Glossary at the back of the textbook, these same terms are defined. Questions in the margin of the text urge students to read carefully for meaning. Questions for review and discussion are provided at the end of each chapter.

One or more of these informational icons may appear by applications at the end of chapters:

Practice Set

The filing practice set that accompanies RECORDS MANAGEMENT, entitled RECORDS MANAGEMENT PROJECTS, Seventh Edition, features a new business and includes a data disk for students to use with database applications. This set of practical learning materials consists of 12 filing jobs in which students practice card filing and correspondence filing in alphabetic, subject, consecutive numeric, terminal-digit numeric, and geographic filing systems. In addition, students will practice requisition/charge-out and transfer procedures.

Study Guide

A Study Guide, which is designed to reinforce the material covered in the textbook, includes review of important terms, sample test questions, and several practical activities to supplement the textbook exercises assigned by the instructor.

Data Disk

A data disk containing files students use to complete end-of-chapter textbook applications and study guide activities is included in the back of the student text. In the textbook, a data disk icon identifies applications that require the data disk.

Instructor's Manual

The instructor's manual that accompanies RECORDS MANAGE-MENT, Seventh Edition, provides instructors with suggested methods of instruction, teaching aids, and time schedules for various teaching situations. Teaching suggestions, answers to the review and discussion questions, and solutions to the end-of-chapter Applications are provided for each chapter. Also, solutions are provided for the Checking Your Knowledge of the Rules activities that appear in Chapters 2 and 3. Detailed solutions for all practice set jobs are also included in the instructor's manual. Finding tests, which students use with the practice set, are included in the manual, as well as the finding test solutions.

Instructor's Resource CD-ROM

An Instructor's Resource CD-ROM is packaged in the back of the Instructor's Manual. Files on the CD-ROM include:

- A course completion certificate,
- Transparency masters for alphabetic filing rules,
- Supplementary activities and solutions for Chapters 1–12,
- Supplementary tests and solutions, and
- *Microsoft PowerPoint* slides for each chapter for use during class discussions.

Electronic Test Package

Instructors can purchase a flexible, easy-to-use test bank and test generator software program that contains objective questions for each test. Test bank questions are included for 12 chapter tests and a final exam. The *Exam View® Pro* software enables instructors to modify questions from the test bank or add instructor-written questions to create printed tests, Internet tests, and computer-based tests.

On-line (Internet-based testing)
- Lets instructors create tests that students can take on the Internet using a browser
- Provides instant feedback to students and instructors via e-mail
- Can create on-line study guides with student feedback for incorrect responses
- Can include any of the test question types

On-line (computer-based testing)
- Allows all or selected students to take a test
- Can create on-line study guides with student feedback for incorrect responses
- Can incorporate multimedia
- Exports student results to a grade book or spreadsheet

Acknowledgments

The authors are grateful to many companies and individuals who assisted in completing this extensive revision of RECORDS MANAGEMENT. Further, we appreciate the help of the filing equipment and supplies manufacturers and vendors who gave time, information, and photos to the authors in their efforts to update this edition effectively.

The authors are especially grateful to the following individuals who served as contributing authors on this edition: Dr. Joyce Logan, University of Kentucky, Lexington, Kentucky; Ms. Marti Fischer, CRM, San Jose, CA; and Ms. Jane Connerton, CRM, Cincinnati, OH.

In addition, special appreciation is extended to our families, friends, co-workers, project manager, consulting editor, and each other, whose encouragement and direction have been invaluable in completing this revision. The result, we believe, is an easily understandable, instructive, up-to-date introduction to the field of records management.

Judy Read-Smith
Mary Lea Ginn

CONTENTS

PART 1

THE FIELD OF RECORDS MANAGEMENT

1 **Records Management in Review**

Part 1 introduces you to the field of records management and to the nature and purpose of records. This first part includes a concise treatment of records management history, current trends in records and information management, and key legislation important to the effective operation of modern business firms. Highlights of the part are the discussion of records management as a key organizational function and careers in records management.

RECORDS MANAGEMENT IN REVIEW

LEARNING OBJECTIVES

1. Describe how records are classified and used in an office.
2. Compare early and modern records management operations.
3. Discuss relevant legislation that affects records management.
4. Describe the management functions necessary to operate a records management program effectively.
5. Identify possible careers in records management.

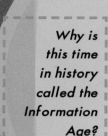

Why is this time in history called the Information Age?

In most jobs today workers are increasing their use of information. This time in our history frequently is called the *Information Age*; this generation often is called the *Information Society*. Computers, so much a part of today's world, are called *information-processing machines* because of their key role in information systems. To survive, businesses and organizations must have up-to-date *information* in the *right form*, at the *right time*, in the *right place* to make management decisions. **Management** is the process of using an organization's resources to achieve specific goals through the functions of planning, organizing, leading and controlling. In other words, information is an important and valuable business resource. Finally, most people use information minute by minute to manage their lives and perform their jobs.

Generally, information is stored on records of various types. A **record** is stored information, regardless of media or characteristics, made or received by an organization that is evidence of its operations and has value requiring its retention for a specific period of time. In turn, records are organized into complex systems. As workers rely more and more on information and as the volume of information increases, the value of records and information also increases. Like all other company "assets," records must be properly managed.[1]

In this overview chapter, you are introduced to records management. **Records management** is the systematic control of all records from their

---

[1]Definitions throughout this textbook are consistent with those in the *Glossary of Records and Information Management Terms*, Second Edition (Prairie Village, KS: ARMA International), 2000; and *A Glossary for Archivists, Manuscript Curators, and Records Managers*, compiled by Lewis J. Bellardo and Lynn L. Bellardo. (Chicago: The Society of American Archivists), 1992.

creation or receipt, through their processing, distribution, organization, storage, and retrieval, to their ultimate disposition. Because information is such an important resource to organizations, the records management function also includes information management. Therefore, records management is also known as *records and information management* or RIM. Records managers are also known as *records and information managers*. You will learn about important records and information management terms and concepts, a brief history of records, current trends in records management, and legislation to control records. You will also learn about the content of records and information management programs and careers in records and information management. Keep in mind that this textbook deals with records in business firms; however, the principles you learn should also help you understand how to use records efficiently in other types of organizations and in your home.

RECORDS: CLASSIFICATION AND USE

Your study of records and information management includes several basic concepts: definitions of key terms, classifications of records, and reasons that records are used and will continue to be used. As you study these concepts, relate them to your personal situation as well as to your job, if you are now employed. By doing so, you will learn more quickly and retain better what you will need for future work in an office.

A record is recorded information, regardless of media or characteristics, created or received, and used in the operation of an organization. The most common records, such as correspondence (letters and memoranda), reports, forms, and books, usually appear on paper. An organization may receive these records through regular mail, facsimile machines (fax), special couriers, or electronically by computer networks. Correspondence, reports, and forms are often created through word processing software programs.

Other types of records to consider are *oral records* that capture the human voice and are stored on cassettes and other magnetic media. Records also are stored on films such as movies, videotapes, photographs, and microfilm. Additionally, records are produced by and stored in computers and on optical disks, which are discussed in Chapter 10. Figure 1–1 on page 4 shows three familiar record forms. Records are valuable property, or resources, of a firm; and, like all other resources, they must be managed properly.

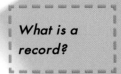

What is a record?

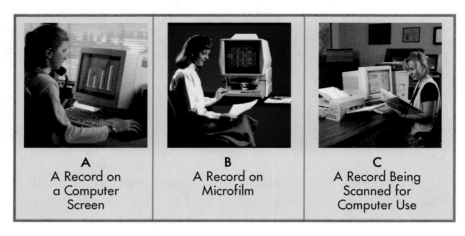

| A | B | C |
| A Record on a Computer Screen | A Record on Microfilm | A Record Being Scanned for Computer Use |

Figure 1-1 Common Record Forms

How Records Are Classified

How are records classified?

Usually, records are classified in three basic ways: (1) by the *type of use*, (2) by the *place where they are used*, and (3) by the *value* of the records to the firm. Each of these classifications is discussed in this section.

Classification by Use

Classification according to records use includes transaction documents and reference documents. A **transaction document** is a record used in a firm's day-to-day operations. These documents consist primarily of business forms. Examples are invoices, requisitions, purchase and sales orders, bank checks, statements, contracts, shipping documents, and personnel records such as employment applications and attendance reports. A **reference document**, on the other hand, contains information needed to carry on the operations of a firm over long periods of time. These records are referenced for information about previous decisions, quotations on items to purchase, statements of administrative policy, and plans for running the firm. Common reference documents, the most frequently used category of records maintained in an office, are business letters, reports, and interoffice memoranda. Other examples include catalogs, price lists, brochures, and pamphlets.

Classification by Place of Use

How do internal and external records differ?

Classification by *place of use* of the records refers to external and internal records. An **external record** is created for use outside a firm. Examples of such records are letters or faxes sent to a customer or client, to an organization's suppliers, or to the various branches of the government. The larger group of records classified by their place of use is that of internal records. An **internal record** contains information needed to operate a firm. Such a record may be created inside or outside an organization. Examples are communications between a firm and its employees (payroll records, bulletins, newsletters, and government regulations) and communications among a firm's departments (inventory control records, interoffice memoranda, purchase requisitions, and reports). Accounting departments maintain important internal records that document the presence and use of assets and liabilities and information essential for local, state, and federal tax purposes.

Classification by Value of the Record to the Firm

From an inventory and analysis of the use of each major record category, a manager determines the *value of the record* to the firm. This evaluation is used to develop a records retention schedule specifying how long to keep the records in the firm. The retention of records, an important part of a records and information management program, is discussed in Chapters 6 and 12.

Some records are so valuable to a firm that they require special measures of protection. Each record maintained by a firm falls into one of four categories that is used to determine *how records should be retained* and the level of protection they require. These categories are (1) vital, (2) important, (3) useful, and (4) nonessential.

Vital records are records that are necessary for the continuing operation of a firm. These records are usually not replaceable. They may be legal papers, such as articles of incorporation and titles to property owned by the firm, which must be retained indefinitely (although all vital records do not require indefinite retention). Reports to shareholders and minutes of important board meetings are also considered vital records because they are the official records of decisions made. These records must be protected to ensure the ongoing operation of the firm. **Important records** are records that assist in performing a firm's business operations and, if destroyed, are replaceable, but only at great cost. Personnel records, sales records, financial and tax records, and selected correspondence and reports are important records. Given the high cost associated with replacement, this category of records should also be protected. **Useful records** are records that are helpful in conducting business operations and may, if destroyed, be replaced at slight cost. General correspondence (letters, memoranda, and faxes) and bank statements are useful records that are easily replaced, or will have minimal impact if they are destroyed. The least valuable records are the nonessential records. **Nonessential records** are records that have no predictable value to the organization after their initial use and should be destroyed after use. Examples of nonessential records are announcements and bulletins to employees, acknowledgments, and routine telephone messages.

What are the four categories of records that determine how records should be retained?

Why Records Are Used

Records serve as the "memory" of a business. They document the information needed for operating the firm. For example, management policies are developed and recorded to furnish broad guidelines for operating a business. Each department (for example, finance, marketing, accounting, and human resources) bases its entire method of operations upon records. Usually, records are used and retained because they have one or more of the following values to a firm:

> **What serves as the memory of a firm?**

1. *Administrative value* in that they help employees perform office operations within the firm. Examples of such records include policy and procedures manuals, handbooks, and organizational charts.
2. *Fiscal value* because records may be used to conduct current or future financial or fiscal business. Fiscal records can document operating funds or serve tax audit purposes. Examples of this type of record include tax returns and records of financial transactions such as purchase and sales orders, invoices, balance sheets, and income statements.
3. *Legal value* because they provide evidence of business transactions. Examples of such records include contracts, financial agreements that are legally binding, deeds to property owned, and articles of incorporation.
4. *Historical value* because they furnish a record of the organization's operations and major shifts of direction over the years. Minutes of meetings, the corporate charter, public relations documents, and information on corporate officers all fall into this records category. In addition, the value of many records increases with the passage of time. Original copies of the Declaration of Independence and the Gettysburg Address are well-known examples, as is the original drawing of Ford's first Model T automobile.

From a personal standpoint, why do you keep your diploma, birth certificate, the title of ownership to your car, or the promissory note that provided you with the money to attend college? The answer is simple: *In today's complex world, people cannot get along without records! They need records for the information records contain.*

> **Why do individuals keep personal records?**

RECORDS MANAGEMENT HISTORY

Museums in the United States or in ancient civilizations, such as those in Greece and Italy, house many examples of early records. Examples include religious scrolls, documents proclaiming control over conquered people, and hieroglyphics describing early lifestyles. Carvings on the walls of caves in Latin America tell about the lives of early inhabitants and how they conducted their business affairs. Tours of early Native American

Hieroglyphics are an example of early records.

dwellings in the western United States provide similar examples or records of early tribal life. Computerized records in a variety of formats (including written, audio, video, and magnetic records) provide information about the population and the way businesses operate in the United States. When comparing the records of earlier periods in history with those of the computer age, records and attitudes toward records have changed significantly.

Early Records

Most of the business records before 1600 were based upon simple trade transactions that provided evidence of moneys received and spent, lists of articles bought and sold, and simple contracts. Such records and any copies were created by hand (that is, *manually*) until the printing press and later the typewriter were invented. These machines increased the speed by which records were created and processed.

Microfilm is an example of a technology ahead of its time. The ability to produce microfilm dates back to the nineteenth century and the birth of photography. Early and notorious uses include filming documents for espionage purposes as well as for ease in transportation. Business, particularly the banking industry, began making widespread use of microfilm in the 1930s. These uses, however, were never a threat to traditional paper records.

Until the 1950s, when computers were first used in business, records were almost entirely paper documents. The most important emphasis during this stage in history was getting the records properly placed in the files. Emphasis on retrieval surfaced later.

Before World War II, management directed its main business efforts toward work performed in factories or plants. Usually the plant work-force was large compared with the office staff. Consequently, managers gave their main attention to the factory because the factory produced the salable products that resulted in profits and against which expenses were charged. In such a setting, management assumed that records should be

What was the common form for most records until the 1950s?

the sole responsibility of the office staff. Little importance or status was granted to records and to management functions.

Modern Records

How have records evolved since the 1950s?

Since the early 1980s, over 60 percent of the Gross Domestic Product (GDP) has been based on information services. This significant change from the 1950s industrial-based economy is evident in the volume and type of records. The majority of business records are no longer just records of accounting transactions. Correspondence and information about customers are prevalent because these records are an important resource about the customer who buys the services a company sells. Additionally, records are stored on magnetic media, microforms, and optical media as well as in paper form. Fast, accurate retrieval helps a business meet customer needs.

Figure 1-2 **Retrieving Records from a Computer**

The process of creating records, the media on which records are stored, and the ways records are used have changed greatly since the 1950s. Newer technology applications have sped up all aspects of the business world—including the rate of change. Additionally, technology has helped create a global marketplace, bringing people closer together for the exchange of goods and services. The scope of managing information in this high-tech environment is creating new challenges and opportunities. The next section discusses some of these trends—merely the next phase in this evolutionary cycle.

Trends in Records and Information Management

Even though more businesses than ever are investing in new technologies, paper usage continues to be a fact of office life. This can be attributed to the increased use of equipment that enables employees to create paper records from electronic media. Copiers, printers, and facsimile machines all have the ability to interface with office computer systems to produce large volumes of paper documents.

Other reasons for continued popularity of paper are more personal and individual: paper requires no additional equipment for viewing; people can write on and annotate paper documents; paper has a presumed permanence. It is also conveniently transportable. In short, it is a user-friendly "technology."

Consequently, records managers must deal with increasing numbers of records—both paper and electronic. What are some of the more common electronic records? Electronic records are discussed in the next section.

Why are paper records so popular?

Electronic Records

An **electronic record** is a record stored on electronic media that can be readily accessed or changed. A piece of equipment is required to view and read electronic records. Until the 1980s, computer records were mostly financial or other statistical data stored on punched cards or reels of tapes. With the development and use of word processing systems, letters, memos, and reports were created electronically; however, the purpose of these systems was to facilitate the creation of paper records. As technology has advanced, true electronic records are in use today; i.e., records created, distributed, used, and stored electronically. The contents of these records are accessible only by machine.

The challenge for the records manager is to ensure that each person responsible for electronic records follows the records management storage and retrieval procedures set up for the office. Consistently following procedures helps protect the company in legal actions. The same benefits of following proper records management procedures for paper records also apply to electronic records: The information is available at the right time to help make effective decisions.

Electronic Mail **Electronic mail (e-mail)** is a system that enables users to compose, transmit, receive, and manage electronic documents and images across networks. A variety of electronic mail systems allow users to write and send messages via computers and software. Many systems allow the user to create electronic folders in which to place messages about a particular subject.

What is electronic mail?

Many questions related to records management and e-mail must be addressed by records managers. How do you maintain the integrity of a record? Can you keep it confidential? How long do you keep an electronic mail message? How should you retain such messages? (Electronically? As paper records?) These questions are only a few of the ones that must be answered as more and more messages are sent and received electronically.

Electronic Data Interchange. **Electronic data interchange (EDI)** is a communication procedure between two companies that allows the exchange of standardized documents (most commonly invoices or purchase orders) through computers. If the two companies have compatible systems, the computers talk to each other through a connection. For example, Company A sends a purchase order to Company B by EDI. When Company B ships the order to Company A, an invoice is created and sent to Company A, again through EDI. Company A can then pay Company B by the transfer of electronic funds by using EDI. Thus, no paper documents are exchanged. Some large companies no longer do business with other firms that do not use EDI. Records managers must ensure that these electronic records are accurate, safe, and secure.

What is EDI?

The Internet. The **Internet** is a worldwide network of computers that allows public access to send, store, and receive electronic information over public networks. The multimedia center of the Internet, the **World Wide Web,** is a worldwide hypermedia system (a network of networks containing hyperlinks) that allows browsing in many databases. Companies, organizations, and individuals create locations, called *Web sites,* that can be accessed by anyone who has an Internet connection. Companies use these sites to share information about themselves and their products. They also conduct business using these sites, where customers can order products, invest in the stock market, and pay their bills. Thus transactional records are being created, which must be managed. This technology poses special challenges as entire transactions take place without the creation of paper records or an easily discernable audit trail.

Document Imaging. **Document imaging** is an automated system for scanning, storing, retrieving, and managing paper records in an electronic format. A paper document is scanned into a computer, thus creating an electronic image of the document. Scanned files are usually large; consequently, optical disk storage (discussed in Chapter 10) is recommended. Textual data can be converted electronically using optical character recognition (OCR) software. Lists of key words are created for each scanned file. An image and text database is developed enabling a search by key words to find a document in a matter of seconds. Once found, the document can be sent to the requester by fax, computer-to-computer communication, or a hard (printed) copy. Chapter 10 includes a discussion of this technology.

What is document imaging?

Many companies integrate microfilming and document imaging technology to provide fast, accurate retrieval of records. Microfilming is a proven technology in terms of integrity and archival quality. The use of hybrid systems that combine computer imaging with microfilming is growing. Records managers must be aware of the need for developing standards, testing legal issues, lowering costs, and viewing imaging from an organizational strategic perspective.[2]

Integrated Electronic Recordkeeping Systems. Companies are creating, storing, and using more electronic records, and the systems used to create and manage these records are increasingly being integrated with each other. Some of these systems, such as enterprise information processing systems, present real challenges to records managers. Enterprise systems often combine capabilities previously found in standalone accounting, payroll, and human resources systems. Other integrated systems incorporate records and information management functionalities and are valuable tools for managing electronic records. An example of this is the convergence of electronic document management (EDM) systems and electronic records management (ERM) systems. EDM systems create, store, and manage electronic documentation, while ERM systems facilitate the application of a company's retention schedule to these electronic records—including electronic mail. You will learn ways to manage electronic files in Chapter 4. Chapter 10 gives more information on managing electronic information.

Knowledge Management

As companies integrate their systems and technologies, they also place a greater emphasis on their knowledge resources. This includes both recorded documentation and unrecorded information, the information that exists through the knowledge and experiences of a company's employees. **Knowledge management** is the effective management and use of an organization's knowledge resources, including the knowledge and experience of its employees.[3] This area provides new opportunities for records and information management professionals, working with other information managers, to harness the power of a company's intellectual capital.

RECORDS MANAGEMENT LEGISLATION

With the changes in the volume of records, the type of media, and the information stored that occurred as a result of World War II, many people were concerned about managing and controlling these records. Questions

---

[2]Carl J. Case, "Imaging Technologies: A Strategic Organizational Solution," *Journal of Systems Management*, July 1993, p. 12-16.

[3]William Saffady, *Knowledge Management: A Manager's Briefing* (Prairie Village, KS: ARMA International, 1998), p. 3.

about retention, who had access, and other concerns regarding privacy, were raised.

The Hoover Commissions

What was a major outcome of the first Hoover Commission?

In 1946, President Truman appointed the first Hoover Commission to study the policy and records needs of the federal government. The Commission's work was responsible for establishing the General Services Administration (GSA) to improve government practices and controls in records management. During this time a highly productive industrial system was in operation with new government regulations that required large volumes of records. The federal government recognized the need for controlling the volume of government records created both during and after World War II.

Later, a second Hoover Commission found that many reports required of business and industry were already available in other government agencies. Also, large numbers of records were submitted to government by industry, but many were never used. As a result, the second Hoover Commission in 1955 concluded that the need for management of governmental records was crucial and continuing. A government-wide records management program was then created under the direction of the GSA to oversee the reduction of paperwork in each government agency.

The federal government's pioneer studies in records management were widely acclaimed. They provided the example and motivation needed by business, industry, and lower levels of government to study the need for records and for setting up programs for their management.

Since the earlier studies, the federal government's concern for properly using and controlling information has continued with the passage of important records legislation. Significant examples of federal legislation affecting records are presented in the next section.

Federal Laws, Rules, and Regulations for Controlling Records

What three factors influence legislation for controlling records?

As the number of records increases dramatically, legislation to balance and protect an individual's right to privacy, the public's access to information, and the quest for national security also increases. When individuals' rights to privacy have been violated, the public's access to information denied, or the national security has been breached, steps need to be taken to protect these three important rights in a democratic society. These three rights are kept in balance by legislation. In the aftermath of the Watergate problems of the early 1970s, which stemmed in part from the lack of control of records, new federal legislation was passed by Congress.

Two laws, the Freedom of Information Act and the Privacy Act, have special meaning to you as a person and as a professional. Both laws aim to protect individuals against the misuse of filed information. As the use of electronic information increases, these laws are being scrutinized to determine if they are still appropriate and viable.

The Freedom of Information Act of 1966 gives you the right to see information about yourself. You may request records kept by private and public organizations such as medical offices, hospitals, dental clinics, law offices, government agencies, counseling clinics, banks, and the human resources (personnel) departments in business firms. You may have access to such records after proper submission of requests to the organization that has this information on file.

The Privacy Act of 1974 (with later amendments) gives you the right to exclude others from seeing records with information about you, as well as the right to know who has had access to your records. Many states have passed additional legislation aimed at protecting the files of individuals.

What does the Privacy Act of 1974 ensure?

As you continue your studies in records and information management, you need to be aware of other legislation affecting the control of records. Of special relevance to this field are (1) the Federal Records Act of 1950 and its later amendments, (2) the Copyright Act of 1976 and its amendments, (3) the Right to Financial Privacy Act of 1978, (4) the Paperwork Reduction Act of 1980, (5) the Video Privacy Act of 1988, (6) the Computer Matching and Privacy Protection Act of 1988, and (7) the Electronics Signature in Global and National Commerce Act of 2000. Also, the Fair Credit Reporting Act allows credit bureau members controlled access to credit- and tenant-bureau files.

As an employee responsible for company files, you need to know the rights of people asking to see the files. You also need to maintain control over the files, such as preparing a log of the names of persons who have read the files. Some firms that maintain a high volume of confidential information develop lists of individuals who may see such files and situations justifying access to their records. For other purposes, such files are off limits.

As companies rely increasingly on information stored on a variety of media, records managers must be certain that their companies' record-keeping systems are legally acceptable to governmental agencies and courts of law. Several rulings and regulations address this issue, including three Internal Revenue Service Revenue Procedures: Revenue Procedure 81-46 (1981) for microfilm records, Revenue Procedure 91-50 (1991) for computer-based systems, and Revenue Procedure 97-22 (1997) for electronic imaging. Also, Rules 1001-1003 of The Uniform Rules of Evidence define original and duplicate records and their admissibility into a court of law. Finally, Rule 26B of the Uniform Rules of Civil Procedure pertains to the scope of litigation discovery and the production of records, in the event of a lawsuit.

RECORDS MANAGEMENT: A KEY ORGANIZATIONAL FUNCTION

As stated earlier, management is the process of using an organization's resources to achieve specific goals through the functions of planning, organizing, leading, and controlling. *Planning* involves establishing goals or objectives and the methods required to achieve them. With the firm's goals in mind, *organizing* takes place, a step that calls for arranging the tasks, people, and other resources needed to meet the goals set in the planning stage. *Leading* refers to managerial behavior (such as training, supervising, and motivating) that supports the achievement of an organization's goals. Finally, *controlling* means measuring how well the goals have been met.

Keep these four functions in mind when you study the management of records. Also, observe how you manage because you, too, perform these steps when you manage your study time, money, and social and professional life.

What is management?

The Life Cycle of Records

As a manager, you must see the whole picture, which involves understanding the four managerial functions discussed earlier and how each relates to the other. In the same way, managing records involves clearly understanding the phases making up the life cycle of a record.

As Figure 1–3 shows, the **record life cycle** is the life span of a record as expressed in the five phases of creation, distribution, use, maintenance, and final disposition. Note how this cycle is carried out. Whenever a letter is produced, a form completed, a cassette tape dictated, or a pamphlet printed, a record is *created*. This record is then *distributed* (sent) to the person responsible for its *use*. Records are commonly used in decision making, for documentation or reference, in answering inquiries, or in satisfying legal requirements.

What are the phases in the record life cycle?

When a decision is made to keep the record for use at a later date, it must be stored, retrieved, and protected—three key steps in the *maintenance* of records. During this phase, the records must be *stored* (filed), which involves preparing and placing records into their proper storage place. After a record is stored, a request is made to *retrieve* (find and remove) it from storage for *use*. When the retrieved record is no longer needed for active use, it may be *re-stored* and *protected*, using appropriate equipment and environmental and human controls to ensure record security. Also involved in the maintenance phase are activities such as updating stored information and purging or throwing away obsolete records that are no longer useful or that have been replaced by more current ones.

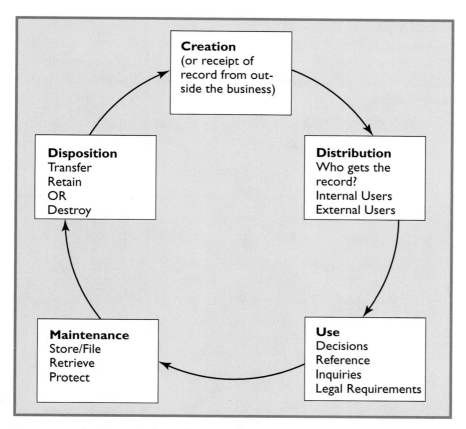

Figure 1–3 **The Record Life Cycle**

The last phase in the record life cycle is *disposition*. After a predetermined period of time has elapsed, records to be kept are *transferred* to less expensive storage sites within the firm or to an external records storage facility. At the end of the number of years indicated in the retention schedule, the records are *disposed of*, either by destruction or by transfer to a permanent storage place. The facilities where records of an organization are preserved because of their continuing or historical value are called the **archives**. The records retention schedule is discussed in detail in Chapter 6.

The record life cycle is an important concept for you to understand. It shows, for example, that *filing is only one part of records and information management*. Many interrelated parts must work together for an effective records and information management program. Knowing the meaning and importance of each part of the *entire* record life cycle, you will be able to understand what is needed to manage all records—those on paper and those stored on other media such as microfilm or magnetic media.

What are archives?

Programs for Managing Records

As mentioned earlier, a records program must be in place to manage all phases in the record life cycle. Although the contents of records and information management programs vary, such programs generally have these features:

1. *Well-defined goals that are understood by all workers.* Figure 1–4 outlines six common goals of successful records and information management programs.

GOALS OF THE RECORDS AND INFORMATION MANAGEMENT PROGRAM AT THE ABC COMPANY

1. To provide *accurate, timely information* whenever and wherever it is needed.
2. To provide information at the *lowest possible cost.*
3. To provide the *most efficient records systems*, including space, equipment, and procedures for creating, storing, retrieving, retaining, transferring, and disposing of records.
4. To *protect information* by designing and implementing effective measures for records control.
5. To determine *methods for evaluating* all phases of the records and information management program.
6. To *train company personnel* in the most effective methods of controlling and using records.

Figure 1–4 Goals of a Records and Information Management Program

What are four common features of a records and information management program?

2. *A simple, sound organizational plan.* Sometimes, the program is *centralized* (records are physically located and controlled in one area); in other cases, it is *decentralized* (records are physically located in the departments where they are created and used). Each plan offers advantages and disadvantages that managers should consider carefully before deciding on an organizational plan. In large firms where work can be specialized, computers and other information systems, as shown in Figure 1–5, play a major role in records and information management.

3. *Efficient procedures for managing each of the five stages in the record life cycle.* (See Figure 1–3.) You will study these procedures in detail in Chapter 12.

4. *A well-trained staff.* See the "Careers in Records Management" section later in this chapter.

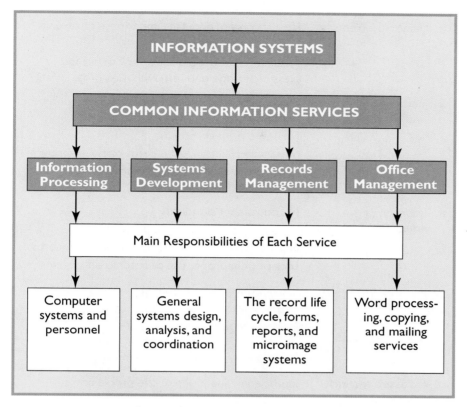

Figure 1–5 Location of Records Management in a Large Organization

Problems in Records Systems

The programs for managing records discussed earlier achieve their goals through the operation of an organization's records system. In this sense, a **records system** is a group of interrelated resources—people, equipment and supplies, space, procedures, and information—acting together according to a plan to accomplish the goals of the records and information management program. Anything that interferes with the operation of one or more of these resources, either individually or in combination, creates a problem in the records system and, therefore, hinders the effectiveness of the records and information management program.

Common problems in records systems and typical symptoms of such problems include:

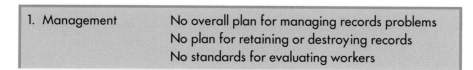

1. Management	No overall plan for managing records problems
	No plan for retaining or destroying records
	No standards for evaluating workers

What is a records system?

What are the
six most
common
problems in
records
systems?

2. Human problems	Lack of concern about the importance of records Hoarding of records Assuming that people know how to use the files for storage and retrieval of records
3. Inefficient filing procedures	Overloaded and poorly labeled drawers and folders Failure to protect records Misfiles resulting in lost records or slow retrieval Records removed from and placed in files without proper authorization
4. Poor use of equipment	No equipment standards No use of fire-resistant equipment Improper type of storage containers for records Lack of or improper use of automated systems
5. Inefficient use of space	Crowded working conditions Poor layout of storage area Inadequate use, or absence, of microfilmed records Resistance to the use of magnetic media
6. Excessive records costs	Inefficiency due to the above problems

To resolve such problems, managers frequently turn to various forms of information technology. Solutions may include company-wide computer systems, microfilm systems, and image systems. These systems, however, are not a panacea for records-related problems. Nor do they eliminate the use of paper. Companies still rely on paper, and this situation will continue because of the ease of producing paper copies with computers and copying machine technology.

Technology aside, the paper records system is the best place to begin a study of records management. Good records and information management principles are universal. They can and should be applied to electronic systems as well. Additionally, the tangible nature of paper records, the fact that paper records are familiar to most people, and that such records can be located easily make the study of paper records the logical introduction to the records and information management field. From such study, you need to understand alphabetic storage and retrieval systems discussed in Part Two along with subject, numeric, and geographic storage and retrieval systems explained in Part Three.

CAREERS IN RECORDS MANAGEMENT

Opportunities to work with records exist in every type and size of office. In a small office with one administrative assistant and an owner/manager, working with records occupies much of the time of both people. In this setting, opportunities for records work are unlimited. The classified ads section of all daily newspapers lists many general positions in small offices.

Another potential career connected to records and information management is the marketing of records supplies and storage equipment. Offices need the paper, folders, file cabinets and shelves, and other supplies and equipment that are necessary for records storage and retrieval. Office supply vendors are an important resource to a records and information management department. A career as a marketing service representative for an office supplies company offers growth opportunities.

Larger firms with more specialized staff often employ records supervisors who direct the work of several records clerks. In major corporations or other large administrative headquarters, such as the City Hall in major cities, you can find the following three levels of records workers as shown in Figure 1–6.

1. *Managerial level*, where the top position is the records manager who is responsible for directing the entire program.
2. *Supervisory level*, which includes specialists responsible for operating the records center, supervising the design and use of business forms, and directing the creation and use of microfilm records.

Where can you find opportunities for working in records and information management?

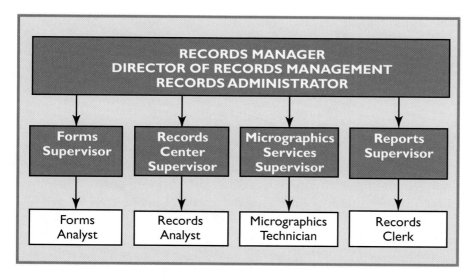

Figure 1–6 Typical Job Levels and Job Titles in Records Management

3. *Operating level*, which includes those workers responsible for routine filing and retrieving tasks, and assisting with vital records and records retention work. Because this is the level of work emphasized in this textbook, we shall concentrate on the basic principles involved in storing and retrieving records.

Companies that place a high value on their information resources have created a new position to oversee all information-related departments, including Records and Information Management. These new positions are variously titled "Chief Information Officer" (CIO) or "Chief Knowledge Officer" (CKO).

In times of economic downsizing, many organizations are outsourcing portions of their records and information management services such as inactive records storage. Because inactive records may be kept for a long period of time but may not be referenced often, records storage facilities are usually located offsite in lower rent districts. Many companies offer storage and retrieval services for several types of businesses. Career opportunities exist in these records and information management service businesses. See Appendix A for more detailed information on careers in records and information management as well as job descriptions for positions in this field.

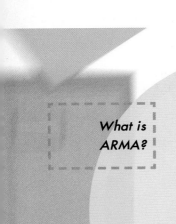

What is ARMA?

You can easily locate information on the records and information management profession by checking the publications and Web sites of the various professional associations specializing in the records and information management profession. **ARMA International (The Association of Records Managers and Administrators, Inc.) (www.arma.org)** is the most important professional group interested in improving educational programs in schools and industry and providing on-the-job knowledge about records and information management. ARMA members receive subscriptions to two publications: *The Information Management Journal* and *Infopro*.

Information on records management jobs can be found in the *Dictionary of Occupational Titles* and in the *Occupational Outlook Handbook*. The Association of Information and Image Management (AIIM) (www.aiim.org) provides members subscriptions to two electronic publications, *e-doc* and *DOC.1,* in addition to an annual technology exposition and career information. The American Health Information Management Association (AHIMA) (www.ahima.org) provides members subscriptions to three publications, the *Journal of AHIMA*, *AHIMA Advantage*, and *Keeping Pace*, as well as information about careers, schools, and on-line courses. Members also receive *E-Alert*—a periodic e-mail supplement to the *AHIMA Advantage* newsletter. Members may participate in *AHIMA Online*—an electronic bulletin board service for discussion groups on a variety of issues. You can find copies of such publications in college, university, and city libraries.

As the United States evolves more and more into a service economy based on information technology, many opportunities will appear for careers including management positions in information systems. Records management, which is a subspecialty of information systems (IS) and information technology (IT), is evolving and changing with the impact of technology. The person who is comfortable with technology and who can apply the principles of records and information management can look forward to a career in this area.

SUMMARY

A record is recorded information, regardless of its form; while records management is the systematic control of all records during their life cycle. The record life cycle includes creation, distribution, use, maintenance, and disposition. Records are classified according to their use, their place of use, or their value to a firm. Records serve as the memory of a company. Early records were physical records of simple transactions; as technology advanced, records have changed shape and form.

Records and information management is influenced by new technologies: electronic mail and the Internet, EDI, electronic imaging, and integration of electronic records systems. Knowledge management expands records and information management concepts to include non-recorded information.

The Hoover Commissions developed regulations to reduce paperwork in government agencies and to manage government records. Computers help to manage records, but the use of computers has raised questions about an individual's right to privacy, the public's access to information, and the quest for national security, which has resulted in federal legislation to control access to individuals' records. Other federal laws, rules, and regulations affect the control of other types of records and records media.

Management of records seeks to use an organization's resources to achieve specific goals through the functions of planning, organizing, leading, and controlling. Records and information management offers many career opportunities.

IMPORTANT TERMS

archives

ARMA International

document imaging

electronic data interchange (EDI)

electronic mail (e-mail)

electronic record

external record

important records

internal record

Internet

knowledge management

management

nonessential records

record

record life cycle

records management

records system

reference document

transaction document

useful records

vital records

World Wide Web

REVIEW AND DISCUSSION

1. Compare and contrast the terms *record* and *records management*. (Obj. 1)

2. What are the main classifications for records? What types of records are commonly found in each classification? (Obj. 1)

3. Compare and contrast the records operations of early offices with those found in modern offices. (Obj. 2)

4. Why does paper continue to be used in offices despite the increasing use of automation and computers? (Obj. 2)

5. What current issues are records managers facing? (Obj. 2)

6. Compare the Freedom of Information Act and the Privacy Act. Why are these acts important to records management? (Obj. 3)

7. List the phases in the record life cycle and describe the activities that occur during each phase. What phases, if any, do you eliminate in your own personal records cycle? Why? (Obj. 4)

8. What are some common problems found in records systems? (Obj. 4)

9. How can you best prepare for work and advancement in records and information management positions? (Obj. 5)

10. Describe two benefits available for members of ARMA. (Obj. 5)

APPLICATIONS (APP)

Collaborate

Critical Thinking

APP 1-1.   Classifying Records (Obj. 1)

1. Work with another student in your class to complete this application.

2. Visit a business and bring to class five examples of its business records. Make a chart similar to the one below, adding enough lines for all the records you collected. Record each business record by name, and place a check mark in the appropriate column(s). What helped you and your partner decide how to classify a record?

Business Record	By Use	By Place of Use	By Value to Firm

3. Make another chart similar to the one below, adding enough lines for all the records you collected. List the records again. Place a check mark in the appropriate column. What helped you decide how to mark a column?

Business Record	Vital	Important	Useful	Nonessential

4. Compare your charts and records with another team in the class. Discuss the reasons for any differences.

5. Analyze the records from the business. Why did the business develop each record? How will each record help that company conduct business?

APP 1-2.   Using Technology (Obj. 2)

1. Write a memorandum to your instructor identifying your goals for this class. Use electronic mail if it is available.

2. Scan a printed letter of your choice and save the image to a floppy disk if a scanner is available. Determine how many bytes your scanned file contains. If you are using a 1.44 MB floppy disk, approximately how many scanned letters of this size could the disk hold?

3. Insert the scanned image into a word processing document and print the resulting document. Compare the quality of this printout to your original letter. Which is better? Do you think that scanning documents is a viable option for records management? Why or why not?

PART 2

ALPHABETIC STORAGE AND RETRIEVAL

Part 2 highlights the rules for alphabetic storage and retrieval systems. The ten rules studied in Chapters 2 and 3 are based on the ARMA Simplified Filing Standard Rules. Chapter 4 discusses applying the rules to computer software applications. Chapter 5 presents the equipment and supplies used in manual and computer filing systems. Principles and procedures for retention, retrieval, and transfer of records are discussed in Chapter 6.

CHAPTER 2

ALPHABETIC INDEXING RULES 1–5

LEARNING OBJECTIVES

1. Explain the necessity for indexing rules in alphabetic storage of names and the importance of following these rules consistently.
2. Index, code, and arrange personal and business names in indexing order of units.
3. Index, code, and arrange minor words and symbols in business names.
4. Index, code, and arrange personal and business names with punctuation and possessives.
5. Index, code, and arrange personal and business names with single letters and abbreviations.
6. Index, code, and arrange personal and business names with titles and suffixes.
7. Apply alphabetic filing procedures.
8. Prepare and arrange cross-references for personal and business names.

NEED FOR ALPHABETIC ORDER

How do business records help decision makers?

Records help a business *do* business. Business records give the decision maker the right information at the right time at the lowest possible cost. To store records in the most efficient way possible, some type of filing or storing method must be used. A **filing method**, sometimes called a **storage method**, describes the way in which records are stored in a container. This text will present alphabetic, subject, numeric, and geographic methods of storage. Alphabetic storage is discussed in Chapters 2–6, subject storage in Chapter 7, numeric storage in Chapter 8, and geographic storage in Chapter 9. The most common method of storage is alphabetic.

The alphabetic storage method is a method of storing records arranged according to the letters of the alphabet. Sounds simple, right? Everyone knows the alphabet! However, consistently accurate alphabetic filing isn't that simple. Look in the telephone books of two major cities and you will find major discrepancies in the order of the listings. Another example is filing under the letters "Mc." Mc is not one of the 26 letters of the alphabet; however, it is included in some alphabetic filing systems and not in others.

ARMA Rules

The most important filing concept to remember is: **All filing is done to retrieve information.** To retrieve information efficiently, a set of rules must be followed. Different businesses have different needs for information retrieval. Not every business follows a universal set of rules for alphabetic filing because the goals and needs of each business vary. The Association of Records Managers and Administrators, Inc. (ARMA International) has published *Alphabetic Filing Rules*, containing standard rules for storing records alphabetically. ARMA is an organization designed to help professionals in records and information management perform their jobs easier and better. By using ARMA's simplified rules, businesses have a place to start setting up an efficient alphabetic storage system.

ARMA's Simplified Filing Standard Rules are shown in Figure 2–1. The rules in this chapter and in Chapter 3 are written to agree with the ARMA Simplified Filing Standard Rules and Specific Filing Guidelines.

The Association of Records Managers and Administrators, Inc. (ARMA International), the professional organization for the records and information management field, recommends the following Simplified Filing Standard Rules for consistency in filing.

1. Alphabetize by arranging files in unit-by-unit order and letter-by-letter within each unit.

2. Each filing unit in a filing segment is to be considered. This includes prepositions, conjunctions, and articles. The only exception is when the word *the* is the first filing unit in a filing segment. In this case, *the* is the last filing unit. Spell out all symbols: e.g., &, $, #, and file alphabetically.

3. File "nothing before something." File single unit filing segments before multiple unit filing segments.

4. Ignore all punctuation when alphabetizing. This includes periods, commas, dashes, hyphens, apostrophes, etc. Hyphenated words are considered one unit.

5. Arabic and Roman numbers are filed sequentially before alphabetic characters. All Arabic numerals precede all Roman numerals.

6. Acronyms, abbreviations, and radio and television station call letters are filed as one unit.

7. File under the most commonly used name or title. Cross-reference under other names or titles that might be used in an information request.

Figure 2–1 ARMA Simplified Filing Standard Rules

Procedures for storing records alphabetically vary among organizations and among departments within organizations. Therefore, the filing procedures to be used in any *one* office must be determined, recorded, approved, and followed with no deviation. Without written rules for storing records alphabetically, procedures will vary with time, changes in personnel, and oral explanations. Unless those who maintain the records are consistent in following storage procedures, locating records will not be possible. **The real test of an efficient records storage system is being able to find records quickly once they have been stored.**

Why are written rules needed for filing?

If you thoroughly understand the rules in this textbook, you will be able to adjust to any exceptions encountered in the specific office where you may work. Records managers who adopt these rules for their offices will find them understandable, logical, workable, and comprehensive enough to provide answers to the majority of storage questions that arise.

In this chapter, you will be using three of the seven steps for storing alphabetically: indexing, coding, and cross-referencing. Chapter 5 explains all seven of the alphabetic storing procedures.

Indexing

Indexing is the mental process of determining the filing segment (or name) by which a record is to be stored or the placing or listing of items in an order that follows a particular system. The **filing segment** is the name by which a record is stored and requested. In alphabetic storage, indexing means determining the name that is to be used in filing.

What is indexing?

The indexing step is more difficult when correspondence is being stored than when cards are being put in alphabetic order. On a card, the name is easily recognized; on correspondence, the name may appear in various places on a record. Because accurate indexing is necessary for quick retrieval, the indexing step is extremely important. *Careful, accurate indexing is perhaps the most exacting step in the storage procedure.* In an alphabetic arrangement, the selection of the right name by which to store (the filing segment) means that the record will be found quickly when it is needed. If the wrong name is selected, much time will be wasted trying to locate the record when it is eventually requested.

What is a filing segment?

To select the filing segment, keep the following in mind: The name most likely to be used in asking for the record, usually the most important one, is the one to be used for storage.

Take a look at the examples in Figure 2–2. Several new terms are introduced in this figure: *Key Unit*, *Unit 2*, *Unit 3*, and *Unit 4*. These units are the **indexing units** of the filing segment; in other words, the

What are indexing units?

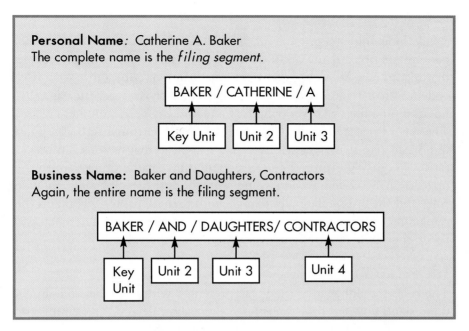

Personal Name: Catherine A. Baker
The complete name is the *filing segment.*

BAKER / CATHERINE / A

| Key Unit | Unit 2 | Unit 3 |

Business Name: Baker and Daughters, Contractors
Again, the entire name is the filing segment.

BAKER / AND / DAUGHTERS/ CONTRACTORS

| Key Unit | Unit 2 | Unit 3 | Unit 4 |

Figure 2–2 Coded Filing Segments, Key Unit, and Succeeding Units

indexing units are the various words that make up the filing segment. The **key unit** is the first unit of the filing segment. Units 2, 3, 4, and so on, are the next units by which the placement of the record is further determined. The use of these terms is helpful when determining how an item is to be filed. By mentally identifying the key and succeeding units, you are making a complex process simpler and easier to handle.

Coding

Coding is the act of assigning a file designation to records as they are classified. For paper records, coding is the physical marking of a record to indicate the name, number, or subject by which it is to be stored. Coding is a physical act, as contrasted with indexing, which is a mental determination. Coding procedures for this book for paper records are to place a diagonal (/) between each word in the filing segment, underline the key unit, and then number each succeeding unit (i.e., 2, 3, 4), which you have mentally identified in the indexing process. When the records are coded, the indexing order of the filing segment is marked. The **indexing order** is the order in which units of the filing segment are considered when a record is stored.

To code properly, a set of rules for alphabetic storage must be faithfully followed. **Indexing rules** are the written procedures that describe how the filing segments are ordered. The indexing rules that follow give you a good start in following appropriate alphabetic storage procedures.

What is coding?

Cross-References

While indexing a record, the filer may determine that the record could be requested by a name other than the one selected for coding. Because that record may be requested by the *other* name or names that were not coded, a cross-reference should be prepared. A **cross-reference** is a notation in a file or list showing that a record has been stored elsewhere. The record is stored under the name the filer determines to be the most important (*key unit*). Cross-referencing is used so that records can be retrieved quickly, even if they are requested by a name other than the one originally coded. Chapter 2 presents the first five alphabetic indexing rules and the cross-references that go with them. Chapter 3 contains the remaining indexing rules and their cross-references. Cross-referencing is mentioned here and is discussed in detail after the rules.

Indexing Rules

The rules for alphabetic storage are presented with examples to help you understand how to apply the rules. Study each rule and the examples of its application carefully; above all, be sure you understand the rule.

Here is an effective way to study the indexing rules:

First, read the rule carefully. Make sure you understand the meaning of the words used to state the rule. Then, look at the examples. Note that the complete name (the filing segment) is given at the left. Then the name is separated into indexing units at the right according to the rule you are studying. Be sure you understand why the name has been separated as it has.

In determining alphabetic order, compare the units in the filing segments for differences. If the key units are alike, move to the second units, the third units, and succeeding units until a difference occurs. The point of difference determines the correct alphabetic order. Marks that appear over or under some letters in different languages are disregarded (such as Señora, Marçal, René, Valhallavägen). In this text, you will find an underscore in each example except the first one. This underscore indicates the letter of the unit that determines alphabetic order. Examples are numbered for ease in referring to them. Be sure you understand each rule before going to the next.

> **What is an effective way to study alphabetic indexing rules?**

RULE 1: INDEXING ORDER OF UNITS

A. Personal Names

A personal name is indexed in this manner: (1) the surname (last name) is the key unit, (2) the given name (first name) or initial is the second unit, and (3) the middle name or initial is the third unit. If determining the surname is difficult, consider the last name written as the surname.

A unit consisting of just an initial precedes a unit that consists of a complete name beginning with the same letter—*nothing before something*. Punctuation is omitted. Remember, the underscored letter in the example shows the correct order.

What does "nothing before something" mean?

Examples of Rule 1A:

Filing Segment	Index Order of Units		
Name	Key Unit	Unit 2	Unit 3
1. William H. Barnes	BARNES	WILLIAM	H
2. Johanna Barns	BARNS	JOHANNA	
3. Phillip A. Barrett	BARRETT	PHILLIP	A
4. A. Bennett	BENNETT	A	
5. Carolyn Bennett	BENNETT	CAROLYN	
6. Z. Lisa Bernard	BERNARD	Z	LISA
7. Jason Blake	BLAKE	JASON	
8. Michael Blake	BLAKE	MICHAEL	
9. Michael Blakely	BLAKELY	MICHAEL	
10. Susan G. Brown	BROWN	SUSAN	G

B. Business Names

Business names are indexed *as written* using letterheads or trademarks as guides. Each word in a business name is a separate unit. Business names containing personal names are indexed as written.

What does "as written" mean?

Examples of Rule 1B:

Filing Segment	Index Order of Units			
Name	Key Unit	Unit 2	Unit 3	Unit 4
1. Bailey Construction Co.	BAILEY	CONSTRUCTION	CO	
2. Barker Metal Working	BARKER	METAL	WORKING	
3. Betsy Weil Law Firm	BETSY	WEIL	LAW	FIRM
4. Bill Barker Consultants, Inc.	BILL	BARKER	CONSULTANTS	INC
5. Billings Home Mortgage	BILLINGS	HOME	MORTGAGE	
6. Blissful Desserts	BLISSFUL	DESSERTS		
7. Blustery Day Kites	BLUSTERY	DAY	KITES	
8. Branson Concert Company	BRANSON	CONCERT	COMPANY	
9. Brown Barber Shop	BROWN	BARBER	SHOP	
10. Brown Telecom Services	BROWN	TELECOM	SERVICES	

Check Your Knowledge of Rule 1

1. On a separate sheet of paper, code items a–j by putting diagonals (/) between each unit in the filing segment, underlining the key unit, and then numbering second, third, and fourth units.

Example: 0. Mark / Kennedy
(with a "2" above Kennedy)

a. Anna Wong
b. Albert Brown Hosiery
c. Elbert Albert
d. Li Wu Wong
e. Elspeth Gregory
f. Greg Barnett Car Company
g. T. F. Sommers
h. E. William Smith
i. Wong Dry Cleaners
j. George Wong Aviation

2. Are the two names in each of the following pairs in correct alphabetic order? If not, explain.

a. Miller Clothing Store
   Charlotte Miller
b. Andrew Rose
   Rose Garden Nursery
c. Rose Dale
   Rosedale Custom Painting
d. Linda Lindsay Natural Foods
   Roy A. Lindsay
e. Allen Todd
   Todd Allen Furniture
   Company
f. Ron Dickinson
   Robert Dickinson
g. Martin Ulbert
   Josephine Urroz
h. Red Robin Restaurant
   Red Robin Bait Shop
i. Pioneer Museum
   Pioneer Cemetery
j. L. G. Baker
   Larry G. Baker

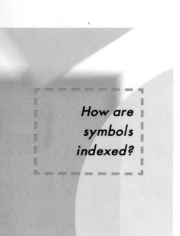

How are symbols indexed?

RULE 2: MINOR WORDS AND SYMBOLS IN BUSINESS NAMES

Articles, prepositions, conjunctions, and symbols are considered separate indexing units. Symbols are considered as spelled in full. When the word "The" appears as the first word of a business name, it is considered the last indexing unit.

Articles:	A, AN, THE
Prepositions:	AT, IN, OUT, ON, OFF, BY, TO, WITH, FOR, OF, OVER
Conjunctions:	AND, BUT, OR, NOR
Symbols:	&, ¢, $, #, % (AND, CENT OR CENTS, DOLLAR OR DOLLARS, NUMBER OR POUND, PERCENT)

Examples of Rule 2:

Filing Segment		Index Order of Units		
Name	Key Unit	Unit 2	Unit 3	Unit 4
1. A Cut Above	A	CUT	ABOVE	
2. An Excellent Shop	AN	EXCELLENT	SHOP	
3. Bonzo the Clown, Inc.	BONZO	THE	CLOWN	INC
4. Dollar Drug Store	DOLLAR	DRUG	STORE	
5. Douglas $ Shop	DOUGLAS	DOLLAR	SHOP	
6. Going My Way Motel	GOING	MY	WAY	MOTEL
7. Golf By The Shore	GOLF	BY	THE	SHORE
8. The Grand Hotel	GRAND	HOTEL	THE	
9. Hunt & Jones, Attorneys	HUNT	AND	JONES	ATTORNEYS
10. # One Drug Store	NUMBER	ONE	DRUG	STORE

Check Your Knowledge of Rule 2

1. On a separate sheet of paper, code items a–j by placing a diagonal between each unit in the filing segment, underlining the key unit, and then numbering second, third, and fourth units.

   a. The Chimney Sweeps
   b. The Crazy Chicken
   c. A Shop of Wonders
   d. An Honorable Mercantile
   e. C & R Office Supplies
   f. The Camp By The Sea
   g. C & R Hot Springs
   h. Clip & Curl Salon
   i. $ Saver Cleaners
   j. Cybersurf By The Hour

2. Write the letters beside the names to indicate the correct alphabetic order for items a–j on the same piece of paper.

RULE 3: PUNCTUATION AND POSSESSIVES

All punctuation is disregarded when indexing personal and business names. Commas, periods, hyphens, apostrophes, dashes, exclamation points, question marks, quotation marks, and diagonals (/) are disregarded, and names are indexed as written.

> *What do you do with punctuation marks when indexing?*

Examples of Rule 3:

Filing Segment	Index Order of Units			
Name	Key Unit	Unit 2	Unit 3	Unit 4
1. Icandoit.com	ICANDOITCOM			
2. Illinois & Indiana Cooperative	ILLINOIS	AND	INDIANA	COOPERATIVE
3. Imagine! Toy Store	IMAGINE	TOY	STORE	
4. Jones' Homestyle Eatery	JONES	HOMESTYLE	EATERY	
5. Kelly Jones-Zeta	JONESZETA	KELLY		
6. Kelly & O'Donnell Realty	KELLY	AND	ODONNELL	REALTY
7. Kelly's Hair Salon	KELLYS	HAIR	SALON	
8. Why Not Travel?	WHY	NOT	TRAVEL	
9. Wiley's Information Service	WILEYS	INFORMATION	SERVICE	
10. Willy-Hill Ice Creamery	WILLYHILL	ICE	CREAMERY	

Check Your Knowledge of Rule 3

1. On a separate sheet of paper, code items a–j by placing a diagonal between each unit in the filing segment, underlining the key unit, and then numbering the second, third, and fourth units.

   a. To-and-Fro Travel
   b. Robin Thompson-Brown
   c. The Spotted Cow Dairy
   d. Inside/Outside Gardeners
   e. Allison Love-Staak
   f. The Ink-a-Do Stamp Store
   g. $ Off Discount Store
   h. In-Town Delivery Service
   i. #s Away Diet Center
   j. Lovely & Thompson Law Firm

2. Are the two names in each of the following pairs in correct alphabetic order? If not, explain.

   a. Yolanda's $ Saver
      Yolanda Doolittle
   b. Rod-N-Reel Store
      Rodriguez & Gonzales Associates
   c. Do-Rite Pharmacy
      Do-Rite Builders
   d. John & Son Electric
      John & Sons Alignment
   e. Colt-Western Company
      Colt Industries
   f. Temp-A-Cure Company
      Temp-Control Mechanics
   g. Nor-West Growing Company
      Nor'Wester Novelties
   h. Ezekial M. Swanson
      The Swan Dive Shop
   i. Heckelman & Perez Law Firm
      Jason Heckelman
   j. Chi Kuo
      Ching-yu Kuo

RULE 4: SINGLE LETTERS AND ABBREVIATIONS

A. Personal Names

Initials in personal names are considered separate indexing units. Abbreviations of personal names (Wm., Jos., Thos.) and nicknames (Liz, Bill) are indexed as they are written.

How do you index abbreviated personal names?

B. Business Names

Single letters in business and organization names are indexed as written. If single letters are separated by spaces, index each letter as a separate unit. An acronym (a word formed from the first, or first few, letters of several words, such as ARMA and ARCO) is indexed as one unit regardless of punctuation or spacing. Abbreviated words (Mfg., Corp., Inc.) and names (IBM, GE) are indexed as one unit regardless of punctuation or spacing. Radio and television station call letters (WBAP, KRDO) are indexed as one unit.

How do you index single letters in business names?

Examples of Rule 4:

Filing Segment		Index Order of Units		
Name	Key Unit	Unit 2	Unit 3	Unit 4
1. A C T Realty	A	C	T	REALTY
2. AT&T Wireless	ATANDT	WIRELESS		
3. K & O Railway	K	AND	O	RAILWAY
4. KKRS Radio Station	KKRS	RADIO	STATION	
5. K-Nine Security	KNINE	SECURITY		
6. KOGO Television	KOGO	TELEVISION		
7. L A D Construction	L	A	D	CONSTRUCTION
8. LADD, Inc.	LADD	INC		
9. U & I Nursery	U	AND	I	NURSERY
10. US Bancorp	US	BANCORP		

Check Your Knowledge of Rule 4

1. On a separate sheet of paper, code items a–j by placing a diagonal between each unit in the filing segment, underlining the key unit, and then numbering the second and succeeding units.

   a. IDEA Corporate Services
   b. I Can Fix It Auto Body
   c. I C A Corp.
   d. I-Can-Dig-It Backhoe Services
   e. I Am Woman, Inc.
   f. I C Clearly Vision
   g. I Buy Antiques
   h. ICAP Inc.
   i. ID Booth Inc.
   j. IBT Associates

2. Write the letter beside the names to indicate the correct alphabetic order for items a–j on the same piece of paper.

RULE 5: TITLES AND SUFFIXES

A. Personal Names

A title before a name (Dr., Miss, Mr., Mrs., Ms., Prof.), a seniority suffix (II, III, Jr., Sr.), or a professional suffix (CRM, DDS, Mayor, M.D., Ph.D., Senator) after a name is the last indexing unit. Numeric suffixes (II, III) are filed before alphabetic suffixes (Jr., Mayor, Senator, Sr.). If a name contains both a title and a suffix, the title is the last unit.

Royal and religious titles followed by either a given name or a surname only (Father Leo, Princess Anne) are indexed and filed as written.

Note: If a person's professional title appears after his or her name, it is referred to as a suffix: e.g., CPA, CRM, CMA, Senator.

> What are some suffixes for personal names?

Examples of Rule 5A:

Filing Segment	Index Order of Units			
Name	Key Unit	Unit 2	Unit 3	Unit 4
1. Father John	FATHER	JOHN		
2. Ms. Ada Johnson, CPA	JOHNSON	ADA	CPA	MS
3. Dr. Ada Johnson	JOHNSON	ADA	DR	
4. Mr. Goro Nagai	NAGAI	GORO	MR	
5. Father Ron Nelson	NELSON	RON	FATHER	
6. Ron Nelson, Jr.	NELSON	RON	JR	
7. Ron S. Nelson	NELSON	RON	S	
8. Ron S. Nelson II	NELSON	RON	S	II
9. Ron S. Nelson III	NELSON	RON	S	III
10. Ron Nelson, Sr.	NELSON	RON	SR	
11. Miss Ruth Nguyen	NGUYEN	RUTH	MISS	
12. Mrs. Ruth Nguyen	NGUYEN	RUTH	MRS	
13. Ms. Ruth Nguyen	NGUYEN	RUTH	MS	
14. Sister Mary Nunamaker	NUNAMAKER	MARY	SISTER	
15. Queen Mary	QUEEN	MARY		
16. Sister Bernadette	SISTER	BERNADETTE		

B. Business Names

Titles in business names are indexed as written.

Examples of Rule 5B:

Filing Segment		Index Order of Units		
Name	Key Unit	Unit 2	Unit 3	Unit 4
1. Aunt Sally's Cookie Shop	AUNT	SALLYS	COOKIE	SHOP
2. Captain Roy Bean's Coffee	CAPTAIN	ROY	BEANS	COFFEE
3. Dr. Carla's Chimney Works	DR	CARLAS	CHIMNEY	WORKS
4. Father Time's Antiques	FATHER	TIMES	ANTIQUES	
5. Mister Oscar's Gym	MISTER	OSCARS	GYM	
6. Mr. Video Connection	MR	VIDEO	CONNECTION	
7. Mrs. Mom's Day Care	MRS	MOMS	DAY	CARE
8. Ms. Salon of Beauty	MS	SALON	OF	BEAUTY
9. Professor Owl's Bookstore	PROFESSOR	OWLS	BOOKSTORE	
10. The Prof's Tutorial Service	PROFS	TUTORIAL	SERVICE	THE

Check Your Knowledge of Rule 5

1. On a separate sheet of paper, code items a–j by placing a diagonal between each unit in the filing segment, underlining the key unit, and then numbering second and succeeding units.

   a. Father Rodney
   b. Ms. Paula Rodriguez, CRM
   c. Mrs. Char. Campbell, DVM
   d. Call/Delivery Company
   e. COR Construction, Inc.
   f. WKRA Radio Station
   g. R & K Drop Box Service
   h. Champs-of-the-Road Trucking
   i. The Roseway Arms Apts.
   j. RK Architects PC

2. Are the two names in each of the following pairs arranged in correct alphabetic order? If not, explain.

   a. The Magic Bean Shop
      Magic $ Saver
   b. Sean Phillips, Sr.
      Sean Phillips, Jr.
   c. Mrs. Carmen Zapata
      Z-Pro Company
   d. XYZ Rentals, Inc.
      X M Chemical Co.
   e. Mrs. C's Chocolates
      MVP Pizza Shop
   f. The Yarn Barn
      Ye Olde Print Shop
   g. L-M Equipment Co.
      L & M Appliance Repair
   h. Sharon's "Of Course"
      Miss Sharon Oest
   i. The Office King
      The Office Doctor
   j. I-Net, Inc.
      I-Freenet Company

3. Are the following names in alphabetic order? If so, indicate by writing "Yes." If not, write "No," then determine the correct alphabetic order and show it by rearranging the numbers beside the names on a separate sheet of paper.

Example: 0. 1. A–Z Rentals
2. AAA Used Cars
3. A. Wilson Enterprises

Answer: No, 3, 2, 1

a. 1. ITC Truck Company
2. In & Out Diner
3. I Do I Do Catering

b. 1. Donald Carter
2. The Carter Company
3. Alice Carter

c. 1. Brother Alfonso Ledford
2. Cynthia Ledford-White
3. Dexter Ledford

d. 1. Ryan Shenkar III
2. Ryan Shenkar
3. Ryan Shenkar II

e. 1. AMPAK, Inc.
2. AMP Factory
3. AMPCO Parking, Inc.

f. 1. Dr. Joji Chiba
2. Joji Chiba, M.D.
3. Mr. Joji Chiba, CMA

g. 1. Queen Anne
2. Annette Queen
3. The Queen's Closet

h. 1. The Professor Book Store
2. Professor Rebecca Bartels
3. Professor T's Academy

i. 1. The Captain's Surf & Turf
2. Captain Cynthia S. Wilson
3. Cap'n Hook's Sea Food

j. 1. Janice Cooper, CPA
2. Ms. Janice Cooper
3. Sister Janice Cooper

ALPHABETIC CARD FILING

Many offices use an alphabetic card file or a computer file to store information that is frequently referenced. Think back to your own experiences when calling for services such as an electrical hook-up. What is the first piece of information asked of you? If you can hear key clicks, chances are the person is using a computer to find your record. More offices are using computers to reference customer records. However, depending on the size and type of office, computers may not be available to everyone. Therefore, you must be prepared to use both manual and computer files.

What Is a Card Record?

In many offices, card record files of the names and addresses of persons and businesses are kept in alphabetic arrangement. A **card record** is a piece of card stock used for storing information that is referenced often. The card stock provides the durability to withstand frequent handling. These cards are prepared according to the style selected by the records manager so that the cards can be handled with maximum efficiency and ease.

To understand the advantages and disadvantages of card records, remember the basic difference between card records and records kept in other forms. One main item or unit of information, such as a telephone number or address, is stored on each card. For this reason, a card has often been called a **unit record** or *unitized record*, which is a record that contains one main item or piece of information. Each card is handled as a single item or unit record.

What is a unit record?

Preparation of Cards

Information contained on each card must follow the same pattern. This pattern helps to ensure consistency and ease in finding the information.

As you read the following explanation, refer frequently to Figure 2–3, which shows one style that is commonly used in either manual or computer-based systems.

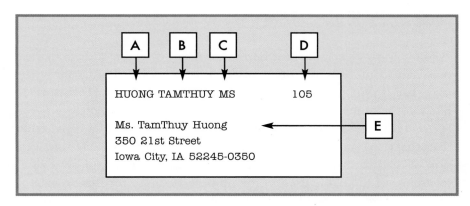

Figure 2–3 **Name Card Preparation**

1. Key the name of the person or business in all caps with no punctuation, in indexing order. Place the name near the left and top edges of the card. The key unit is always the first word keyed, (see A in Figure 2–3) followed by the second and succeeding units (see B in Figure 2–3). A person's title should be keyed if it is known (see C in Figure 2–3).
2. Key the name and address below the indexed name using upper and lower case letters and punctuation (see E in Figure 2–3). Leave a blank line before the name and address.
3. Key the number code in the upper right corner of the card if the name on the card is to be used with a numeric system (see D in Figure 2–3).

Using Database Software

When customer names and other information are stored in a database, the user locates information using the search or query functions of the software. The filing segment is integrated into the fields of the database in a variety of ways. For example, the units of a personal name might be entered in database fields such as Last Name, First Name, Middle, Title, and Suffix. The entire name written in indexing order might be keyed in a field called Indexing Order. The fields containing individual units of the name might be used for applications such as mail merge letters or creating a query using the Suffix field (to find all doctors in the data table, for example). The Indexing Order field might be used to sort merged letters in filing order. Chapter 4 discusses other methods of using the database fields.

Electronic cross-referencing can follow the manual method described next or is not needed because the search feature of the database application is extensive. Also, entire records are visible when a search result shows on the screen.

CROSS-REFERENCING

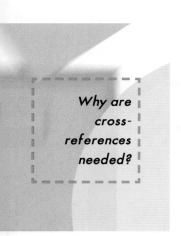

Why are cross-references needed?

Some records of persons and businesses may be requested by a name that is different from the one by which it was stored. This is particularly true if the key unit is difficult to determine. When a record is likely to be requested by any of several names, an aid called a *cross-reference* is prepared. A cross-reference shows the name in a form other than that used on the original record, and it indicates the storage location of the original record. The filer can then find requested records regardless of the name used in the request for those records. A cross-reference card may be identical with all other cards in size and color, or it may be distinctively different in color so that it will stand out clearly from the other cards. Cross-reference cards are discussed in this chapter. Cross-reference sheets, used with correspondence records, are discussed in Chapter 5.

Cross-referencing must be done with discretion. Too many cross-references crowd the files and may hinder retrieval rather than help. Each cross-reference requires valuable time to prepare, creates at least one additional card or computer entry that must be stored, and therefore requires additional space in a file.

Four types of personal names should be cross-referenced:

1. Unusual names.
2. Hyphenated surnames.
3. Alternate names.
4. Similar names.

Also, nine types of business names should be cross-referenced. Four will be presented in this chapter; the remainder, in Chapter 3.

1. Compound names
2. Abbreviations and acronyms
3. Popular and coined names
4. Hyphenated names

An explanation of the procedure to be followed in cross-referencing each of these kinds of names follows.

Personal Names

Cross-references should be prepared for the following types of personal names.

1. ***Unusual names.*** When determining the surname is difficult, use the last name written as the key unit on the original record. Prepare a cross-reference with the first name written as the key unit.

   On the original card for Allen Todd, Todd is the key unit, and Allen is the second unit. However, a request might come in for Todd Allen. The cross-reference would show Allen as the key unit and Todd as the second unit. Someone looking under Allen would find the cross-reference under A for Allen. Study the examples in Figure 2–4.

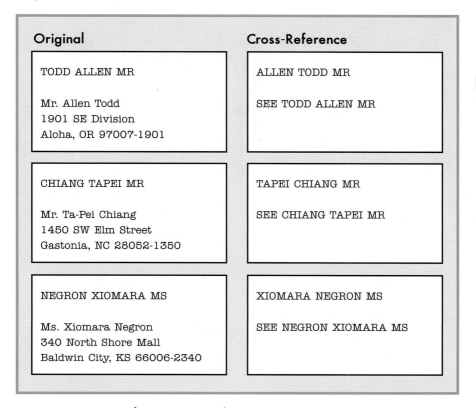

Original	Cross-Reference
TODD ALLEN MR Mr. Allen Todd 1901 SE Division Aloha, OR 97007-1901	ALLEN TODD MR SEE TODD ALLEN MR
CHIANG TAPEI MR Mr. Ta-Pei Chiang 1450 SW Elm Street Gastonia, NC 28052-1350	TAPEI CHIANG MR SEE CHIANG TAPEI MR
NEGRON XIOMARA MS Ms. Xiomara Negron 340 North Shore Mall Baldwin City, KS 66006-2340	XIOMARA NEGRON MS SEE NEGRON XIOMARA MS

How do you cross-reference a hyphenated surname?

Figure 2–4 **Cross-Reference: Unusual Names**

2. ***Hyphenated surnames.*** Hyphenated surnames often are used by married women. With hyphenated surnames, a request for records could be in either of the two surnames. A cross-reference enables retrieval in either case. An example is Terri Palmer-Green shown in Figure 2–5. Remember that punctuation is ignored.

   Many men use hyphenated surnames that are their family names, and they are known only by their hyphenated surnames. A cross-reference is not necessary. Some men choose to adopt a hyphenated surname when they marry and may, in that case, be known by more than one name. A cross-reference is needed for accurate retrieval of records when a man changes his surname to a hyphenated surname. See Tim Mitchell-Phillips shown in Figure 2–5. You will be told when a cross-reference is needed for a man's name, otherwise, a cross-reference will not be required.

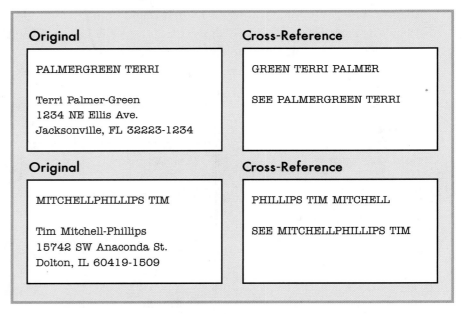

Figure 2–5 **Cross-Reference: Hyphenated Surnames**

3. ***Alternate names.*** When a person is known by more than one name, you need to make cross-references. Examples are Sarah Starkinsky doing business as Sarah Star; Sally Reardon, DVM, who is also known as Sally Reardon-Woods, Mrs. Forrest Woods, and Mrs. Sally Woods. (See Figure 2–6.)

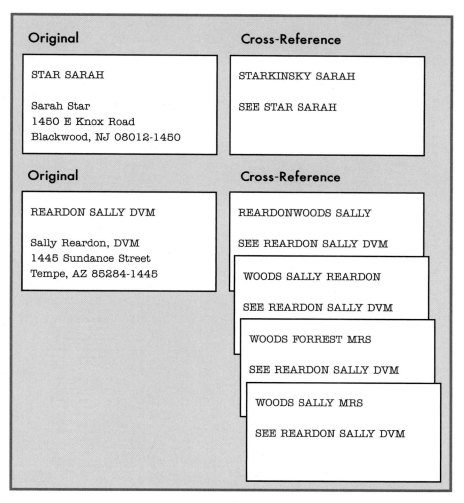

Figure 2–6 **Cross-Reference: Alternate Names**

4. ***Similar names.*** A variety of spellings exist for some names like Brown and Johnson. A SEE ALSO cross-reference is prepared for all possible spellings. If the card isn't found under one spelling, the filer checks the SEE ALSO card for other possible spellings. Figure 2–7 on page 44 illustrates see also cross-references for similar names.

Business Names

Cross-references should be prepared for the following types of business names. The original name is the name appearing on the letterhead.

1. ***Compound names.*** When a business name includes two or more individual surnames, prepare a cross-reference for each surname other than the first. See Figure 2–8 on page 44 for an example using Moore, Ruse, and Sullivan Attorneys.

How many cross-references are needed for a business that has three individual surnames?

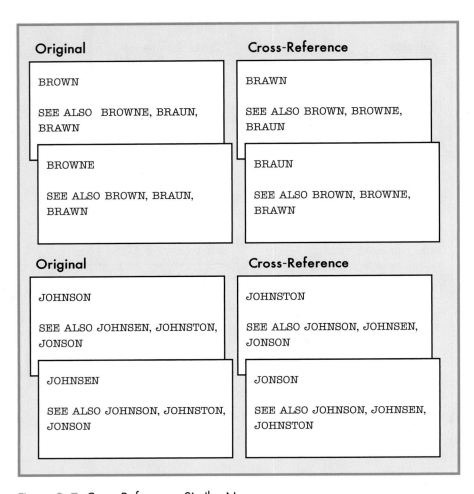

Figure 2–7 Cross-Reference: Similar Names

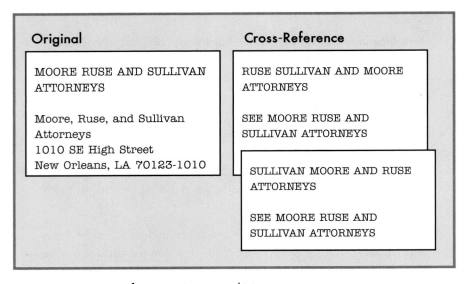

Figure 2–8 Cross-Reference: Compound Names

2. ***Abbreviations and acronyms.*** When a business is commonly known by an abbreviation or an acronym, a cross-reference is prepared for the full name. Examples are IBM (International Business Machines Corporation) and MADD (Mothers Against Drunk Driving) shown in Figure 2–9.

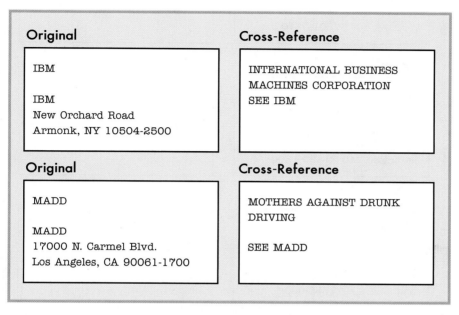

Figure 2–9 Cross-Reference: Abbreviations and Acronyms

3. ***Popular and coined names.*** Often a business is known by its popular and/or coined name. A cross-reference will assist in retrieval. Figure 2–10 on page 46 shows cross-references for Freddy's (Fred Meyer Department Store), Penney's (JCPenney Company, Inc.), and Granny's (Grandma's Home Cooking Restaurant).

4. ***Hyphenated names****. Just as in personal names, business surnames with hyphens need to be cross-referenced for each surname combination. Examples are shown in Figure 2–11 on page 46.

Check Your Knowledge of Cross-Referencing

Which of the following names should have cross-references? Prepare cross-references as needed on a separate sheet of paper.

1. WKKP Radio Station
2. IBM
3. Black-Dodson Cattle Company
4. Nelson Allen
5. Mrs. Joanna Childer-Evans
6. The Riverside Terrace
7. Akeo Saga, M.D.
8. Mom's (Mom's Cafe & Concert Hall)
9. Nelson, Winter & Wakui Brokerage
10. BBCC (Big Bend Community College)

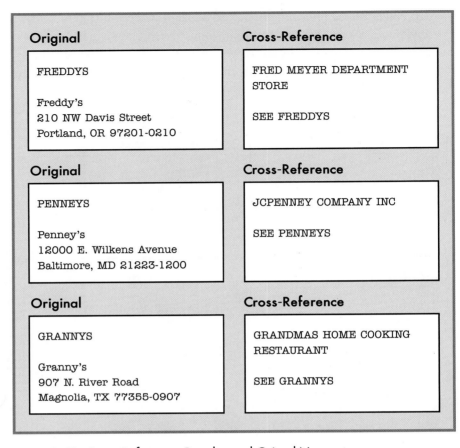

Figure 2–10 Cross-Reference: Popular and Coined Names

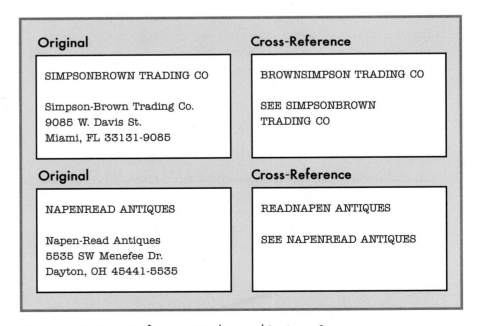

Figure 2–11 Cross-Reference: Hyphenated Business Surnames

Coding Cross-References

The name on the first line of a card is always used to determine placement in a file. The rule applies to original cards and to cross-reference cards. If the names on the cards are coded, diagonals are placed between the units, the key units are underlined, and the remaining units are numbered.

SUMMARY

A set of written rules helps make filing consistent. When filing is consistent, retrieving records is easier. The ten indexing rules presented in this textbook are based on the ARMA Simplified Filing Standard Rules.

Indexing is the mental process of determining the filing segment or the name by which the record is to be stored. Coding is the physical process of marking the filing segment into indexing units. Insert diagonals between units, underline the key unit, and then number each succeeding unit when coding.

Personal names are indexed by the surname, the given name, and then middle name or initial. Business names are indexed as written on the letterhead. Minor words and symbols in business names are indexed as written and are considered separate indexing units. Spell out any symbols. When the word "The" is the first word in a business name, consider it the last indexing unit. All punctuation marks are ignored when indexing personal and business names.

Single letters and abbreviations are indexed as written for both personal and business names. When single letters in a business name are separated by spaces, each letter is considered a separate indexing unit. Personal titles and suffixes are indexed after the surname and given name. A suffix is indexed before a personal title when a person's name contains both. Titles in business names are indexed as written.

Card records can be prepared manually or by computer; in either case, consistency of format is important. Cross-reference personal names that are unusual, hyphenated surnames, alternate names, and similarly spelled names. Cross-reference business names that contain more than one surname, abbreviations and acronyms, popular and coined names, and hyphenated surnames.

IMPORTANT TERMS

card record

coding

cross-reference

filing or storage method

filing segment

indexing

indexing order

indexing rules

indexing units

key unit

unit record

REVIEW AND DISCUSSION

1. Why is consistency in filing important? (Obj. 1)

2. Why are indexing rules important when filing names alphabetically? (Obj. 1)

3. In personal names, what is the key unit? (Obj. 2)

4. How is the key unit of a business name determined? (Obj. 2)

5. Code and arrange the following names in alphabetic order. Justify your arrangement. (Obj. 2)
   a. Norman Andrews
   b. Norm's Painting Company
   c. Norma Anderson
   d. Norton Printing Company

6. Code and arrange the following names in alphabetic order. Justify your arrangement. (Obj. 3)
   a. Pitt & Aniston Produce
   b. The Pitfall Deli & Restaurant
   c. A/J E-Mail Express
   d. $ Off Store

7. Code and arrange the following names in alphabetic order. Justify your arrangement. (Obj. 4)
   a. Audrey Kelley-O'Neal
   b. Kelly's Mercantile
   c. Kwik Copies, Inc.
   d. Kelley-Evans Hardware Store

8. Code and arrange the following names in alphabetic order. Justify your arrangement. (Obj. 5)
   a. JMR, Inc.
   b. J M R Associates
   c. Will Jones
   d. Wm. S. Jones

9. Code and arrange the following names in alphabetic order. Justify your arrangement. (Obj. 6)
   a. Mr. John Miller, Jr.
   b. Ms. Julie Miller
   c. Mrs. John Miller, CPS
   d. Mr. John Miller, Sr.

10. Can you have too many cross-references? Explain. (Obj. 8)

11. Give two examples of types of personal names that should be cross-referenced. (Obj. 8)

12. Give two examples of types of business names that should be cross-referenced. (Obj. 8)

APPLICATIONS

APP 2-1.   Create an Alphabetic Card File (Objs. 2-8)

1. On 5" by 3" cards or on slips of paper of that size, key or print in indexing order the names listed below. Key or print the number beside the name in the top right corner of the card. Key the name and address below the indexed name.

2. Prepare cross-reference cards where necessary according to the guidelines provided in this chapter. On the cross-reference card, key or print the number of the original name plus an "X" in the top right corner.

3. Arrange all cards, including cross-references, in alphabetic order.

4. In a vertical column on a separate sheet of paper, list the numbers on the cards that you have now arranged in alphabetic order.

5. Save the cards for use in Chapter 3.

Example Cards:

MEJIA SANTOS 5 Santos Mejia 1750 S. Sunnyvale Providence, RI 02909-1435	SANTOS MEJIA 5X SEE MEJIA SANTOS

Names:
1. L. M. Kale, CPA, 1351 West Losey, Hartford, CT 06110-6033
2. Sister Doreen Mellman, 106 S. Elm Street, Chicago, IL 60680-3425
3. Arun Lakra, M.D., 888 Bayou Lane, Baton Rouge, LA 70802-2322

4. Jane Kemp, 302 Sitka St., Juneau, AK 99802-6195
5. Santos Mejia, 1750 S. Sunnyvale, Providence, RI 02909-1435
6. Life-Time Gate Company, 4845 S. Bellevue Crescent, Chevy Chase, MD 20815-1101
7. K & M Inc., 742 Pine St., Galesburg, IL 61401-3425
8. Layla's Salon of Beauty, 100 S. Potter Street, Jackson, MS 39202-1763
9. Donna Little, 1602 Wade St. SE, Pittsburgh, PA 15217-1123
10. K L M Services, 404 Spring Park Blvd., Lansing, MI 48912-6766
11. Lace-N-Satin Boutique, 414 W. Seventh Street, Andover, NH 03216-2233
12. Lawson, Kemp, and Mason Attorneys, 2350 N. Montgomery Ave., Austin, TX 78705-3245
13. Miller Hardware, Inc., 4700 E. Morningside Dr., Cincinnati, OH 45227-6511
14. Kemp-Mason Associates, 890 Francis Ave., Boston, MA 02199-3682
15. Lay-Away Furniture Store, 44 Hillcrest, South Burlington, VT 05401-2217
16. M/K Corporation, 455 SE Vineyard Lane, Lincoln, NE 68501-1273
17. Lynda Kemper Brokerage, 450 NW Lovejoy, San Francisco, CA 94102-6722
18. MRI, Ltd., 1650 Northern Avenue, Bangor, ME 04401-1014
19. La-Di-Da Salon, 217 S. Douglas Street, Dover, DE 19901-2235
20. "Move-It" Trading Co., 126 W. Grant Lane, Little Rock, AR 72211-5452

APP 2-2.   Arrange Personal and Business Names in Alphabetic Indexing Order (Objs. 2-8)

Write or key in indexing order the units of the filing segments for the names below. Then write or key the number by each filing segment to indicate correct alphabetic order for the names.

No.	Filing Segment
1.	KRTV Television Station
2.	LTL Trucking (Little, Trent, and Lyle)
3.	Mayor John Miller
4.	Northwest Nannies Institute
5.	Keebler-Martin Consulting
6.	Martin's Electronics
7.	Little Ones' Nursery
8.	Lyle Business College
9.	Ken's Construction Company
10.	# One Printer
11.	N-R-Getic Delivery Service
12.	Nu-Hope Natural Foods
13.	Ms. Mary Newton-Little
14.	Karen Keebler Bakery
15.	Nu-Skin Facial Care

16. Josefina Lugo, CPA
17. North/South Distribution, Inc.
18. Mr. San-li Liang
19. KKJZ Radio Station
20. Little/Big Clothing Store
21. Keep'em Flying
22. Miss Lucinda Martin
23. Joseph H. Karner
24. Señor Juan Medina
25. Mrs. Laura Little

APPLYING THE RULES

Job 1, Card Filing, Rules 1-5. All supplies necessary for completing Job 1 and all other jobs in *Records Management Projects*, 7th ed., are contained in the practice set.

CHAPTER 3

ALPHABETIC INDEXING RULES 6–10

LEARNING OBJECTIVES

1. Index, code, and arrange personal and business names with articles and particles.
2. Index, code, and arrange business names with numbers.
3. Index, code, and arrange the names of organizations and institutions.
4. Index, code, and arrange personal and business names that are identical.
5. Index, code, and arrange government names.
6. Prepare and arrange cross-references for business names.
7. Select appropriate subject categories to be used within an alphabetic arrangement.

RULE 6: PREFIXES—ARTICLES AND PARTICLES

What are examples of foreign articles or particles in names?

A foreign article or particle in a personal or business name is combined with the part of the name following it to form a single indexing unit. The indexing order is not affected by a space between a prefix and the rest of the name, and the space is disregarded when indexing.

Combine prefixes with the following word—DELEUROPE.

Examples of articles and particles are: a la, D', Da, De, Del, De la, Della, Den, Des, Di, Dos, Du, E', El, Fitz, Il, L', La, Las, Le, Les, Lo, Los, M', Mac, Mc, O', Per, Saint, San, Santa, Santo, St., Ste., Te, Ten, Ter, Van, Van de, Van der, Von, Von der.

Examples of Rule 6:

Filing Segment	Index Order of Units			
Name	Key Unit	Unit 2	Unit 3	Unit 4
1. Arthur A'Costa, DMD	A<u>C</u>OSTA	ARTHUR	DMD	
2. A'Costa's Pizza Parlor	ACOSTA<u>S</u>	PIZZA	PARLOR	
3. Ms. Maria De Abreu	<u>D</u>EABREU	MARIA	MS	
4. Mario De La Torres, Jr.	DE<u>L</u>ATORRES	MARIO	JR	
5. Thomas DelFavero, CPA	DEL<u>F</u>AVERO	THOMAS	CPA	
6. LaVoy & McNeil Attys	<u>L</u>AVOY	AND	MCNEIL	ATTYS
7. Mr. Timothy O'Brien	<u>O</u>BRIEN	TIMOTHY	MR	
8. O'Brien's Public House	OBRIEN<u>S</u>	PUBLIC	HOUSE	
9. St. Anne's Arts & Crafts	<u>S</u>TANNES	ARTS	AND	CRAFTS
10. Edward Ste. Cyr	ST<u>E</u>CYR	EDWARD		
11. Eric Ten Eyck	<u>T</u>ENEYCK	ERIC		
12. Ms. Lorraine TenPas, Ph.D.	TEN<u>P</u>AS	LORRAINE	PHD	MS
13. Mr. Pieter VanAmerongen	<u>V</u>ANAMERONGEN	PIETER	MR	
14. VanCamp's Sports & Hobby	VAN<u>C</u>AMPS	SPORTS	AND	HOBBY
15. Lt. Jason Van de Hoef	VAN<u>D</u>EHOEF	JASON	LT	

Check Your Knowledge of Rule 6

1. On a separate sheet of paper, code items a–j by placing diagonals (/) between each unit in the filing segment, underlining the key unit, and then numbering the second, third, and fourth units.

   a. MacCafferty & McCabe Consultants
   b. O'Hanlon's Barber Shop
   c. McAdoo's Web Design
   d. Martin O'Hanlon
   e. Pamela O'Connor
   f. Maureen O'Boyle's Networking Co.
   g. Colleen K. O'Donnell
   h. Mr. Mitchell McAdam
   i. Gov. Tom McCall
   j. Macadam's Road Building

2. Write the letters beside the names to indicate the correct alphabetic order for items a–j on the same piece of paper.
3. Which of the examples for Rule 6 needs a cross-reference?

RULE 7: NUMBERS IN BUSINESS NAMES

Numbers spelled out (Seven Acres Inn) in business names are filed alphabetically. Numbers written in digits are filed before alphabetic letters or words (B4 Photographers comes before Beleau Building Co.). Names with

Which is filed first—numbers spelled out or numbers written as figures?

numbers written in digits in the first units are filed in ascending order (lowest to highest number) before alphabetic names (229 Club, 534 Shop, Bank of Chicago). Arabic numerals are filed before Roman numerals (2, 3, II, III).

Names with inclusive numbers (33–37) are arranged by the first digit(s) only (33). Names with numbers appearing in other than the first position (Pier 36 Cafe) are filed alphabetically and immediately before a similar name without a number (Pier and Port Cafe).

When indexing numbers written in digit form that contain *st*, *d*, and *th* (1st, 2d, 3d, 4th), ignore the letter endings and consider only the digits (1, 2, 3, 4).

Examples of Rule 7:

		Index Order of Units		
Filing Segment				
Name	Key Unit	Unit 2	Unit 3	Unit 4
1. 7 Day Food Mart	7	DAY	FOOD	MART
2. 21st Century Graphics, Inc.	21	CENTURY	GRAPHICS	INC
3. 24 Carrot Cake Bakery	24	CARROT	CAKE	BAKERY
4. 405 Auto Repairs	405	AUTO	REPAIRS	
5. 500-510 DeLaRose Court	500	DELAROSE	COURT	
6. The 500 DeLaRose Shop	500	DELAROSE	SHOP	THE
7. 1001 Book Store	1001	BOOK	STORE	
8. 12500 Windows, Inc.	12500	WINDOWS	INC	
9. XXI Club	XXI	CLUB		
10. Fifth Dimension, Inc.	FIFTH	DIMENSION	INC	
11. Highway 395 Cafe	HIGHWAY	395	CAFE	
12. I-90 Road Services	I90	ROAD	SERVICES	
13. I-205 Towing, Inc.	I205	TOWING	INC	
14. One Main Place	ONE	MAIN	PLACE	
15. Sixty-Six Grand Ave. Apts.	SIXTYSIX	GRAND	AVE	APTS

Check Your Knowledge of Rule 7

On a separate sheet of paper, code the following names by placing diagonals between each unit in the filing segment, underlining the key unit, and then numbering the second and succeeding units. Write "Yes" if the names are in alphabetic order. Write "No" if the names are not in alphabetic order and show the correct order by rearranging the numbers. Item a has been coded and alphabetized for you.

a. 1. <u>EL-CO</u>/Enterprises²
   2. Colleen/<u>Eller-McKinstry</u>²
   3. <u>El Dorado</u>/Hotel²
  Ans: No, 1, 3, 2

f. 1. Janet de la Cross
   2. Janet DeLacey
   3. John DelaCruz

b. 1. 50% Off Shop
   2. V Roman Way
   3. 21st Century & Beyond Shop

c. 1. Labels 4 All, Inc.
   2. LaBelle Salon of Beauty
   3. Robert LaBelle

d. 1. Mackenzie M. Minten
   2. McKenzie Building Co.
   3. McKenzie's Café

e. 1. Philip TenEyck, Sr.
   2. 10 Minute Delivery
   3. Philip TenEyck, Jr.

g. 1. # 1 Delivery Express
   2. A-1 Auto Sales
   3. 10 # Line Shop

h. 1. Frank Van Camp
   2. Walter Vander Camp
   3. Wm. VanCamp

i. 1. Daniel LaDew
   2. Ladybug Day Care
   3. Joellen LaDuc

j. 1. The Elegant Gallery
   2. El Rancho Florists
   3. Ms. Anna Ellis

RULE 8: ORGANIZATIONS AND INSTITUTIONS

How do you index the names of organizations and other institutions?

Banks and other financial institutions, clubs, colleges, hospitals, hotels, lodges, magazines, motels, museums, newspapers, religious institutions, schools, unions, universities, and other organizations and institutions are indexed and filed according to the names written on their letterheads.

Examples of Rule 8:

	Filing Segment		Index Order of Units		
	Name	Key Unit	Unit 2	Unit 3	Unit 4
1.	1st National Bank	1	NATIONAL	BANK	
2.	Assembly of God Church	ASSEMBLY	OF	GOD	CHURCH
3.	Assn. of Iron Workers	ASSN	OF	IRON	WORKERS
4.	Associated Electric Workers	ASSOCIATED	ELECTRIC	WORKERS	
5.	The Bank of Mississippi	BANK	OF	MISSISSIPPI	THE
6.	Bank of Nova Scotia	BANK	OF	NOVA	SCOTIA
7.	College of the Rockies	COLLEGE	OF	THE	ROCKIES
8.	Disabled American Veterans	DISABLED	AMERICAN	VETERANS	
9.	Eastern Living Enrichment Center	EASTERN	LIVING	ENRICHMENT	CENTER
10.	Federated Farm Workers	FEDERATED	FARM	WORKERS	
11.	First Church of Christ	FIRST	CHURCH	OF	CHRIST
12.	Foundation for the Blind	FOUNDATION	FOR	THE	BLIND
13.	Hands and Feet Artists	HANDS	AND	FEET	ARTISTS
14.	Institute of Better Living	INSTITUTE	OF	BETTER	LIVING

Filing Segment	Index Order of Units			
Name	Key Unit	Unit 2	Unit 3	Unit 4
15. Jewish Historical Society	JEWISH	HISTORICAL	SOCIETY	
16. JFK High School	JFK	HIGH	SCHOOL	
17. Journal of Photography	JOURNAL	OF	PHOTOGRAPHY	
18. New York Times	NEW	YORK	TIMES	
19. Pacific University	PACIFIC	UNIVERSITY		
20. Public Employees Union	PUBLIC	EMPLOYEES	UNION	
21. Roosevelt High School	ROOSEVELT	HIGH	SCHOOL	
22. Rotary Club of Detroit	ROTARY	CLUB	OF	DETROIT
23. The Sandman's Hotels	SANDMANS	HOTELS	THE	
24. School of the Arts	SCHOOL	OF	THE	ARTS
25. Spokane Community College	SPOKANE	COMMUNITY	COLLEGE	
26. St. Vincent's Medical Center	STVINCENTS	MEDICAL	CENTER	
27. Temple Beth Israel	TEMPLE	BETH	ISRAEL	
28. University of Iowa	UNIVERSITY	OF	IOWA	
29. Western Society of Jesus	WESTERN	SOCIETY	OF	JESUS
30. Western X-Ray Technicians Assn.	WESTERN	XRAY	TECHNICIANS	ASSN

Check Your Knowledge of Rule 8

1. On a separate sheet of paper, code items a–j by placing diagonals between each unit in the filing segment, underlining the key unit, and then numbering the second and succeeding indexing units.

   a. Western Business and Information Technology Educators
   b. International Brotherhood of Electricians
   c. Church of Religious Science
   d. Vicksburg Episcopal Church
   e. St. Peter's Catholic Church
   f. Temple Beth Israel
   g. Boise Medical Center
   h. Union Gospel Missionaries
   i. University Hospital
   j. Purdue University

2. On the same sheet of paper, indicate whether the following pairs of names are in correct alphabetic order. If not, explain.

   a. International Organization of Masters, Mates & Pilots
      International Pentecostal Church
   b. Habitat for Humanity
      International Habitat for Endangered Species
   c. American Red Cross, Wisconsin Chapter
      American Baptist Churches of Montana

<ol type="d" start="4">
<li>American Legion Post 52
American Legion Post 32</li>
<li>American Association of Retired Persons, Chapter 78
American Association of University Women</li>
</ol>

RULE 9: IDENTICAL NAMES

When personal names and names of businesses, institutions, and organizations are identical (including titles as explained in Rule 5), filing order is determined by the addresses. Compare addresses in the following order:

1. City names.
2. State or province names (if city names are identical).
3. Street names, including *Avenue, Boulevard, Drive, Street* (if city and state names are identical).

   a. When the first units of street names are written in digits (18th Street), the names are considered in ascending numeric order (1, 2, 3) and placed together before alphabetic street names (18th Street, 24th Avenue, Academy Blvd.).

   b. Street names with compass directions (North, South, East, and West) are considered as written (SE Park Avenue, South Park Avenue). Numbers written as digits after compass directions are considered before alphabetic names (East 8th, East Main, Sandusky, SE Eighth, Southeast Eighth).

4. House or building numbers (if city, state, and street names are identical).

   a. House and building numbers written as digits are considered in ascending numeric order (8 Riverside Terrace, 912 Riverside Terrace) and placed together before spelled-out building names (The Riverside Terrace).

   b. If a street address and a building name are included in an address, disregard the building name.

   c. ZIP Codes are not considered in determining filing order.

<aside>
When names are identical, which indexing units are compared next?
</aside>

Examples of Rule 9:
Names of Cities Used to Determine Filing Order

Filing Segment	Index Order of Units			
Name	Key Unit	Unit 2	Unit 3	Unit 4
1. Snooze Inn Middlebury, Connecticut	SNOOZE	INN	MIDDLEBURY	
2. Snooze Inn New Haven, Connecticut	SNOOZE	INN	NEW	HAVEN

Names of States and Provinces Used to Determine Filing Order

	Filing Segment	Index Order of Units				
Name		Key Unit	Unit 2	Unit 3	Unit 4	Unit 5
3.	William H. Miller Nelson, BC (British Columbia)	MILLER	WILLIAM	H	NELSON	BC
4.	William H. Miller Nelson, PA	MILLER	WILLIAM	H	NELSON	PA
5.	Nacho Mama's Franklin, NJ	NACHO	MAMAS	FRANKLIN	NJ	
6.	Nacho Mama's Franklin, OH	NACHO	MAMAS	FRANKLIN	OH	

Names of Streets and Building Numbers Used to Determine Filing Order

	Filing Segment	Index Order of Units						
Name		Key Unit	Unit 2	Unit 3	Unit 4	Unit 5	Unit 6	Unit 7
7.	Ron's Deli 6570 – 8 St. Atlanta, GA	RONS	DELI	ATLANTA	GA	8	ST	
8.	Ron's Deli 4560 – 48 St. Atlanta, GA	RONS	DELI	ATLANTA	GA	48	ST	4560
9.	Ron's Deli 16450 Carter Ave. Atlanta, GA	RONS	DELI	ATLANTA	GA	CARTER	AVE	
10.	Ron's Deli 12800 Carter St. Atlanta, GA	RONS	DELI	ATLANTA	GA	CARTER	ST	12800
11.	Ron's Deli 18800 Carter St. Atlanta, GA	RONS	DELI	ATLANTA	GA	CARTER	ST	18800
12.	Ron's Deli 255 SW 15 St. Atlanta, GA	RONS	DELI	ATLANTA	GA	SW	15	ST
13.	Ron's Deli 576 SW Eighth St. Atlanta, GA	RONS	DELI	ATLANTA	GA	SW	EIGHTH	ST
14.	Ron's Deli 6224 SW Pecan Dr. Atlanta, GA	RONS	DELI	ATLANTA	GA	SW	PECAN	DR

Check Your Knowledge of Rule 9

On a separate sheet of paper, code each of the following names by placing diagonals between each unit in the filing segment, underlining the key unit, and then numbering the succeeding units. Are the pairs in correct alphabetic order? If not, explain.

a. St. Peter's Episcopal Church
   1250 SE Concord
   Salisbury, MA

   St. Peter's Episcopal Church
   2725 N 48 Street
   Salisbury, VT

b. Tiffany Reardon
   4550 SE Flavel St.
   Salem, OR

   Tiffany Reardon
   975 Cedar Street
   Salem, MA

c. The Inquirer
   870 N Main Street
   Granite, OK

   The Inquirer
   370 Main Street
   Granite, OR

d. The Corner Mart
   1015 – 17 Street
   Pittsburgh, PA

   The Corner Mart
   11500 – 8 Street
   Pittsburgh, PA

e. Mike's $ Saver
   8th and Grand Streets
   Milan, WA

   Mike's $ Saver
   16875 Main Street
   Milan, NH

f. US National Bank
   210 N Elgin Blvd.
   St. Louis, MO

   US National Bank
   150 S Elgin Ave.
   St. Louis, MO

RULE 10: GOVERNMENT NAMES

Government names are indexed first by the name of the governmental unit—country, state, county, or city. Next, index the distinctive name of the department, bureau, office, or board. The words "Office of," "Department of," "Bureau of," etc., are separate indexing units when they are part of the official name.

Note: If "of" is not a part of the official name as written, it is not added.

> **What are the first three indexing units of federal government agency names?**

A. Federal

The first three indexing units of a United States (federal) government agency name are *United States Government.* Note that the examples start with Unit 4.

		Key Unit	Unit 2	Unit 3		
		UNITED	STATES	GOVERNMENT		
Filing Segment			**Index Order of Units**			
Name	**Unit 4**	**Unit 5**	**Unit 6**	**Unit 7**	**Unit 8**
1. Houston Office					
General Accounting Office	GENERAL	ACCOUNTING	OFFICE	HOUSTON	OFFICE
2. Antitrust Division					
Justice Department	JUSTICE	DEPARTMENT	ANTITRUST	DIVISION	
3. Bureau of Prisons					
Justice Department	JUSTICE	DEPARTMENT	PRISONS	BUREAU	OF

Check Your Knowledge of Rule 10A

1. On a separate piece of paper, index and code items a–e by placing diagonals between each unit in the filing segment, underlining the key unit, and then numbering all succeeding units.

   a. National Park Service, Department of the Interior (federal government)

   b. Boise Field Office, Food and Nutrition Service, Department of Agriculture (federal government)

   c. Water Quality Section, Environmental Protection Agency (federal government)

   d. Pacific NW Regional Center, National Archives and Records Administration (federal government)

   e. Gifford-Pinchot National Forest, U.S. Forest Service, Department of Agriculture (federal government)

2. Write the letters beside the names to indicate the correct alphabetic order for items a–e on the same piece of paper.

B. State and Local

How are city government names indexed?

The first indexing units are the names of the state, province, county, parish, city, town, township, or village. Next, index the most distinctive name of the department, board, bureau, office, or government/political division. When the words "State of," "County of," "City of," "Department of," etc., are in a name, each word is a separate indexing unit.

Examples of Rule 10B:

Filing Segment	Index Order of Units					
Name	Unit 1	Unit 2	Unit 3	Unit 4	Unit 5	Unit 6
1. Banking Office Dept. of Commerce (State Government) Juneau, AK	ALASKA	COMMERCE	DEPT	OF	BANKING	OFFICE
2. Cincinnati Bridge Maint. Engineering Dept. Cincinnati, OH (City Government)	C<u>I</u>NCINNATI	ENGINEERING	DEPT	BRIDGE	MAINT	
3. Highway Div. Marin County (County Government) San Raphel, CA	M<u>A</u>RIN	COUNTY	HIGHWAY	DIV		
4. Dept. of Public Safety Baltimore, MD (State Government)	MAR<u>Y</u>LAND	PUBLIC	SAFETY	DEPT	OF	
5. Planning Commission Wheatland Municipal Dist. Strathmore, AB (Alberta)	<u>W</u>HEATLAND	MUNICIPAL	DIST	PLANNING	COMMISSION	

Check Your Knowledge of Rule 10B

1. On a separate piece of paper, index and code items a–e by placing diagonals between each unit in the filing segment, underlining the key unit, and then numbering all succeeding units.

    a. Beaverton Police Dept., Beaverton, Alabama
    b. Baker County Public Works, Baker City, Oregon
    c. Assessments and Taxation, Washington County, Hillsboro, Virginia
    d. Finance Division, Iowa Dept. of Revenue, Des Moines, Iowa
    e. Des Moines Fire Dept., Des Moines, Iowa

2. Write the letters beside the names to indicate the correct alphabetic order for items a–e on the same piece of paper.

C. Foreign

The distinctive English name is the first indexing unit for foreign government names. Then, index the balance of the formal name of the government, *if needed,* and if it is in the official name (CHINA REPUBLIC OF). Branches, departments, and divisions follow in order by their distinctive names. States, colonies, provinces, cities, and other divisions of

How are foreign government names indexed?

foreign governments are followed by their distinctive or official names as spelled in English.

Examples of Rule 10C:

Foreign Government Name	English Translation in Indexed Order*
1. Republik of Österreich	AUSTRIA REPUBLIC OF
2. Druk-yul	BHUTAN KINGDOM OF
3. République Gabonaise	GABON REPUBLIC OF
4. Jamhuri ya Kenya	KENYA REPUBLIC OF
5. Al-Joumhouriya al-Lubnaniya	LEBANON REPUBLIC OF
6. Repobli Kan'l Madagasikara	MADAGASCAR REPUBLIC OF

Check Your Knowledge of Rule 10C

1. On a separate piece of paper, code the English translation of items a–e by placing diagonals between each unit in the filing segment, underlining the key unit, and then numbering all succeeding units.

Foreign Government	English Translation
a. République de Guinée	Republic of Guinea
b. Bundesrepublik Deutschland	Federal Republic of Germany
c. Republika Hrvatska	Republic of Croatia
d. República del Ecuador	Republic of Ecuador
e. Nippon	Japan

2. Write the letters beside the names to indicate the correct alphabetic order for items a–e on the same piece of paper.

★Note: The *United States Government Manual* and the *Congressional Directory*, published annually, report a current list of United States government agencies and offices. *Countries, Dependencies, Areas of Special Sovereignty, and Their Principal Administrative Divisions*, published by the U.S. Department of Commerce, National Bureau of Standards, provides a list of geographic and political entities of the world and associated standard codes. The *State Information Book* by Susan Lukowski provides an up-to-date list of state departments and their addresses. The *World Almanac and Book of Facts*, updated annually, includes facts and statistics on many foreign nations, and is helpful as a source that gives the English spellings of many foreign names. A good Internet source for countries is Lycos infoplease.com (http://lycos.infoplease.com/countries.html). Your local and/or college library should have these reference books. Search the Internet for "US government." Many Internet sources show a breakdown of the departments, bureaus, and offices of the U.S. government, for example, the National Technology Transfer Center (http://www.nttc.edu/gov/departments.html).

What source will help you correctly index a federal government agency name?

Check Your Knowledge of Rules 6–10

1. On a separate sheet of paper, code the following names. Place diagonals between each unit in the filing segment, underline the key unit, and then number all succeeding units.

   a. Nat'l Assn. of Sheet Metal Workers
   b. Independent Order of Moose
   c. 1st Methodist Church
   d. The Green Bay Register Guard
   e. International Dunes Hotel
   f. American Federation of Teachers
   g. Building Dept., Athens, GA (City Government)
   h. Bureau of Tourism, Lyoveldio Island (Iceland)
   i. American Society of Engineers
   j. International Association of Diabetics
   k. Ernest L. A'Costa
   l. Sisters of Mercy Medical Center
   m. Bureau of Land Management, Department of the Interior (federal government)
   n. Brotherhood of Iron Workers
   o. Neighbors of Woodcraft

2. Write the letters beside the names to indicate the correct alphabetic order for items a–o on the same piece of paper.

3. On a separate sheet of paper, code the following names by placing diagonals between each unit in the filing segment, underlining the key unit, and then numbering the succeeding units. Next, indicate whether the pairs are in correct alphabetic order. If not, explain.

   a. St. Mary's Academy
      St. Mary's Church
   b. 21st Century Gallery
      The 21 Club
   c. Astor Elementary School
      Astoria Community College
   d. Water Dept. Buxton, ND
      Water Dept. Buxton, NC
   e. Central State Bank
      1430 Plymouth St.
      Redmond, UT

      Central State Bank
      350 E First Avenue
      Redmond, WA

   f. Daily News, Combs, KY
      Daily News, Combs, AK
   g. Elliniki Dimokratia
      (Greece Democracy)
      Towanda Greco
   h. School of Arts and Crafts
      School of the Arts
   i. San Carlos Apartments
      Mr. Tatsumi Sanada
   j. Freedom Museum
      Historical Commission
      Cheyenne, WY (State Govt.)

      Archives & Records
      Historical Commission
      Cheyenne, WY (State Govt.)

CROSS-REFERENCES, BUSINESS NAMES (CONTINUED)

In Chapter 2, you learned that cross-references should be prepared for business names that are (1) compound names, (2) abbreviations and acronyms, (3) popular and coined names, and (4) hyphenated names. In this chapter, you will learn to prepare cross-references for the following types of business names:

5. Divisions and subsidiaries
6. Changed names
7. Similar names
8. Foreign business names
9. Foreign government names

An explanation of the procedure to be followed in cross-referencing each of these kinds of names follows.

The original record is stored in one place according to the alphabetic rules being used. A cross-reference is made, if necessary, for any of the reasons discussed here and in Chapter 2. The cross-reference will, in all probability, be on a label affixed to the tab of a guide or on a sheet of paper inserted into a folder. The cross-reference guide or the cross-reference sheet may be a distinctive color so that it is easy to find.

Divisions and Subsidiaries

When one company is a subsidiary or a division or branch of another company, the name appearing on the letterhead of the branch or subsidiary is the one indexed on the original record. A cross-reference is made under the name of the parent company. Examples are shown in Figure 3–1.

Changed Names

A company may change its name. Records must then be changed to indicate the name change and to ensure that the new name will be used for storage purposes. If only a few records are already in storage, they are usually refiled under the new name, and the former name is marked as a cross-reference. If many records are filed under the former name, a permanent cross-reference is placed at the beginning of the records for the former name. Any new records are placed under the new name. Examples are shown in Figure 3–2: Paragon Cable changed its name to AT&T Cable Services, and GTE changed its name to Verizon Communications.

Similar Names

Similar names for a business include examples like Northwest or North West, Southeast or South East, Goodwill or Good Will, and All State or Allstate. If a name could be considered either as one unit or as two units, it

How is a cross-reference for a division of a company prepared?

If a company changes its name, how is the cross-reference prepared?

Original

ONE STOP MORTGAGE

One Stop Mortgage
(A div. of National Bancorp)
555 Oregon Bldg.
San Francisco, CA 94102-0555

Cross-Reference

NATIONAL BANCORP

SEE ONE STOP MORTGAGE

Original

PLATINUM VISA SERVICES

Platinum VISA Services
(A subsidiary of National
    Bancorp)
2250 SE Main St.
Chicago, IL 60680-2250

Cross-Reference

NATIONAL BANCORP

SEE PLATINUM VISA SERVICES

Figure 3–1 **Cross-Reference: Divisions and Subsidiaries**

Original

ATANDT CABLE SERVICES

AT&T Cable Services
1650 SW Broadway
Boston, MA 02174-1650

Cross-Reference

PARAGON CABLE

SEE ATANDT CABLE SERVICES

Original

VERIZON COMMUNICATIONS

Verizon Communications
16540 SE Jennings Ave.
Lansing, MI 48912-1650

Cross-Reference

GTE

SEE VERIZON COMMUNICATIONS

Figure 3–2 **Cross-Reference: Changed Names**

is a good candidate for a cross-reference. A SEE ALSO cross-reference is used to remind the filer to check the files for other possible spellings. The complete business name is not cross-referenced—only the similar name. For example, Allstate Road Supply is the complete name of the business; a SEE ALSO cross-reference is prepared for All State. (See Figure 3–3.)

What is an example of similar business names?

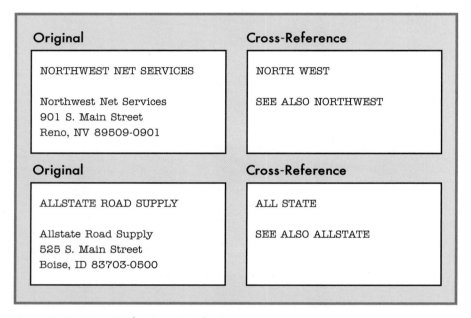

Original

NORTHWEST NET SERVICES

Northwest Net Services
901 S. Main Street
Reno, NV 89509-0901

Cross-Reference

NORTH WEST

SEE ALSO NORTHWEST

Original

ALLSTATE ROAD SUPPLY

Allstate Road Supply
525 S. Main Street
Boise, ID 83703-0500

Cross-Reference

ALL STATE

SEE ALSO ALLSTATE

Figure 3–3 Cross-Reference: Similar Names

Foreign Business Names

The original spelling of a foreign business name is often written in the foreign language, which is then translated into English for coding. The English translation is written on the document to be stored, and the document is stored under the English spelling. When a request for records is written in the native language, the filer will find that a cross-reference bearing the original spelling is an aid in finding the records. Special care should be taken to ensure the correct spellings and markings because they may differ greatly from the English form. Examples are shown in Figure 3–4.

In what language is the original record of a foreign business name filed?

Foreign Government Names

The name of a foreign government and its agencies, like foreign businesses, is often written in a foreign language. Write the English translation of the government name on each document to be stored. Store all documents under the English spelling. A cross-reference is prepared using the foreign spelling. Examples are shown in Figure 3–5.

In what language is a cross-reference prepared for a foreign government name?

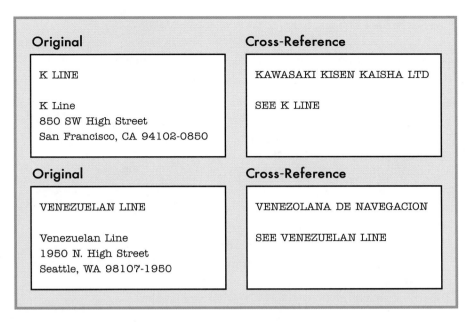

Figure 3–4 Cross-Reference: Foreign Business Names

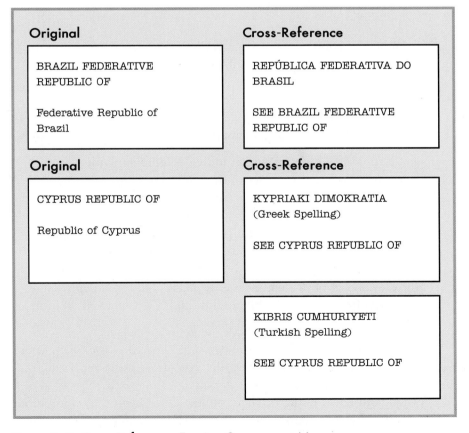

Figure 3–5 Cross-Reference: Foreign Government Names

Check Your Knowledge of Cross-References of Business Names

On a separate sheet of paper, prepare a cross-reference for each name that should have a cross-reference.

1. Societe Europeene des Satellite
   Translated: European Society of Satellites
2. Dade County Public Works, Miami, Florida
3. St. Catherine Catholic Church
4. New Orleans Police Department
5. Northwest Security Systems
6. Tech-N-Go Co., A Div. of Systems Solutions Corp.
7. Anchorage Daily News
8. Ministry of Defense, Dominion of Canada
9. Thao Huong Distributing Company changed its name to Huong Distribution, Inc.
10. All State Mfg. Co.

SUBJECTS WITHIN ALPHABETIC ARRANGEMENT

Within an alphabetic arrangement, records may sometimes be stored and retrieved more conveniently by a subject title than by a specific name. Beware, however, of using so many subjects that the arrangement becomes primarily a subject arrangement with alphabetic names as subdivisions! A few typical examples of acceptable subjects to use within an otherwise alphabetic name arrangement are:

- *Applications*. The job for which individuals are applying is more important than are the names of the applicants.
- *Bids or projects*. All records pertaining to the same bid or the same project are kept together under the project or bid title.
- *Special promotions or celebrations*. All records relating to a specific event are grouped together by subject.
- *Branch office memos and other information sent to many different offices.* Material of this nature is grouped together to keep storage containers from becoming filled with duplicate records filed in many different places.

The filing procedure for the subject storage method is explained in detail in Chapter 7. Its application in this chapter consists of writing the subject title on the record if it does not already appear there.

When coding a record, the main subject is the key unit. Subdivisions of the main subject are considered as successive units. The name of the correspondent (individual or company name) is considered last.

In what situations would you find records grouped by subject in an alphabetic file?

For example, on all records pertaining to applications, the word *APPLICATIONS* is written as the key unit. The specific job applied for is a subdivision of that main subject and is the next unit (*ASSISTANT* in the first example and *CASHIER* in the third example). The applicant's name is coded last.

Examples of Subjects Within Alphabetic Arrangement:

		Index Order of Units		
Key Unit	Unit 2	Unit 3	Unit 4	Unit 5
1. APPLICATIONS	ASSISTANT	ADAMS	LOREN	
2. APPLICATIONS	ASSISTANT	CHUNG	KAREN	
3. APPLICATIONS	CASHIER	CLERK	OWINGS	CHERYL
4. APPLICATIONS	CASHIER	CLERK	PACE	JANICE
5. APPLICATIONS	DATA	ENTRY	GEORGE	SUE
6. APPLICATIONS	DATA	ENTRY	JORDAN	VICKY
7. APPLICATIONS	RECORDS	CLERK	AMOS	PENELOPE
8. APPLICATIONS	RECORDS	CLERK	BAKER	MARGARET

SUMMARY

The second half of the alphabetic filing rules addresses additional kinds of personal and business names as well as government names. A prefix (article or particle) is combined with the part of the name following it regardless of space.

Numbers spelled out in business names are alphabetized. Numbers written in digit form are filed numerically in ascending order before alphabetic names. Arabic numbers are filed before Roman numerals. Inclusive numbers are filed by the first digit(s) only.

Organizations and other institutions are indexed as written on letterheads. When names are identical, use the addresses to determine filing order. Start with the city, then state; use the street name last. If a difference still has not occurred in these units of the name, use the house or building number to determine the order.

Government names are indexed first by the name of the governmental unit (country, state, county, or city). The first three indexing units in federal government names are UNITED STATES GOVERNMENT. The next units are the distinctive name of the department, office, or bureau. The words "Office of," "Department of," etc., are separate indexing units only when those words are part of the official name.
Continued

Cross-references are prepared for businesses that are a division or subsidiary of another company, changed business names, similar names, foreign business names, and foreign governments.

Within an alphabetic file, subject files are appropriate for applications, bids or projects, special promotions or celebrations, or branch office memos.

REVIEW AND DISCUSSION

1. Code and arrange the following names in alphabetic order and justify your arrangement. (Obj. 1)
   a. Frederick Van der Sanden
   b. V-A-N Delivery Service
   c. Frederic Van Der Sanden
   d. John Vander-Sanden
   e. Vance's Web Design

2. Code and arrange the following names in alphabetic order and justify your arrangement. (Obj. 2)
   a. 3 Rs Tutoring
   b. 7 Gnomes Mining Co.
   c. 5 Star Movie Producers
   d. 405 Interstate Inn
   e. 1 Stop Shopping

3. Code and arrange the following names in alphabetic order and justify your arrangement. (Obj. 3)
   a. St. Peter's Orthodox Church
   b. St. Paul First National Bank
   c. The St. Paul Times
   d. St. Peter's Children's Home
   e. St. Paul's Chapter of the American Red Cross

4. What determines the alphabetic arrangement of common names that are identical such as John Smith or Lincoln High School? (Obj. 3 and 4)

5. Index, code, and arrange the following federal government names in alphabetic order. Hint: The first three units in each name are the same. (Obj. 5)
   a. Animal Damage Control, Animal and Plant Health Inspection, Department of Agriculture
   b. Air Quality Section, Nevada Operations Office, Environmental Protection Agency

c. Customs Service, Department of the Treasury (federal government)
   d. Bureau of Export Administration, Department of Commerce
   e. Federal Aviation Administration, Department of Transportation
   f. Federal Protective Service, General Services Administration
   g. Bureau of Engraving and Printing, Department of the Treasury
   h. Bureau of Public Affairs, Department of State
   i. Energy Sciences Network, Department of Energy
   j. Department of the Navy, Department of Defense

6. When arranging city, county, province, or state government names, what are the key units? (Obj. 5)

7. Which of the following items need cross-references? Explain why cross-references are needed and prepare the necessary cross-references. (Obj. 6)
   a. Transportacion Maritima Mexicana (Mexican Shipping Line)
   b. O'Connor Construction changed its name to Buildings by O'Connor
   c. Southwest Computer Institute
   d. Modular Housing, a subsidiary of St. Cyr Construction Company, Inc.
   e. Koninkrijk Belgie (Kingdom of Belgium)

8. Why are subject categories sometimes used in an alphabetically arranged name file? Give at least two examples of subjects that might be found in an alphabetic file. (Obj. 7)

APPLICATIONS (APP)

APP 3-1.   Create an Alphabetic Card File (Objs. 1-6)

1. On 5" by 3" cards or on slips of paper of that size, key or print in indexing order the names listed below. Key or print the number beside the name in the top right corner of the card. Key or print the name and address below the indexed name.

2. Prepare cross-reference cards where necessary according to the guidelines provided in this chapter. On the cross-reference card, key or print the number of the original name plus an "X" in the top right corner.

3. Arrange all cards, including cross-references, in alphabetic order.

4. In a vertical column on a separate sheet of paper, list the numbers on the cards that you have now arranged in alphabetic order. Check your answers as your instructor directs.

5. Combine the cards you created in Chapter 2, APP 2-1, with the cards you created for this application. Arrange the cards so all 40 names and their cross-references are shown in alphabetic order. Check your answers as your instructor directs.

Example Cards:

```
┌─────────────────────────────────────────────────┐
│                                                   │
│  MOZAMBIQUE REPUBLIC OF              33           │
│  TOURISM DEPARTMENT OF                            │
│                                                   │
│                                                   │
│                                                   │
└─────────────────────────────────────────────────┘
```

```
┌─────────────────────────────────────────────────┐
│                                                   │
│  REPUBLICA DE MOCAMBIQUE             33X          │
│                                                   │
│  SEE MOZAMBIQUE REPUBLIC OF                       │
│  TOURISM DEPARTMENT OF                            │
│                                                   │
└─────────────────────────────────────────────────┘
```

Names:
21. Keene Baptist Church, 330 Beech Ave., Keene, NH 03435-0330
22. 9 to 5 Uniform Shop, 1250 S Mill St., Dutton, VA 23050-5142
23. Richard LaBelle, 2800 Bowman Rd., Baskett, KY 42402-3801
24. Transportation Dept., République Islamique de Mauritanie, (Translation: Islamic Republic of Mauritania)
25. LaBelle Beauty Shop, 145 Ross St., Lebanon, MO 65536-1089
26. Leadoff Investment Co., 350 N. Silas St., Auburn, AL 36830-4521
27. The Kelso Times, 3560 Main St., Kelso, WA 98626-3560
28. Memo, a div. of Mason Office Products, 6354 N. Vineyard, Marion, NY 14505-6543
29. Kent Fire Dept., 250 N. Main St., Kent, TX 79855-0250
30. The Kelso Times, 9520 Ashton Way, Kelso, CA 92309-9520
31. 57 Street Club, 19450 - 57 Street, Somerton, AZ 85350-5700
32. Lenox Public Works Dept., 220 S. Main Street, Lenox, MA 01240-0220
33. Department of Tourism, República de MoÇambique (Translation: Republic of Mozambique)
34. Lenox Police Dept., 35 Greenway Plaza, Lenox, IA 50851-0035
35. Ms. Colleen McNamara, CPS, 442 Lark Avenue, San Antonio, TX 78263-4400
36. LaBelle Beauty Shop, 450 S. Harris Street, Lebanon, IL 62254-4700
37. Keene Brotherhood of Iron Workers, 255 Exeter, Keene, NY 12942-0255
38. Life Center Institute, 16750 S. McLoughlin, Marion, NC 28752-1675
39. Kent's Barber Shop, 30250 N. Harris Street, Montgomery, IN 47558-4350
40. Kent Police Dept., 4350 Cedar Street, Kent, CT 06757-4350

Write or key in indexing order the units of the filing segments for the
names below. Then write or key the number by each filing segment
to indicate correct alphabetic order for the names.

No.	Filing Segment
1.	2 for 1 Paperback Books
2.	K-2 Construction (A div. of Karvonen & Kelly, Inc.)
3.	Little Owl's Bookstore Providence, RI
4.	McGregor Public Works Dept. (city government)
5.	Meade County Historical Society
6.	LaFont, Martin & Newton Lawyers
7.	North-West Services Co.
8.	Ms. Lorrie La Font
9.	Señor Juan Medina
10.	21 Manchester Market
11.	M/A Computer Systems
12.	Little Owl's Bookstore Bangor, ME
13.	MMK (Martin, McGregor & Keebler Studios)
14.	New Hope Church
15.	Keep In Touch Florists
16.	Sathalanalat Paxathipatai Paxaxon Lao (Translation: Lao People's Democratic Republic)
17.	New Hope Fire Dept.
18.	Keep'em Flying
19.	Museum of Tall Ships
20.	Ms. Noriko Nagai
21.	LaFontana Downtown Hotel
22.	205 Shopping Center
23.	Little Owl's Bookstore Bangor, PA
24.	Natural Cosmetics (name change for Nancy's Beauty Shop)
25.	Ken Keebler Bake Shop
26.	Mrs. Melanie LaFont-Newton
27.	Maitres-Fourreurs Associes (Translation: Master Furriers Association)
28.	Nu-Hope Natural Foods
29.	Little Rock Fire Dept.
30.	Little Owl's Bookstore Bangor, MI

APPLYING THE RULES

Job 2, Card Filing, Rules 6–10.

Practice Set

CHAPTER 4

ALPHABETIC INDEXING RULES FOR COMPUTER APPLICATIONS

LEARNING OBJECTIVES

1. Describe how databases can be used in records management.
2. Describe how ASCII values affect computer sorting.
3. Analyze and adjust filing segments for input into computer applications software.
4. Describe and apply simple electronic file management.

USING DATABASES

An electronic **database** is a collection of related data stored on a computer system that can be manipulated or extracted for use with various applications but managed independently of them. Databases are organized especially for rapid search and retrieval of specific facts or information. People have been using databases on large mainframe computers for many years. A variety of database programs are available for personal computers as well.

A database is composed of tables containing records and fields. A **field** is a set of one or more characters treated as a unit of information. The combination of characters forms words, numbers, or a meaningful code. Your first name, middle name, and last name could each be entered in a separate field. Your date of birth, social security number, telephone number, the day you started school, and the month and year you finished high school are all examples of facts about you, and each fact could be entered in a separate field.

What is a field?

All the fields related to one person or organization make up a **record** (sometimes called a *computer record* to distinguish it from a paper record). Records related to one subject or topic (customers, students, orders) make up a **table**. A database can contain several tables and other objects such as forms and reports. Figure 4–1 shows a database created with *Microsoft Access*.

What is a record?

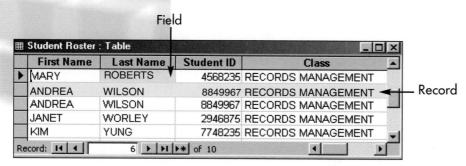

Figure 4–1 **Database Table**

A field has a unique name and a specified number of characters, and it contains a defined type of information. Typical field types include text fields (sometimes called *alphanumeric fields* for letters, numbers, symbols, and punctuation) and number fields (for numbers only). In a more sophisticated database program, the field types can include date fields and logical fields.

When using database software, a unique or key field may be specified. Each record in the database can have a unique identifier. For example, when you change a service to your telephone, the person making the change asks for your phone number (which is unique to you). Your phone number is entered into the database, which then finds and displays your personal information.

Word processing and spreadsheet software can contain simple databases. A relational database program such as *Microsoft Access* allows more flexibility in working with the information in the database. When the document is set up in database form with fields (whether the document is in a word processing, spreadsheet, or database program), sorting on any field is possible. The procedures vary depending on the software. Usually a field or column is selected. The type of sort is defined: ascending (A–Z, 1–10) or descending (Z–A, 10–1). The sort command is carried out, and the list is placed in alphabetic or numeric order by the chosen field. Several words can be entered in the same field and the correct alphabetic order is maintained.

> *Can you use a word processing program to create a database ?*

Finding Information in a Database

Finding a specific piece of information in a database is easy! Use the Find feature to enter the name, address, phone number, or data. Tell the database to search all fields, give the command to start the search, and the information will display on the screen within seconds. What if you don't know the exact name for the database to find? In this case, you can enter the first few letters of the last name. When that information displays on the screen, scroll through the records until you find the correct one. You may need other information to validate that the name is the correct one.

A database is useful for sorting various fields alphabetically. As you learned in Chapters 2 and 3, an alphabetic listing of customer names makes it much easier to look up a particular customer. Database software can sort any field in the database. If you want to sort the database by the city in which customers live, simply sort the City field. If you want to sort the database by the postal code for a large customer mailing, sort on the Postal Code field. If you want to sort the database by the city then alphabetically by customer, the database will return this information with the proper query. Remember that the purpose of filing is for retrieval—finding and using information again. A **query** is a database object used to instruct the program to find specific information. For example, Figure 4–2 shows the design view of a query in *Microsoft Access* and the resulting query table.

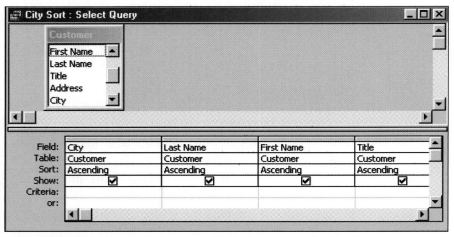

Design View

Query Results

Figure 4–2 **Access Query**

Figure 4–3 shows a partial report based on the query shown in Figure 4–2. Customers are grouped alphabetically by city, and then sorted by name.

City Sort

City	Last Name	First Name	Title
Albany			
	Kelly	Arnold	Mr.
	Lilly	Camille	Ms.
	Read	Timothy	Mr.
	Smith	Richard	Mr.
Aloha			
	Little	Denise	Mrs.
Beaverton			
	Kale	Ed	Mr.
Corvallis			
	Clarkson	William	Mr.

Figure 4–3 Access Report

Queries also help a user summarize information. For example, a video store has a database of customer names, addresses, phone numbers, video rentals organized by types of movies, and the dates of rentals. The store manager wants to know which category of movies had the most rentals last month. The query would ask the database to sort the Movie Category field, and then identify the beginning and ending dates of the last month in the Date Rented field. The database would return a list of customers in sorted order by the Movie Category field for the last month.

Video stores use databases to store movie titles, customer information, and dates of rentals.

How could this information be used? The store manager could count the number of rentals for a specific category of movie. If comedies were rented more often than dramatic movies, the manager could obtain more comedies. Keeping track of the rental dates will help the store manager know which days are the busiest. Would you guess Fridays and Saturdays? The database will return a listing of days of the week so that the store manager has solid data to use in making decisions.

Using Databases to Assist in Records Management

Many records departments create a database index of their paper and/or nonpaper records. For example, a database is created that contains the names, addresses, and telephone numbers of customers of the symphony. The actual records are sales records in paper form. An electronic database allows rapid creation of mailing labels to notify customers of special concerts or other events to help generate more sales.

Local area networks (LANs) are common in many businesses. The use of a LAN allows the sharing of correspondence, forms, and other computer records. A database index listing the names of the files and their locations is helpful in maintaining order in the electronic files. Chapter 10 discusses LANs and other automated records in more detail.

HOW COMPUTERS SORT DATA

Why use a computer for office operations?

A computer performs sorting operations quickly and can store a great amount of data in a small space. It pays great attention to detail and can retrieve information faster and more accurately than humans—*if* the input is accurate.

In Chapters 2 and 3, you were introduced to standard alphabetic indexing rules for personal and business names. In this chapter, you will learn about how to enter names into a computer to achieve correct alphabetic order when the names are sorted.

The As Written column in Example 1 on page 79 shows a computer sort of example names from Rules 1 – 10 in Chapters 2 and 3. The names were keyed into the computer as they were written. Example 2 shows the same list of names (in all caps with no punctuation) keyed in indexing order. Notice the difference in the alphabetic order of the examples. What causes the difference? Part of the change is due to placing the words in indexing order. To understand some other factors contributing to the difference, you need some background on how the computer recognizes information.

Example 1	Example 2
As Written	**Indexing Order**
"A-OK" Smart Shop	003 RS NURSERY SCHOOL
# Off Diet Center	026 HIGHWAY SERVICE
$ Value Store	405 SHOPPING CENTER
405 Shopping Center	AOK SMART SHOP
3 Rs Nursery School	DOLLAR VALUE STORE
26 Highway Service	LABELLE FASHION BOUTIQUE
LaBelle Fashion Boutique	LARRYS RESTAURANT
Larry's Restaurant	POUNDS OFF DIET CENTER

ASCII Values

The American Standard Code for Information Interchange (**ASCII**, pronounced "Ask E") was developed to give computers a standard and logical way to recognize character data. ASCII assigns specific numeric values to the first 128 characters of the 256 possible character combinations. Each space, symbol, number, uppercase, and lowercase letter has a unique numeric value. Notice the order of the decimal numbers and the ASCII characters in the ASCII Values Chart shown in Figure 4–4 on page 80.

Sort by ASCII Values

What do the ASCII values have to do with alphabetic indexing rules? When you manually sort a list of names, you look at the letters to determine the order. A computer reads each character as an ASCII value. Because these ASCII values are numbers, the computer places the lowest value, or number, first. Then the numbers are sorted from lowest to highest. Symbols such as $, %, and /, are sorted before numbers written as digits because symbols have a lower numeric value. Capital letters have a lower value than lowercase letters and thus are placed before lowercase letters in a sort.

If a filing segment begins with a number, it would be sorted before any filing segment that begins with an uppercase letter. If two filing segments were the same, but one was in uppercase letters and the other was in lowercase letters, the uppercase letters would be sorted and listed before the lowercase letters.

By understanding how a computer reads the ASCII values, you can make your computer input more accurate and the output more predictable.

> *According to the ASCII values, which comes first—an uppercase A or a lowercase a?*

Decimal Number	ASCII Character	Decimal Number	ASCII Character	Decimal Number	ASCII Character
*32	Space	64	@	96	'
33	!	65	A	97	a
34	"	66	B	98	b
35	#	67	C	99	c
36	$	68	D	100	d
37	%	69	E	101	e
38	&	70	F	102	f
39	'	71	G	103	g
40	(	72	H	104	h
41	)	73	I	105	i
42	*	74	J	106	j
43	+	75	K	107	k
44	,	76	L	108	y
45	-	77	M	108	m
46	.	78	N	110	n
47	/	79	O	111	o
48	0	80	P	112	p
49	1	81	Q	113	q
50	2	82	R	114	r
51	3	83	S	115	s
52	4	84	T	116	t
53	5	85	U	117	u
54	6	86	V	118	v
55	7	87	W	119	w
56	8	88	X	120	x
57	9	89	Y	121	y
58	:	90	Z	122	z
59	;	91	[	123	{
60	<	92	\	124		
61	=	93	]	125	}
62	>	94	^	126	~
63	?	95	_	127	DEL

* The first 31 decimal characters are reserved for nonprinting characters, sometimes known as control characters.

Figure 4–4 ASCII Values Chart

APPLYING INDEXING RULES TO COMPUTER APPLICATIONS

Whether you are indexing and coding filing segments for a manual storage system or for computerized storage, the choice of the filing segment is vitally important. Careful attention to detail, consistent application of the alphabetic indexing rules, and knowledge of how a computer processes data are important points to remember. This section deals with the considerations for computer input of filing segments.

For computer input of filing segments:

- Follow Rules 1 – 10 from Chapters 2 and 3 with the modifications described in the following sections.
- Key indexing units used to determine filing order in uppercase letters with no punctuation. (Data entered in other fields might be entered in all caps or in upper- and lowercase with or without punctuation depending upon the intended use of the data.)
- Spell out all symbols.
- Format numbers for proper sorting. (See Rule 7: Numbers in Business Names that follows.)

Rule 5: Titles and Suffixes

Names with titles and suffixes are indexed according to Rule 5, Chapter 2. Numeric suffixes (I, II) are filed before alphabetic suffixes (CPA, Jr. Sr.). The computer reads Roman numerals as letters and sorts them after numbers. Key Roman numerals as Arabic numbers (1, 2, 3, etc.) so suffixes will be placed in the correct filing order. The following table shows examples of suffixes with Roman numerals keyed as Arabic numbers and as letters and how they sorted. In Example 1, CPA is filed before Roman numeral II. This list is *not* in correct order because Roman numerals were keyed as letters. The list in Example 2 is in correct order.

> *How do you key Roman numerals?*

Example 1 Incorrect Order			Example 2 Correct Order		
Last Name	First Name	Title/Suffix	Last Name	First Name	Title/Suffix
MILLER	JOHN	CPA	MILLER	JOHN	2
MILLER	JOHN	II	MILLER	JOHN	3
MILLER	JOHN	III	MILLER	JOHN	CPA
MILLER	JOHN	JR	MILLER	JOHN	JR
MILLER	JOHN	MAYOR	MILLER	JOHN	MAYOR
MILLER	JOHN	MR	MILLER	JOHN	MR
MILLER	JOHN	SR	MILLER	JOHN	SR

Rule 7: Numbers in Business Names

When entering data in a text field, numbers written as digits should be keyed so that all numbers have an equal number of digits and align on the right. A zero added to the front of a number to have it sort in numeric order is known as a **leading zero**. Most people know that 2 comes before 10. To the computer, which reads from left to right, 1 comes first, then 10 through 19, then 2, followed by 20 through 29, continuing to 99. By adding a zero before a one-digit number, you are forcing the computer to read the number as a two-digit number. In Example 1, the numbers 14, 7, and 205 are out of order because leading zeros have not been added. In Example 2, the numbers with leading zeros sort correctly.

How many leading zeros are entered for the number 7 in a list containing numbers 10, 407, and 1250?

Example 1	Example 2
Company Name	**Company Name**
14 CARROT BAKERY	007 SEAS RESTAURANT
205 AUTO SERVICE	014 CARROT BAKERY
7 SEAS RESTAURANT	205 AUTO SERVICE

Rule 9: Identical Names

Identical names are indexed according to Rule 9, Chapter 3. Remember, the address is used to determine alphabetic order; first by the city name, then the state, then the street name, and last the building number. A database structure to match Rule 9 includes Address, City, State, and Street fields. If a building number will determine a filing order, a Building Number field is also needed. Add leading zeros in a building number field if the field is a text field. If the field is a number field, the numbers will sort correctly without leading zeros.

In Example 1, the Address field contains both the building numbers and the street name. The data in the Address field is sorted by the numbers, which does not result in the correct order. In Example 2, the building number is in a separate field and leading zeros are used. The database table is sorted first by the Address field, then the City field, then the State field, and then the Bldg No field. The sort is now correct.

What fields are needed to sort identical names correctly?

Example 1				Example 2		
Address	**City**	**St**	**Bldg No**	**Address**	**City**	**St**
145 CEDAR STREET	SELMA	AL	025	ASH STREET	SELMA	AL
201 ASH STREET	SELMA	AL	201	ASH STREET	SELMA	AL
25 ASH STREET	SELMA	AL	145	CEDAR STREET	SELMA	AL

ELECTRONIC FILE MANAGEMENT

Electronic records are proliferating at an exponential rate. As the number of computer files increases, the need to organize these files is more important than ever. For example, how many disks do you have for your homework? Do you know where your last essay is stored and the name of the file? This section gives a background on file naming rules, and then gives suggestions for organizing files.

Working with a Computer Operating System

Whether an application program is run from a mainframe, minicomputer, or microcomputer, it performs according to the operating system of the computer. An **operating system** is an organized collection of software that controls the overall operations of a computer. It is the link between the computer hardware, the user, and the application software. A common operating system for microcomputers is *Windows*, developed by Microsoft. *Windows* is an operating system and an interface for humans at the same time. The *Windows* program was designed to help people interact more efficiently with the computer. Other operating systems specific to the type of computer and microprocessor are also available. For instance, the Apple Macintosh operating system is called *Mac OS*. Another operating system gaining popularity is *Linux*. *Linux* is an open source operating system, which means that the programming code is available for anyone, i.e., not owned by any one company.

When you work with any computer application software, each file you create must have a filename. A **filename** is a unique name given to a file stored for computer use; the filename must follow the computer's operating system rules. For common operating systems, characters can include all letters of the alphabet; digits 0 through 9; and special characters such as ! @ # $ % ^ & ( ) - _ { } ~ `. You may not use some mathematic and punctuation symbols. Some operating systems restrict filenames to eight characters in length. *Windows 95* and higher versions allow longer filenames, as does *Mac OS* and *Linux* operating systems.

A three-letter extension can be used in filenames. In some application programs, the extension is assigned by the program and cannot be changed. For example, a file that contains database records may have an extension of *mdb*, a spreadsheet may have an extension of *xls*, and a word processing file may have an extension of *doc*. Extensions can be helpful in identifying files stored on your disk.

Large hard drives of 10, 20, or 30 gigabytes or more are common in today's personal computers. By convention, floppy drives are indicated by an A or a B. Hard drives are indicated by a C, D, or E. Typical personal

> **What is an operating system on a computer?**

Large hard drives of 30 gigabytes or more are common in today's personal computers.

computers have one floppy drive, one hard drive, and one CD-ROM or CD-RW drive. The floppy drive is called Drive A, the hard drive is called drive C, and the CD drive is called drive D.

Organizing Folders and Files

What is a directory or folder on a computer?

Dividing disk space into directories or folders is an important part of managing your computer's information. A **directory** or **folder** is a subdivision of a disk created by the operating system of a computer. Each set or group of records created for a specific purpose should be in a separate folder. Each folder can contain many files. For example, you might have a directory for this class called Records Management on your computer's hard drive C. You might create a file called *Chapter 4.doc* and save it to the Records Management directory. The full path and filename for this document would be C:\Records Management\Chapter 4.doc. Notice that a backwards diagonal (\) is used to separate the drive, the folder, and the filename. This notation is called the *path* to indicate where the file is stored.

Creating folders on your floppy or hard disk is easy. You can even have folders within folders. Your folder structure is more effective if it is shallow (many folders at the same level) rather than deep (folders within folders within folders). Seeing the logic of folders can be difficult when several layers of folders are used.

Choosing meaningful names for folders and files is important for quick retrieval of files. While you are in college, folders can be named for the classes you are taking. When you create files for your classes, simply store the file in the correct class folder. Figure 4–5 shows an example of a typical student's file system.

When you study Chapter 7, Subject Records Management, you will be introduced to records stored by subjects. An example of an administrative assistant's file system for a hard drive organized by the main subjects of the business is shown in Figure 4–6.

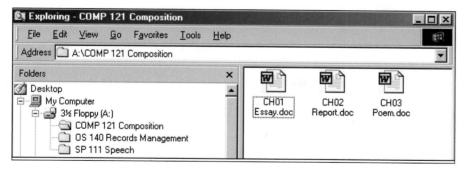

Figure 4–5 Typical Student's Folders

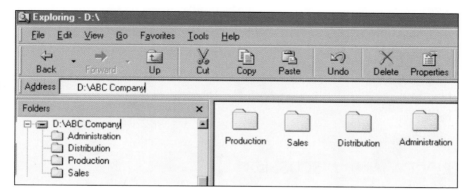

Figure 4–6 Folders for the ABC Company

SUMMARY

In a database, a record contains one or more fields about one person or subject. Records related to one subject or person (customers, students, orders) make up a table. When sorting, you must choose the field by which to sort and the order of the sort (ascending or descending).

A computer sorts data based on the numeric values of the letters or digits as determined by the ASCII values. Numbers are sorted before capital letters. Capital letters are sorted before lowercase letters. The sort order for symbols varies with the symbol. Whether you are indexing and coding for a manual or computer filing system, attention to detail, consistent application of the alphabetic indexing rules, and knowledge of how a computer processes data are important points to remember.

When keying indexing units to be used in determining filing order, use all caps with no punctuation and spell out all symbols. In addition, key Roman numerals as Arabic numbers. In text fields, add leading zeros so that numbers align on the right. For identical names, enter data in fields for the city, state, street name, and building number. Use these fields in determining the proper filing order.

Continued

When creating a computer file, you must save it by giving it a file-name. The specific rules for naming the file are determined by the computer's operating system. A file extension may be added automatically by the application program. Creating directories or folders on the computer's hard disk or a floppy disk helps you better manage the information contained on the disk.

IMPORTANT TERMS

ASCII	leading zero
database	operating system
directory	query
field	record
filename	table
folder	

REVIEW AND DISCUSSION

1. Describe how a database could be used to assist in records management. (Obj. 1)
2. Describe the relationship among a database and its tables, records, and fields. (Obj. 1)
3. What is the purpose of a database query? (Obj. 1)
4. What does an ASCII value represent? (Obj. 2)
5. Based on your knowledge of ASCII values, what adjustments to your input into a computer do you think are necessary? (Obj. 2)
6. Write each name in indexing order as you would key it into a computer application. Describe the adjustment made for computer input. (Obj. 3)
   a. #1 Rentals
   b. 21st and Main Cafe
   c. 110 Main Place Gallery
   d. $ Days Again!
   e. KOST Radio Station
   f. Dan's Diving Supplies
7. Write each name in indexing order as you would key it into a computer application. Describe the adjustment made for computer input. (Obj. 3)
   a. U & I Antiques, Inc.
   b. Henry Hastings, CRM

c. St. Andrew's Elementary School

d. 35 North Plains Mall

e. $ and ¢ Store

f. Henry Hastings III

g. Mary Miller, 123 First Street, Gordon, Alaska

h. Mary Miller, 123 Cedar Street, Gordon, Alaska

8. You are taking the following classes: WR 121 English Composition, SOC 104 Introduction to Sociology, HST 201 History of Western Civilization, and BA 244 Records Management. List the folders you will create for your disk to store files for each of your classes. (Obj. 4)

9. What is a computer directory or folder? (Obj. 4)

10. Is a shallow or a deep folder structure more effective? Why? (Obj. 4)

APPLICATIONS

Data Disk

APP 4-1.   Input and Manipulate Database Records (Obj.3)

1. Open the *Access* file APP 4-1.mdb from the data disk.

2. Open the table App 4-1. Enter the names from the list below. Enter the number in the CustID field. In the Indexing Order field, key the entire personal or business name in correct indexing order in all capitals. In the Indexing Order field, make adjustments for computer entry of data as needed. For personal names, enter data as written using the First Name, Last Name, Middle, Title, and Suffix fields. If there is no data for a field, such as Middle or Suffix, leave it blank. For company names, enter the company name as written in the Company Name field. Enter the address, city, state, and postal code for each name in the appropriate fields. Two records have been entered in the database for you as examples.

3. Sort the table in ascending order by the Indexing Order field.

4. Create a query based on the App 4–1 table to include the CustID, City, Indexing Order, and State fields. Design the query to sort the records in ascending order first by the City field, then by the Indexing Order field, then by the State field. Print the sorted query table.

Names:

1101, Archie Abbott, 4110 SW Oak St., Portland, OR 97223-0410

1102, KPDX Radio Station, 120 W. Skyline Blvd., Portland, OR 97201-0120

1122, 1 Way Direct, 301 E. 6th Street, Portland, OR 97203-0301

1159, 2001 Net Works, 5505 E. Burnside, Portland, OR 97233-5500

2107, K. A. Abbott III, 11044 Overlook Dr. W, Bellevue, WA 98005-0411

2115, Early Bird Installers, 2400 Hunters Point, Bellevue, WA 98004-2400

2690, KATZ Communications, P.O. Box 1255, Bellevue, WA 98005-1255

2980, Keep It Beaming, 401 Ellis St., Bellevue, WA 98004-0400

3109, Earnest Satellite Installations, 3800 N. 10th Street, Boise, ID 83713-8300

3119, David Demarco, 300 Front Street, Boise, ID 83702-4400

3127, KBOS Television Station, 125 S. Lewis Street, Boise, ID 83703-0125

3149, 99 TV & Appliance, 45015 S. Hwy. 97, Boise, ID 83702-4501

3163, 180 Stations, Inc., 49 South Main St., Boise, ID 83701-0049

4108, B-N Handy Company, 117 Circle Drive, Sparks, NV 89431-0117

4114, "Demand the Best" Co., 1431 Pinewood Dr., Sparks, NV 89434-1400

4122, Catch-A-Dish, Inc., 1652 Springhill Dr., Sparks, NV 89434-1600

4135, 360 Dish, Inc., 8850 Pyramid Lake, Sparks, NV 89436-8800

4970, Miss Vicky McAllister, 5500 S. Grand St., Sparks, NV 89431-0050

APP 4-2.   Create a Database Report (Obj. 3)

1. Open the *Access* file APP 4–1.mdb that you updated in APP 4-1.

2. Create a query to include the Indexing Order, Address, City, State, and Postal Code fields. Design the query to sort the customer names in ascending order and to display only customers from Boise, ID, and Portland, OR. *Hint: Which field will you sort to ensure alphabetic order of customer names?*

3. Create a report based on the query you created in step 2. Design the report to group the data by city and sort the cities in ascending order. Sort in ascending order by the Indexing Order field within each city. Include all fields from the query. Name the report *Boise and Portland Customers.* Print the report.

APPLYING THE RULES

Job 3, Card Filing Review, Rules 1–10.

CHAPTER 5

ALPHABETIC RECORDS MANAGEMENT

LEARNING OBJECTIVES

1. Explain terms used in correspondence records management systems.
2. Identify the basic types of equipment and supplies for correspondence records storage.
3. Explain five considerations for selecting storage equipment and supplies.
4. Discuss the advantages and disadvantages of the alphabetic method of records storage.
5. Describe six types of information that should be determined before selection and design of an alphabetic records system.
6. Explain how color can be used in correspondence records storage.
7. Apply the six procedures for storing correspondence.
8. Explain how a tickler file is used.

CORRESPONDENCE RECORDS STORAGE

As you studied the first four chapters of *Records Management*, Seventh Edition, you learned to index, code, and cross-reference names and addresses. Beginning with this chapter, you will work with correspondence—the type of records found in all kinds of businesses. Business letters, forms, reports, and memorandums are all part of the daily correspondence that businesses transact. Although the use of electronic records is growing rapidly in business offices, the numbers of paper documents and all forms of recorded information are increasing. The greatest volume of records continues to be paper documents.[1] Paper records are estimated to comprise about 80 percent of all records in the average organization. Business offices continue to use paper as a medium for all or part of their records. Thus, the discussion in this chapter focuses on the use of equipment and supplies for paper records. Chapter 10 discusses electronic systems used in records management; Appendix B discusses other types of records and their equipment and supplies.

[1] Mark, Langemo, "Strategies for Developing and Strengthening Records Management Programs," *Records Management Quarterly*, Vol. 31, No. 3, July 1997.

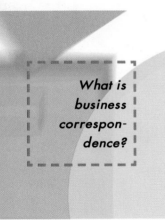

As you complete this chapter, you will apply the ten alphabetic indexing rules learned from Chapters 2 and 3 to indexing, coding, and cross-referencing correspondence. In addition, you will learn three other steps in alphabetic storage procedures: inspecting, sorting, and storing.

Information requirements make systematic storage and retrieval of records increasingly important. Businesses use records to complete transactions, to communicate with customers or clients, and to document compliance with laws and regulations. You have discovered that a set of written rules for alphabetic indexing provides consistency for storing and retrieving records. Consistent application of the alphabetic indexing rules is only one part of an efficient records management program. Using effective, appropriate equipment and supplies is another. This chapter introduces a variety of available records storage equipment and supplies and describes selection criteria.

You are familiar with some of the specific terms and meanings pertaining to the storage and retrieval of records. The following terms and definitions will help you understand the information in this chapter:

- **Records management** is the systematic control of all records from their creation, or receipt, through their processing, distribution, organization, storage, and retrieval to their ultimate disposition. The goal of records management is to get the right record to the right person at the right time at the lowest possible cost.
- **Storage** is the actual placement of records, according to a plan, into a folder, on a shelf, or in a file drawer. Also, storage can be electronically saving a record to a medium readable by a computer. The term *filing* may be used to mean storage, but filing is usually associated with paper records only.
- A **storage method** is a systematic way of storing records according to an alphabetic, subject, numeric, geographic, or chronologic plan. A specific system for organizing and arranging records can be referred to as a records management system or filing system. Often these terms are used synonymously.
- **Alphabetic records management** is a method of storing and arranging records according to the letters of the alphabet.
- **Storage procedures** are a series of steps for the orderly arrangement of records as required by a specific storage method or records management system.

The storage method or system discussed here and in previous chapters is alphabetic. Records management professionals do not agree on the number of records storage systems. Some say there are just two: alphabetic and numeric. Subject and geographic methods are not considered separate methods because the subjects and geographic names are filed alphabetically. Other records professionals add alphanumeric as a third system. Still others add a fourth—chronologic. In this text, alphabetic, subject, numeric, and geographic are considered as four records management systems. With the exception of chronologic storage, each of these methods uses alphabetic concepts in its operation. Subject, numeric, and geographic records are described in detail in Chapters 7, 8, and 9.

ARMA International (Association of Records Managers and Administrators, Inc.), a professional organization for records management, offers many helpful publications designed to simplify records management procedures. In this chapter, you will note references to ARMA's *Filing Procedures Guideline*. ARMA committee members prepared this guideline, which addresses the best and most efficient storage procedures. As with the ARMA *Alphabetic Filing Rules*, the *Filing Procedures Guideline* describes procedures to help achieve the consistency so important to records storage and retrieval efficiency.

RECORDS STORAGE EQUIPMENT AND SUPPLIES

You have heard the adage, "A place for everything, and everything in its place." The records manager or person in charge of purchasing the equipment and supplies for the records center must certainly heed this advice! To have a proper place for various types of records requires a knowledge of equipment for records processing and storage. What type of equipment and supplies are used most often in offices? What is the specific vocabulary for records management equipment and supplies? The ARMA Web site (www.arma.org) links to a number of records management and office products companies. In addition, you can use an Internet search engine to locate Web sites for vendors of filing equipment and supplies. Viewing information on these Web sites can help familiarize you with the array of available records management equipment and supply products. This section of the chapter describes characteristics of these different types of products and their uses.

Storage Equipment

Types of storage equipment commonly used for paper records are: (1) vertical file cabinets, (2) lateral file cabinets, (3) shelf files, and (4) mobile shelving. Other types of storage equipment and their special uses for records management are discussed in later chapters.

Vertical File Cabinets

A **vertical file cabinet** is storage equipment that is deeper than it is wide. Generally, the arrangement of documents in the file drawers is from front to back. Vertical file cabinets are the conventional storage cabinets in one- to five-drawer designs. (See Figure 5–1a on page 92.)

Two rows of vertical file cabinets may be placed back to back in a large central storage area with aisle space on either side. The type and volume of records to be stored will determine the width, depth, number, and size of drawers. The two-drawer file is desk height and sometimes used beside a desk for additional workspace, as well as ready access to frequently used records. The most common widths of vertical file cabinet drawers are appropriate for letters, legal-size documents, and cards.

Lateral File Cabinets

A **lateral file cabinet** is storage equipment that is wider than it is deep—records are accessed from the side (horizontally). Records can be arranged in the drawer from front to back or side to side. Because the long (narrow) side opens, lateral file cabinets are particularly well suited to narrow aisle spaces. They are available in a variety of sizes, depending on the number and depth of the drawers. Figure 5–1b shows a lateral file cabinet with roll-back drawer fronts and one with pull-out drawers.

Shelf Files

A **shelf file** is open-shelving equipment in which records are accessed horizontally from the open side. Shelf files may be an open style or have roll-back or roll-down fronts. They may be stationary shelves (see Figure 5–1c) or shelves arranged in rotary form (see Figure 5–1d). Rotary shelf files make space available in the back of a cabinet by rotating the bank of shelves so that records can be stored and accessed from both sides of the shelves.

Figure 5–1a Vertical File Cabinets

Figure 5–1b Lateral File Cabinets

Figure 5–1c Shelf Files

Figure 5–1d Rotary Shelf File

Mobile Shelving

Areas with limited space may use mobile banks of shelves that move as needed for storage and retrieval. **Mobile shelving** is a series of shelving units that move on tracks attached to the floor for access to files. In some movable shelving equipment, the shelves slide from side to side as shown in Figure 5–2a. The records on shelves behind the moved shelves are then exposed for use. The units may operate with electric power or may be moved manually by the operator. Because aisle space is not constantly maintained between each unit, mobile shelving can approximately double the storage capacity of an area. One type of mobile shelving, the **mobile aisle system** (see Figure 5–2b), consists of rows of shelving used for compact storage, situated on wheel-fitted carriages that travel on tracks and allow one or more aisles to be opened to access the system.

Figure 5–2a **Side-to-Side Mobile Shelving**

Figure 5–2b **Mobile Aisle System**

Motorized rotary storage is a unit that rotates shelves in the unit around a central hub to bring the files to the operator. Figure 5–3a shows correspondence power files that have an automated keypad-driven retrieval system. This system uses overhead storage with the rotation of the files moving horizontally around a central core to bring files to the operator, and it provides access at a height that can accommodate persons with a disability requiring a wheelchair. Figure 5–3b shows a system of no-walk carousels with banks of vertical shelves rotating for access by an operator.

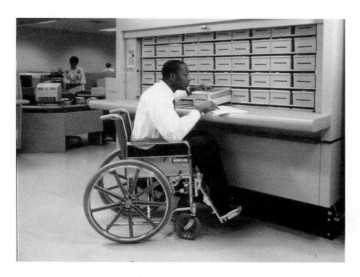

Figure 5–3a **Power Files that Comply with the Americans with Disabilities Act (ADA)**

Figure 5–3b **No-Walk Carousels**

File Capacity and Space Requirements

When choosing storage cabinets or shelves, a comparison of file capacity and floor space requirements helps determine cost effectiveness. An estimated capacity for a standard four-drawer file cabinet is about 10,000 records (calculated at about 100 sheets per linear inch including guides and folders). Three to four inches of space should be left as working space at the end of a file drawer or shelf section to allow easy removal and replacement of file folders. A letter-size vertical cabinet drawer measures 15 by 28 inches and, therefore, holds about 25 linear inches of records. A lateral file drawer is 18 by 36 inches with a file capacity of 33 linear inches. Pull-out drawer space for vertical files requires about two feet; lateral file drawers use approximately one foot of pull-out space. Shelf files require less floor space because they need no drawer-pull space, are not as deep as file cabinets, and hold records that can be readily accessed up to seven shelves high. Figure 5–4 illustrates the capacity and floor space requirements for these three types of storage equipment.

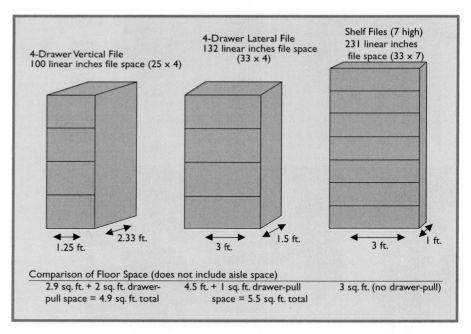

Which type of cabinet requires the least amount of aisle space?

Figure 5–4 Comparison of Filing Equipment Storage Capacity and Floor Space

Shelf files save filer time as well as floor space because there are no drawers to open before records can be accessed; however, open-shelf filing for confidential or vital records must be placed in a records vault for security. File drawers and closed-front cabinets can be purchased with locks. Fire protection is a safety consideration. Vital records can be duplicated and kept in off-site storage. Fireproof storage cabinets can be purchased for important records; these cabinets are heavier and higher in cost than standard file cabinets.

Storage Supplies

Efficient storage and retrieval requires the use of the right equipment and the right supplies. The principal supplies used in manual storage of paper records are discussed briefly in this section.

Guides

A **guide** is a rigid divider with a projecting tab to identify a section in a file and to facilitate reference to a particular record location. Guides are made of heavy material such as pressboard, manila, or plastic. Some guides have reinforced tabs of metal or acetate to give added strength for long wear. Tabs and tab cuts are discussed in detail on page 101.

The proper placement of guides eliminates the need to spend time searching through similar names to find the part of the alphabet needed. The same set of guides may be used year after year with no change, or they may be added to or changed as the quantity of records expands. Because of their thickness and sturdy construction, guides also serve to keep the contents of a container (drawer or box) upright. Keeping contents upright promotes efficient storage and retrieval.

Guides serve as signposts and speed location of records. Too few guides result in unnecessary time spent looking for the correct place to store or find a record. Too many guides that are unevenly distributed throughout the files can slow storage and retrieval because the eye must look at so many tabs to find the right storage section. Several filing authorities recommend using about 20 guides for each file drawer or for each 28 linear inches of stored records.

Primary Guides. A **primary guide** is a divider that identifies a main division or section of a file and always precedes all other material in a section. In Figure 5–5 on page 98, the NAMES WITH NUMBERS, A, and B guides in first position are primary guides. Remember Rule 7 about business names beginning with numbers? Numbers are filed before letters of the alphabet; the NAMES WITH NUMBERS guide and NAMES WITH NUMBERS folder are filed before the A guide. A small volume of stored correspondence with many individuals or firms requires only primary guides to indicate the alphabetic sections. Systems that use color extensively may use only primary guides with the letters of the alphabet because blocks of colored folders act as a visual guide to a section of the alphabet.

Guide sets that divide the alphabet into many different segments are available from manufacturers of filing supplies. The simplest set is a 23- or 25-division set, the latter having a tab for each letter from A to W, a

> **What purpose do guides serve?**

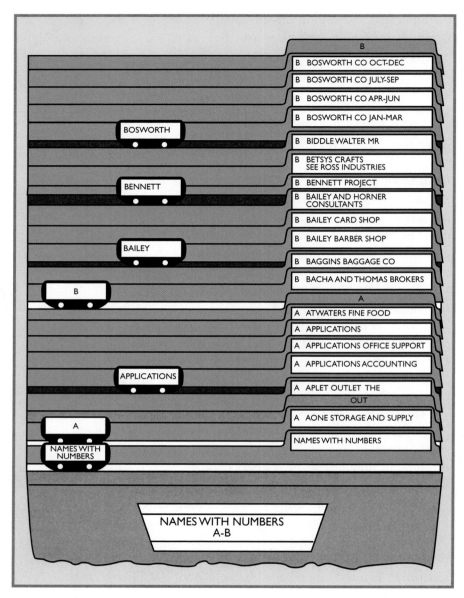

Figure 5–5 One Section of an Alphabetic Arrangement

tab labeled Mc, and a last tab with the combination XYZ. Figure 5–6 compares an 80-division and a 120-division breakdown of guides printed by manufacturers.

The number of alphabetic guides furnished by different manufacturers can vary even though each plan may divide the alphabet into 40 subdivisions. Manufacturers may elect to omit Mc, subdivide letters differently, or combine different letters. Before purchasing a set of guides, the records manager should examine the manufacturer's alphabetic subdivisions to see if the subdivisions fit specific office requirements.

80 Div. A to Z				120 Div. A to Z					
A	1	L	41	A	1	Gr	41	Pe	81
An	2	Le	42	Al	2	H	42	Pi	82
B	3	Li	43	An	3	Han	43	Pl	83
Be	4	Lo	44	As	4	Has	44	Pr	84
Bi	5	M	45	B	5	He	45	Pu	85
Bo	6	Map	46	Bar	6	Hen	46	Q	86
Br	7	McA	47	Bas	7	Hi	47	R	87
Bro	8	McH	48	Be	8	Ho	48	Re	88
Bu	9	McN	49	Ber	9	Hon	49	Ri	89
C	10	Me	50	Bl	10	Hu	50	Ro	90
Ce	11	Mi	51	Bo	11	I	51	Rog	91
Co	12	Mo	52	Br	12	J	52	Ru	92
Coo	13	N	53	Bre	13	Jo	53	S	93
Cr	14	O	54	Bro	14	K	54	Sch	94
D	15	P	55	Bu	15	Ke	55	Scho	95
De	16	Pl	56	C	16	Ki	56	Se	96
Do	17	Q	67	Car	17	Kl	57	Sh	97
Dr	18	R	68	Ce	18	Kr	58	Shi	98
E	19	Re	59	Ci	19	L	59	Si	99
En	20	Ro	60	Co	20	Lar	60	Sm	100
F	21	S	61	Com	21	Le	61	Sn	101
Fi	22	Sch	62	Cop	22	Len	62	Sp	102
Fo	23	Se	63	Cr	23	Li	63	St	103
G	24	Sh	64	Cu	24	Lo	64	Sti	104
Ge	25	Si	65	D	25	M	65	Su	105
Gi	26	Sm	66	De	26	Map	66	T	106
Gr	27	St	67	Di	27	McA	67	Th	107
H	28	Sti	68	Do	28	McD	68	Tr	108
Har	29	Su	69	Du	29	McH	69	U	109
Has	30	T	70	E	30	McN	70	V	110
He	31	To	71	El	31	Me	71	W	111
Her	32	U	72	Er	32	Mi	72	Wam	112
Hi	33	V	73	F	33	Mo	73	We	113
Ho	34	W	74	Fi	34	Mu	74	Wh	114
Hu	35	We	75	Fo	35	N	75	Wi	115
I	36	Wh	76	Fr	36	Ne	76	Wil	116
J	37	Wi	77	G	37	No	77	Wim	117
K	38	Wo	78	Ge	38	O	78	Wo	118
Ki	39	X-Y	79	Gi	39	On	79	X-Y	119
Kr	40	Z	80	Go	40	P	80	Z	120

Figure 5–6 Comparison of Guide Sets for A to Z Indexes

Alphabetic guides can be purchased with preprinted tabs or tabs with slotted holders for the insertion of labels. (The guides in Figure 5–5 are slotted holders.)

Special Guides. A **special** or **auxiliary guide** is a divider used to lead the eye quickly to a specific place in a file. Use special guides to:

1. Indicate location of an individual or a company folder with a high volume of correspondence. In Figure 5–5, the guides labeled BENNETT and BOSWORTH are special (auxiliary) name guides.
2. Introduce a special section of subjects, such as Applications, Bids, Conferences, Exhibits, Projects, or Speeches. Figure 5–5 shows a special subject guide, APPLICATIONS, placed in alphabetic order in the A section. Correspondence concerning applications for positions in accounting and office support is stored behind APPLICATIONS, in properly labeled folders.
3. Identify a section reserved for names with the same first indexing unit. In Figure 5–5, the BAILEY special name guide leads the eye to the section with numerous folders labeled with BAILEY as the first indexing unit.

The tabs on guides for open-shelf equipment are at the side (see Figure 5–7). Because materials stored in open-shelf equipment are visible at one edge instead of across the top (as is true in drawer files), the alphabetic or other divisions must extend from the side of the guide so that they can be seen easily. The printing on these side-guide tabs may be read from either side.

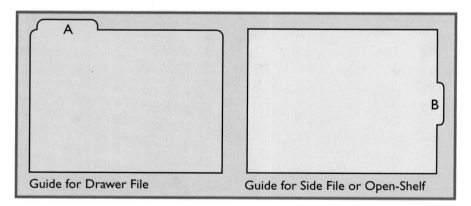

Guide for Drawer File   Guide for Side File or Open-Shelf

Figure 5–7 Guides Used in Drawer Cabinets and Open-Shelf Files

Folders

A **folder** is a container used to hold and protect the contents of a file together and separate from other files. Folders are usually made of heavy material such as manila, Kraft, plastic, or pressboard and can have either top or side tabs in varying sizes. Folders are creased approximately in half; the back is slightly higher than the front. A folder may be reinforced across the top of the back edge because that is the place receiving the greatest wear, as a folder is usually grasped by that edge.

A **tab** is a projection for a caption on a folder or guide that extends above the regular height or beyond the regular width of the folder or guide. Folder and guide tabs are available in different sizes or *cuts*. A **tab cut** is the length of the tab expressed as a proportion of the width or height of the folder or guide. A tab extending across the complete width of a folder is called *straight cut* (see Figure 5–8). One-third cut tabs extend only one third the width of a folder and may be in any of three positions as shown in Figure 5–8.

How are folders used in records storage?

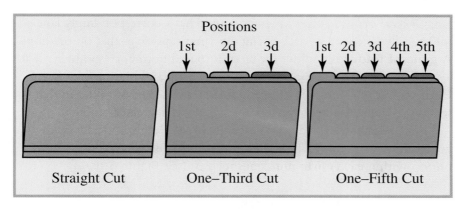

Figure 5–8 Folder Cuts and Tab Positions in a File Drawer

Position refers to the location of the tab across the top or down one side of a guide or folder. First position means the tab is at the left; second position means the tab is second from the left; and so on. **Straight-line arrangement** is a system that aligns folder tabs in one position; for example, all folder tabs are third position (see Figure 5–5). **Staggered arrangement** is a system that follows a series of several different positions of folder tabs from left to right according to a set pattern (see Figure 5–8). Straight-line position is preferred because of ease in reading label captions; the eye travels faster in a straight line than when it jumps back and forth from left to right. The most efficient position for folders is third, with third-cut tabs; and the most efficient position for guides is either first or second with fifth-cut tabs as shown in Figure 5–5.

Tabs on folders for open-shelf equipment are on the side edge (see Figure 5–9 on page 102) in various positions according to the manufacturer's system or the customer's preference.

Folders behind every guide are used to keep like records together. The three main types of folders used in alphabetic storage are general folders, individual folders, and special folders.

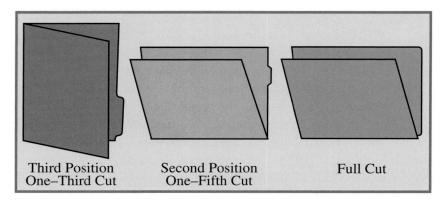

Third Position
One–Third Cut

Second Position
One–Fifth Cut

Full Cut

Figure 5–9 Folder Cuts and Tab Positions for Open-Shelf Files

General Folders. Every primary guide has a correspondingly labeled folder, called a *general folder,* bearing the same caption as that on the guide. A **general folder** is a folder for records to and from correspondents with a small volume that does not require an individual folder or folders. In Figure 5–5, the A folder is a general folder and is the last folder in that section. General folders often are color coded for greater visibility.

Records are arranged inside a general folder alphabetically by the correspondents' names. Then, the most recently dated record is placed on top within each correspondent's records (see Figure 5–10).

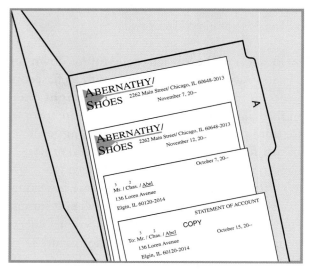

Figure 5–10 Arrangement of Records in a General Folder

Individual Folders. An **individual folder** is a folder used to store the records of an individual correspondent with enough records to warrant a separate folder. Records are arranged chronologically within an individual folder with the most recently dated record on top. In Figure 5–5, all individual folders are third cut, third position.

Records pertaining to one correspondent are removed from the general folder and placed in an individual folder when the number of records accumulates to a pre-determined number. Individual folders are placed in alphabetic order between the primary guide and its general folder.

Special Folders. A **special folder** is a folder that follows an auxiliary or special guide in an alphabetic arrangement. In Figure 5–5 three special folders are shown: two behind APPLICATIONS and one behind BENNETT. Within the APPLICATIONS ACCOUNTING folder, all records pertaining to accounting positions are arranged first by the names of the applicants. If an applicant has more than one record in the folder, those records are arranged by date with the most recent date on top. Within the BENNETT PROJECT folder, records are arranged by date, the most recent one on top.

Care of Folders. Proper care of folders will help make stored records readily accessible. When records start to "ride up" in any folder, too many papers are in the folder. The number of records that will fit into one folder obviously depends on the thickness of the papers. Records should never protrude from the folder edges and should always be inserted with their tops to the left. The most useful and most often recommended folders have score marks. **Score marks** are indented or raised lines or series of marks along the bottom edge of a folder to allow for expansion (see Figure 5–11). As it becomes filled, the folder is refolded along a score mark and expanded to give it a flat base on which to rest. Most folders can be expanded from $3/4$ to 1 inch. Refolding a folder at the score marks reduces the danger of folders bending and sliding under others, avoids curling papers, and results in a neater file.

What is a general folder? an individual folder? a special folder?

Why are score marks on file folders?

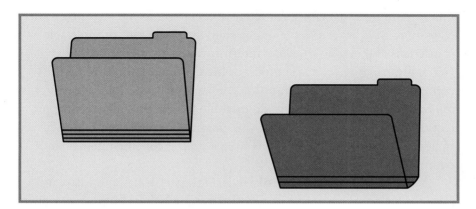

Figure 5–11 **Flat Folder and Expanded Folder**

A folder lasts longer and is easier to use if it is not stuffed beyond its capacity. If too many papers are in an individual folder, prepare a second folder for that correspondent. Then label the folders to show that the records are arranged chronologically in them (see the four BOSWORTH CO folders in Figure 5–5). Sometimes papers in a folder are redistributed by adding subject folders instead of subdividing by dates, as is the case with APPLICATIONS in Figure 5–5.

New folders may be needed because:

When are new folders needed?

- A new group of names is to be added to a file.
- Older folders have become full and additional ones must be added to take care of the overload.
- Enough records have accumulated for certain correspondents so that their records can be removed from the general folders and put into individual folders.
- Folders have worn out from heavy use and must be replaced.
- The regular time of the year has arrived for replacing folders and transferring infrequently used folders to inactive storage. Chapter 6 further explains records transfer.

Types of Folders. Other folders frequently used in offices are a suspension or hanging folder, a bellows folder, and a pocket folder. These folder types can be useful for particular types of records within a records management system.

The **suspension** or **hanging folder** is a folder with built-in hooks on each side that hang from parallel metal rails on each side of a file drawer or other storage equipment. The main advantage of hanging folders over conventional folders is their added support for holding records in a neat, upright position due to support of both the front and back of the folder with hooks on the drawer rails. If your file cabinet does not have built-in rails for hanging folders, you can purchase drawer frames with rails that adjust for letter or legal-size filing. Hanging folders have up to 10 slots across the upper edge for placement of insertable plastic tabs and can hold several interior folders to subdivide a file. Generally, hanging folders should not leave a file drawer. Placing the contents of these folders in interior conventional-type folders or interior folders that are shorter than traditional file folders provides records protection and facilitates removal or placement of records (see Figure 5–12). In addition, some hanging folders have a pocket for small items like computer disks, notes, or receipts.

A **bellows (expansion) folder** is a folder that has a top flap and sides to enclose records in a case with creases along its bottom and sides that allow it to expand like an accordion. These folders usually come with dividers inside for subdividing the records and are used when the

Figure 5–12 Hanging or Suspension File Folders

volume of stored records is small. In Figure 5–13, the bellows folder is on the left.

A **pocket folder** is a folder with partially enclosed sides and more expansion at the bottom than an ordinary folder (Figure 5–13, right). A pocket folder is useful for transporting as well as for storing records. Also, these folders can be used to store records such as bound reports or other records media with more bulk than can be easily fitted into a traditional file folder.

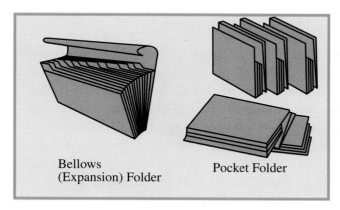

Bellows
(Expansion) Folder

Pocket Folder

Figure 5–13 Special Folders for Storing Paper Records

Follower Blocks or Compressors

Failing to use proper means to hold drawer contents upright causes folders to bend and slide under one another. The proper number of guides and correct use of a follower block behind the guides and folders keeps folders upright. A **follower block** (or **compressor**) is a device at the back of a file drawer that can be moved to allow contraction or expansion of the drawer contents (see Figure 5–14). A follower block that is too loose will allow the drawer contents to sag; one that is too tight will make filing and retrieving a folder difficult. In an over-compressed drawer, as in an overcrowded drawer, locating and removing a single sheet of paper is almost impossible. Instead of follower blocks, some file drawers have slim steel upright dividers placed permanently throughout the file drawer to keep the contents vertical. Also, shelf files use a series of metal upright dividers to hold records upright. A lateral or vertical file with metal rails and hanging folders do not require the use of a follower block; the suspension of each folder on the drawer rack holds records upright.

Figure 5–14 **Follower Block (Compressor)**

> *What is the purpose of a follower block in a file drawer?*

OUT Indicators. An **OUT indicator** is a control device that shows the location of borrowed records. These indicators contain a form for writing the name of the person borrowing the record, the date it was borrowed, a brief statement of the contents of the record, and the due date for return to storage. When a borrowed record is returned to storage, the OUT indicator is removed, to be reused, thrown away, or saved and later used to check the activity at the files or to determine which records are active or inactive. Commonly used indicators are OUT guides, OUT folders, and OUT sheets; examples are shown in Figure 5–15.

> *What is an OUT guide? OUT folder? OUT sheet?*

OUT Guides. An **OUT guide** is a special guide used to replace any record that has been removed from storage and to indicate what was taken and by whom. When the borrowed record is returned, the filer can quickly find the exact place from which the record was taken. An OUT guide is made of the same sturdy material as other guides with the word OUT printed on its tab in large letters and a distinctive color. In Figure 5–5, an OUT guide is located between the AONE STORAGE AND

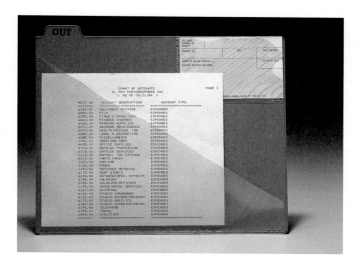

Figure 5–15a **OUT Folder with Pocket**

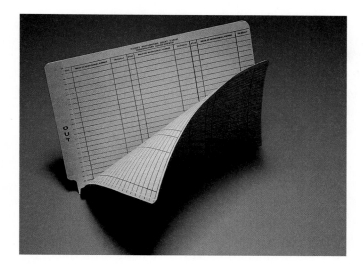

Figure 5–15b **OUT Folder**

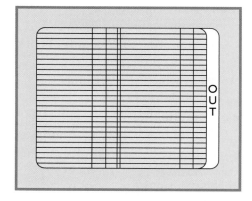

Figure 5–15c **OUT Sheet**

SUPPLY and the APLET OUTLET THE individual folders. The guides can have preprinted charge-out forms on both sides or a plastic insert pocket to hold a charge-out form. Some OUT guides have a pocket for temporarily holding documents to be replaced in the folder when it is returned to the file.

OUT Folders. An **OUT folder** is a special folder used to replace a complete folder that has been removed from storage. This folder has a pocket or slot into which a small card is placed bearing the same information concerning who took the folder, the date it was taken, its contents, and the date the folder should be returned to storage. The OUT folder remains in the file as a temporary storage place for records that will be transferred to the permanent folder when it is returned to storage.

OUT Sheets. An **OUT sheet** is a form that is inserted in place of a record removed from a folder. An OUT sheet is often the same size and color as an OUT guide, but its thickness is that of a sheet of paper. An OUT sheet remains in the file folder until replaced with the returned record.

Labels

Containers, guides, and folders that help you store records efficiently must be labeled to guide the eye to the appropriate storage location. A **label** is a device that contains the name of the subject or number given to the file folder contents. It may have other pertinent information, be color-coded to denote its place in an overall filing system, or have a bar code. A **caption** is a title, heading, short explanation, or description of a document or records. Label captions may be typewritten or computer printed.

Container Labels. The labels on drawers, shelf files, or other storage containers should be clearly but briefly worded and inclusive enough to represent the contents. The containers usually have holders on the outside where card stock labels can be inserted. Various colors are available on perforated card stock sheets. The ARMA *Filing Procedures Guideline* recommends centering the information for the container in all caps with no punctuation. The caption on the drawer illustrated in Figure 5–5 reads NAMES WITH NUMBERS A–B, indicating that records of correspondents whose names are within the A and B sections of the alphabet are stored in that drawer. Names in which the key units are numbers written as digits are filed before all alphabetic names. For example, 123 Builders comes before Albany Builders.

Guide Labels. Labels on guides consist of words, letters, or numbers (or some combination of these items). In Figure 5–5, the guides shown have window tabs into which keyed captions have been inserted (NAMES WITH NUMBERS, A, APPLICATIONS, B, BAILEY, BENNETT, BOSWORTH). Some guides (alphabetic or numeric guides) are available with preprinted information. The ARMA *Filing Procedures Guideline* recommends placing guide captions near the left margin of the label and as near as possible to the top. Print captions in all capital letters with no punctuation. Single letters of the alphabet may be centered on guide labels if preferred.

Folder Labels. Folder labels come as pressure-sensitive adhesive labels in continuous folded strips or on sheets that can be prepared with computer software and affixed to folders. A colored stripe across the top is often used on a white or buff-colored label. Sheets of labels for computer generation usually have columns of labels across an $8\frac{1}{2}$ by 11-inch sheet. Most word processing software has settings for different label sizes that match common label product numbers. Also, packaging that comes with the labels often has instructions for required software settings. Many supply vendors have computer software programs that generate labels or they will provide a service for custom-printed labels. Some vendors have printers that print durable laminated labels. Figure 5–16 illustrates a computer-generated labeling system.

Figure 5–16a **Computer-Generated Labeling System**

Figure 5–16b **Colorflex Labels**

Bar codes can be generated along with a name on a label. Use of a bar code tracking system keeps a record of a file location at all times. When a file is checked out, a scanner reads the bar code. Bar code technology is discussed in detail in Chapter 10. Information about the file and who checked it out is then updated and recorded in a computer program. Sometimes another label strip is generated for OUT indicators. Use of a bar code tracking system can improve retrieval rates up to 99 percent. Refer to Chapter 6 for more on bar code tracking.

As noted previously, the ARMA *Filing Procedures Guideline* recommends placing folder labels near the left edge and as near the top of the label or the bottom of the color bar as possible. Wrap-around side-tab labels for open-sided lateral file cabinets or shelf filing are placed both above and below the color bar separator so that the information is readable from both sides of the folder. Word processing software with automatic label settings places information in the proper location on the label. For alphabetic filing, the letter of the alphabet is keyed first, followed by about $1/2$ inch of blank space, then the filing segment. In all cases, the label is keyed in capital letters with no punctuation as shown in Figure 5–17.

> **What format does ARMA recommend for folder labels?**

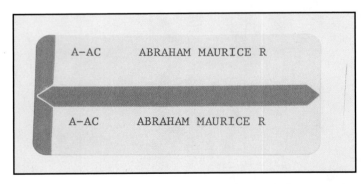

Figure 5–17a **Caption Location on a Folder Label**

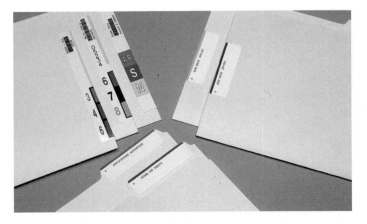

Figure 5–17b **Preprinted Label Captions**

When new folders are prepared, make sure the placement of the labels and the caption format are the same as those on other folders. Consistency in the placement and format of labels helps achieve faster retrieval of a required folder. One way to achieve uniform placement of labels is as follows: When a new box of folders is opened, remove all the folders, keep them tightly together, and stand them upright on a flat surface. Place a ruler or stiff card over the tab edges at the spot where all the labels are to be affixed. Make a pencil mark across the top edge of all the tabs. A very small pencil mark will show on each of the tabs at the same place and will serve as a guide for attaching all the labels.

Sorters

A **sorter** is a device used to arrange records into alphabetic or numeric categories and to hold records temporarily prior to storage. The records are organized alphabetically in the order they will be stored to improve the speed and accuracy of actual storage in the records system. The type of sorter used depends on the volume of record flow in the office.

Figure 5–18 shows one sorter that accommodates records with one dimension as large as ten inches such as checks, sales slips, time cards, correspondence, and ledger sheets.

Figure 5–18 **General-Purpose Sorter**

Other specialized supplies are discussed in later chapters of the text, as their use becomes necessary. The supplies just explained and illustrated are basic ones and applicable to all storage methods.

Selection of Storage Equipment and Supplies

Every office has its own records management system; and the right equipment, supplies, and filing accessories can improve document-handling efficiency. Proper selection of equipment can result in saving space and time, both factors that can reduce operating costs. Records managers should keep updated on new and improved products by reading business periodicals and trade magazines; viewing vendor catalogs and brochures; attending business shows; and participating in professional records management association meetings.

Appropriate selection of storage equipment and supplies requires consideration of the following factors:

What are the benefits of using the right type and quality of storage equipment and supplies?

1. *Type and volume of records to be stored and retrieved.* An inventory of what is to be stored is a basic step in making the best choice of storage equipment and supplies. Records in different formats or media such as papers, cards, books, computer disks, microrecords, videos, architectural drawings, or computer printouts have special storage needs. A records inventory also shows the current volume of stored records. Future volume must be forecast as well as any anticipated changes in method of storage; for example, consider the possibility of microfilming or imaging records. Chapter 6 presents more detailed information about records inventory.

2. *Degree of required protection of records.* Confidential or classified records require equipment with locks or location in a records vault; records vital to the operation of the business need fireproof or fire-resistant storage equipment.

3. *Efficiency and ease of use of equipment and systems.* The ease with which records can be found is a major consideration. The simpler the system is to understand, the easier it is to use. Also, less training of new employees is needed when the system is a simple one. Time saved by personnel who store and retrieve records means dollars saved. The ease of expansion or modification of a system or the addition of compatible equipment will be important to meet the changing needs of an organization.

4. *Space considerations.* Floor-weight restrictions, usage of space to the ceiling (air space), or the advisability of counter-type equipment or something in between, and the possibility of transferring part of the records to off-site storage facilities affect space which, in an office, is costly. The effect of new equipment on present layout and workflow should be considered, also.

5. *Cost.* After all other criteria have been examined, cost and the company budget may be the final determinants as to which equipment and supplies may be acquired. The astute records manager realizes that the least expensive equipment and supplies may not provide the most economical records storage. Quality in construction and materials is important; inferior materials or lightweight stock may need frequent and costly replacement. In determining costs, keep in mind the following points:

   • Cost of the personnel needed to work with the records.
   • Compatibility of supplies and equipment.

- Advisability of using local vendors rather than purchasing from out-of-town vendors.
- Possibility of discounts for quantity purchases.
- Feasibility of choosing used rather than new equipment.
- Volume of records that can be stored within the equipment. Lateral, shelf, or rotary equipment can house more square feet of records than can conventional drawer file cabinets in the same square footage of floor space.

What factors need to be considered when choosing a storage system?

Special needs of your organization could add other factors to your list of considerations. Also, consult users of equipment under consideration for purchase to learn about benefits, problems, or special considerations associated with the equipment.

CORRESPONDENCE STORAGE PROCEDURES

This last section of the chapter looks at the advantages and disadvantages of alphabetic records management; some criteria for selecting an alphabetic storage system; and finally, procedures for storing correspondence alphabetically.

Advantages and Disadvantages of Alphabetic Records Management

The advantages of alphabetic records management are as follows:

- Alphabetic filing does not require an index and is, therefore, a direct access filing method. **Direct access** is a method of accessing records by going directly to the file without first referring to an index or a list of names for location in the files.
- All records for correspondent names that begin with numbers written as digits are filed before all alphabetic names according to alphabetic indexing Rule 7. Knowing this rule facilitates storage and retrieval.
- The alphabetic dictionary (A to Z) order of arrangement is simple to understand.
- Storage is easy if standard procedures are followed.
- Misfiles are easily checked by examining alphabetic sequence.
- The direct access feature can save time and, thus, reduce costs of operation.
- Related records from one name, either a company or an individual, are grouped together.

The disadvantages of alphabetic records storage are as follows:

- Misfiling is prevalent if rules for alphabetic storage are not established and followed.
- Similar names may cause confusion, especially when spellings are not precise.
- Transposition of some letters of the alphabet is easy, causing filing sequence to be out of order.
- Filing under the wrong name can result in lost records.
- Names on folders are seen instantly by anyone who happens to glance at an open storage container. Consequently, confidential or classified records are not secure.
- Related records with different correspondent names are filed in more than one place.

Selection and Design of an Alphabetic Records Management System

At the time a new office is opened, the company must decide on the kind of storage system to be selected or designed. For established offices, the system in use may prove to be ineffective because it no longer serves the needs of those who request records. If records are requested by names of individuals, businesses, and organizations with few subjects, then an alphabetic system is best for that office.

When selecting the alphabetic method of storage, utmost care should be exercised in the selection or design because, once installed, it is likely to be used for a long time. To select an alphabetic system, or to redesign one, the records manager should know:

1. The total volume of records to be stored.
2. The number of records in each alphabetic section and which letters of the alphabet contain a large number of records.
3. The expected activity in the files—an estimate of how many times records may be requested.
4. The length of time records are to be kept.
5. The efficiency of the filing personnel.
6. Time and resources available for training personnel.

What information does the records manager need to know before talking to a manufacturer of storage systems?

In some cases, the person in charge of the records may seek the help of a records management consultant or a representative of a filing system manufacturer to determine the best records management system. These people study the information needs of the office, consult with the person in charge of the records, and make recommendations.

The person in charge of the records must keep the needs of the office in mind and not be swayed by the beauty of a system, the expert sales techniques of a representative, or the apparent low cost of a system.

The ultimate test of any successful storage system (alphabetic or any other) is whether records that have been stored within the system can be found quickly when needed.

Examples of Records Storage Systems

Many different manufacturers create storage supplies and systems. The use of color enhances the effectiveness of a records storage system. For instance, all key units that begin with A are stored in blue folders with red labels. If you see a yellow folder among the blue folders, you know that something is misfiled, and you can immediately place the yellow folder with other yellow folders.

The use of color has two meanings: (1) **Color coding** is using color as an identifying aid in a filing system (for example, different colors might be used to divide the alphabetic sections in the storage system); and (2) **color accenting** is the consistent use of different colors for different supplies in the storage system—one color for guides, various colors for folders, one color for OUT indicators, and specific colors of labels or stripes on labels. Both color coding and color accenting are found in the systems illustrated here (see Figure 5–19). Blocks of colored folders act as a visual guide to lead you quickly to a section of the alphabet. Use of a contrasting color for special folders such as key customers, current projects, or unpaid bills makes them easy to locate.

For an alphabetic system, color bars can correspond to the first letters of the correspondent's name to create blocks of colors. Another use of color shows the same first color for alphabetic letter guides and

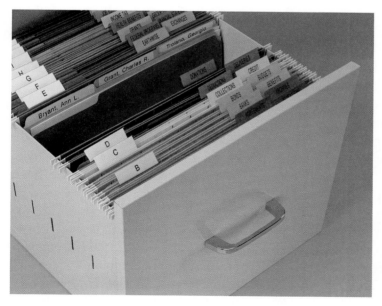

Figure 5–19 Color-Coded Files for Categories of Records

a different second color on the label for secondary guides. Another use of color assigns a letter and color for the key unit of the filing segment, a second color for the second letter of the key unit, and a third color for the first letter of the second unit.

The use of color speeds retrieval because it eliminates the need to stop and read letters. Misfiles stand out visually when the color pattern is broken.

Many manufacturers produce trade-named alphabetic systems with special characteristics intended to speed records storage and retrieval and to provide a double check against misfiling. These systems use color extensively, as you will see in the following illustrations. Other trade-named alphabetic systems are available; the ones shown here are only representative of the many systems available. To gain understanding of each system, study the text material carefully and refer to the illustrations frequently.

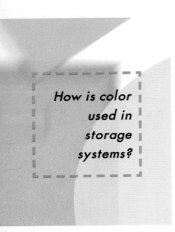

How is color used in storage systems?

TAB Products Co.

TAB Products Co. (www.tab.com) is an example of a company that provides equipment, supplies, and services for filing systems using color coding and color accenting in a variety of records systems ranging from simple to complex. TABQUIK products allow you to produce and apply color-coded file folder labels. You can purchase label-printing software to color code floppy disks, backup tapes, videos, books, binders, or file folders. This software can be used with a variety of printers for label printing. TAB's FileTracker software package allows you to track document location through use of bar codes and bar code readers. Bar code readers enable you to check items in or out or transfer them to a new location without manual data entry. The FileTracker software links with TABQUIK to print color-coded labels with bar codes. Figure 5–20 illustrates a TAB color-coded system.

Smead Manufacturing Company

Smead Manufacturing Company (www.smead.com) uses color in its filing systems and products. Smead's color-coded top tab or end tab folders have a large wrap-around color bar printed on the top and end tab of each folder with reverse numerals 0 through 9 spaced in half-inch intervals on the back of the tabs. Ten different printed colors are used to indicate the first primary filing digit. The second primary filing digit is indicated by wrapping a colored tape around the tab in a position corresponding to the numeral. Their Alpha-Z® TTN color-coded system uses a large letter and color bar to identify all subjects beginning with the same letter. Thirteen colors code all 26 letters of the alphabet. The position of the color bar distinguishes the second half of the alphabet from the first. A band of color is created for all subjects beginning with the

Figure 5–20 TAB's Color-Coded Filing Supplies

same letter (see Figure 5–21 on page 118). Smead Manufacturing Company also offers ColorBar software for printing color labels and ImageTrax® Express for managing and tracking folders and records using software that integrates with an *Access* database structure. Another Smead product, Smeadlink™, integrates document management for electronic, paper, and microfilm records.

For alphabetic filing of 1,000 records or less, a color band plus the alphabetic letter in the same color is enough for effective color coding shown in the upper-right corner. Larger systems use an additional colored label for the second character of the folder title to break the color line for the different letter.

Procedures for Storing Correspondence Records

The actual storing operation is an exacting responsibility that must be done with concentration and the knowledge that a mistake can be costly. No matter whether records storage is centralized, decentralized, or centrally controlled, the filing procedures remain the same: Records must be (1) inspected, (2) indexed, (3) coded, (4) cross-referenced if necessary, (5) sorted, and (6) stored. Therefore, the filer must enjoy detailed work, be dexterous, have a good memory, be willing to follow procedures consistently, be interested in developing new and better procedures, and realize the importance of correctly storing all records so that they may be found immediately when needed. The following section gives details about each of these steps.

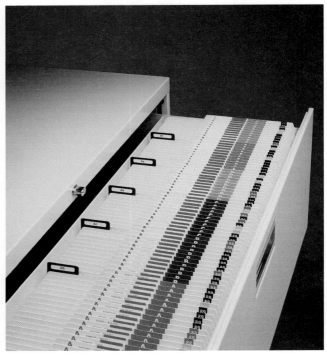

Figure 5–21 Smead's Alpha-Z System (Open-Shelf and Lateral File)

Inspecting

Checking a record for its "readiness to be filed" is known as **inspecting**. A business record must not be stored until someone with authority marks it to be released for filing. Whatever action the record requires must be taken or noted prior to storage. Anyone storing records must be certain that action has been taken or noted in a reminder system such as a tickler file. Notation in a reminder system assures that the record will be brought to the attention of the proper person at a future date. (See page 124 for more information on tickler files.) Storing records before their contents are noted and before appropriate action has been taken can sometimes cause embarrassment to a business and can directly or indirectly result in financial loss or loss of goodwill.

The copy of an outgoing letter or other communication would appear ready to be stored when it is received by the filer for storage. But in most offices every original (or incoming) record to be stored must bear a release mark. A **release mark** is an agreed-upon mark such as initials or a symbol placed on a record to show that the record is ready for storage (see "JJ" on Figure 5–22). The person who prepared the reply or otherwise handled the matter usually puts this release mark on the letter. Types of marks used are initials, a code or check mark, a punched symbol, a stamped notation, a lightly drawn pencil line through the contents, or some other agreed-upon mark. A missing mark is a signal to the filer to inquire why the release mark is missing. A date/time stamp (see OCT 23, 20-- 10:30 AM in Figure 5–22) is not a release mark. The person who opens mail often stamps the correspondence for reference purposes with a date/time stamp showing the date and time received.

A cardinal rule that all filers must observe, therefore, is:

Be sure the record to be stored has been released for storage.

Indexing

Because you indexed filing segments in applications for Chapters 2, 3, and 4, you know that indexing is a mental process. On correspondence, the name (filing segment) may appear in various places. As you know, the selection of the right name by which to store the record means that the record will be found quickly when it is needed. If the wrong name is selected, much time will be wasted trying to locate the record when it is eventually requested.

Keep these rules in mind when indexing incoming correspondence:

1. On incoming correspondence, the name for storage purposes is usually in the letterhead.
2. If a letterhead has no relationship with the contents of the letter, the writer's location or the writer's business connection is used. The letterhead name is disregarded for filing purposes. An example is a letter written on hotel stationery by a person who is out of town on a business trip.
3. Incoming correspondence on plain paper (paper without a letterhead—usually personal) most likely will be called for by the name in the signature line, so this name is the one used for storage.
4. When both the company name and the name of the writer seem to be of equal importance, the company name is used.

Keep these rules in mind when indexing outgoing correspondence:

1. On the file copy of an outgoing letter, the most important name is usually the one contained in the letter address.
2. When both the company name and the name of an individual are contained in the letter address of the file copy of an outgoing letter, the company name is used for filing unless the letter is personal or unless a name in the body is the correct name to index.

How do you know when a record is ready to be stored?

How do you index incoming and outgoing correspondence?

3. On a copy of a personal letter, the writer's name is usually the most important and should be used for storage.

If a special subject is used in an alphabetic arrangement (such as Applications), the subject is given precedence over both company and individual names appearing in the correspondence. Often, the subject name is written on the correspondence at the top right.

Sometimes two names seem equally important. One name is selected as the name by which the record is to be stored and the other name is cross-referenced according to the rules learned in Chapters 2 and 3. In case of real doubt about the most important name, request clarification from the records supervisor or the department from which the record came. Consult a records manual if one is in use in the office.

Coding

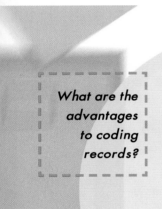

What are the advantages to coding records?

Often the filer is responsible for coding the record. The filing segment can be coded in any one of several ways. Figure 5–22 shows diagonals placed between the units, the key unit underlined, and the remaining units numbered. In some offices, a colored pencil is used for coding to make the code stand out; in other offices, coding is done with a pencil, to keep distracting marks at a minimum.

Coding saves time when refiling is necessary. An uncoded record removed from storage and returned at a later date to be refiled must be indexed and coded again.

Cross-Referencing

The same cross-reference rules learned in Chapters 2 and 3 apply for storing correspondence. Here's an example:

Assume that the letter shown in Figure 5–22 comes to the filer for storage. The record is indexed and coded for Investment Strategies, Inc., by placing diagonals between the units, underlining the key unit, and numbering the other units. The letter is then coded for cross-referencing because it is likely to be called for by Trotter Poll Company. A wavy line is drawn under Trotter Poll Company, diagonals are placed between the units, all units are numbered, and an X is written in the margin. The cross-reference coding marks are slightly different from those used for the regular coding of a record. Figure 5–23 shows the cross-reference sheet prepared for the letter shown in Figure 5–22.

A separate cross-reference sheet, as shown in Figure 5–23, may be prepared for an alternative name, or an extra copy of the original record can be coded for cross-reference purposes. The cross-reference sheet shown in Figure 5–23 is a type that can be printed in quantity and used as needed. Note that the name at the top of the cross-reference sheet is coded for storage in exactly the same way as for any record—diagonals

Figure 5–22 Letter Properly Released and Coded

Investment/
Strategies,/Inc.

150 SW Salmon Ave., Suite 200
Portland, OR 97202-0015
(503) 555-0992
(503) 555-0991 FAX

October 21, 20--

OCT 23, 20-- 10:30 AM

Ms. Joan Jensen, Manager
1040 Tax Express
1500 SW Cedar Ave.
Portland, OR 97204-1500

Dear Ms. Jensen:

We are very interested in forming a type of partnership for your customers. We would like to help your customers by offering advice in investments for both short-term and long-term goals.

To help us get an idea of what your customers need, we have hired the Trotter/Poll/Company to conduct a survey of the investment objectives of your customers.

In the near future Trotter Poll Company will send to each of your customers a questionnaire that will provide spaces for the listing of annual income, approximate annual expenses, amount available for saving and investment, financial objectives, and other pertinent information. Trotter Poll Company will analyze the data received from all those who return the questionnaire and will then make recommendations for type of investments your customers should make.

We shall greatly appreciate your cooperation in this matter.

Sincerely yours,

James Washington

James Washington
Investment Counselor

pas

CROSS-REFERENCE SHEET

Name or Subject
Trotter/Poll/Company

Date of Records
October 21, 20--

Regarding
Survey of customers regarding investment objectives

SEE

Name or Subject
Investment Strategies, Inc.

Date Filed 10/23/20--   By J. Phelps

Figure 5–23 Cross-Reference for Letter Shown in Figure 5–22

are placed between the units, the key unit is underlined with a straight line, and succeeding units are numbered.

At times a permanent cross-reference replaces an individual folder to direct the filer to the correct storage place. A **permanent cross-reference** is a guide with a tab in the same position as the tabs on the individual folder and is placed in a location that is frequently assumed to be the location of that folder. The caption on the tab of the permanent cross-reference consists of the name by which the cross-reference is filed, the word SEE, and the name by which the correspondence folder may be found. In Figure 5–5, a permanent cross-reference guide for BETSYS CRAFTS SEE ROSS INDUSTRIES appears in proper alphabetic sequence in the file drawer.

A permanent cross-reference can be used, for instance, when a company changes its name. The company's folder is removed from the file, the name is changed on the folder, and the folder is refiled under the new name. A permanent cross-reference guide is prepared under the original name and is placed in the position of the original folder in the file. For example, assume that EMORY AND PHILLIPS changes its name to RIVERSIDE DISTRIBUTION CO. The EMORY AND PHILLIPS folder is removed from the file, the name on the folder is changed to RIVERSIDE DISTRIBUTION CO, and the folder is filed under the new name. A permanent cross-reference guide is made and filed in the E section of the file:

EMORY AND PHILLIPS
SEE RIVERSIDE DISTRIBUTION CO

Sorting

Sorting is the arrangement of records in the sequence in which they are to be filed or stored. In most instances, a sorting step precedes the actual storing. Sorting should be done as soon as possible after coding and cross-referencing, especially if storage must be delayed. Sometimes coding and rough sorting are done in sequence. **Rough sorting** is arranging records in approximately the same order as the filing system in which they will be placed. After each record has been coded, it is rough sorted into a pile of like pieces—all A, B, Cs are together, all D, E, Fs are together, and so on. Records having filing segments that are numbers written as digits are rough sorted into 100s, 200s, and so on. Coordination of inspection, indexing, coding, and sorting means handling each record only once. If a record is needed before it has been filed, it can be found with less delay if records have been rough sorted instead of being put in a stack on a desk or in a "to-be-filed" basket.

A delay in sorting until all records have been coded means handling each record twice, consumes more time and energy, and results in greater record-handling costs. If sorting is delayed until all coding is finished, the records can then be grouped into another rough-sort arrangement: all the As together in no special order, all the Bs together at random, all the Cs together in mixed order, all 100s in random order, all 200s in random order, and so forth. Sorting can be done on a desk or table top, with the records placed in separate piles. Use of a desktop sorter that has holders or pockets for various sections of the alphabet makes sorting easier.

After rough sorting the records according to alphabetic sections, the filer removes them section by section, alphabetizes them properly within each section, and replaces them in order in the sorter for temporary storage. This step is often called fine sorting. **Fine sorting** is arranging records in exact order of the filing system in which they will be placed. This alphabetizing of records in all sections makes them ready to be stored. Fine sorting records with numeric key units arranges them in numeric order prior to storing. Then the records are removed in sequence from all divisions of the sorter and taken to the files for storage.

Using these rough and fine sorting procedures saves time. By handling each paper once when inspecting, indexing, coding, cross-referencing, and rough sorting, wasted motion will be minimized because all records are in strict alphabetic or numeric order. The greater the number of records to be stored, the more precise or fine the sorting should be to make the work easier, quicker, and less tiring.

What is the difference between rough sorting and fine sorting?

Storing

Storing is the actual placement of records into storage containers, a physical task of great importance in an office. A misfiled record is often a lost record; and a lost record means loss of time, money, and peace of mind while searching for the record.

The time at which records are actually put into the storage containers depends on the workload during the day. In some offices, storing is the job performed first in the morning; in others, all storing is done in the early afternoon; in others, storing is the last task performed each day. In still other offices, storing is done when records are ready and when a lull in other work occurs. In a centralized filing department, storage takes place routinely throughout the day every day—storing, retrieving, and re-storing.

Prior to the actual storage of records, the filer must remember to:

1. Remove paper clips from records to be stored.
2. Staple records together (if they belong together) in the upper right corner so that other records kept in the folder will not be inserted between them by mistake.
3. Mend torn records.
4. Unfold folded records to conserve storage space unless the folded records fit the container better than when unfolded.

Before placing the record in its storage location, the filer should:

1. Glance quickly at the container label to locate the place to begin storage.
2. After locating the place, scan the guides until the proper alphabetic section is reached. All records having numeric key units will be stored at the front of the alphabetic file.
3. Pull the guides forward with one hand, while the other hand searches quickly for the correct folder.
4. Check for an individual or a special folder for the filing segment. If none of these folders is in the file, locate the general folder.
5. Slightly raise the folder into which the record is to be placed. Avoid pulling the folder up by its tab, however, as continual pulling will separate the tab from its folder. Raising the folder ensures that the record will be inserted into the folder and not in front of or behind it.
6. Glance quickly at the label and the top record in the folder to verify further the correct placement of the document because all records in the folder will bear the same coded name.
7. Place each record in the folder with its top to the left. When the folder is removed from storage and placed on a desk to be used, the folder is opened like a book with the tab edge to the right; all the records in it are then in proper reading position.
8. Jog the folder to straighten the records if they are uneven.
9. Never open more than one drawer in a cabinet at the same time; a cabinet can fall forward when overbalanced by having two or three loaded drawers open.

What preparation is needed before a record is stored?

Special points to remember include:

1. The most recently dated record in an individual folder is always placed at the front and, therefore, is on top when the folder is opened. The record bearing the oldest date is the one at the back of the folder.
2. Records that are removed from a folder and later refiled must be placed in their correct chronologic sequence, not on top of the contents of the folder.
3. Records within a general folder are arranged first alphabetically by correspondents' names and then by date within each correspondent's records. The most recently dated record is, therefore, on top of each group (see Figure 5–10).

Using a Tickler File

A **tickler file** is a date-sequenced file by which matters pending are flagged for attention on the proper date. This chronologic arrangement of information "tickles" the memory and serves as a reminder that specific action must be taken on a specific date. Other names sometimes used to describe such a file are *suspense file* and *pending file.* The basic arrangement of a tickler file is always the same: chronologic by current month and day. A manual arrangement usually takes the form of a series of 12 guides with the names of the months of the year printed on their tabs. One set of guides or folders with tabs printed with 1 through 31 for the days of the month is also used. A computer tickler file is usually in the form of entries in a database with a reminder list showing on the screen or printed in sort order by action date. Figure 5–24a shows a manual tickler file and Figure 5–24b on page 126 shows a list of OUT files due dates from a database. An example of a manual tickler file would be one for holding correspondence that requires specific action to be taken before being placed in the alphabetic correspondence file.

Many office workers use a tickler system to remind them of events that happen yearly such as birthdays and anniversaries; membership expiration dates and dues payments; insurance premium payments; weekly, monthly, or annual meetings; subscription expiration dates; and the dates on which certificates of deposit or bonds are due. In records management, tickler files can be used to keep track of due dates for records that are borrowed or to keep track of records that do not have a release mark.

On the last day of each month, the person in charge of the tickler file checks through the date cards/folders to be certain that nothing has been inadvertently overlooked during the month. Then, all the papers from behind the next month's guide are removed and redistributed behind the daily guides (numbered 1 through 31). At the end of October, for instance, the spaces behind all the daily guides would be checked, the October guide would be moved to the back of the file, and the November guide would be put in the front. All reminders that were

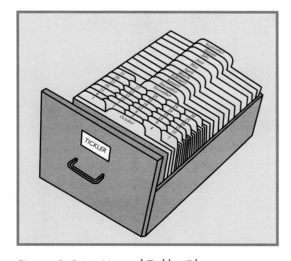

Figure 5–24a **Manual Tickler File**

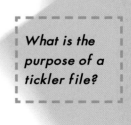

What is the purpose of a tickler file?

DATE DUE	REQUESTED BY	PHONE	DEPARTMENT	RECORD TYPE	CORRESPONDENT NAME	RECORD DATE
10/6/00	THOMAS LOGAN	5-8966	ADMINISTRATION	RECORD	MILES LAW OFFICE	1/30/00
10/9/00	MARGARITA SHELBY	5-9912	ADVERTISING	RECORD	WAXI RADIO	5/15/00
10/10/00	MARY NEISMITH	5-8999	ACCOUNTING	FOLDER	MARTIN AUTO PARTS	
10/12/00	DAVID SMELSON	5-8875	MARKETING	RECORD	MARGARET JACKSON	3/17/00
10/12/00	JUAN CARLOS	5-9986	ADVERTISING	RECORD	ADVO SYSTEMS	7/18/00
10/13/00	SUE BELL	5-3264	ACCOUNTING	RECORD	MIDATLANTIC BOXES INC	5/16/00
10/17/00	MARY JANE HILTON	5-7792	PURCHASING	RECORD	JONES SUPPLY CO	9/16/00
10/19/00	JACK KLINE	5-8865	MARKETING	FOLDER	IKOHOTO TRADE CENTER	
10/19/00	WANDA ADAMS	5-8921	TRAINING	RECORD	MISTY WATERS	2/17/00
10/22/00	JOHN FRYMIRE	5-8632	PURCHASING	RECORD	J P SMITH	1/10/00

Figure 5–24b Tickler Database OUT File

filed behind November would then be redistributed behind the daily guides according to the dates on the reminders.

The tickler file must be the first item checked each day by the person in charge of it. Information on the notes found in the tickler file serves as a reminder to act or follow through on specific instructions.

Misfiled and Lost Records

A lost or misplaced record often delays or affects the work of more than a dozen people. Estimates suggest that executives spend an average of three hours per week looking for missing information.[2] Reducing the number of misfiled documents results in considerable cost savings. Every "filing mistake" costs over $100 in lost time and reduces an organization's effectiveness in serving customers. Prompt, high-quality service to customers and clients is made possible with almost instant access to data and documents related to their transactions.[3] Improvements in records management can bring measurable increases in staff productivity.

If storage is done haphazardly or with little concern for the importance of following consistent procedures, lost records are numerous. Lack of attention to spelling, careless insertion of records into the storage equipment, and distractions often cause records to be misfiled and, therefore, "lost."

Experienced filers use the following techniques in trying to find missing records:

1. Look in the folders immediately in front of and behind the correct folder.
2. Look between the folders.
3. Look under all the folders, where the record may have slipped to the bottom of the drawer or shelf.
4. Look completely through the correct folder because alphabetic or other order of sequence may have been neglected due to carelessness or haste.
5. Look in the general folder in addition to searching in the individual folder.
6. Check the transposition of names (DAVID MILLER instead of MILLER DAVID).
7. Look for the second, third, or succeeding units of a filing segment rather than for the key unit.
8. Check for misfiling because of misreading of letters—such as, e for i, n for m, t for l, k for h, and C for G.

---

[2]Smead Manufacturing Company, "The Business Benefits of a Smead Shelf Filing System," July 2000. [On-line]. Available: http://www.smead.com/main3f.html.

[3]Mark Langemo, "Strategies for Developing and Strengthening Records Management Programs." *Records Management Quarterly*, Vol. 31, No. 3., July 1997.

9. Check for alternate spellings (JON, JAHN).
10. Look under other vowels (for a name beginning with Ha, look also under He, Hi, Ho, and Hu).
11. Look for a double letter instead of a single one (or the reverse).
12. Look for Anglicized forms of a name (Miller, Moller, or Muller for Mueller).
13. Check for transposition of numbers (35 instead of 53).
14. Look in the year preceding or following the one in question.
15. Look in a related subject if the subject method is used.
16. Be aware that the records may be en route to storage.
17. Look in the sorter.
18. Ask the person in whose desk or briefcase the record may be to search for it!

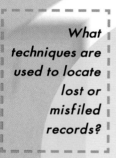

What techniques are used to locate lost or misfiled records?

If every search fails to produce the missing record, some records managers try to reconstruct the record from memory, rekeying as much as is known. This information is placed in a folder labeled LOST along with the name on the original folder. This new folder is stored in its correct place as a constant reminder to the filer to be on the alert for the missing record.

Efficient correspondence records storage is the result of:

- Good planning to choose the right equipment, supplies, and system.
- Proper training of personnel who recognize the value of the release mark, know and consistently apply the rules for alphabetic indexing, code papers carefully, prepare cross-references skillfully, invariably sort papers before storing, and carefully store records in their proper location.
- Constant concerned supervision by records managers or others responsible for the storage and retrieval functions.

SUMMARY

The volume of recorded information is rapidly increasing. More and more electronic records are being created, but paper records still make up about 80 percent of all records. Information in this chapter describes equipment, supplies, and processes used in storage and retrieval of paper records. Included throughout the chapter are definitions and descriptions of common terms used for records management materials, equipment, and procedures.

The four most common types of filing equipment are the vertical file, lateral file, shelf files, and mobile shelf files. Types of supplies used for correspondence storage include guides, folders, labels, and OUT indicators. Considerations for selection of equipment and supplies require information on a number of related factors: type and volume of records to be stored and retrieved; degree of protection required; efficiency and ease of use of equipment and systems, space requirements, and cost.

Alphabetic records management is appropriate for correspondence files with a low to moderate volume of records and names of correspondents when records are requested by names of individuals, businesses, and organizations. This system is a direct access method; and attention to detail, along with consistent application of written rules, makes this method easy to use.

Many manufacturers of storage supplies use color as a means to increase efficiency in storing and retrieving records. Color can be used to visually separate sections of the file or to call attention to special folders. Consistent filing procedures follow these six steps for storing correspondence records: inspecting, indexing, coding, cross-referencing, sorting, and storing.

Tickler files can be manual or computer based and are used as a reminder for tasks to be done daily. Tips for finding lost or misfiled records included looking around, under, between, and in other folders; checking for alternate spellings, other vowel combinations, and double letters; and being aware that the record may be temporarily in the sorter or in transit to storage.

IMPORTANT TERMS

alphabetic records management	label
bellows (expansion) folder	lateral file cabinet
caption	mobile aisle system
color accenting	mobile shelving
color coding	motorized rotary storage
direct access	OUT folder
fine sorting	OUT guide
folder	OUT indicator
follower block (compressor)	OUT sheet
general folder	permanent cross-reference
guide	pocket folder
individual folder	position
inspecting	primary guide

records management

release mark

rough sorting

score marks

shelf file

sorter

sorting

special (auxiliary) guide

special folder

staggered arrangement

storage

storage (filing) method

storage procedures

storing

straight-line arrangement

suspension (hanging) folder

tab

tab cut

tickler file

vertical file cabinet

REVIEW AND DISCUSSION

1. Compare and contrast the terms *storage, filing, storage method,* and *records management*. (Obj. 1)

2. List and briefly describe four kinds of commonly used storage equipment for correspondence records. (Obj. 2)

3. List and briefly describe five important supplies used in records storage. (Obj. 2)

4. Why is the straight-line arrangement of tabs on folders and guides easier to use than the staggered arrangement? (Obj. 2)

5. What five criteria should be considered when choosing storage equipment and supplies? (Obj. 3)

6. Discuss the advantages and disadvantages of the alphabetic storage method. (Obj. 4)

7. What types of information should be gathered before selecting and designing an alphabetic storage system? (Obj. 5)

8. Explain how color can be used in correspondence records storage. (Obj. 6)

9. List and briefly describe (in order) the six steps to store a record properly. (Obj. 7)

10. What kinds of release marks might you find on records that are ready to be stored? (Obj. 7)

11. List at least five procedures to try to locate a "lost" or a "misfiled" record. (Obj. 7)

12. What is a tickler file and how is one arranged? (Obj. 8)

APPLICATIONS (APP)

APP 5-1.   Coding Correspondence (Obj. 7)

Correctly index and code the following outgoing letters to be filed in an alphabetic correspondence records system. Place a diagonal between units of the name by which the record is to be stored. Underline the first indexing unit and number other units in their order for arrangement in the storage system.

Dr. Joyce Phosgene, President
Callous Records Equipment, Inc.
Coney Towers #47
Dallas, TX 75202-1847

Jaymire Communications Systems
1812 Roswell Avenue
Albuquerque, NM 87201-1254

J.C. Wilshire, Advertising Director
Johnson Office Supplies
Yuma, AZ 88364-6943

1-2-3 Tailor-made Publications
87 West Second Street
Sacramento, CA 95801-9985

Oney Jasmine
First Street, NE
Brenham, TX 77833-5415

Collaborate

APP 5-2.   Changing Storage Equipment (Objs. 2, 3, and 5)

You and one or two of your classmates have formed a records management consulting company. The Wilson Charter Co. has asked your company for a consultation about their storage equipment. You and your team visited the Wilson office and noted the following:

- Correspondence is stored alphabetically in traditional four-drawer vertical file cabinets.
- Everyone in the office has access to the file cabinets.
- Ten to 20 stored records are retrieved daily, one paper at a time.

1. Along with your team members, analyze the Wilson Charter Co.'s current equipment and determine whether anything should be changed. Would open-shelf files work better? Why do you think so? What factors would contribute to your decision? What other resources are available to help your team assemble the facts needed to propose a solution for Wilson Charter Co.?

2. Create a proposal for the Wilson Charter Co. giving your team's recommendations for changing their filing equipment or procedures.

Collaborate

APP 5-3.   Observe Records Storage Equipment and Supplies in Use (Objs. 2, 3, 5, and 6)

Arrange for you and one or two of your classmates to visit a local office to observe the records storage equipment and supplies. Make a list of the equipment and supplies that the office is using to store paper records. If office workers are available, ask the following questions. Be prepared to give an oral summary of your visit to the class.

1. What types of supplies are used? Are the current supplies adequate for the usage?

2. What type of equipment is being used? Is the current equipment adequate for the usage?

3. What changes would you make in terms of equipment or supplies?

4. Do you have input when equipment or supplies are purchased? If so, what types of choices did you make and how did you make your choices?

5. Do you use tickler files; if so, for what purposes?

Practice Set

APPLYING THE RULES

Job 4, Correspondence Filing, Rules 1–5.
Job 5, Correspondence Filing, Rules 6–10.
Job 6, Correspondence Filing, Rules 1–10 and Tickler File Usage.

CHAPTER 6

RECORDS RETENTION, RETRIEVAL, AND TRANSFER

RECORDS RETENTION

Phases of the records life cycle include *creation, distribution, use, maintenance,* and *disposition.* The last two phases, as they relate to the retention, retrieval, and transfer of records, are discussed in this chapter. *Maintenance* includes storing, retrieving, and protecting records; *disposition* includes transferring, retaining, or destroying records.

A sound records and information management (RIM) program includes policies and procedures to assure that records that continue to have value to the organization are retained (kept). A **records retention program** consists of policies and procedures relating to *what* documents to keep, *where* the documents are kept, and *how long* these documents are to be kept. Ideally, the retention of a record is known when the record is created. Retention is part of the *disposition phase* in the records life cycle. Another facet of retention is determining where and in what condition and environment documents are stored. This process is part of the *maintenance phase* of the records life cycle.

Retention policies also allow destruction of records that no longer have value to the organization. Storing records no longer needed is costly in floor space, storage supplies and equipment, and labor. Retaining some records longer than necessary could be costly in legal expenses as well.

Records Inventory

A **records inventory** is a detailed listing that could include the types, locations, dates, volumes, equipment, classification systems, and usage data

What is records retention?

Why is a records retention program important?

of an organization's records. It usually involves a survey conducted by each department in the organization. A member of each department is assigned the task of inventorying its records and documenting important information about those records. Survey information from all departments is incorporated into an organization-wide records retention schedule. A **records retention schedule** is a comprehensive list of records, indicating the length of time records are to be maintained.

Survey information includes types of records (official, record copy, or nonrecord) and their media—paper, electronic, or image. An **official record** is a significant, vital, or important record of continuing value to be protected, managed, and retained according to established retention schedules. The official record is often, but not necessarily, an original. In law, an official record has the legally recognized and judicially enforceable quality of establishing some fact. The **office of record** is an office designated to maintain the *record* or *official* copy of a particular record in an organization. Another name for an official record is **record copy**, or the official copy of a record that is retained for legal, operational, or historical purposes, sometimes the original. For example, a document printed from an electronic file is often considered the "official record" rather than the file stored on electronic media because of its readability, durability, and ease of use. The electronic file must still be retained for a week or two, and the printed document may be saved for two or three years, depending on the content.

A **nonrecord** is an item not usually included within the scope of official records such as a convenience file, day file, reference materials such as dictionaries, and drafts. Typically, nonrecords are created, modified, and destroyed without formal RIM procedures and are not included in a records retention program. Nonrecords should not be retained past their usefulness.

Electronic mail (e-mail) messages sent and/or received within one organization may be considered nonrecords even though these messages are usually stored in the organization's computer system for some time. E-mail messages sent to or received from external correspondents may or may not be considered records. Many managers understand that the volume of e-mail messages, internal and external, can clog the system and cause it to slow down. For this reason, e-mail messages might be included on a records retention schedule and deleted from the system after a predetermined length of time.

E-mail is often a means of transmitting other information rather than being a record in and of itself. For example, an e-mail message to inform the recipient that a report is attached to the message is not important and does not need to be kept. If an e-mail message contains information the recipient needs to keep, a copy can be printed, and the original message deleted from the system. The printed copy becomes the official record.

What is the difference between official records and nonrecords?

Records managers must work with the information services department in their organization to develop official policies regarding e-mail retention. Some organizations routinely purge all e-mail after thirty days. Other organizations allow each user to determine what to retain as long as the user is following the organization's policy regarding retention. E-mail users must be trained to purge unneeded documents. (See Chapter 10 for more about e-mail policies.)

A records inventory is a valuable tool for helping managers decide which filing method (alphabetic, subject, numeric, or geographic) to use. Information obtained from a records survey and inventory usually include the following:

- Name and dates of records series.
- Records location by department or office, then building, floor, and room, if necessary.
- Equipment in which records are stored—cabinets, shelves, or vaults.
- Number of cabinets, shelves, or other storage containers.
- How often records are referenced—daily, weekly, monthly, or annually—and why.
- Records media—paper, microfilm, electronic, or optical.
- Records size—letter, legal, tab/checks, other.
- Records housing—folders, binders, disks, reels, etc.
- Records value—vital, important, useful, nonessential.
- Retention requirements.

Figure 6–1 on page 136 shows a sample records inventory worksheet that would be prepared by a member of each department. Records are identified by series. A **records series** is a group of related records that normally are used and filed as a unit and can be evaluated as a unit to determine the records retention period. For example, invoices for the month of October illustrate a records series, as do bank statements retained for a year.

After the records inventory is completed, the records manager determines the value of each record and then determines how long records are to be kept (retained). Appropriate retention periods are determined and included in a records retention schedule. (See Figure 6–2.) The retention schedule contains a comprehensive list of records series titles, indicating for each series the length of time it is to be maintained. It may include retention in active office areas, inactive storage areas, and when and if such series may be destroyed or formally transferred to another entity such as an archives for historical purposes. Managers base records destruction decisions on the records retention schedule. Consequently, records are destroyed regularly as certain records reach the end of their usefulness. Chapter 12 contains more information about the role that records retention plays in a comprehensive RIM program.

How is a records retention schedule used?

RECORDS INVENTORY WORKSHEET

Department: Contracts   **Division:** Sales   **Date:** January 1, 2001

Records Series/Description	Record Date	Location	Qty	Usage*					Value**				Current Retention
				D	W	M	S	A	1	2	3	4	
CONTRACTS CALDWELL AND LOWE, LLC	1/99–12/99	104	2 fldrs			M				2			3 years
CONTRACTS CAUDLE PRINTERS	1/99–12/99	104	1 fldr			M						4	1 year
CONTRACTS CHANDLER LIGHTING COMPANY	1/99–12/99	104	2 fldrs			M					3		3 years
CONTRACTS COX, DENHAM, AND FORTNER	1/99–12/99	104	3 fldrs			M				2			3 years
CONTRACTS CROWDER, CYNTHIA S.	1/99–12/99	104	2 fldrs			M				2			3 years
CONTRACTS C (GENERAL FOLDER)	1/99–12/99	104	2 fldrs			M				2			3 years

Form 203 (Rev. 00)

* D – Daily	S – Semi-annual	** 1 – Vital	3 – Useful
W – Weekly	A – Annually	2 – Important	4 – Nonessential
M – Monthly			

Figure 6–1 Records Inventory Worksheet

Creating the records retention schedule is a cooperative effort among several departments in an organization: legal, tax, information management, records management, as well as various departments that own the records. The length of time may be determined by law for statutory, regulatory, or tax purposes. For other records, such as general correspondence, the length of time may be limited to the record's actual time of use. Each department has unique needs the retention schedule must meet. Without cooperative input from all departments in an organization, the records retention schedule will not serve its purpose. In addition, the records manager must consider each of the following interrelated aspects when developing a records retention schedule.

1. How long will the records be used?
2. In what form should the records be kept? How accessible should the records be?
3. When should the records be determined inactive? Which records should be transferred offsite and when? How will such records be accessed? Will transferred records maintain their integrity and security?

RECORDS RETENTION SCHEDULE

Record	Years in Office/Active	Years in Storage/Inactive	Total Years
Accounting and Fiscal			
Accounts payable invoices	3	3	6
Accounts payable ledger	3	3	6
Accounts receivable ledger	3	3	6
Balance sheets	3	3	6
Bank deposit books and slips	3	3	6
Bank reconciliations and statements	3	3	6
Financial reports–annual	3	P	P
Financial reports–monthly	1	P	P
Administrative			
Correspondence–Executive	1	P	P
Correspondence–General office	1	4	5
Legal			
Contract documentation	3	20	20
Leases, property	3	20	20
Mortgages, property	3	20	20
Patents and related data	3	P	P
Trademarks	3	P	P
Office Supplies and Services			
Inventories	1	–	1
Office equipment records	3	3	6
Requisitions–Supplies	1	–	1
Personnel			
Applications, changes, terminations	1	–	1
Attendance records	3	4	7
Time cards	3	3	6
Training manuals	3	P	P
Public Relations and Advertising			
Advertising activity reports	2	3	5
News releases	1	P	P
Publicity photographs	1	–	1
Speeches	3	–	3
Records Management			
Records destruction documentation	3	P	P
Records inventory	1	–	1
Records management procedures	1	P	P

Form 220 (Rev. 00)

P = Permanent

Source: Adapted from *Olsten Temporary Services Pocket Retention Guide*, 1993, and Donald S. Skupsky, *Recordkeeping Requirements*. Denver: Information Requirements Clearinghouse, 1988.

Figure 6–2 Records Retention Schedule

4. What are the applicable federal, state, and local laws?
5. What are the comparative costs for keeping the records or not keeping the records?
6. When and how will the records be disposed of?

Once a record is stored, it may not be stored forever. Just think of the thousands of storage containers and shelves that would be required in offices if that were the case! One critical part of creating the records retention schedule is estimating the value of a record to an organization and determining how long the record is useful. The next section discusses the value of records.

The Value of Records

Remember the four uses of records first discussed in Chapter 1? Records serve as the memory of an organization, and their purpose is administrative, fiscal, legal, or historical. Classifications of records were also discussed in Chapter 1. The classification by value of the record to the firm is useful for making retention decisions. The following four categories of records values are useful when determining which records should be retained (and for how long) and which records should be destroyed.

What is a
vital record?

1. *Nonessential—records that are not worth keeping.* These records, such as bulk mail announcements, simple acknowledgments, routine telephone message forms, and bulletin board announcements, have no predictable value to an organization after their initial use. Some e-mail or fax messages may be useful when received but become nonessential after action is taken.
2. *Useful—records for short-term storage* of up to three years. These records are helpful in conducting business operations and, if destroyed, may be replaced at slight cost. This category is used mainly for active files of business letters and interoffice memorandums, business reports, and bank statements.
3. *Important—records for long-term storage* of approximately seven to ten years. These records contain information pertinent to an organization that would need to be re-created or replaced if lost or destroyed. This category includes important financial and sales data, credit histories, and statistical records.
4. *Vital—records for permanent storage* such as student transcripts, customer profile records, and business ownership records that have lasting value. These records are essential for the continuation or survival of an organization if a disaster strikes. Such records are necessary to re-create an organization's legal and financial status and to determine the rights and obligations of employees, customers, stockholders, and citizens.

Information needed to create and keep a records retention schedule up-to-date can be obtained at little or no cost from various sources. The U.S. Government annually publishes the *Guide to Records Retention Requirements*, which is available from the Superintendent of Documents, U.S. Government Printing Office. Each of the fifty states has developed statutes of limitations that specify the time after which legal rights cannot be enforced by civil action in the courts. When a record reaches an age beyond which the statute of limitations applies, the record has no value as evidence in a court of law.

Records retention and destruction schedules are based on the value of the *information* contained in the records and not on the storage media. However, as discussed in Chapters 10 and 11, the life span of the media is important for long-term retention. All records media—paper, electronic, and image—need retention schedules. Storage conditions and environment are also important considerations for each type of records media. Records users often refer to records that are not electronic records as *visible records* or *visible media*. In some organizations, a separate retention schedule is maintained for electronic records. See Chapter 10 for more about electronic records retention schedules.

What records media are included on a records retention schedule?

All records users need to comply with the records retention schedule adopted by their organization. Many organizations emphasize the importance of records by conducting "Records Week" activities centered around cleaning out old records, transferring records, and destroying records. By adhering to transfer and destruction timetables, an organization can reduce clutter and improve retrieval time because fewer records will be contained in storage. Additional space will be available for current records needed for day-to-day decision making. The records retrieval process is discussed next.

RECORDS RETRIEVAL

Retrieval is the process of locating and removing a record or file from storage. It is also the action of recovering information on a given subject from stored data. In this section, you will learn how to retrieve records by following standard procedures. Although the procedures discussed here are primarily for paper-based systems, the same procedures apply for electronic and image records. For example, finding a name and telephone number in a telephone directory or database is a common storage and retrieval activity. The storage method is an alphabetic listing of names on the pages of a book or in rows in a computer database. The system is a table search (scanning of tabulated telephone lists) according to name. Similarly, nonfiction library books are stored on shelves in numbered sequence; you must search the shelves by reference number to retrieve a desired book.

What is retrieval?

A record or information from it can be retrieved in three ways:

1. *Manually.* A person goes to a storage container and removes by hand a record wanted or makes a note of the information requested from it.
2. *Mechanically.* A person uses some mechanical means, such as pressing the correct buttons to rotate movable shelves to the correct location of a record, remove the record manually, or record information requested from it.
3. *Electronically.* A person uses some means, such as a computer, to locate a record. The physical record may not need to be removed from storage. The requester is informed as to where it can be found, or the information requested is shown to the requester in some way, perhaps on a screen in a database or electronic mail file.

How are records requested?

Requests for stored records may be made orally (from the next desk, over the telephone or intercom, or by messenger) or in writing (by fax, e-mail, memo, letter, or a special form). The request may be delivered in person, sent by some mechanical means, such as a conveyor system, or sent electronically by fax or e-mail. A typical request, for example, might be, "Please find the most recent letter from Organic Growers that forecasts the number of tons of soybeans that will be produced next quarter." Or, "Please pull the videotape of the chairman's annual report to stockholders." Or, perhaps, "Please retrieve the microfiche of the current price list for patio enclosures." All these records have previously been stored manually according to an established method of storage. The letter, videotape, or microfiche must be retrieved from storage and given to the requester quickly. Every minute of delay in finding a record is costly—in user or requester waiting time and in filer searching time—and could possibly lead to loss of money for the business.

If filer and requester use the same filing segment for storing and requesting a record, the system works well. If, for instance, records relating to a company named Stanford Refrigeration were stored under *Stanford* but requested under *Air Conditioner Company*, the searcher would find retrieval extremely difficult because he or she would look in the A section of storage instead of the S section. Consequently, good cross-referencing is necessary.

Retrieval and Re-storage Cycle

The same basic steps for retrieving are used for handling all manual records. Only the specific operating procedures differ. The crucial step, the point at which a problem is most likely to arise, is in Step 1 with the words used to request a record. Ideally, the person who stores a record is also the one who searches for and removes it from storage when it is requested. Realistically, however, a record may be stored by one person and retrieved by someone else when that record or information is requested. Steps in the retrieval process include:

1. Request for stored record or records series—requester or records center personnel prepares requisition form.
2. Check index for location of stored record(s).
3. Search for record or records series.
4. Retrieve (locate) record or records series.
5. Remove record(s) from storage.
6. Charge out record(s) to requester. Insert OUT indicator in place of record(s) removed from storage. Complete charge-out log.
7. Send record(s) to requester.
8. Follow-up borrowed record(s).
9. Receive record(s) for re-storage.
10. Store record(s) again. Remove OUT indicator. Update charge-out log.

Effective records control enables the records manager or filer to retrieve requested records on the first try and to answer correctly these questions:

1. *Who* took the records?
2. *What* records are out of storage?
3. *When* were the records taken?
4. *Where* will the records be refiled when they are brought back to storage?
5. *How long* will the records be out of storage?

Requisition, Charge-out, and Follow-up Procedures

Effective records control includes following standard procedures for requesting records, charging them out, and seeing that they are returned. These procedures are referred to as *requisition, charge-out,* and *follow-up.* These procedures may be completed manually or by using an automated system.

Requisition Procedures

Preparing a requisition is the first step in the retrieval process. A request is an in-person, mail, telephone, fax, or e-mail inquiry for information about or from records stored in a records center or an archives. A **requisition** is a written request for a record or information from a record. Even if the borrower orally requests the information or record, that request is put into writing and referred to as a *requisition.* The form may be prepared by the requester or completed by the filer from information given orally or in writing by the requester. An organization that is networked through the Internet or an intranet may post a variety of forms,

Why is a requisition form used?

including records requisition forms, which users may complete and transmit electronically. Two types of these forms are described next.

Requisition Form. One of the most frequently used requisition forms is a 5″ by 3″ or 6″ by 4″ card or slip of paper printed with blanks to be filled in. Figure 6–3 shows an example of such a requisition. A requester or filer may complete a similar computer form in an automated system.

RECORDS REQUEST	
Name on Record	Date on Record
Date Taken	Date to be Returned
Requester	Extension
Department	E-mail
White copy in folder; blue is reminder copy.	
Form 209 (Rev. 00)	

Usually prepared in duplicate—original stays in folder; copy serves as a reminder.

Figure 6–3 **Requisition Form**

When the requisition form is completed, the filer will have answers to the five records retention questions (Who? What? When? Where? How Long?) discussed previously. This form may be prepared in duplicate: The original stays in the folder from which the document was retrieved to serve as an OUT indicator. The copy (usually placed in a tickler file as discussed in Chapter 5) serves as a reminder to assure the record is returned on time. In an automated system, a copy of a computerized requisition form may be printed to serve as an OUT indicator in a paper file. The filer may also be able to insert an electronic flag into the records database to indicate that a record is out of the records center. The form is then sent to an electronic tickler file.

On-Call (Wanted) Form. Occasionally, another user will request a record that has already been borrowed. A requisition form replaced the record in the file, and it identifies who has the record and when it will be returned. The filer should notify the second requester that the record is on loan and state when it is scheduled for return to storage. If the second request is urgent, the filer will notify the original borrower that someone else wants the record and ask that it be returned to storage. Notification may be made orally, in writing on an on-call form or a wanted form, or by fax or e-mail. An **on-call form** (or **wanted form**) is a written request for a record that is *out* of the file. (See Figure 6–4.) This form is similar to an OUT form. A computerized form may also be completed and transmitted by fax or e-mail to the records center.

ON CALL

WANTED BY		RECORDS WANTED		DELIVERED
DATE	NAME	DATE	DESCRIPTION	DATE
7-6	K.C. Costa	5-20	McMillan Co. Sun Coast Mall Drawings	7-6

Form 205 (Rev. 00)

Prepared as a duplicate—one copy to borrower; one copy is attached to the original OUT indicator in storage.

Figure 6–4 On-Call (or Wanted) Form

Two copies of an on-call form are made—one copy goes to the borrower; the other copy is attached to the original OUT indicator in storage. When the borrowed record is returned to storage, it is charged out to the second borrower by the standard method of charge-out or by writing on the on-call form the date on which the record was delivered to the second borrower. (Note the "Delivered Date" column on the card in Figure 6–4.)

In some optical disk and microfilm storage systems, requested information is retrieved and sent to the requester electronically. The optical disk record is retrieved on a computer terminal and faxed or e-mailed to the requester. Microfilm is scanned into a computer terminal and faxed or e-mailed to the requester. In both cases, the official record is not removed from its file. No follow-up procedures are needed because the official record is still in storage. Requesters may be instructed to destroy the borrowed record when they have completed their work with it. Note also that manual records (paper) can be scanned and transmitted by e-mail or fax. Paper records also can be faxed through a conventional fax machine. The official record is returned to the file, and the user may destroy the fax copy after use.

Confidential Records Requests. All stored records are considered valuable or they would not be stored. Some are so valuable that they are stamped *Confidential, Classified, Secret, Vital,* or *Personal.* Do *not* release these types of records from storage without proper authorization following established procedures. In some offices, a written request bearing the signature of a designated officer of the organization is required for release of such records. In an electronic system, access to confidential records is limited to those users who know the password. If a copy of a confidential record is sent electronically, it might be encrypted (the words are scrambled into code using a software program) to prevent

What procedures are followed for borrowing confidential records?

unauthorized access. When the requester receives the encrypted file, he or she must unscramble the file to read it.

Some records may be so valuable or confidential that they are not to be removed from storage under any circumstances. These records must be inspected only at the storage container. The signature of someone in authority is required before the inspection is allowed. A requisition form is usually not needed; however, a record of the persons inspecting the records may be kept.

Charge-Out Procedures

Charge-out is a control procedure to establish the current location of a record when it is not in the records center or central file, which can be a manual or automated system. A record is charged-out to the borrower who is held responsible for returning it to storage by an agreed-upon date. A standard procedure for charging out and following up records should be observed in every instance, regardless of who removes material from storage. Less than one minute is needed to note the name of a person borrowing a record, but hours can be spent searching for a lost or misplaced record. Borrowers seem to be more conscientious about returning records to storage when they know that records have been charged out in their names. Typically, the supplies needed to charge-out records consist of the following:

Why use a charge-out procedure?

1. OUT indicators to show that records have been removed from storage.
2. Carrier folders to transport borrowed records while the original folder remains in the file.
3. Charge-out log.

In automated systems, records are indexed and bar coded to identify their places in the file and other information. When the requester has presented his or her bar code identifier and the file is located, the bar code on the record is scanned. An electronic form is created that indicates which record is checked out to whom and for how long. Copies of the form may be printed or kept electronically. A bar code of the form may be printed to be affixed to an OUT indicator and placed in the file where the requested record should be refiled. When the record is returned, the bar code is scanned again, the OUT indicator located, the record returned to the file, and the requester "cleared" of any borrowed records.

OUT Indicators. When a requested record is found, it is removed from storage and an OUT form is inserted in place of the record. An OUT form shows where to refile the record when it is returned. OUT indicators are explained in Chapter 5.

Disposing of OUT Indicators. When a borrowed record is returned to storage, the OUT form inserted while the record was gone must be

In automated systems, bar codes are used to identify and track records.

removed immediately. If the charge-out information was written on the OUT form itself, this information is crossed out, and the form is stored for reuse. In some offices, OUT forms are kept for tallying purposes—to see how many records are being requested, to determine the workload of employees, and to see which records are being used frequently and which are not. Totals may be kept daily, weekly, monthly, or yearly as determined by the standard procedure in effect. Requisition forms removed from files may be destroyed. Any duplicate copies of OUT forms should be located and immediately destroyed. Any forms filed in electronic ticker files may also be deleted.

Follow-up Procedures

Whoever is responsible for retrieving records from storage and charging them out is also responsible for checking in the records on their return. **Follow-up** is a system for assuring the timely and proper return of materials charged out from a file. The length of time records may be borrowed from storage depends on (1) the type of business, (2) the number of requests received for the records, (3) the use of a copying machine, and (4) the value of the records.

Experience shows that the longer records remain out of the files, the more difficult their return becomes. Many organizations stipulate a week to ten days, with two weeks being the absolute maximum amount of time records may be borrowed. Other organizations allow less time because records can be copied easily and quickly, and the original may be returned to storage within a few hours. Extra copies should be destroyed when they are no longer needed. Following up on a borrowed record

Why perform follow-up procedures?

may mean calling a borrower or sending a written request as a reminder that borrowed records must be returned to storage. If no other requests for the same records have been received, the date the records are to be returned may be extended.

Following Up Confidential Records. The rule concerning confidential records is generally that the records (if they may be borrowed) must be returned to storage each night. A special reminder often is used to assure that these records are returned. This reminder may be a note prominently displayed, a special flag, or some other type of signal. The same charge-out procedures used for other records are also used for confidential records. However, an *additional* reminder to obtain the record before the end of the day also is used. Because the memory jogger must remind the filer that confidential records are out of storage and must be returned, it must be something unusual.

Charge-out Log. Usually, an organization will have a charge-out log on which to record information for all records as they are removed from storage. A **charge-out log** is a written or electronic form used for recording the following information:

What purpose does a charge-out log serve?

1. *What* record was taken (correspondent name or subject title on the record and date on the record).
2. *When* the record was taken (date borrowed).
3. *Who* took the record (name of person, extension number, e-mail address).
4. Date due.
5. Date returned.
6. Date overdue notice was sent.
7. Extended date due.

The charge-out log should be kept current and used in the follow-up procedure. Refer to Figure 6–5 for an example of a portion of a charge-out log.

CHARGE-OUT LOG								
Name on Record	Date on Record	Name of Person Borrowing Record	Ext. or E-mail	Date Borrowed	Date Due	Date Returned	Date Overdue Notice Sent	Extended Date Due
Albermarl Photo Equipment	1/15	A. Castro	acast@xyz.net	2/1	2/8	2/4		
Zyphone, Inc.	12/28	R. Franklin	rfrank@xyz.net	2/2	2/9	2/9		
Biagio's Restaurant	1/30	J. Thompson	4378	2/3	2/10		2/10	2/17
Claymore Gardens	1/27	M. Tran	5260	2/4	2/11	2/5		
FORM 211 (Rev. 00)								

Figure 6–5 Charge-out Log

RECORDS TRANSFER

The final phase of the records life cycle is disposition. **Records disposition** is the final destination of records after they have reached the end of their retention period in active and/or inactive storage. Records may be transferred to an archives for retention or destroyed. Inactive storage may be housed on-site or off-site. **On-site storage** is storage of inactive (usually) records on the premises of an organization. **Off-site storage** is a potentially secure location, remote from the primary location, at which inactive or vital records are stored. Off-site storage is sometimes referred to as *remote storage*. **Archives** are the records created or received and accumulated by a person or an organization in the conduct of affairs and preserved because of their historical or continuing value. Archives also may refer to the building or part of a building where archival materials are located.

As indicated on the sample records retention schedule shown in Figure 6–2, records may be stored in an active records area for a period of time before being moved to another storage area when they are no longer accessed regularly. **Records transfer** is the act of changing the physical custody of records with or without change of legal title. In other words, it is the relocating of records from one storage area to another. The basis for making the decision to transfer records is the frequency of use of the records. As records age, they are less frequently accessed. Consequently, dates on the records are also considered when deciding to transfer records. Records analysts define three degrees of records activity:

1. **Active record**—A record needed to perform current operations. It is subject to frequent use and is usually located near the user. An active record can be accessed manually or on-line via a computer. Active records are accessed three or more times a month. Such records are stored in very accessible equipment in the active storage area or on-line.
2. **Inactive record**—A record that does not have to be readily available but which must be kept for legal, fiscal, or historical purposes. Inactive records are referred to less than fifteen times a year. Inactive records are stored in a less expensive storage area.
3. **Archive record**—A record that has continuing or historical value to an organization and is preserved permanently. Archives can have many uses: to maintain public relations; to prepare commemorative histories; to preserve corporate history; to provide financial, legal, personnel, product, or research information; or to provide policy direction. Archive records are stored in less expensive storage areas, often at an off-site location.

> What is the difference between inactive and archive records?

Careful management of stored records requires that established procedures be followed. Procedures to handle all situations should be described in the policies and procedures manual developed for the organization. In most cases, the current year's records plus those of the past year are all that are needed in the active files. However, several other factors must be considered when making transfer decisions.

First, transfer helps to reduce equipment costs because inactive records may be stored in less expensive cardboard containers. Second, cabinets or shelves formerly used by the transferred files provide additional space for new active files. Finally, efficiency of storage and retrieval of active files is improved because crowding of files has been eliminated; and, as a result, the space in drawers, cabinets, shelves, or computer storage has been increased.

In the disposition phase of the records life cycle, decisions are made to (1) destroy a record, (2) retain a record permanently, or (3) transfer a record to inactive storage. Records transfer is made according to a retention schedule as described earlier. If records are transferred, the main basis for making that decision is often the active or inactive use of the record. Sometimes records transfer decisions are made on the basis of dates on the records. The following reasons also greatly influence when and why transfer takes place:

When should a records transfer take place?

1. No more active records storage space is available.
2. Costs of more storage equipment and extra office space are rising and less costly areas of nearby storage or off-site storage become attractive alternatives.
3. Stored records are no longer being requested and, therefore, are ready for transfer.
4. Workloads have lightened, and time is available for records transfer activity.
5. Case or project records have reached a closing or ending time (the contract has expired, the legal case is settled or closed).
6. Established organizational policy requires every department to transfer records at a stated time.

Once transfer is decided upon, the records manager must find answers to four important questions:

1. *What* records are to be moved?
2. *How* are the records to be prepared for transfer?
3. *When* are the records to be transferred?
4. *Where* are the transferred records to be stored?

Answers to the first three questions will depend on the transfer method selected and the organization's records retention schedule. The answer to *where* will depend on the method selected *and* on the availability of in-house or off-site records storage areas. After answering those questions, the records manager then follows perpetual or periodic transfer procedures to move the selected records.

Transfer Methods

Two of the most commonly used methods of transferring records are the perpetual transfer method and the periodic transfer method. Each is discussed in this section along with the procedure required to ensure efficient records transfer.

Perpetual Transfer Method

Under the **perpetual transfer method**, records are continually transferred from active storage to inactive storage areas whenever the records are no longer needed for reference. Examples of records that can be transferred by the perpetual method include student records after graduation, legal cases that are settled; research projects when results are finalized; medical records of cases no longer needing attention; prison and law-enforcement case records; and construction or architectural jobs that are completed.

The perpetual transfer method is often used for medical records.

Electronic records and nonrecords should be perpetually transferred from storage on a hard drive to storage on microfilm or floppy disks. E-mail messages should be routinely deleted if they are not official records. The perpetual transfer method is not recommended for business correspondence or records that are referred to often and that must be available quickly.

Periodic Transfer Method

The **periodic transfer method** is a method of transferring active records at the end of a stated period of time, usually one year, to inactive storage. Records are removed from current files into inactive storage sites on a scheduled basis. Guides remain in the active storage containers. However, new folders are made for records that are then allowed to accumulate in active storage until the next transfer period. A commonly used periodic method of transferring records at the end of one period of time, usually once or twice a year, is called the **one-period transfer method**. Records are transferred at the end of *one period of time*, (six months or a year). The main advantage of this method is the ease of operation. The main disadvantage is that some frequently requested records will be in inactive storage, making frequent trips to the inactive storage area necessary. Records of some correspondents will occasionally need to be retrieved from both active and inactive storage if the requested records cover several time periods.

How do the perpetual and the periodic transfer methods differ?

Transfer Procedures

After the transfer method is determined, transfer procedures are communicated to every department. The records manager must ensure that adequate storage equipment is available and at the correct location to receive transferred records before the actual transfer begins.

Records are transferred to inactive or archive (permanent) storage. Inactive storage indicates the record may be infrequently referenced; at the end of the retention period, inactive records are destroyed. The **retention period** is the length of time that records must be kept according to operational, legal, regulatory, and fiscal requirements. The estimate of the frequency of use for current and anticipated business is also important. This time period usually determines how long records should be retained in offices or records centers before they are transferred to an archives or otherwise disposed of.

Records stored in an archives must be kept permanently; however, the records may still be referenced. Because some of the records may have historical value, a special display area may be created for those records. Often, records are transferred to a **records center**, which is a low-cost centralized area for housing and servicing inactive records whose reference rate does not warrant their retention in a prime office area. Whether the records are classified as inactive or archival, the transfer procedures are the same.

Preparing records for transfer involves completing the necessary forms (see Figure 6–6) and boxing the records for inactive or archival storage. The forms used will vary; Figure 6–6 shows a records transmittal form. Note that the form should be keyed or clearly handwritten because it will be attached to the outside of a storage box and used to locate

What is the purpose of a records transmittal form?

RECORDS TRANSMITTAL TO RECORDS CENTER

Department
Administration

Office
Purchasing

Address
Main building, Rm. 201

Shaded Areas for
Records Mgmt. Use Only

Box Number		Description of Records (Exact description of content of each box)	Records Disposal Auth. No.	Department Schedule Item No.	Year of Record		Location in Records Center	Ret. Per.	Disp. Year	Disp. Date
Current Year	Sequential Number				Beg	End				
20--	3478	*Purchase Requisitions*	125	*PUR 110*	98	98				
20--	3479	*Purchase Orders*	125	*PUR 120*	99	99				

Date Transferred *1/06/20--*	Signature of Person Releasing Records *K. A. Kaminski*	Telephone: *3290* E-mail: *kak@xyz.com*	Received in Records Center By: *Olivia Chan*	Date: *1/06/20--*

Form 210 (Rev. 00) Distribution: White & Yellow – Records Center: Pink – File Copy

Figure 6–6 Records Transmittal Form

inactive records that may be requested at a later date. Also note that information on the form is about the contents of a box such as a description of the records, the time span the records cover, the department name, and retention information.

At the time records are transferred, the transferring department completes a multicopy set of the records transfer form. The transferring department retains one copy while the box is in transit to storage. The original and two copies accompany the box to inactive storage where the box is logged in and its location on the storage shelves is noted on all copies of the transmittal form. One copy of the form is returned to the sending department for reference when a record from that box is required. The copy that was first retained in the department is now destroyed.

Information from the records transfer form is either keyed or read into automatic equipment. Bar codes (discussed further in Chapter 10) make this process go much faster. When records are borrowed from inactive or archival storage, the same controls are needed as are used in active storage—requisition, charge-out, and follow-up.

If the records center does not provide boxes of uniform size in which to store records to be transferred, the records manager must ensure that all departments use the same size box, to facilitate stacking and to use space most economically. A **records center box** or *carton* or *container* is usually made of corrugated cardboard that is designed to hold approximately one cubic foot (12 inches high by 12 inches wide by 12 inches deep) of records, either legal or letter size. Using uniform-size boxes makes stacking the boxes on storage shelves much easier and looks neater. These boxes may have lift-up or lift-off tops or lift-out sides. Records center boxes are shown in Figure 6–7.

 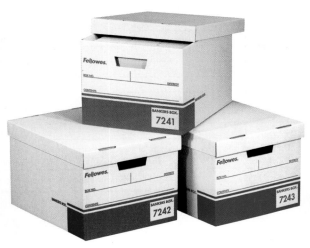

Figure 6–7 Transferring Records to an Inactive Records Storage Center

RECORDS CENTER CONTROL PROCEDURES

Whether inactive or archival records are stored off-site or within the same building as active records, several control procedures should be in place to ensure the appropriate security and accession of the records.

Inactive Records Index

First and most important, the records must be located. A commercial records center may house several different organization's records; an in-house records center contains records for all departments of one organization. In either case, many different records series are stored on a space-available basis. Therefore, like records series with different dates probably will not be stored near each other. If a request is made for an inactive record, the filer must locate the box of records quickly to find the requested record.

In records and information management, various indexes are useful in locating stored records. An **index** is a systematic guide that allows access to specific items contained within a larger body of information.

A records center will maintain an index to assist filers in locating inactive records. An **inactive records index** is an index of all records in the inactive records storage center. This index contains details about the inactive records: the dates the records were created, a description of the records series, the department that owns the records, an authorization for transfer to inactive storage, their location in the records storage center, the retention period, and the disposition date.

What is the purpose of an inactive records index?

This information can be manually or electronically maintained and is often a continuation of the records transmittal form (see Figure 6–6). The transmittal form contains all information needed for an inactive records index. A records center employee completes the location part of the form by checking the available space in the center and assigning space for the box(es). A copy of the records transmittal form is affixed to the box containing the records; and another copy of the transmittal form is filed in the destruction date file (discussed later).

Charge-out and Follow-up File

As with active records, charge-out and follow-up procedures must be followed for inactive and archive records. When someone from the accounting department requests accounts payable records for July 1, 2000, through December 31, 2000, a requisition form is completed. The filer scans the inactive records index, noting the location of the requested box of records. Then the filer physically goes to that location in the records center, finds the correct box, and removes the correct record. One copy of the requisition form is used as an OUT indicator and is placed inside the box. Last, the requisition information is entered into the charge-out and follow-up file.

A **charge-out and follow-up file** is a tickler file that contains requisition forms filed by dates that records are due back in the inactive records center. If a record is not returned by the date due, written reminders, telephone calls, faxes, or e-mail messages are used to remind the borrower to return the record(s) to the center.

Destruction Date File

Records destruction is the disposal of records of no further value by incineration (burning), maceration (soaked in a chemical solution to soften the paper, then bailed), pulping (shredded and mixed with water, then bailed), or shredding. Destruction is the definitive obliteration of a record beyond any possible reconstitution; i.e., nothing can possibly be recovered from the record. Shredders can shred not only paper records but also microrecords, magnetic tape, floppy disks, compact disks, and optical disks. Some records that do not contain confidential information may be sold for recycling. Many organizations find that contracting with service providers to destroy their records is more cost-effective than purchasing the supplies and equipment and hiring workers to carry out the destruction.

An important part of the control procedures in a records center is to maintain records documenting the destruction of records. A **destruction date file** is a tickler file containing copies of forms completed when records are received in a records center. Destruction dates are determined when a records retention schedule is created. The destruction date is recorded on the records transmittal form (see Figure 6–6). Another copy of the transmittal form can be placed into the destruction date file.

Before the destruction date arrives, the records center will send a notice of the pending records destruction to the department that owns the records. A **destruction notice** is a notification (memo, listing, form, etc.) of the scheduled destruction of records. This notice reminds departmental employees that some of their records will soon be destroyed. The manager of the department that owns the records signs a records destruction authorization form when the records are transferred to the records center. That authorization form is kept on file in the records center. Notice that the fourth column on the records transmittal form in Figure 6–6 identifies a records disposal authorization number. This number is assigned when the records are transferred to the records center. If a written authorization is on file, the number in that column is all that is needed to proceed with the destruction. If, however, the department manager determines that the inactive records continue to have value, the destruction may be suspended. A **destruction suspension** is a hold placed on the scheduled destruction of records that may be relevant to foreseeable or pending litigation, governmental investigation, audit, or special organizational requirements. Records for which destruction has been suspended are often referred to as *frozen records*.

Why is a destruction date file used?

Destruction File

Whether the records are destroyed by a service provider or by records center employees, the actual destruction must be witnessed or proof provided by a certificate of destruction. A **destruction file** contains information on the actual destruction of inactive records. Usually, the type of destruction is determined at the time the records are transferred to the records center. This information is recorded on the forms in the destruction date file, which are moved to the destruction file after the records are destroyed. These forms are filed by department names and dates the destruction was carried out.

Records managers maintain and dispose of records as part of the records life cycle. Proper control procedures ensure that the right record is available to the right person at the right time.

RECORDS CENTER SOFTWARE

The volume of records on all media continues to grow along with the increased demand to retrieve records faster. The need to manage and retrieve records as quickly as possible has led to the development of RIM software. Records and information management software can help manage electronic, imaged, microfilmed, and paper records in active records systems and in inactive records centers and archives.

Many records center software programs provide some of the same capabilities: bar code tracking, cross-referencing, global searching, off-site storage control, label generation, document indexing, check in/out, spell checking, report generation, audit trails, and more. (Records audits are discussed in Chapter 12.) Some programs allow users to generate a **pick list**—a list containing specific records needed for a given program or project. A filer can use a pick list to retrieve all records on the list. The records are then sent as a group to the requester. The same list can be used to return the records to the proper files/locations.

Records center software is often referred to as *records management software* and is commonly used for the following applications:[1]

- Indexing and cross-referencing records on all media in active systems and inactive systems and archives.
- Maintaining records inventories for assuring information about the different types of records on all media.
- Developing records retention schedules and programs through legal research.
- Including records retention schedules for computer-based records retention.
- Incorporating bar coding to track physical records media (file folders, individual documents, boxes, film cartridges, and others).
- Preparing on-demand, printed, computer-generated indexing with color-coded, bar-coded, adhesive strip labels for active records.
- Integrating electronic imaging (scanned images of paper and other records) so that imaged documents can be managed with all other forms of information.
- Producing reports for use in organization-wide records and information management.

Often, records tracking systems use bar codes to help in retrieval and to eliminate the need for keying input each time a record is requested. Because pertinent information is not keyed each time, input errors are virtually eliminated when bar codes are used. Whether the record is classified as active, inactive, or archival, a tracking system allows instant recall

What are some uses for records management software?

[1]Mark Langemo, "Records Management Software," *OfficeSystems 99*, October, 1999, pp. 22–26.

of facts, location, and in some cases, the record itself. Most tracking systems use a database setup where management at the document, folder, or box level is possible.

Figure 6–8 illustrates Zasio's Versatile Enterprise tracking software (www.zasio.com; Boise, Idaho). With this software, records managers can handle physical and electronic records. Note that with the space management feature, filers can assign locations for records as they enter a records center. Filers also can find records on the computer when they need to retrieve specific records. The ability to research retention information when preparing retention schedules is incorporated into the software as well.

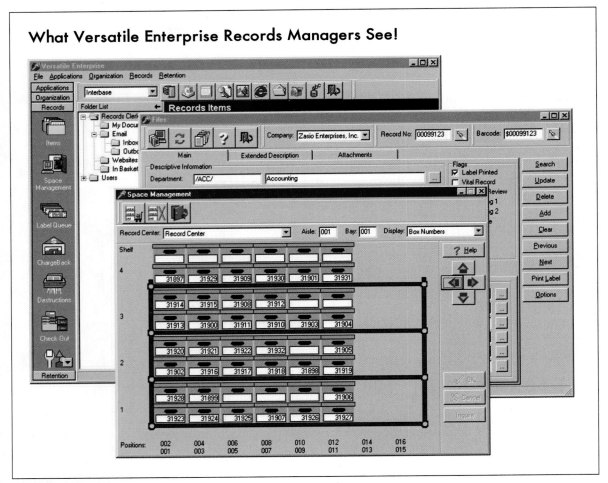

Source: *ZASIO Versatile Enterprise.* Zasio. 15 August 2000. http://www.zasio.com/WhatRMSee.Htm.

Figure 6–8 Records Tracking Software

SUMMARY

Records retention, retrieval, transfer, and disposition of records are important elements of an organized RIM program. The first step in developing a records retention policy is to conduct a records inventory to determine the frequency of use, location, size, and other facts about official records. From the completed inventory, create a records retention schedule showing how long a records series needs to be retained. Create a retention schedule for all official records regardless of the media on which they are stored.

Records retrieval in its simplest form is retrieving information from a record or file. Standard retrieval procedures should be in place to ensure protection of the records. When a request for a record is made, complete a requisition form. Find the record and send it to the requester. If a record is removed from a storage container, the filer prepares a charge-out form. After a specified length of time, perform follow-up procedures to ensure the proper return of the record to its storage container.

By following a records retention schedule, records that are no longer active are transferred to inactive storage by perpetual transfer or periodic transfer methods. Again, follow procedures to ensure proper tracking of the records. Final transfer of records is either to archival storage or destruction.

Records centers use an inactive records index to keep track of the location of the records and destruction dates. Similar charge-out and follow-up procedures are needed in records centers. In addition, records centers have destruction date files so that records are destroyed according to the records retention schedule. A destruction file is maintained to provide proof of records destruction.

Records management and records center software is available to keep track of records at the document, folder, or box level. Records management software programs that combine document tracking software and bar coding are used more often for faster, more accurate retrieval.

IMPORTANT TERMS

active record	charge-out and follow-up file
archive record	charge-out log
archives	destruction date file
charge-out	destruction file

destruction notice

destruction suspension

follow-up

inactive record

inactive records index

index

nonrecord

office of record

official record

off-site storage

on-call (wanted) form

on-site storage

one-period transfer method

periodic transfer method

perpetual transfer method

pick list

record copy

records center

records center box

records destruction

records disposition

records inventory

records retention program

records retention schedule

records series

records transfer

requisition

retention period

retrieval

REVIEW AND DISCUSSION

1. Why is a records retention program useful to an organization? What is the purpose of a retention schedule? How is it created? (Obj. 1)

2. How is a retention schedule used? How can using a retention schedule contribute to cost savings? (Obj. 1)

3. What is retrieval? Name at least three ways that requests for stored records are made. (Obj. 2)

4. Explain the steps in a manual charge-out procedure. (Obj. 2)

5. What is the purpose of using follow-up procedures? (Obj. 2)

6. Explain three categories of file activity. (Obj. 3)

7. Why is transferring records necessary? (Obj. 3)

8. What four important questions need to be answered before records transfer takes place? (Obj. 3)

9. Describe the two most commonly used methods of records transfer. (Obj. 3)

10. Explain the steps for making a records transfer. (Obj. 3)

11. What is the purpose of an index? Why is an inactive records index used? (Obj. 4)

12. Describe the records center control provided by a charge-out and follow-up file. (Obj. 4)

13. Explain procedures followed when records are destroyed. (Obj. 4)

14. What are five important uses served by records center software? (Obj. 5)

APPLICATIONS

Critical Thinking

APP 6-1.   Records Retention Schedule (Objs. 1, 4)

1. Use your database software to create a records retention schedule. Create a new database table with the following fields:

   Records Series
   Record
   Years Active
   Years Inactive
   Total Years

2. Determine a records series name for each of the records listed below. For example, accounts payable invoices might be part of the records series, Accounting and Fiscal.

3. Create a record in the database for each of the items listed below. For each record, enter a records series name in the Records Series field and the item description in the Record field. Enter numbers in the Years Active, Years Inactive, and Total Years fields or enter P for Permanent. Refer to the records retention schedule in Figure 6–2, page 137, to assist your decisions.

4. Sort the table by the Records Series field and then by the Record field.

5. Create and print a report to show the records retention schedule. Group the records by records series.

6. Create a query to show all records with P in the Years Total field. Print the query results.

   Office equipment records
   Balance sheets
   Trademarks
   Time cards
   Accounts payable invoices
   News releases
   Monthly financial reports
   Bank deposit books
   Supplies requisitions
   Records destruction documentation

APP 6-2.   Solving Retrieval Problems (Objs. 1-3)

You and two other students are consulting with Dinsmore & Frankel, a small architecture firm where two senior architects, one junior architect, and two administrative assistants work. The two administrative assistants are responsible for keeping the records stored so that they can be found quickly. All five people in the office have access to the files—removing and refiling records as needed. The two administrative assistants do the refiling about fifty percent of the time.

Because the office is small, no controls are presently being used; no one knows who has a client's records. Misfiling occurs frequently because someone is in a hurry when records are refiled, and the administrative assistants spend unproductive time searching for records that should be in storage but are not.

What kind of records procedures would you recommend? Would additional supplies or equipment provide adequate control of records?

Work with your team members to prepare a list of recommendations to help Dinsmore & Frankel become more productive in records management.

APP 6-3.   Recommending Records Transfer Methods (Obj. 3)

Which transfer method—perpetual, periodic, or one-period—would you recommend for each of the following records situations? Explain your decision.

1. Department store: Employment applications; general correspondence; property mortgages.

2. Medical clinic office: Medical case files of deceased patients.

3. Law office: Client folders from the last ten years.

4. Radio Station: All folders relating to advertising activity. Folders contain news releases, publicity photographs, and advertising activity reports. All records were created in the current year.

5. Shopping center developer: All folders related to a shopping center that has recently been completed, all space is rented, and the Grand Opening was held the last Saturday of last month. The folders contain records of contractors, lessees, insurance carriers, and governmental agencies that issued required permits.

APPLYING THE RULES

Job 7, Requisition and Charge-out Procedures.
Job 8, Transfer Procedures.

PART 3

SUBJECT, NUMERIC, AND GEOGRAPHIC STORAGE AND RETRIEVAL

7 **Subject Records Management**

8 **Numeric Records Management**

9 **Geographic Records Management**

Part 3 focuses on subject, numeric, and geographic records management. The subject and geographic methods are extensions of the alphabetic records storage method. Numeric records storage is truly indirect access filing and is portrayed as a method especially adaptable to electronic records storage. All three filing methods represent essential skills for organizing information in a records management program.

CHAPTER 7

SUBJECT RECORDS MANAGEMENT

LEARNING OBJECTIVES

1. Define subject records management.
2. Give examples of situations and records appropriate for subject records management.
3. List advantages and disadvantages of storing and retrieving records by subject.
4. Compare the dictionary and encyclopedic subject file arrangements.
5. Describe the guides, folders, and labels used for subject records storage.
6. Describe four indexes and their use for subject records management.
7. Use computer software to prepare an index for subject records.
8. Store and retrieve records following subject records procedures.

SUBJECT RECORDS STORAGE AND RETRIEVAL

In Part 2 of this textbook, you studied the alphabetic method of storing and retrieving records by name—names of individuals, businesses, and organizations. Two other alphabetic storage methods are also used: (1) subject and (2) geographic records management systems. In this chapter, you will learn how and when to use subject records management. In Chapter 9, you will study geographic records management, a filing system with records arranged by geographic location.

The Subject Records Management System

Subject records management is an alphabetic system of storing and retrieving records by their subject or topic. File users expect records that pertain to the same subject or topic to be stored together. Arranging records by subject categories, such as topic, department, service, product, or project, is logical and improves findability for certain records. **Findability** refers to how quickly and accurately records can be located. Even when you file records alphabetically by name, certain records are kept together under subject headings, such as APPLICATIONS, PROJECTS, and BRANCH OFFICE MEMOS, because use of these records would require such grouping. This chapter describes a subject filing system.

As you study a variety of filing systems, however, you will learn how components of one or more filing systems can be combined for efficient records storage and retrieval.

Use of Subject Records Storage

The ARMA International *Subject Filing Guideline* describes subject records storage in detail. This document recommends using subject filing when other systems will not be effective or when documents cannot be filed by any other single filing characteristic. For example, logically, you may expect all information related to filing equipment to be stored together in one file location. If you file letters, memoranda, brochures, flyers, and other material related to filing equipment by personal or business names that appear on those documents, you scatter this information throughout the filing system. With alphabetic name filing, finding all records that you need to make a decision about ordering filing equipment would be difficult. Instead, filing all information related to filing equipment under the subject FILING EQUIPMENT, or as a subdivision of OFFICE EQUIPMENT, would keep the records together and improve findability. Although all records do not contain personal or business names, all records do refer to a topic, project, or subject. Subjects are easy to recall, and subject records storage is the only logical, efficient method of storing and retrieving certain records. A rule of thumb for choosing an appropriate records management system is to match the system to the most logical way for file users to request records.

Think about how you use the telephone directory. Imagine each of these situations: (1) You go to your basement, find a broken water pipe, and are knee-deep in water. (2) You need help completing your income tax return. (3) You want to buy a new car. (4) You need to talk to a lawyer. (5) You want to locate a bank near your home. The white pages of a telephone directory list alphabetically names of individuals and businesses that could help you. Were you thinking of names in those situations? More than likely, you were thinking PLUMBER, ACCOUNTANT or INCOME TAX, AUTOMOBILE, LAWYER, and BANK. To locate help under these topics, you would look for these topics in the telephone directory Yellow Pages.

You can locate a nearby bank in the Yellow Pages of metropolitan telephone directories by looking up the subject BANKS. Banks are listed alphabetically under this subject. Often, suburban banks are listed by their location (geographic filing) and, finally, alphabetically by bank name. With this combination of subject, geographic, and alphabetic name arrangement, you can find a local bank quickly. When you look for a particular subject, you might be directed to search elsewhere for it. For example, when you look up LAWYERS in the Yellow Pages, you are

> **Why store records by subject?**

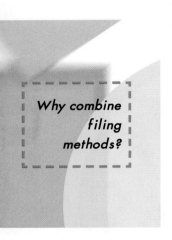

directed to see the alternate term ATTORNEYS. Office workers also sometimes use alternate, synonymous terms for a single topic when filing by subject. Therefore, cross-references and indexes are necessary with subject filing and are explained later in the chapter. For now, remember these important subject filing guidelines:

Why combine filing methods?

1. Select subject titles that best reflect stored records and are easy to remember.
2. Provide for the occasional use of alternate, synonymous, or related subject titles.
3. Consider combining filing methods when subdividing and sub-sorting records in large subject filing systems. For example, subdivide records first by subject and then alphabetically by location or name, numerically by record or document number, or chronologically by date.

Examples of Subject Records Storage

Whether you are in the kitchen using a cookbook or in the office at your computer doing research on the Internet, you are likely using some type of subject arrangement of records. Subject records storage is used in some way in almost every office. Subject filing can be used for filing correspondence, reports, catalogs, clippings, research data, inventory lists, or product development plans, just to name a few examples. Subjects or topics are used frequently with Internet searches to locate information. The following list illustrates how subject records storage may be used for different types of organizations:

Who stores records by subject?

1. Department stores file records together for subjects such as advertising, appliances, clothing, customers, home furnishings, housewares, special promotions, store maintenance, and window displays.
2. School offices store records according to subjects such as accidents, accreditation, athletics, budget, cafeteria, curriculum, graduation, library, personnel, and student records.
3. Airplane manufacturers store records according to the types of planes manufactured.
4. Construction companies store records by types of construction such as apartment buildings, bridges, condominiums, houses, office buildings, townhouses, and roads.
5. Office equipment companies keep records by subjects such as chairs, credenzas, desks, file cabinets, and storage cabinets.

Subject filing is appropriate for both electronic and manual records. Electronic records are often categorized appropriately by subject, topic, product, or particular business function. Electronic folders can be created with subject filenames used to store related correspondence, reports, or other records. Just as a manual file guide can be labeled with the subject title ADVERTISING, a computer file folder or directory may also be named ADVERTISING. Information stored on computer disks, microforms, videotapes, or other electronic records requires the same considerations as paper records when selecting a filing method. Subject records storage is just as easy and simple to implement or use with such records. In fact, with computer search or find functions, a subject is often the means used to locate a record. Usually, computer files are arranged alphabetically under subject folders with titles such as CORRESPONDENCE, CUSTOMER ACCOUNTS, INVENTORY, REPORTS, and SALES PROJECTIONS. Because information stored on electronic media is not readable without special equipment, the subject titles must describe the media contents in a way that clearly reflects the information stored and is easy to remember.

How are computer files stored by subject?

ADVANTAGES AND DISADVANTAGES OF SUBJECT RECORDS STORAGE

Many people think records are best remembered and retrieved by subject. Finding records filed by subject can be a problem, however, because users might not remember the exact subject titles selected to file the records. Using subject files can be difficult for people who are unfamiliar with the topics in the filing system. This section describes advantages and disadvantages of a subject management system.

Advantages

The main advantage of storing records by subject is that this method makes finding related records quicker and easier than scattering them throughout the file alphabetically by name. This is true when records related to a specific topic, product, or project are likely to be requested by subject rather than by name because managerial decisions require a group of records. Another advantage of subject files is the ease of expanding files by adding subdivisions to main subjects. For example, if OFFICE EQUIPMENT were a main subject and COPIERS, CHAIRS, DESKS, and FILES were subdivisions, new subdivisions for COMPUTERS, LASER PRINTERS, and SCANNERS could be added easily.

How can related records be located quickly?

Disadvantages

Main subject titles and subdivisions in subject files have a tendency to grow until subjects begin to overlap. Selecting subject titles that are concise, clearly defined, and uniformly stated can be difficult. Without consistent use of selected subject titles to code records, filers will find storage and retrieval difficult. Because of the importance of selecting the most logical subjects for the filing system, development and installation of a subject records system may require the assistance of an experienced records analyst to examine stored records and to create well-defined subject titles for them. The subject method of storage is the most expensive method to maintain because it requires experienced filers. In addition, preparation of materials for subject filing takes longer than for other methods because the content of every record must be read thoroughly and carefully. Although finding a variety of related records takes less time with this system than with others, *indexing* and *coding* records takes longer.

The disadvantages of the subject method can be many if the file is poorly planned and maintained. The disadvantages are minimized, however, when you select an appropriate arrangement of guides and folders, prepare the necessary indexes, and apply proper procedures to store and retrieve records. The next section explains the arrangement of records by subject and procedures for indexing and coding.

Why is subject records storage expensive?

ARRANGEMENT OF RECORDS BY SUBJECT

Two alphabetic arrangements for subject storage are (1) the dictionary arrangement and (2) the encyclopedic arrangement. The definitions of these two terms are easy to remember when you relate them to the arrangement of words in a dictionary versus the arrangement of information in an encyclopedia. Both subject arrangements are explained and illustrated in the following paragraphs.

Dictionary Arrangement

In the **dictionary arrangement**, subject folders are arranged behind A-to-Z guides in correct alphabetic order by subject title. Generally, the dictionary subject arrangement is not recommended if the volume of records is greater than could be stored in two file drawers. If the nature of the records makes it possible to identify subject topics that do not require subdivisions, however, the dictionary arrangement is used regardless of the number of records. Figure 7–1 shows a small office file arranged in straight dictionary order. A-to-Z guides are one-fifth cut and occupy first position in the file. Special guides are one-fifth cut and are in second position. Two special guides in Figure 7–1 are CREDIT CARDS and TAXES. These special subject guides mark exceptionally active subjects, making them conspicuous and, therefore, easier to find. All general folders with subject topics and OUT guides are one-third cut and occupy the third position in the file. So far, subdividing general subjects into more specific subdivisions has not been necessary. If records accumulate

What is a dictionary arrangement?

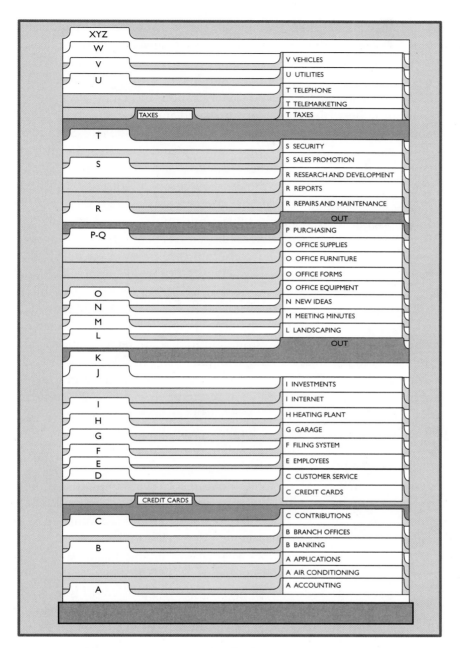

Figure 7–1 **Dictionary Arrangement of Subjects**

and make dividing the general subjects into more specific subdivisions necessary, the arrangement would no longer be considered a dictionary arrangement.

Encyclopedic Arrangement

The **encyclopedic arrangement** is a subject filing arrangement in which broad main subject titles are arranged in alphabetic order with subdivisions arranged alphabetically under the title to which they relate. Figures 7–2a and 7–2b show encyclopedic arrangements of the subject file shown in Figure 7–1. As the number of records increases, the file arrangement requires specific subject subdivisions for quicker access to filed records. Study the guide and folder captions in Figures 7–2a and 7–2b. Main subject labels have been prepared and inserted into the metal holders of the one-fifth cut, first-position, primary guide tabs. Secondary guides are in second position. The secondary guides are also one-fifth cut tab guides with labels bearing the *subdivisions* of the main subject. The secondary guides may include the primary guide captions such as those illustrated in Figure 7–3 on page 172. Because guides are not removed from the file, repeating the main subject title on the secondary guide is not necessary. Sometimes in subject filing, less is better; reading lengthy and unnecessary labeling is time-consuming.

On the other hand, the *folder* label captions include complete subject titles: main, secondary, and, if necessary, specific subject titles. A comprehensive folder label helps assure that a borrowed folder will be returned to its correct file location. The tab cut of the folders depends on the length of the subject titles. One-third cut folders are recommended, but unusually long subject titles may require half-cut folders.

Most of the general subject folders have been maintained in the encyclopedic file arrangement shown in Figure 7–2a and 7–2b on pages 169 and 170. Specific subject folders have been added, however, where subjects have been subdivided. Note the general subject folder for TAXES in Figure 7–2b. Although subdivision folders for FEDERAL, SALES, and STATE taxes have been added, the general taxes folder remains. The general TAXES folder holds records pertaining to any other tax information; for example, city tax, import and export tax. Apparently, the number of records for any other tax topics has not accumulated to the predetermined number that warrants a specific folder.

The secondary subject guides have accompanying specific subject folders. See OFFICE SUPPLIES in Figure 7–2b. The general subject folder for OFFICE SUPPLIES appears at the end of the OFFICE SUP-PLIES section and is used for storing information that does not fit in any of the established subdivisions. Subdivisions have been added for CATA-LOGS, COMPUTER DISKS, and FILING. Each subdivision has a specific subject folder. In addition, two individual folders have been added for individual vendor catalogs: one for The Stationery Center and one for Wholesale Supply Company. Can you spot other individual folders added to the system? Store any information other than that related to the specific subject folders in the OFFICE SUPPLIES general folder placed at the end of the section. General folders should be checked from time to time to see whether the number of records for a specific subject category should be transferred to a more specific subject subdivision or individual folder, especially for frequently requested records.

What is an encyclopedic arrangement?

Why subdivide main subject titles?

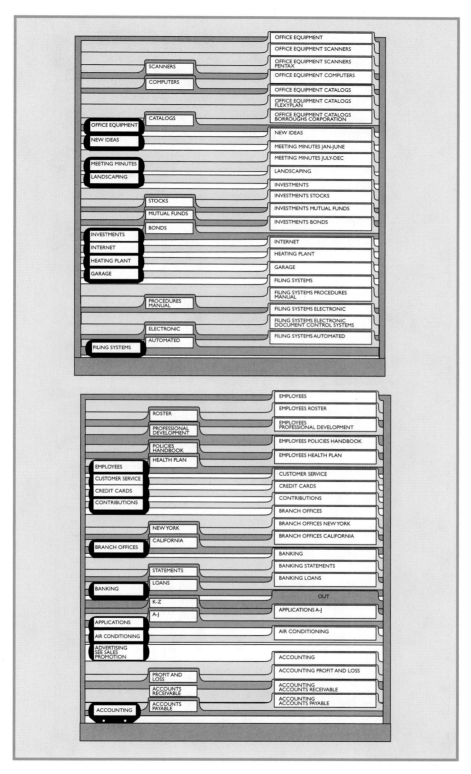

Figure 7–2a Encyclopedic Arrangement of Subjects

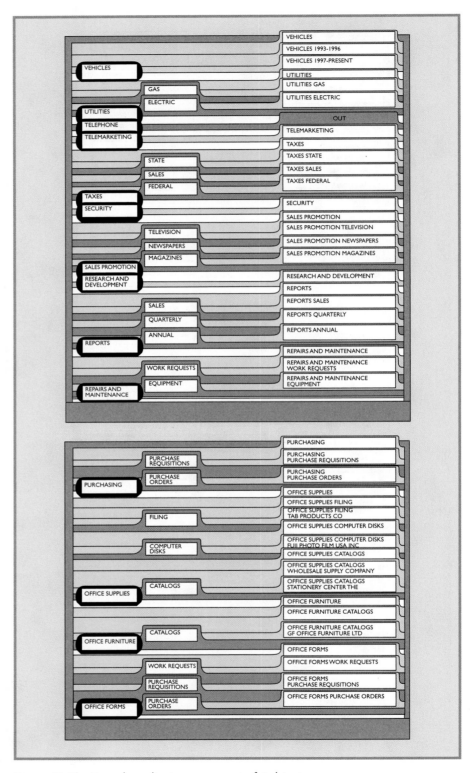

Figure 7–2b Encyclopedic Arrangement of Subjects

When general folders become crowded and no specific subject subdivisions are possible, other means of subdividing records may be used. Notice that the APPLICATIONS general folders are subdivided alphabetically A to J and K to Z in Figure 7–2a. In Figure 7–2b, the VEHICLES general subject is subdivided by the model years of the vehicles. Although a specific folder for each type of vehicle could have been prepared, apparently infrequent retrieval of records by type does not warrant specific folders.

As you can see from studying the file illustrations, predicting the subjects and subject subdivisions that will be needed in an office file is unlikely. The nature of the organization, the kinds of records stored, and how the office staff uses and requests stored information determine the subject titles and subdivisions of stored records.

OUT indicators are in third position with all folders. These third-cut OUT guides are usually of some distinctive color and stand out to show the location of a removed folder. Color can be used effectively with subject filing. Very often, each subject will have a color band that is repeated on all guides and folders of that subject. Sometimes, all captions of one subject will be one color, the color changing when the subject title changes. A third possibility is that each subject will have guides and folders of only one color, with a change of color used for guides and folders of the next subject. Using a colored folder for all general subject folders can also be effective. Although the use of color can speed the filing process and reduce misfiles in any filing system, using color does not take the place of careful selection of meaningful subject titles in a subject filing system.

> How is color used in a subject file?

SUPPLIES FOR SUBJECT RECORDS SYSTEMS

Supplies used for the subject arrangement of files include guides, folders, labels, and OUT indicators, which were explained in Chapter 5. Because more information is keyed on guide and folder label captions for subject filing than for alphabetic name files, preparation is slightly more challenging.

Guides and Labels

Guide labels used in subject records storage are determined by the subject titles used. If subject titles are long, subject codes or abbreviations can be used. Subject coding is explained in more detail on pages 179–181. Figure 7–3 on page 172 shows an example of primary and secondary guides. The primary guide caption contains the main subject title; the secondary guide contains the main subject and its subdivision. Because guides are not removed from a storage container, a primary guide caption can be omitted on a secondary guide, as shown in Figures 7–2a and 7–2b.

> Why do subject folder captions include both main titles and subdivisions?

Subject filing requires customized labeling of guides and folders that matches subjects and subdivisions for the specific filing system. Adhesive labels from suppliers such as Avery come in a variety of sizes and colors. These label packages include directions for using the built-in label function in popular word processing software programs such as *Lotus® Ami Pro*, *Microsoft Word*, and *WordPerfect*. The software program label function enables preparation of many different label sizes and styles. Blank tab inserts for one-third or one-fifth cut metal or plastic tab sizes can be purchased in strips for attaching computer-generated adhesive labels.

Be consistent in spacing and styles of captions in label preparation. All primary guide label captions should begin near the left edge and near the top of the label. The label function of software (word processing or database) uses preset margins for each label selection. When using these settings, be sure the label captions begin at the same point on all labels. Labels are easier to read with information in a straight line rather than staggered. Key the information in all capitals with no punctuation. Key secondary guide *subdivisions* about 0.5 inches to the right of the main subject title *or* under the first letter of the first line. Decide whether to use complete subject titles, abbreviated titles, or subject codes and follow this format consistently. Mixing the styles of the captions complicates filing and finding records.

Why does subject filing require customized guide and folder labels?

Where are captions printed on guide labels or inserts?

Figure 7–3 **Primary and Secondary Guide Labels**

Folders and Labels

Folder label captions include the main subject title and all necessary subdivisions. As discussed previously, comprehensive label captions help assure that borrowed folders are returned to the correct file locations. One-third cut folders are preferred. Adhesive file folder labels can be used for computer preparation of folder label captions. File folder labels should match the tab cut of the folder. Use the label function of word processing software for preparing labels, or follow the directions for label formatting that comes with the labels. The main subject title should begin near the left margin and as near as possible to the top of the label or the bottom of a color bar on the label. Key the subdivision 0.5 inches to the right of the main subject title or under the first letter of the first

Where are captions printed on folder labels?

line. Key the label in all capitals with no punctuation as shown in Figure 7–4. Be precise and consistent with folder label preparation. Attention to this detail creates a neat, readable, straight-line filing system.

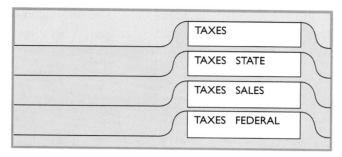

Figure 7–4 **Subject Folder Labels**

Color code folder labels for each subject guide to reduce misfiles. Bar codes can be added for electronically tracking records. Bar codes and color codes for folders and labels in subject records storage relate to the first, second, and, sometimes, third letters in subject titles. Supplies and services for color coding and bar coding are available through companies offering records management products. These can be located through the telephone Yellow Pages or on the Internet. The ARMA Web page (www.arma.org) has a buyer's guide listing vendors of filing supplies and records management products.

Companies such as Smead Manufacturing Company (www.smead.com), TAB (www.tabproducts.com), and Pendaflex (www.pendaflex.com) offer records management products and services applicable to subject records systems, as well as other records systems. Many of these Web sites not only provide information about their companies but also give helpful hints for setting up and maintaining records management systems.

Smead's VIEWables™ Labeling System software creates unique labels for three-sided hanging folder tabs.

OUT Indicators

An OUT guide appears in the file sample in Figure 7–1. You may want to review briefly OUT indicators and the charge-out and follow-up procedures discussed in Chapters 5 and 6. Follow the same procedures for subject filing that you applied in alphabetic name filing. The only difference is that you will use subject titles, rather than individual or organization names, to identify records.

INDEXES FOR SUBJECT RECORDS SYSTEMS

The selection of a word or phrase to use as a subject title (the filing segment) is of prime importance when using the subject storage method. One person should be responsible for selecting subject titles. That person must be thoroughly familiar with the material to be stored and have considerable knowledge of every phase of the operations and activities of the business. If all file users have authority to add subject titles to a subject filing system, the same type of record content soon becomes stored under two or more synonymous terms. Such storage of related records in two or more places separates records that should be stored together and makes retrieval of all related records difficult.

The subject title must be short and clearly descriptive of the material it represents. Once a subject title has been chosen, it must be used by everyone in the organization. Additional subject titles must be chosen so that they do not duplicate or overlap any subject previously used.

Need for Indexes

Good subject selection requires *agreement* by file users on the subjects to be used, *flexibility* to allow for growth within the selected subjects and for expansion to add new material, and *simplicity* so that records users can understand the system. Once subject titles have been selected, they must be used consistently by all file users. Preparation and use of necessary indexes ensure consistent use of selected subject titles.

As you learned in Chapter 6, an *index* is a systematic guide that allows access to specific items contained within a larger body of information. Because you may not know all subjects used in a subject file, you cannot go directly to a file to locate a record. A subject file requires an index and, therefore, is considered an indirect access filing method. **Indirect access** is a method of locating records that requires prior use of an index. Users must refer to an index to determine the subject and the location of a record before they can store or retrieve the record from the main file. Alphabetic name files discussed in Part 2 are considered **direct access** because a specific name in a file can be found without first referring to an index to find its location.

Why are indexes necessary?

Preparation of Indexes

Indexes are electronic or printed lists. Lists can be printed on sheets of paper, cards, or some kind of visible file (described in Appendix B). An index prepared on sheets of paper or using a visible card file is easier to see at a glance than are indexes keyed on individual cards. Adding or deleting subjects on visible strips or cards is easier, however, than adding and deleting from printed sheets. Computer-prepared indexes allow you to make additions, deletions, and corrections quickly and easily. Because the computer can be used to sort the index, maintaining an up-to-date index is easy. The search function of your computer software also makes finding a specific subject quick and easy.

These four types of indexes are valuable, and often necessary, when using the subject records storage method:

- Master index
- Relative index
- Numeric index
- Name index

The master index is also referred to as the *master list*, *subject index*, or *subject list*. Even if computer access to the master index and relative index is available, keep an updated printed copy in front of the file drawer with the manual files. This practice is important to maintain consistent coding and filing of records by subject. Without frequent referrals to these indexes, misfiles and duplicate subject titles are likely to occur. For a large volume of records in a complex filing system, use of electronic indexes saves time in locating specific records.

Master Index

A **master index** is a printed alphabetic listing in file order of all subjects used as subject titles in the filing system. The index should be updated as new subjects are added and old ones are eliminated or modified. When new subjects are added, refer to the index to avoid any subject title duplications. Figure 7–5 on page 176 is a master index of the portion of the file illustrated in Figure 7–2. For manual filing systems, store a copy of the index at the beginning of the file for ready access to all users as an outline of the file contents. Without a master index, file users would have to scan drawers of records to locate subject titles. New file users can familiarize themselves with the subject storage system quickly by referring to a master index. In addition, reference to the master index assures that only pre-selected subject titles are used for filing and retrieving records.

What is a master index?

Relative Index

A more complex subject file may require a relative index. A **relative index** is a dictionary-type listing of *all* possible words and combinations of words by which records may be requested. The word *relative* is used

Accounting	Heating Plant	Repairs and Maintenance
Accounts Payable	Internet	Equipment
Accounts Receivable	Investments	Work Requests
Profit and Loss	Bonds	Reports
Air Conditioning	Mutual Funds	Annual
Applications*	Stocks	Quarterly
Banking	Landscaping	Sales
Loans	Meeting Minutes*	Research and Development
Statements	New Ideas	Sales Promotion
Branch Offices	Office Equipment	Magazines
California	Catalogs	Newspapers
New York	Computers	Television
Contributions	Scanners	Security
Credit Cards	Office Forms	Taxes
Customer Service	Purchase Orders	Federal
Employees	Purchase Requisitions	Sales
Health Plan	Work Requests	State
Policies Handbook	Office Furniture	Telemarketing
Professional Development	Catalogs	Telephone
Roster	Office Supplies	Utilities
Filing Systems	Catalogs	Electric
Automated	Computer Disks	Gas
Electronic	Filing	Vehicles*
Procedures Manual	Purchasing	
Garage	Purchase Orders	
	Purchase Requisitions	

*Not necessary to show divided folders in the master index.

Figure 7–5 Subject File Master Index

What is a relative index?

because the index includes not only all of the actual subject titles used in the system but also synonyms for subjects or any *related* subject titles that filers might consider logical topics for storing and retrieving records. Study the relative index in Figure 7–6. Notice the entry for Advertising. (Advertising is not used as a subject title in the system.) The relative index refers the filer to Sales Promotion—the subject title selected for storing and retrieving advertising materials. This type of index serves as a vast cross-reference device because it contains all the subjects by which a record might be requested. When someone requests a record by a subject that is not the one selected for use in the system, check the relative index to see if that requested subject has been included. If not, add the requested subject to the index listing with the correct subject title beside it. The relative index often contains both SEE and SEE ALSO cross-references. These notations help to suggest related materials and alternate file locations.

Subject Title	Filed Under	Subject Title	Filed Under
Accounting	Accounting	Meeting Minutes	Meeting Minutes
Accounts Payable	Accounting	Mutual Funds	Investments
Accounts Receivable	Accounting	New Ideas	New Ideas
Advertising	Sales Promotion	New York Branch	Branch Offices
Air Conditioning	Air Conditioning	Newspaper Advertising	Sales Promotion
Annual Reports	Reports	Office Equipment	Office Equipment
Applications	Applications	Office Forms	Office Forms
Automated Filing Systems	Filing Systems	Office Furniture	Office Furniture
Banking	Banking	Office Supplies	Office Supplies
Bonds	Investments	Policies Handbook	Filing Systems
Branch Offices	Branch Offices	Professional Development	Employees
Building Maintenance	Repairs and Maintenance	Profit and Loss	Accounting
California Branch	Branch Offices	Purchase Orders	SEE Office Forms Purchasing
Cars	Vehicles		
Catalogs	SEE Office Equipment Office Furniture Office Supplies	Purchase Requisitions	SEE Office Forms Purchasing
Computer Disks	Office Supplies	Purchasing	Purchasing
Computers	Office Equipment	Quarterly Reports	Reports
Contributions	Contributions	Repairs and Maintenance	Repairs and Maintenance
Credit Cards	Credit Cards		
Customer Service	Customer Service	Reports	Reports
Electric	Utilities	Research and Development	Research and Development
Electronic Filing Systems	Filing Systems	Roster	Employees
Employee Roster	Employees	Sales Promotion	Sales Promotion
Employees	Employees	Sales Reports	Reports
Equipment	Office Equipment	Sales Taxes	Taxes
Equipment Repair	Repairs and Maintenance	Scanners	Office Equipment
		Security	Security
Federal Taxes	Taxes	State Taxes	Taxes
Filing Equipment	Office Equipment	Statements	Banking
Filing Procedures Manual	Filing Systems	Stocks	Investments
Filing Supplies	Office Supplies	Taxes	Taxes
Filing Systems	Filing Systems	Telemarketing	Telemarketing
Forms	Office Forms	Telephone	Telephone
Garage	Garage	Television Advertising	Sales Promotion
Gas	Utilities	Utilities	Utilities
Health Plan	Employees	Vans	Vehicles
Heating Plant	Heating Plant	Vehicles	Vehicles
Internet	Internet	Work Requests	SEE Office Forms Repairs and Maintenance
Investments	Investments		
Landscaping	Landscaping		
Loans	Banking		
Magazine Advertising	Sales Promotion		

Figure 7–6 Subject File Relative Index

Numeric Index

The numeric index will become more meaningful to you after you study Chapter 8 and learn to assign numbers to subject file headings. Numbers are faster to file and retrieve than words or letters because you can read numbers more quickly. When numbers are used to identify specific subjects, a numeric index is needed. A **numeric index** is a current list of all files by the file numbers. Such an index shows the numbers assigned to subject titles and avoids duplication of numbers when new subjects are added to the storage system.

Name Index

Why is a name index necessary?

Customarily, subject records storage does not require an alphabetic index of names of individuals or companies. However, correspondence filed in a subject arrangement *does* require a name index. A **name index** is a listing of correspondents' names stored in a subject file. The name and address of each correspondent are included in the index, as well as the subject under which each name is stored. The names are arranged alphabetically on printed sheets, on cards, or in a computer file. Because records are sometimes requested by the name of an individual or a company, a name index containing this information can save time that would otherwise be spent searching for a record by subject.

STORAGE AND RETRIEVAL PROCEDURES

All the steps studied in Chapters 5 and 6 for storing and retrieving correspondence records are as important in the subject method as they are in any other storage method. A brief description of each step, together with an explanation of its application to the subject method, follows.

Inspecting

In any records management system, inspect every record to see that it has been released for filing. Do not store a record until a written notation by someone with authority indicates that it is ready for storage. In Figure 7–7 on page 180, JJ is the release mark used to indicate that the letter is ready for storage.

Indexing

Indexing, or classifying, is deciding the filing segment to be used in storing a record. This step takes more time with the subject method than with other storage methods. Examine the contents of each record carefully to determine the filing segment. If a record relates to only one subject, indexing is simple. Select the correct subject from the master index. If someone else has previously indicated the subject under which a record is to be stored, recheck the accuracy of the subject selection. If a record contains information about more than one subject, you must determine the most important subject by which to store the record. Then cross-reference the other subject(s). Indexing is the mental process of determining the subject filing segment prior to coding the record.

Coding

In Chapter 5 you learned that coding means marking the filing segment on the record. Code the main subject title and any subdivisions by placing diagonals between the units, underlining the key unit, and numbering the remaining units in the selected words (filing segment) where they appear on the record. Code the correspondent's name by placing diagonals between the units and continuing the numbering of the units. If the subject is not mentioned, write it legibly at the top of the record. Some filers prefer to write the filing segment in color in the upper right margin of the record. The subject title is, therefore, more visible in the file. When more than one subject is indicated, code only the most important one; cross-reference all other subjects in some distinctive manner. For example, the subject to cross-reference in Figure 7–7 is underscored with a wavy line, and an X is placed in the margin opposite the subject. The correct cross-reference subject title and subtitle SALES PROMOTION/ TELEVISION are written and coded in the margin. Diagonals are placed between the units, and all filing units are numbered.

> **How do you code a record for subject filing?**

Do not rely on memory to determine the subject under which a record should be stored. Consult the master or relative index to be sure that you have selected and coded the filing segment correctly.

Coding in an alphabetic subject filing system may include an entire subject title such as PERSONNEL. However, abbreviations can simplify coding in a complex subject filing system. Create an abbreviation with the first alphabetic character of the subject title followed by the next one or two consonants such as PRS for PERSONNEL, or use the first character of each word in a multiple-word subject heading such as RRS for RECORDS RETENTION SCHEDULE. Consistency is essential when developing a subject code system in which two- to six-character abbreviations are used. Everyone using the system must understand the codes and how to develop new ones when necessary. If abbreviations are used, the master index should show codes as well as complete subject titles. Be sure to write subject letter codes on each record and include them on individual folder label captions, along with the subject title.

Cross-Referencing

Cross-references help locate stored records. When file users call for a record under a topic other than its subject title, add a cross-reference under that topic. Code the document as suggested previously and prepare

Martinez/Advertising/Agency

1220 Park Avenue, New York, NY 10128-5701

April 12, 20--

APR 15, 20-- 11:00 AM

Ms. Joanna Shelden
Shelden K & R, Inc.
600 E. 52 St.
New York, NY 10022-2844

Dear Joanna

The magazine advertising media kit you requested for *Decorators' International* magazine is on its way. Note that the new full-color page rate is $12,450; the black/white page, $8,275. A copy of your ad is enclosed and ready for your approval. We should meet the publication deadline for the June issue with no problem.

If you are still considering television, you might be interested in WCB-TV's monthly advertising schedule for May. *Oprah Winfrey* and *Inside Edition* rates are easily within your budget. We will be happy to show you some ideas for 30-second commercials if you think you want to pursue TV advertising.

Decorators' International is offering an incentive to first-time advertisers. It is offering an 8 percent discount to all advertisers booking space in the next two issues. An 18 percent discount is offered to advertisers contracting space in the next four issues. We can discuss these issues at our meeting on Tuesday.

Sincerely

Bill Berta

Bill Berta
Advertising Director

lms

Enclosure

TEL 212 555-0177 FAX 212 555-0136

Figure 7–7 Record Coded for Subject Records Storage

Why cross-reference records?

a cross-reference sheet such as the one shown in Figure 7–8. File users looking for the document under its alternate subject title SALES PROMOTION/TELEVISION are sent to the original record file location SALES PROMOTION/MAGAZINE. If a record refers to several important subjects, consider filing photocopies of the record under the different subject titles involved. This procedure eliminates the need for preparing cross-reference sheets for that record. Sometimes a permanent cross-reference guide is placed in the storage container. In Figure 7–2a, for example, a permanent guide labeled ADVERTISING, SEE SALES PROMOTION has been placed in the file in the primary guide position after

```
                         CROSS-REFERENCE SHEET
        Name or Subject
        Sales / Promotion / Television / Martinez / Advertising / Agency
                  2          3          4           5             6
        _____

        _____

        _____


        Date of Record
        April 12, 20--
        _____

        _____


        Regarding
        Magazine and television advertising
        _____

        _____

        _____

        _____


                                SEE

        Name or Subject
        Sales Promotion Magazine Martinez Advertising Agency
        _____

        _____

        _____



        Date Filed ____4/15/20--_____  By ____JJ_____
```

Figure 7–8 **Cross-Reference Sheet for Subject Records Storage**

ACCOUNTING. Do not file records behind the permanent SEE guide. The SEE guide is there only to direct you to the correct storage location.

Sorting

Sorting arranges records in filing order according to the records management system used. Use some kind of A-to-Z sorter to sort records to be stored alphabetically by subject. Sort records by main subject titles; then sort records by subdivisions as well. Time spent sorting records before filing saves filing time. You will be able to file by moving in one direction through a filing system rather than moving backward and forward through stored records.

Why sort records before storing?

Storing

Storing (also called filing) places the hard copy or saves the computer record in an appropriate location. For manual filing of records, careful placement into folders is always important. Be sure the folder label subject caption agrees with the filing segment coded on the record. Raise the folder slightly before inserting the record to be sure the record enters the folder completely. Remove papers that are in disarray, jog them, and return them neatly into the folder. Records in shelf-stored folders need constant straightening. Papers sticking out of folders can obscure guide and folder label captions.

When filing correspondence in subject folders, file records in alphabetic order according to the names of the correspondents. Then for each correspondent, arrange the records by the date of the document with the *most recent date in front.*

Retrieving

Understanding the subject records system is critical to finding and removing (retrieving) records from storage. Use indexes to help locate records. In addition, follow the retrieval procedures described in Chapter 6. As with other methods of records storage, retrieval procedures for subject records management make use of OUT indicators to show information about records that have been removed from storage. Knowing who has taken the records, the contents of those records, when the records were borrowed, and when the records will be returned is the only way to maintain control over a retrieval system. Follow-up also is necessary to assure that records are returned, to extend the charge-out time, or to direct attention to any matters needing future action or consideration.

SUBJECT RECORDS MANAGEMENT SOFTWARE

The types of records management software discussed in Chapter 6 apply to subject records systems as well as other records storage systems. However, some computer software features are especially helpful for labeling and indexing records stored with encyclopedic alphabetic arrangement. This system uses labels for guides and folders that are unique to the records topics for a specific office. Alphabetic and numeric sets of guides are readily available for purchase; however, customizing labels for subject filing requires special preparation. Offices with a low-to-medium volume of records are likely to prepare these labels in-house using the label function of word processing software as described earlier in this chapter. If records information is stored in a database, labels can be printed using the label feature. Another option is to purchase special software for printing labels such as *TABQUIK* or *Smead® ColorBar.*

Businesses with large volumes of records are likely to contract printing of labels with records management production services.

Subject records management works well with electronic files stored on computers. Software programs, including most e-mail software, allow users to set up electronic folders. Subject names for folders generally work well with computer files. Figure 7–9 shows how folders and subfolders can be set up in *Windows Explorer* with subject titles arranged alphabetically and records stored alphabetically in folders. The portion of the files illustrated in Figure 7–9 includes the same label captions as a section of the file drawer in Figure 7–2b. Comparison of the computer folder subject arrangement with the manual subject file lets you see their similarity. Notice that a general folder is set up for each subfolder as well as for each major folder. The software automatically arranges these general folders in alphabetic order with other folders rather than placing them at the end of the section. Because of limited screen space, subject folder names sometimes are abbreviated. In Figure 7–9 captions for the Office Supplies and Purchase Orders general folders are abbreviated. The right column of the display screen shows the contents of the PO General folder.

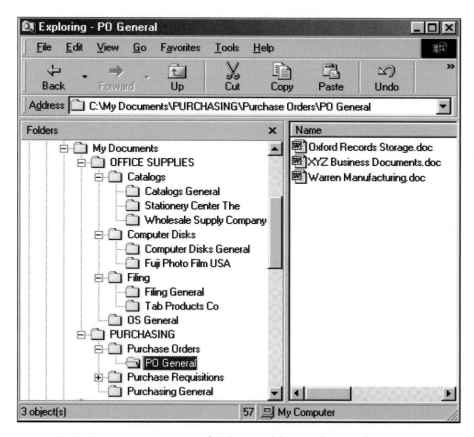

Figure 7–9 Computer Directory of Subject Folders and Records

Be consistent in applying the procedures described in this chapter to naming and storing electronic as well as manual files. Setting up a master index and keeping it current is important for an efficient manual or electronic subject filing system. Too often, electronic folders or file names are added to computer files without a planned system, thus complicating retrieval.

SUMMARY

Subject records management is the best choice for classifying and storing records if the records will be requested by subject or topic. Storing records by subject keeps together records that are related to a particular topic. Benefits of storing like records in one location are numerous. However, subject records systems become highly individualized if they are not carefully controlled and monitored by an individual who understands the operation of the office and is familiar with the office records and the information needs of the staff.

The dictionary and encyclopedic arrangements are used in subject records storage systems. Deciding which arrangement to use depends on the nature of the records and the volume of records. Use the dictionary arrangement when main subject titles do not require subdivisions and when the volume of records does not make this method cumbersome. The encyclopedic arrangement is usually the choice for large subject records storage systems. Faster information retrieval is possible in a large system if primary subject titles are subdivided into more specific subject categories.

Supplies used for the subject arrangement of files include guides, folders, labels, and OUT indicators. Subject filing requires customized labeling of guides and folders that matches subjects and subdivisions for the specific filing system. Comprehensive label captions help assure that borrowed folders are returned to the correct file locations. Bar codes and color-coded folder labels can help reduce misfiles. The same procedures are followed for using OUT indicators for subject filing as for alphabetic name filing.

The subject records storage method requires the use of indexes and is, therefore, considered an indirect access filing method. The master index is an outline of the file and lists all subject titles and subdivisions in alphabetic order as they appear in the file. The relative index lists *all* subject titles and subdivisions in a straight alphabetic, dictionary order. Alternate, synonymous titles by which some filers may request subjects are listed, as well, and refer the file user to the correct subject file location. Correspondence files that assign numbers to the subject titles require an alphabetic name index.

How are electronic filing and manual filing similar?

Maintain control over the records storage system by carefully inspecting, indexing, coding, cross-referencing, sorting, and storing records. Keep a charge-out record of all borrowed records and a follow-up system that ensures their safe return to storage.

Prepare indexes using a computer if possible. The sorting and searching functions of software simplify preparation and maintenance of updated file indexes. In a high-volume, complex filing system, information can be obtained more quickly from a computer file than from a paper index. Keeping a paper copy of the master and relative indexes with the manual file is advisable, however, in addition to keeping an electronic file of these indexes for updating and searching for subject titles.

Companies specializing in records management products and services can be helpful with preparing customized labels, bar coding, and color coding of subject files. Computer software application packages, as well as software specifically for label preparation, add a professional look to file labels.

Frequently, subject filing is used for computer files of e-mail messages and other computer records. Effective use of computer files requires the same systematic procedures and guidelines as paper files.

IMPORTANT TERMS

dictionary arrangement	master index
direct access	name index
encyclopedic arrangement	numeric index
findability	relative index
indirect access	subject records management

REVIEW AND DISCUSSION

1. Define subject records management and explain why this system is the best choice for certain records. (Obj. 1)

2. Give two reasons why an organization might have a subject filing arrangement for records rather than arranging their records alphabetically by individual or company names. (Obj. 1)

3. Describe two examples of records storage situations or types of records appropriate for use of subject records management. (Obj. 2)

4. How can subject records management be used with electronic records? (Obj. 2)

5. List three advantages and three disadvantages of the subject records storage method. (Obj. 3)

6. What do you consider the most important advantage and the greatest disadvantage to arranging records by subject? (Obj. 3)

7. Name two alphabetic arrangements of subject records storage and explain how the two arrangements are alike and how they differ. (Obj. 4)

8. What two criteria determine which alphabetic arrangement to use for a subject records system? (Obj. 4)

9. What supplies are needed when using the subject storage method? Describe the placement of subject titles on guide and folder labels captions. (Obj. 5)

10. Explain how color can be used with labels or folders to help locate records and reduce misfiles. (Obj. 6)

11. Name and describe four indexes used with subject records storage. (Obj. 6)

12. Which two indexes are essential for all subject files? Name two types of computer software that can be used to prepare subject file indexes. (Objs. 6 and 7)

13. Explain the procedure for storing records, including letters and memos, in a subject records storage system. (Obj. 8.)

14. When filing correspondence in subject folders, how are records arranged in the folder? (Obj. 8)

APPLICATIONS (APP)

Critical Thinking

APP 7-1.   Use the Internet to Locate Supply Vendors (Obj. 5)

If an Internet connection is available, go to the ARMA Web site (www.arma.org). Locate the Buyer's Guide section. From this Guide, select two vendors of records management supplies and two vendors of software that have a Web address shown. Go to these vendor Web sites and review products. Write a summary paragraph of what you learned by reviewing these sites.

If you do not have Internet access, locate local office supply vendors from the telephone directory. Go to two of these companies and look for types of filing supplies that you would need for subject filing. Write a summary paragraph describing these products.

Data
Disk

APP 7-2.   Prepare a Master Index for a Subject File (Objs. 6 and 7)

Use your database software to complete a master index for subject record files for a small business. Some of the records have already been entered in the database. You will add records and sort the database, query the database to show only a portion of the master index, and create a report showing the complete index.

1. Open the *Access* file APP 7-2.mdb from the data disk.

2. Enter records in the Master Index table for the remaining files listed below. For main subject titles, enter only the main subject title in the Main field. For subdivisions of main titles, enter the main title in the Main field and the subdivision title in the Sub field. (You will add subdivisions for some main titles already in the index.) Save the table.

3. Sort the table by the Main field then by the Sub field to place the index in alphabetical order.

4. Create a query to show all records with *Accounting* in the Main field. Print the query results.

5. Create and print a report to show all the data in the Master Index table. The data should be sorted by the Main field then by the Sub field.

Main Title	Subdivision	Main Title	Subdivision
Utilities		Reports	
Utilities	Gas	Reports	Annual Reports
Utilities	Electric	Reports	Quarterly Reports
Utilities	Water	Reports	Monthly Reports
Telephone		Internet	
Telephone	Voice Lines	Internet	Internet Service Provider
Telephone	Data Lines	Internet	Web Page
Telephone	Telephone Rate Plans	Taxes	
Accounting	Credit Cards	Taxes	State Tax
Accounting	Loans	Taxes	Federal Tax
Vehicles		Taxes	Sales Tax

Critical
Thinking

APP 7-3.   Create a Relative Index (Objs. 6 and 7)

1. Open the *Access* file APP 7-2.mdb, which you updated in APP 7-2.

2. Make a copy of the Master Index table (structure and data) and save it as Relative Index.

3. Open the Relative Index table.

Data
Disk

4. Change the Main field name to Filed Under. Change the Sub field name to Subject Title.

5. Sort the table by the Filed Under field then by the Subject Title field.

6. For records that have data only in the Filed Under field (Accounting, Applications, etc.), key an identical entry in the Subject Title field.

Filed Under	Subject Title
Accounting	Accounting

7. Add the records below to include other titles by which records might be requested.

Filed Under	Subject Title
Applications	Resumes
Vehicles	Cars
Vehicles	Trucks
Contributions	Charities
Accounting	Banking

8. Add at least five records of your choice to include other titles by which you think records might be requested.

9. Make other changes as you think are needed to clarify the information. For example, key *Promotions* or *Advertising* or *Commercials* after Internet, Print, Radio, and Telephone in the Promotions division.

10. Create and print a report to show all the data in the Relative Index table. Show the Subject Title data in the first column of the report and the Filed Under data in the second column of the report. The data should be sorted by the Subject Title field.

Critical Thinking

APP 7-4.   File or Retrieve Records by the Subject Method (Obj. 8)

Refer to Figures 7–2a and 7–2b, the Encyclopedic Arrangement of Subjects, to file/retrieve the records described below. Indicate where each of these records would be located by giving the complete folder label caption for each. If more than one subject location is possible, list other subjects that should be used for cross-referencing. Place an X in front of each cross-reference title.

1. A newspaper advertisement promoting a new product.

2. A bulletin explaining a new provision in the health plan for employees.

3. An application form from Maria Alvarez.

4. A letter from TAB Products Co. about filing supplies.

5. A notice of price change on an order you have placed for filing cabinets.

6. A sales report.

7. Last month's electric bill.

8. A research and development report.

9. A form to fill out for a work request.

10. A price quote from a lawn and garden center to landscape a recreational area.

APPLYING THE RULES

Job 9, Subject Correspondence Filing.

CHAPTER 8

NUMERIC RECORDS MANAGEMENT

LEARNING OBJECTIVES

1. Define numeric records management and list three reasons for its use.
2. Give examples of businesses that use numbers to locate records.
3. List and describe the basic components of a consecutive numbering method.
4. Explain the storage and retrieval procedures for a consecutive numeric method.
5. Describe how to convert an alphabetic records arrangement to a consecutive numeric records arrangement.
6. List advantages and disadvantages of consecutive numeric records storage.
7. Compare and contrast consecutive, terminal-digit, and middle-digit numeric storage.
8. Define chronologic records storage and explain its use.
9. Compare and contrast block-numeric, duplex-numeric, decimal-numeric, and alphanumeric coding.
10. Explain how computer indexes and database software can be used with numeric records management.

NUMERIC RECORDS STORAGE AND RETRIEVAL

The records management systems studied in previous chapters used alphabetic storage; arrangement of records was alphabetical by name or subject. This chapter explains how to use numeric arrangements for records storage and location. As its name suggests, **numeric records management** is a systematic arrangement of records according to numbers. The numbers used in this filing system are assigned to records to identify their location in a file. The number can be part of the record itself (such as a purchase order or invoice number) or it may be a number assigned to the record based on the type of numeric filing arrangement. Records are filed by number in ascending order. This chapter describes numbering methods for numeric filing that are categorized as consecutive numbering, nonconsecutive numbering, and numeric coding used in combination with geographic or subject filing. The basic components and procedures for filing are similar for all numeric records management systems.

Several reasons for using a numeric records system will become evident as you study this chapter. Major reasons include the volume of records, confidentiality of records, and numbers on records already used for identification.

Expanding files is easy with a numeric filing system. An unlimited set of available numbers (compared with the limitation of 26 *alphabetic* characters) allows the addition of numbers, folders, and storage units without transferring current files. In an alphabetic file, adding files in one section of the alphabet requires moving folders in all drawers or on all shelves that follow the expanded section.

Numbers are impersonal; the information they represent is dependent on the numbering system and is not immediately accessible to persons other than users of the system. Anyone else who may see an open file drawer, file shelf, or file folder cannot readily identify the contents.

The use of numbers for identification and classification of data is part of everyday work routines. Most people appreciate the speed and accuracy of using numbers. Understanding and recording numbers is easier than pronouncing and spelling names.

In numeric storage, a record can be assigned a code number that is already used as an identifying number. Numerous examples can be cited. If information about you is already in a company's database, your computer record is located by a search of one or more data fields in the record. ZIP Codes, telephone numbers, social security numbers, credit card numbers, and birth dates are examples of this use. When you order a pizza, the order clerk at your local pizza shop asks for your telephone number. Your name, address, and the kind of pizza you last ordered shows on the computer screen when your telephone number is entered into the computer. A video store clerk enters your telephone number into a computer and scans the bar code on a movie jacket to make an electronic record of the movie rental. When you call to ask about an invoice received for merchandise, you are asked for the invoice number. Debit and credit card scanners read identification numbers that allow stores to check information and verify sufficient funds for a purchase.

Why use numeric storage?

USES OF NUMERIC RECORDS STORAGE

Who uses numeric records storage?

Companies with a high volume of records and a concern for protecting the confidentiality of information often choose numeric records storage, particularly when identifying numbers are used in daily routines. Types of organizations that use numeric records management include the following:

1. Physicians, hospitals, clinics, dentists, and other medical-related organizations assign numbers to patient history records and to X-ray records.

2. State automobile license departments and social security offices arrange records by number because of their large-scale operations.
3. Human Resource departments commonly store personnel records by either employee numbers or social security numbers.
4. Banks and other financial institutions, such as savings and loan associations and credit unions, store records by customer account numbers.
5. Lawyers and architects assign numbers to clients to ensure identification of all pieces of correspondence and other records pertaining to a case or a project.
6. Building trade firms use contract or job numbers.
7. Social welfare agencies maintain records by case numbers.
8. Insurance companies store records by policy and claim numbers.

The remaining sections in this chapter describe various numbering methods for numeric records management. Basic components and filing procedures are discussed, and advantages and disadvantages are presented.

CONSECUTIVE NUMBERING METHOD

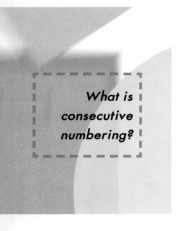

What is consecutive numbering?

The most frequently used method of numbering records for storage assigns numbers to records in sequence. Also called *serial* or *sequential numbering*, the **consecutive numbering method** is a method of numbering records in the order received and arranging them in *ascending* number order—from lowest to highest numbers. Numbers begin with 1, 100, 1000, or any other number and progress upward. Office forms such as invoices, sales tickets, and purchase orders are numbered consecutively. Although these forms may be filled out at various locations within a business, they come together in the file in consecutive numeric sequence.

What is indirect access?

Consecutive numbers are often assigned to customers and clients, and their correspondence is stored by consecutive numbers. Because a record may be requested by a name or topic rather than by a number, an index must be referenced to locate a numbered record. A numeric records management system is considered an **indirect access** system because an index is used to locate a record in the file. As an indirect access system, numeric filing is ideal for storing disks, tapes, cassettes, and other electronic records where label space for record identification is limited. Look at the Dataware® numeric label designs for the optical disk and magnetic tape cartridges in Figure 8–1.

An index is prepared to show the contents of the records and their assigned file code numbers. The index lists records by name, subject, creator, date, department, location, function, or a combination of these. Indexes are necessary to locate the records, just as indexes are needed to find books in your library. The books are labeled with an alphanumeric

Figure 8–1 Dataware® Media Labels for Optical and Magnetic Records

code and stored in sequential order. To locate the books, you reference an electronic or card index by title, author, or key words. The specific indexes required for numeric records storage are discussed in detail later in the chapter.

As noted in the beginning of this chapter, numbers are used frequently to locate information in electronic databases. A large database, used for reports that combine information from different tables, requires a common field in each table that is unique to the individual record. In most cases, an identifying number is used for this field because names, addresses, or other terms may not be unique and can refer to more than one individual or record. A number, such as an account number or social security number, can be used as an identifier, or the database software can assign sequential numbers. This same number, also called a *record number* or *ID number*, can be used as a common field in other tables in the database. Using this common field, reports can be created that include information from more than one table.

Consider a database for a catalog merchandising company as an example of using numbers as unique identifiers. The database could have a table that lists contact information on prospective customers, each with a customer record number in one data field. Another table in the database may include order information for customers. Using the customer record number as a common field in both tables would enable a database query to select information from both tables to be combined in one list or report. The results of the query could be viewed on the screen or printed. For example, the report generated from these two tables could show the date of the order and the item ordered from one table and the customer's name and address from another table.

How are database tables linked?

Consecutive Numbering Components

The components of the consecutive numbering method consist of (1) a numbered file, (2) an alphabetic file, (3) an accession log, and (4) an alphabetic index. Manual files use the following supplies for this filing method:

1. Numbered guides and folders for the numbered file records storage.
2. Alphabetic guides and folders for the general alphabetic file.
3. Database software (or index cards) for an accession log.
4. Database software (or index cards) for an alphabetic index.

Numbered Guides and Folders

Figure 8–2 shows a file drawer of consecutively numbered individual correspondent file folders in a straight-line arrangement. Primary guides, numbered 100 and 110, divide the drawer into easy-to-find numeric segments. In Figure 8–2 consecutively numbered individual folders 100 through 109 are placed behind corresponding guide number Section 100. Usually, one guide is provided for every ten folders. Folders can show the names of the correspondents on the right of the label if secrecy is not a factor. However, when office policy requires names in addition to assigned code numbers, the names are not in alphabetic order. Folders are arranged in consecutive numbered order; therefore, someone with unauthorized access to files would have difficulty locating a particular person's file.

Guide captions are available in a variety of formats: Guides may have numbers already printed on their tabs; numbered labels may be inserted into blank slots on the tabs; self-adhesive numbers may be attached to blank tabs; or numbers may be keyed on guide labels. Filing supply companies can produce customized labels directly from an organization's data saved to a disk from their database. Alternately, software packages, such as *Ames Create-a-File®*, can be purchased that interface with database software to produce custom labels and designs. Figure 8–3 on page 196 illustrates computer-produced labels with color-coded numbers. The numbers and colors call attention to misfiles, and bar codes provide an electronic tracking of records. Avoid handwriting or hand printing on guide labels. Handwriting lacks uniformity of placement and style, making the numbers difficult to read and unattractive.

Alphabetic Guides and Folders

Perhaps you wonder what a general alphabetic file is doing in numeric records storage. A general alphabetic file, found in many numeric arrangements, holds records of correspondents whose volume of correspondence is small. Some offices prepare individually numbered folders for correspondents as they enter the file. With this procedure, a general alphabetic file is not needed. In most offices, individually numbered

How can you create custom labels?

Why have an alphabetic file in a numeric storage system?

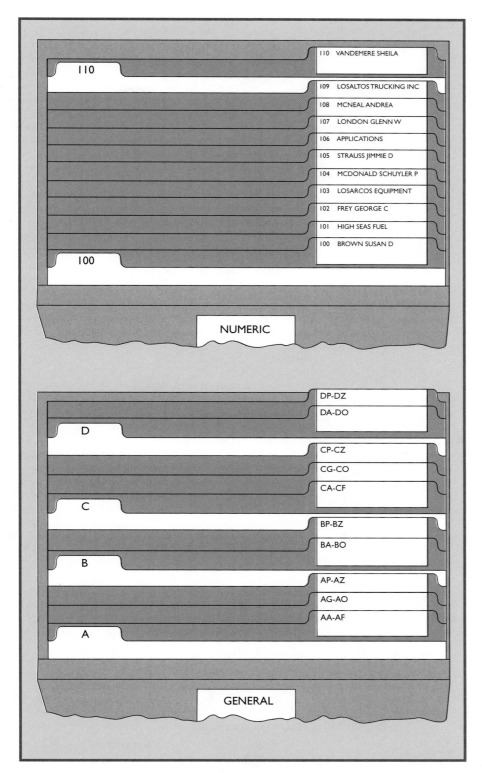

Figure 8–2 Consecutive Numbering Arrangement

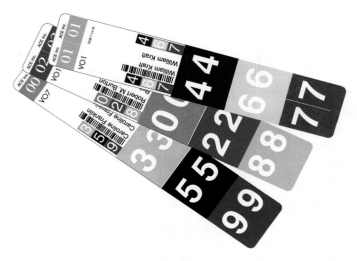

Figure 8–3 Ames Color-Coded Strip Labels for Shelf Files

folders are not prepared until a predetermined number of pieces of correspondence (usually 5 or more) have accumulated for one correspondent or when a correspondent's file is expected to be active. Until an individual numbered folder is prepared, correspondence is stored in general alphabetic folders in a general alphabetic file in the same manner as names stored by the alphabetic method.

The general alphabetic file should be placed at the beginning of the numeric file because expansion occurs at the end of a consecutively numbered arrangement. In Figure 8–2 the general alphabetic file contains a centered primary guide labeled GENERAL. In large records systems, alphabetic-lettered guides follow this primary guide to show the alphabetic divisions. In small systems, alphabetic-lettered guides may not be needed; instead, folders with alphabetic captions are arranged in alphabetic order behind the GENERAL guide. The general alphabetic folders hold records of correspondents who have not yet been assigned numbers.

Accession Log

The **accession log**, also called an *accession file* or *numeric file list*, is a serial list of numbers assigned to records in a numeric storage system. This log provides the numeric codes assigned to correspondents, subjects, or documents and the date of the assignment. The next number available for assignment comes from this log. An accession log prevents a filer from assigning the same number twice. Figures 8–4 shows an accession log created from a computer database.

Although index cards or a book could be used for the accession log, a computer-generated log is simpler to prepare, use, and update. Database software programs such as *Microsoft Access* are preferred because of their flexibility in producing different indexes and reports. You can store

ACCESSION LOG		
ASSIGNED CODE	INDEXED NAME	DATE
212	A TOUCH OF CLASS	5/18/--
213	FOWLER WEBSITE SERVICES	5/10/--
214	A1 PLUMBING SERVICE	7/12/--
215	EZ SERVICE CENTER	11/22/--
216	JOHNSON DAVID	4/21/--
217	DANIELLE EVAN	2/2/--
218	CARDONA JUAN	10/15/--
219	MORALES ANDRES	9/18/--
220	ASPEN TILE COMPANY	8/15/--
221	DELISO JAMES D SR	12/2/--
222	CARROLTON MAKITA	9/1/--
223	JONES OLDTYME BARBEQUE	4/10/--
224	LIANG YANG	8/17/--
225	HAIRSTYLES INC	5/21/--
226	KERSEY WALTER	7/20/--

Figure 8–4 Accession Log

numerous items of information about each record in one or more tables and use the Query or Report functions to generate lists or reports that show all or any part of this information.

Alphabetic Index

A numeric records storage system cannot function without an alphabetic index. An **alphabetic index** is a list of correspondent names or subjects for a numeric file. The assigned file codes are listed for records stored in the numbered file or a G is entered as the code for records stored in the general alphabetic file. Filers reference the alphabetic index to determine where records for correspondents are located in the filing system. Although an index card file can be used for the alphabetic index, a computer file is recommended for its speed and efficiency in locating records. The same database table can be used to store information for an accession log and an alphabetic index. Figure 8–5 on page 198 shows a partial alphabetic index generated from a database.

When an alphabetic card index file is used rather than a computer alphabetic index, filing practice may omit the names of those correspondents whose records are in the general alphabetic file. This practice would eliminate the need to prepare an alphabetic index card until assigning a numeric code. In some cases, however, such a practice could require extra time because filers would have to look in two files to locate a record. To retrieve a correspondent's record, the first source of location information would be the alphabetic card index to see if a code has been assigned. If a code is not found, the filer would check the general alphabetic file to

Why use a computer index?

ALPHABETIC INDEX		
A TOUCH OF CLASS	212	
A1 PLUMBING SERVICE	214	
ASPEN TILE COMPANY	220	
CARDONA JUAN	218	
CARROLTON MAKITA	222	
DANIELLE EVAN	217	
DELISO JAMES D SR	221	
DELSEY DONNA C	G	
DEMPSEY ROGER	G	
EASY SERVICE CENTER	**215X**	**EZ SERVICE CENTER**
EZ SERVICE CENTER	215	
FOWLER A J JR	**213X**	**FOWLER WEBSITE SERVICES**
FOWLER WEBSITE SERVICES	213	
HAIRSTYLES INC	225	
JOHNSON DAVID	216	
JONES OLDTYME BARBEQUE	223	
KERSEY WALTER	226	
LIANG YANG	224	
MILLER MARION	G	
MORALES ANDRES	219	
SISTER MARY CATHERINE	G	
WISHYWASHY LAUNDRY	G	

Figure 8–5 Alphabetic Index

locate the record. Because rapid retrieval of a record can be important, keeping all names in one index is more efficient than looking in multiple locations. With all names in the index, a filer follows the same pattern for all records. Each correspondent in the index has a different file code number or the letter G. Because the alphabetic index serves as the records location source for all file users, the index should be accurate and up to date.

When information about each correspondent or subject is stored in a database, locating information about that correspondent or subject is quick and easy using the database Find or Query functions. Because of the ease of obtaining information from a database, you may want to add addresses or other information. This information in a database is useful for printing mailing labels.

When creating a database, you can use the AutoNumber feature to assign record numbers automatically. If you want to use another numbering system, simply include a record number field and enter the number. The data can be sorted on the record number field in descending order so that the highest number shows on the first line of the list, allowing you to quickly determine the next number for assignment. The data can also be sorted by name to create an alphabetic name index.

What is an advantage of using computer databases for indexes?

The database can be used for an onscreen check of the assigned number for a correspondent or subject. Using the Find feature, you can go directly to an individual record to obtain information.

Storage and Retrieval Procedures

The steps for storage (inspecting, indexing, coding, cross–referencing, sorting, and storing) and retrieval (requisitioning, charging out, and following–up) are as important in the numeric method as they are in all other storage methods. The procedures to follow in storing and retrieving records in numeric systems are discussed next.

Inspecting and Indexing. Inspect records for release marks. Then index to determine the name or subject by which to store each record.

Coding. If a record is being filed that has been coded previously, check the coding for accuracy. If the coding has not been done, check to see if a cross-reference is needed. If so, code the cross-reference name or subject, and mark a notation on the record (usually, an X).

Code each record for numeric storage in two steps: (1) Code the filing segment and (2) assign a file code number or the letter G (GENERAL) by marking it in the upper right margin of the record. Consult the alphabetic index to see whether a file code number or the letter G (GENERAL) has been assigned. For correspondents or subjects with numbers already assigned, code the record with the file code number by writing this number at the top right margin of the record. Place the coded record in a numeric sorter for later storage. The letter in Figure 8–6a on page 200 shows the name coded and the number already assigned to the name of that organization. Number 122 is written in the upper right corner of the letter.

For correspondents or subjects with the letter G already assigned, the record will be stored in the general alphabetic file. Code the record with a G in the upper right corner. Then place the record in an alphabetic sorter for later storage in the general alphabetic file.

For new correspondents or subjects with no assigned numeric code, write the letter G in the upper right corner of the document. The letter in Figure 8–6b on page 201 shows a document coded for the general alphabetic file. Make a computer or card entry for the new correspondent or subject and indicate the file location to be G.

To assign file code numbers to a correspondent or subject, follow these steps:

1. When using a database, create a new record. Key the correspondent's name or subject and current date (and other information that is needed) in the appropriate fields and assign the next number. If a computer record is not kept, make entries in the manual accession log to record the assigned number and in the alphabetic card index to show the number or the letter G for the name or subject.

How are records coded?

Figure 8–6a **Coded Correspondence for Numeric Method, Numbered Files**

2. Write the assigned code number on the record in the upper right corner.

3. If any cross-references are needed, enter the cross-reference name or subject in the computer database with the assigned number followed by an X at the end of the name (i.e., 122X). Key the name in the SEE field for the location of the record in the file. If an alphabetic card index is kept instead of a computer file, prepare a cross-reference entry in this index file with the cross-reference name at the left margin and the numeric code at the right margin. Below the

How are numeric records cross-referenced?

Michael| D.| Larson| Group
3909 21 St., New York, NY 10022-1445 (212) 555-0197

December 18, 20--

DEC 21, 20-- 3:15 AM

Ms. Joanna Shelden
Shelden K & R, Inc.
600 E. 52 Street
New York, NY 10022-2844

Dear Ms. Shelden

Last week I met with your friend Joel Duffy regarding the renovation of our office complex at 3909 21 St., here in the city. He suggested that I look at your work on the Theater Arts Building because he thought it was close to the kind of makeover we are thinking about doing here.

Well, several of us toured the building last week and agreed it is an impressive piece of work. We would like to know what you and your staff would propose for us. We have very specific needs in mind and some creative projects that we would like to leave to you.

Let me know how you would like to proceed. We would prefer a meeting at our location, where we can show you the kinds of changes in layout, in communication services, and office equipment we have in mind. We are also eager to hear your suggestions and hope that you can prepare a proposal by the end of January.

Now that we have agreed to renovate, we are eager to get started. We are looking forward to an early meeting time that will be convenient for your people and our staff.

Sincerely

Michael D. Larson

Michael D. Larson

jmo

Figure 8–6b **Coded Correspondence for Numeric Method, Alphabetic File**

cross-reference name, add the word *SEE* and the name of the original record. Figure 8–7a on page 202 shows a database record and a cross-reference. Figure 8–7b on page 202 shows an index card and its cross-reference card in an alphabetic index.

4. Prepare a new folder with the file code number on its tab. Add the correspondent's name or the subject to the tab label if office policy requires this information.

5. Place the record in the folder with the top to the left, and place the folder in the sorter for later storage in the numbered file.

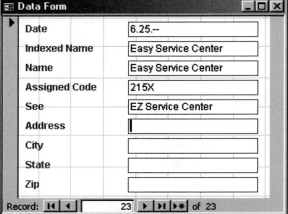

Figure 8–7a Record and Cross-Reference in a Computer Database

EZ SERVICE CENTER 215	EASY SERVICE CENTER 215X
EZ Service Center 123 Seymore Street Providence, RI 02940-2387	SEE EZ SERVICE CENTER

Figure 8–7b Record and Cross-Reference in an Alphabetic Card Index

Cross-Referencing. Follow the same rules and procedures explained in Chapters 2 and 3 to cross-reference names or subjects. Do not store cross-references in numbered file folders. Instead, enter all necessary cross-references in the computer database or in the card index as described previously in Step 3 and illustrated in Figure 8–7. To call attention to cross-referencing, consider using all capitals or bold type to show cross-references in a database name file or a distinctive-colored card in a manual index file.

Sorting. If rough sorting was done as you prepared the records, move the sorter and its contents to the storage area. However, if you prefer to perform like tasks together, sort all records after you have indexed, coded, and prepared necessary cross-reference entries. A quick sort before storage saves time. Stacking the records in random groups by hundreds, for example, eliminates moving back and forth from drawer to drawer or shelf to shelf while storing records.

Storing. Store all records coded with numbers in correspondingly numbered folders with the most recent date on top. Store records coded G in the general alphabetical folders. Store them first alphabetically according to the units in the filing segments and then by dates within each name group with the most recent date on top.

Why are records sorted before filing?

Office policy determines the point at which accumulated records in the general alphabetic file require the assignment of a permanent code number. When that accumulation has occurred, remove the records from the general file and take the following steps:

1. Consult the accession log to determine the next available number. Enter the name of the correspondent or the subject and the numeric code number in the database file or the manual log. Record the current date.
2. Locate the correspondent's name in the alphabetic index. Replace the G with the numeric code number.
3. Locate all cross-references for the subject or correspondent's name. In the computer database or in the alphabetic card index file, change the G on all cross-reference entries to the numeric code number followed by an X.
4. Recode all records removed from the General file by crossing out the G and writing the assigned number above or beside it.
5. Prepare a new folder with the assigned number on its tab (and, possibly, the correspondent's name or the subject).
6. Place all records in the new folder. Place the record with the most recent date on top.
7. Place the numbered folder in its correct numeric sequence in storage.

Retrieving. When you remove records from numeric storage, use requisitions, charge-out cards or slips, and OUT indicators in the same way you used them for alphabetic and subject records storage. With a computer database table, you can include an OUT Date field, Borrower's Name field, and Date Borrowed field in the database table to record OUT information. When a record is removed from the file, a computer entry is made in the database table. Follow-up procedures to locate borrowed records include the use of a tickler file or another reminder system. To ensure the safe return of borrowed records, follow the same procedures described in Chapter 6. If OUT information is kept in the computer database, a filter or query could be used to show all borrowed OUT files, sorted by date.

Conversion from Alphabetic Storage to Consecutive Numeric Storage

An organization may decide that a numeric arrangement would provide quicker records storage and retrieval than an existing alphabetic arrangement. Security reasons may be another consideration for a decision to change from alphabetic storage to consecutively numbered storage. A number on a storage container or file folder does not convey information to inquisitive persons; a name on a folder is instantly recognizable to

How are records transferred from a general to a numbered file?

Why convert from alphabetic to numeric storage?

anyone who sees it. File users in an office may prefer an indirect access storage method that allows for a variety of useful indexes to locate stored records such as a database master file. Whatever the reason for a conversion, the procedure is time consuming but not difficult.

The following steps convert an alphabetic file arrangement to a consecutively numbered arrangement:

How can you convert from alphabetic to numeric arrangement?

1. Prepare numbered guides for every 10 folders in storage according to the sequence of numbers decided upon, such as 1–10–20, 100–110–120, 1000–1010–1020, etc.

2. Remove each individual folder from storage and assign a code number from the accession log. Make the filing segment notation (the name of each correspondent or of any subject) in the computer database or in a manual accession log beside the assigned number. Record the date.

3. Prepare a numbered label and affix it to the folder or add the newly assigned number to the older label. *Caution*: Do not remove general folders from alphabetic storage; the reason will be explained later in the chapter.

4. Key each filing segment for cross-references in a computer database or on cards in the manual alphabetic card index. Key the assigned numeric code and an X in the computer entries or on cross-reference cards.

5. Remove cross-reference sheets and SEE ALSO references from the individual folders because the computer entries or cross-reference cards now take the place of those sheets. Place any cross-reference index cards in their alphabetic location in the card index. Computer entries can be sorted as needed or located without sorting through use of the Find function with record entries.

6. Remove any permanent cross-reference guides within the group of folders being converted to the numeric method, and make computer entries or index card entries with the information that was on the guides. Place any cross-reference index cards in their alphabetic location in the card index.

7. Code each record in every folder with its newly assigned file code number in the upper right margin of the record.

8. Return the numbered folders to storage in correct numeric sequence.

9. Create the general alphabetic file by coding all remaining records with the letter G. (All individual folders from alphabetic storage were converted to numbered folders and filed numerically.)

10. Key a computer entry in the database or prepare an index card for the name of each correspondent or subject in every general folder. If index cards are used, place these cards in the index file in alphabetic sequence. Computer records can be sorted as needed or located with the Find function without sorting.

Advantages and Disadvantages of Consecutive Numbering

Every storage method has advantages and disadvantages. Consecutive numbering is no exception.

Advantages. This indirect access method has advantages for storing electronic records such as tapes, cassettes, and disks, where labeling space is often limited. A numeric code identifies the records. A computer database record for each item shows this number, along with the originator's name, department, subject, special project, or any other meaningful category. The database record can be as comprehensive as necessary to identify and locate records. Even when disks and tapes are reused, the file code number remains the same; only the information in the record fields is updated. These computer database files could be searched by any of the fields of information to find a particular record. Numeric computer files are used frequently for inventories of equipment and supplies. Each item is assigned an identifying number, and pertinent fields of information are added to the database for data entry and retrieval.

The consecutive numeric method offers many advantages to paper records storage. Some of the advantages apply to electronic records media as well. Advantages include the following:

1. Refiling of numerically coded records is rapid because people recognize number sequences better and faster than alphabetic sequences.
2. Expansion is easy and unlimited. New numbers can be assigned without disturbing the arrangement of existing folders or other stored records media.
3. Transfer of inactive records is easy, especially in offices where case numbers or contract numbers are used. The oldest cases or contracts or the oldest cassettes or disks have the lowest numbers and are stored together.
4. All cross-references are in the database general alphabetic name file or the alphabetic card index and do not congest the numbered records files in drawers or on shelves.
5. Numeric captions on guides, folders, electronic records, and other records storage media are secure from curious eyes or intentional information seekers. When storage security is needed for medical patients, research projects, or client names, such information is excluded from label captions.
6. Orders, invoices, ledger accounts, and correspondence for one customer all bear the same numeric code, keeping related records together. Fewer errors may occur when matching invoice and payment, for example.
7. A complete list of correspondents' names, addresses, and other information is available from the alphabetic index or a correspondent database.

> *What are advantages of consecutive numbering for electronic records?*

> *What are consecutive numbering advantages for paper records?*

8. Time and effort in labeling is minimized because numbers can be affixed much more quickly than can names, subjects, or project titles. Available folders and electronic records media may be numbered in advance of their use.
9. Misfiled records are detected easily because numbers out of sequence are usually easier to detect than are misfiled records arranged alphabetically.

Disadvantages. Disadvantages of the consecutive numbering method include the following:

1. Numeric storage access is indirect because reference to an alphabetic index is necessary. When more steps are required to store records, more mistakes can occur.
2. More guides are necessary for the numeric method than for other methods; therefore, the cost of supplies for numeric storage can be higher.
3. If a manual alphabetic card index is used, congestion around this file can occur when frequent reference to its contents is made by more than one person. This problem may or may not occur with this information in computer database records, depending on how many computers can access this information.
4. Use of a manual alphabetic index involves double sorting of records, requiring extra time. Because each record is checked against an alphabetic index, the records must first be sorted alphabetically and then resorted numerically prior to storage. This resorting is eliminated with a computer database and use of the Find function to locate specific names or numbers in the records file.
5. Because new records are added in consecutive order, records with the highest numbers are typically the most current and most active records. Reference to the current records by several people simultaneously can cause congestion in the storage area.

NONCONSECUTIVE NUMBERING METHODS

Nonconsecutive numbering is a system of numbers that has blocks of numbers omitted. The records arrangement based on these numbers uses a sequential order that differs from a consecutive order of numbers normally read from left to right. This section explains the use of three of these methods: terminal-digit, middle-digit, and chronologic storage.

Terminal-Digit Storage
Terminal-digit storage breaks large numbers into groups of digits and overcomes the disadvantage of congestion that can occur at the end of a

What are disadvantages of consecutive numbering?

Why might there be traffic congestion at the end of a storage area?

What is meant by nonconsecutive numbering?

consecutive numeric storage area. The terminal-digit storage method is used most effectively with thousands of folders whose numbers have reached at least five digits (10,000 or more). The words *terminal digit* refer to the end digits of a number (091 38 <u>0297</u>). Numbers may be assigned sequentially or the digit groups may mean something specific. For example, the first group of numbers can be a customer identification number, the second group can indicate a sales district, salesperson, or department; the third group can indicate a date, branch office, or department. The number may be a product number in which various groups of numbers refer to a sales department and/or a particular manufacturer or wholesaler. The numbers can have a variety of meanings, or they can be simply a sequentially assigned numeric code number.

Terminal-digit storage is a numeric storage method in which the last two or three digits of each number are used as the primary division under which a record is filed. Groups of numbers are read from right to left. The digits in the number are usually separated into groups by a space or hyphen. The groups of numbers are identified as primary, secondary, and tertiary numbers reading from right to left.

02	24	51
(tertiary)	(secondary)	(primary)

What is terminal-digit storage?

An arrangement of numbers in terminal-digit sequence would look like the following; the numbers in bold determine the correct numeric order in the file:

786 67 **1258** (front of file)	303 **99** 2891	502 64 **9284**
231 55 **2187**	947 28 **6314**	498 64 **9485**
189 40 **2891**	287 **29** 6314	**502** 64 9485 (file end)

The primary numbers usually indicate a drawer or shelf number. If the volume of records stored is great, more than one drawer or shelf may be needed to hold all records with numbers ending in the same terminal digits. Figure 8–8a shows the arrangement of folders in a portion of drawer 51. The secondary numbers determine the primary guide captions. The section of the drawer shown begins with guide 24–51; actually, if space had permitted, the entire 51 section would show guide 00–51 at the beginning of the drawer. The records are arranged behind each guide by the tertiary numbers; remember, these are the digits at the extreme *left* of the number.

Which numbers determine file order behind guides in terminal-digit storage?

As new folders are stored, new guides are added to separate each group of 10 folders. The first section of the file shown in Figure 8–8a on page 208 (the 24–51 section) has been expanded in Figure 8–8b on page 208 by the addition of folders numbered <u>10</u>–24–51 through <u>19</u>–24–51. The tertiary numbers have increased from 00 through 07 to 00 through 22. Therefore, secondary guides 00, 10, and 20 were added in first position, and the primary guides moved to the prominent center position of the file drawer.

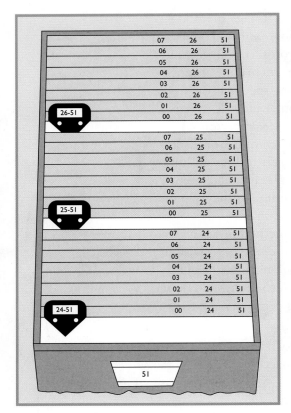

Figure 8–8a **Terminal-Digit Arrangement**

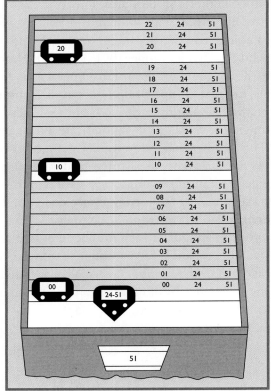

Figure 8–8b **Expansion of Terminal-Digit Arrangement**

When sequentially numbered records, such as 02 25 51 and 02 25 52, are added to terminal-digit storage, these new and typically more active records are filed in *different* file locations. Distributing current records throughout a storage area avoids congestion in one particular storage area. Remember, in consecutive numeric storage these records would be stored next to each other at the end of the storage area.

Do not confuse terminal-digit storage with the consecutive numeric storage of large, six-digit numbers often used in electronic records media storage. When six-digit numbers are stored *consecutively*, the last two digits in the number become rack numbers—the number placed on the rack just below a stored cartridge, cassette, or tape. The last two digits 01 in the number 78 92 01 do not occur again until 78 93 01 (100 records away). Therefore, once you have arrived in the file section of 7893, the last two digits fixed to the storage rack become the important numbers for record identification.

Middle-Digit Storage

Middle-digit storage is another method of nonconsecutive numbering. Like terminal-digit storage, using this method avoids working with large numbers and overcomes the disadvantage of congestion at the end of the storage area. The words *middle-digit* refer to the middle group of digits in a large number.

Middle–digit storage is a numeric storage method that uses the middle two or three digits of each number as the primary division under which a record is filed. Groups of numbers are read from the middle to left to right. Numbers to the left are secondary; numbers to the right are tertiary, or last.

┌─────────────┐
│ *What is*   │
│ *middle-digit* │
│ *storage?* │
└─────────────┘

02	24	51
(secondary)	(primary)	(tertiary)

An arrangement of numbers in middle-digit sequence would look like the following; the numbers in bold determine the correct numeric order:

947 **28** 6314 (front of file)	331 **55** 2187	502 **64** **9485**
287 **29** 6314	498 **64** 9485	786 **67** 1258
189 **40** 2891	**502** 64 9284	303 **99** 2891 (file end)

In Figure 8–9, all records with middle digits 33 are stored in one section. The digits on the left determine record sequence within the 33 drawer, followed by the digits on the right. The left digits determine the primary guide captions **05**–33, **06**–33, and **07**–33.

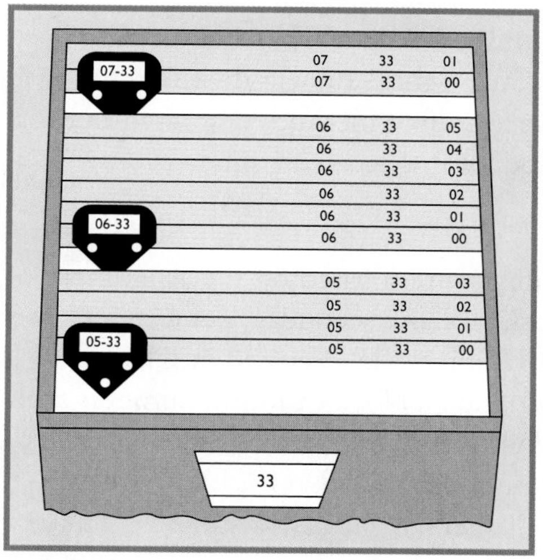

┌─────────────┐
│ *How can*   │
│ *middle-digit* │
│ *numbering* │
│ *keep related* │
│ *records*   │
│ *together?* │
└─────────────┘

Figure 8–9 **Middle-Digit Arrangement**

In the middle–digit method, blocks of sequentially numbered records are kept together. However, records are distributed through the files in blocks of 100. Records numbered 10 <u>34 </u>00 to 10 <u>34 </u>99 are filed together in one section; 10 <u>35 </u>00 to 10 <u>35 </u>99, in the next file section. The middle-digit method has additional value when the middle digits identify someone or something specific and related records need to be kept together. If the middle digits represent a sales representative or a sales district, for example, all records for that individual or location are kept together in one block.

Chronologic Storage

What is chronologic storage?

Chronologic storage is filing records by calendar date in reverse sequence (with the most recent date on top) or forward sequence (with the earliest date on top). Exact chronologic storage is not well suited to correspondence because of the need to keep together all records from, to, and about one individual or organization. Chronologic storage is often used for daily reports, deposit tickets, freight bills, statements, and order sheets, which may be best stored by date.

The chronologic principle is followed in all methods of storage as records are placed in their folders. The most current records are at the front or back of the folder, thereby keeping the most recent records easily accessible. Tickler files are one form of chronologic storage. You may want to refer to the discussion of tickler files in Chapter 5.

OTHER NUMERIC CODING SYSTEMS

Numbers are sometimes added to encyclopedic arrangements of subject and geographic filing methods. Numbers help to eliminate misfiles in subject and geographic files that contain main subject divisions and numerous subdivisions. The numeric coding methods described in this section of the chapter allow for coding the necessary subdivisions.

Block-Numeric Coding

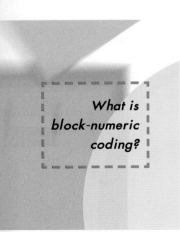

What is block-numeric coding?

Block-numeric coding is a coding system based on the assignment of groups of numbers to represent primary and secondary subjects such as the encyclopedic arrangement of a subject file discussed in Chapter 7. The major subject divisions are assigned a block of round numbers such as 100, 200, 300. Then, each subdivision is assigned a block of numbers within the major block of round numbers such as 110, 120, 130. The more file expansion expected, the larger the blocks of numbers will be. The subdivision 110, for example, allows for additional subject subdivisions of subjects (111 to 119). If blocks of numbers were assigned to the subject file illustrated in Figure 7–2a, p. 169, the block number allotments might look like this:

```
100   ACCOUNTING
      110   ACCOUNTS PAYABLE
      120   ACCOUNTS RECEIVABLE
      130   PROFIT AND LOSS
```

```
150   AIR CONDITIONING
200   APPLICATIONS
250   BANKING
      260   LOANS
      270   STATEMENTS
300   BRANCH OFFICES
```

Duplex-Numeric Coding

Like block-numeric coding, duplex-numeric coding is also used in
subject or geographic filing systems that contain major categories
and subdivisions. **Duplex-numeric coding** is a coding system using
numbers (or sometimes letters) with two or more parts separated by a
dash, space, or comma. An unlimited number of subdivisions is possible
with this coding system. Subject subdivisions are added sequentially,
however, and may not follow a strict alphabetic order. Notice that
PAST BUDGETS comes before FUTURE NEEDS in the following
example because FUTURE NEEDS was added to the file *after* PAST
BUDGETS:

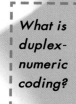

What is duplex-numeric coding?

```
10   BUDGETS
      10–1 ACCOUNTING DEPARTMENT
            10–1–1   PAST BUDGETS
            10–1–2   FUTURE NEEDS
            10–1–3   RECEIPTS
      10–2 DATA PROCESSING DEPARTMENT
            10–2–1   PAST BUDGETS
            10–2–2   FUTURE NEEDS
      10–3 ENGINEERING DEPARTMENT
            10–3–1   PAST BUDGETS
```

Decimal-Numeric Coding

Decimal-numeric coding is a method of coding records numerically
in units of ten. An unlimited number of subdivisions is permitted
through the use of digits to the right of the decimal point. This method
is used for classifying library materials and is called the Dewey Decimal
System. The system has nine general classes or main divisions (100–900).
A tenth division (000) is used for records too general to be placed in
any of the nine main divisions. Each main division can be divided into
nine or fewer parts (110, 130, to 190). These nine parts can be divided
further into nine additional groups (111, 112, to 119). Decimals are
added for further divisions (111.1, 111.1.1). The Dewey decimal classification is not commonly used in an office. However, the use of decimals
to subdivide records is a practical alternative to the dashes, spaces, and
commas used in duplex-numeric coding to subdivide records.

What is decimal-numeric coding?

Alphanumeric Coding

What is alphanumeric coding?

Alphanumeric coding is a coding system that combines alphabetic and numeric characters. Main subjects are arranged alphabetically, and their subdivisions are assigned a number. After all main subjects are determined, they are given a number (usually in groups of 10 or 100 to provide for expansion). More elaborate variations of this system may use both letters and numbers and have numerous subdivisions.

```
MGT – MANAGEMENT
    MGT-01    RECORDS MANAGEMENT
        MGT-01-01    FILING EQUIPMENT
        MGT-01-02    FILING SYSTEMS
            MGT-01-02-01    AUTOMATED
            MGT-01-02-02    ELECTRONIC
            MGT-01-02-03    PROCEDURES MANUAL
        MGT-01-03    RETENTION SCHEDULE
    MGT-02    SALES MANAGEMENT
        MGT-02-01    ADVERTISING
```

COMPUTER INDEXES

Earlier in this chapter, you read about how a database program can simplify creating the accession log and indexes that a numeric file requires. All necessary information can be kept in one table for ready access and updating. When you design database queries to sort numeric codes for the accession log, remember that the computer sorts within a database field from left to right.

With terminal-digit or middle-digit numeric coding storage, use a separate field for each part of the number to aid in sorting and preparing the accession log and indexes. For example, with terminal-digit numbering, set up three fields in the database table for the numeric code: Tertiary, Secondary, and Primary. Enter the numeric code for each group of numbers in its correct field. Data entry is simplified and less prone to error if the order of the numeric codes in the table matches the normal left-to-right reading sequence.

How are terminal-digit numbers sorted in a database?

To sort these numbers as an accession log and determine the next number to be assigned, create a query to display fields in this order: Primary, Secondary, and Tertiary. Then sort each of these three columns in descending order. The query results would be displayed as shown in Figure 8–10.

Note that the numbers are in reverse order to the numeric code to allow the last four digits (Primary field) to be sorted first, the middle digits (Secondary field), second, and first three digits (Tertiary field), last.

Terminal Digit Sort : Select Query

Primary	Secondary	Tertiary	Name	Date
9485	64	502	FREY GEORGE C	9/04/--
9485	64	498	STRAUSS JIMMIE D	9/18/--
9284	64	502	LONDON GLENN W	10/2/--
6314	29	287	MCNEAL ANDREA	10/3/--
6314	28	947	MCDONALD SCHUYLER P	9/11/--
2891	99	303	HIGH SEAS FUEL	9/03/--
2891	40	189	LOSARCOS EQUIPMENT	9/04/--
2187	55	231	APPLICATIONS	9/24--
1258	67	997	LOGAN DANIEL G	3/17/--
1258	67	786	BROWN SUSAN D	9/30/--

Record: 11 of 11

Figure 8–10 Accession Log Query for Terminal Digit Numbering

A list similar to that used for terminal-digit numbering can be generated to produce a sorted list of numeric codes for middle-digit numbering. Numeric codes for middle-digit numbering would be entered on the query design with the middle set of numbers (Primary field) first; the left-most set of numbers (Secondary field), second; and the last group of numbers (Tertiary field), third. Sorting for these three fields would follow the same order. The middle-digit numbers could be sorted from only two fields (by combining the primary and secondary numbers into one field since they read from left to right and would be sorted in that order); however, using the same practice for either method of numbering reduces confusion, and, also, increases the flexibility to change later to a terminal-digit or consecutive numbering without changing the table.

How are middle-digit codes entered in a database table?

When using the accession log for a nonconsecutive numbering system, the number on the top line of the query results table may not tell you the next number to be assigned. Remember that in a particular office, the primary number may indicate a drawer or shelf, the secondary number the section of the shelf or drawer, and the tertiary number the order of the file in that section. Another office may have different categories assigned for the number groupings. For example, the first group of numbers could indicate a customer identification number; the second, a branch office; and the third, a department. The specific record's appropriate grouping would determine where to look on the database generated accession log to locate the next number to be assigned. For a large volume of records, however, you may need to use the database Filter function to show only the categories that pertain to the group of records that you are coding.

Another convenient feature of the Sort function for database records is the ability to sort and print mailing labels. Mailing labels must be presorted to take advantage of bulk mailing rates. The computer-generated mailing labels can be sorted by ZIP Code without entering parts of the ZIP Code in separate fields because these numbers are sorted in sequential order as read from left to right.

Computers use numbers to identify the location of paper documents that are scanned or microfilmed for storage in an electronic image records system. These systems have an automatic indexing system to locate records. In Chapter 11, you will learn more about paper documents that are scanned or microfilmed as image records.

SUMMARY

You use numbers in so many ways that a personal index is almost a necessity to remember all of them. Telephone numbers, voice mail access, social security numbers, ZIP Codes, credit or debit card numbers, birth dates, house numbers, post office box numbers, safe deposit box numbers, and numerous other numbers identify specific aspects of our lives. These numbers allow speedy identification for different purposes. Numbers in a numeric records management system identify the location of specific records.

Records can be numbered consecutively, numbered in combination with geographic locations or subjects, or stored in nonconsecutive filing arrangements. Although numeric records storage is an indirect system that requires an accession log and indexes, the computer makes this indirect system much quicker and easier to update and use than manual access and index lists. Files in a numeric system can be expanded without moving records that are already in the file.

Color-coded numeric file labels reduce misfiles of records. When visually scanning open-shelf files or an open file drawer, you can quickly see an odd color or number out of sequence.

Nonconsecutive numbering systems keep current records from accumulating in one section of a shelf or drawer, thus avoiding crowded use of these files by multiple filers in a work setting with a high volume of records. Terminal-digit storage creates an even distribution of consecutively numbered records throughout a numeric system, and middle-digit storage allows blocks of related records to be stored together sequentially. Chronologic storage is used in some aspect of almost every filing method. Records from the same correspondent are arranged in folders by date, and tickler files are arranged by date to serve as reminders of due dates. Block-numeric coding and duplex-numeric coding combine numeric codes with subject or geographic categories, and alphanumeric coding uses alphabetic subject abbreviations with a numbering system.

Computer databases are important for efficient numeric records storage. Improved efficiency of records management comes from the computer's ability to select particular records quickly, to identify their numeric code, to sort records so that a specific record or numeric code is located quickly, and to prepare lists and reports from stored information in a variety of formats.

IMPORTANT TERMS

accession log

alphabetic index

alphanumeric coding

block-numeric coding

chronologic storage

consecutive numbering method

decimal-numeric coding

duplex-numeric coding

indirect access

middle-digit storage

nonconsecutive numbering

numeric records management

terminal-digit storage

REVIEW AND DISCUSSION

1. List three reasons for storing records by the numeric method. (Obj. 1)

2. Why is expansion easier with numeric than with subject filing? (Obj. 1)

3. What types of organizations use numeric records storage? (Obj. 2)

4. How are records arranged with the consecutive numbering method? (Obj. 3)

5. What is meant by indirect access? (Obj. 3)

6. What are the four components of the consecutive numbering method and what is the purpose of each? (Obj. 3)

7. When are records transferred from the general alphabetic file to the numbered file? (Obj. 3)

8. Why is it recommended that a general alphabetic file be placed at the beginning, rather than at the end, of a consecutively numbered storage arrangement? (Obj. 3)

9. What are the procedures for storing records by the consecutive numbering method? (Obj. 4)

10. Explain why records in numeric storage may be coded with either the letter G or a number. (Obj. 4)

11. How are cross-references prepared in the consecutive numbering method? How are they numbered? (Obj. 4)

12. In converting from an alphabetic arrangement to a consecutively numbered arrangement, you will not assign numbers to the general folders in the alphabetic file. Where will these folders be located in the numeric storage arrangement? Will records in these folders be coded with a number? Why or why not? (Obj. 5)

13. Explain at least three advantages and three disadvantages of consecutive numeric records storage. (Obj. 6)

14. Explain how numbers are sorted in consecutive numbering, terminal-digit numbering, and middle-digit numbering. (Obj. 7)

15. Give at least one way that terminal-digit and middle-digit numbering are alike and one way they are different. (Obj. 7)

16. Explain chronologic storage and how it is used. (Obj. 8)

17. Give at least one way that block-numeric, duplex-numeric, decimal-numeric, and alphanumeric coding are alike and one way they are different. (Obj. 9)

18. What are two ways that computer database software makes numeric data storage and use easy and fast? (Obj. 10)

APPLICATIONS (APP)

APP 8-1. Develop Plans for Organizing Records (Objs. 9, 10)

Milburn Watson, a colleague, asks for your help in setting up a filing system for electronic files saved on floppy disks. He brings disks, numbered 1 to 5, for your review and suggestions. Milburn had no difficulty finding files when he had just one or two disks. Now that the disks are accumulating, finding files is time-consuming. He asks for your help in creating a system that allows him to find his files *without* moving any files.

The following data files are on each of the five disks:

DISK 1
   Sales Forecast Report 12-10.xls
   Annual Sales Report.xls
   McKay Letters 8-15.doc
   Jansen Letters 8-24.doc
   Administrative Budget.xls

DISK 2
   War Memorial Contract 6-18.doc
   Medical Arts Bldg Contract 7-1.doc
   Young and Lewis PO 4-25.xls
   Stationery Center PO 9-9.xls
   Administration Report 1-10.doc
   McKay Email 1-15.eml

DISK 3

    Prospective Customer Database.mdb
    Employee Database.mdb
    Client Database.mdb
    McKay Letters 8-22.doc
    Abbrahm Letters 8-24.doc
    Quarterly Sales Report 4-24.xls
    Kaufman Proposal 6-2.doc

DISK 4

    Willis Memo 9-5.doc
    Computer Center Budget.xls
    Sales and Marketing Budget.xls
    Quarterly Sales Report 7-24.xls
    Theatre Arts Bldg Bid 6-12.doc
    Smead PO 5-19.xls
    WalMart Proposal 11-7.doc
    Theatre Arts Bldg Contract 6-28.doc

DISK 5

    Company Annual Report.doc
    McKay Letters 12-4.doc
    Abbrahm Letters 12-8.doc
    PR Corp Bid 6-8.doc
    Delaney Chemical Bid 6-1.doc
    IBM PO 2-2.xls
    Kaufman Invoice 3-15.xls
    Hart Builders Invoice 10-18.xls
    Sales Promotion Budget.xls

Milburn has tried to use meaningful file names. He explains that the files include the following types of documents:

Budgets
Bids
Contracts
Correspondence (Letters, memos, e-mail)
Databases
Forms (POs and invoices)
Proposals
Reports

1. Work with a classmate to complete this project.

2. Based on what you know about subject and numeric filing and useful indexes, use your database software to create an index for the files on the disk. Use Milburn's eight types of documents as major divisions for the index.

3. Print a table or report showing the index in a format that will make locating files easy for Milburn. The index should show the major file divisions, any subdivisions, each file's place within the system, and the disk on which the file is located.

4. Now help Milburn organize his paper documents. Assume the headings on the index printed in Step 3 refer to paper documents that are stored manually in a records storage system. Use this index to convert subject files to a block-numeric coding system. Write numeric code numbers on the index to the left of each subject or record name. For this application, assign numbers to the main subject headings in blocks of 100 with subdivisions in blocks of 10. Filenames that are the same but with different dates would be considered a subset of the subdivision. You may want to review the section on block-numeric coding on p. 210 in this chapter.

APP 8-2.   Arrange Files by Terminal-Digit, Middle-Digit, and Consecutive Numbering (Obj. 7)

1. Manually arrange the numbers below in terminal-digit order.

2. Manually arrange the numbers below in middle-digit order.

3. Manually arrange the numbers below in consecutive order.

24 15 38	18 31 01	16 74 34	17 34 60	27 11 82	21 32 71
21 33 71	26 00 02	17 33 60	19 31 01	27 10 82	20 33 70
29 17 50	16 74 32	29 17 51	18 31 02	17 31 01	27 11 42

4. The numbers above have been entered in a database table so they can be sorted for terminal-digit, middle-digit, and consecutive numbering. The first group of two digits is in the GROUP 1 field, the second group of two digits is in the GROUP 2 field, and the third group of two digits is in the GROUP 3 field.

5. Open the *Access* database APP 8-2.mdb.

6. Create a query based on the APP 8-2 table to sort the numbers in terminal-digit filing order. Print the query results.

7. Create a query based on the APP 8-2 table to sort the numbers in middle-digit filing order. Print the query results.

8. Create a query based on the APP 8-2 table to sort the numbers in consecutive filing order. Print the query results.

9. Use the query results to check your answers for steps 1 – 3.

APPLYING THE RULES

Job 10, Consecutive Numeric Correspondence Filing.
Job 11, Terminal-Digit Numeric Correspondence Filing.

CHAPTER 9

GEOGRAPHIC RECORDS MANAGEMENT

LEARNING OBJECTIVES

1. Explain the need for geographic records management.
2. Name the kinds of businesses that might use the geographic method of storage.
3. List advantages and disadvantages of geographic records management.
4. Compare dictionary and encyclopedic arrangements of geographic records.
5. Explain the differences between the lettered guide plan and the location name guide plan.
6. Describe an arrangement of guides and folders in the geographic storage method.
7. Explain the use of an alphabetic index in the geographic storage method.
8. Describe how indexing and coding for the geographic storage method differ from indexing and coding for the alphabetic storage method.
9. List the types of cross-references used in the geographic storage method and how they are stored.
10. Describe the effect that e-commerce is likely to have on geographic records storage.

THE GEOGRAPHIC RECORDS STORAGE METHOD

In this age of *e-commerce* and *dot.com companies,* communication and commerce, even for small businesses, can involve a world–wide audience. A New York organization conducts business activities as easily in Mexico, Japan, or Germany as it does in Ohio, California, or Idaho. The United States produces more goods and services than can be consumed locally or domestically. Government agencies, businesses, and organizations interact with markets in countries throughout the world.

Large companies have operated branch offices and set up production internationally for decades, but now this practice is standard operating procedure for an array of organizations. The automobile industry is an example of a widespread international business operation. American automobile manufacturers such as General Motors and Ford do not limit their markets or purchase of components to this country, and companies from countries such as Japan produce and sell a wide variety of cars in the United States. Even state and local governments establish branch offices in other countries to promote foreign trade. Clearly, the global economy creates business opportunities that extend to locations all around the world. High-tech communications and satellite networks increase interactions for multiple locations worldwide.

The importance of diverse locations in the day-to-day decisions of big business is clearly evident. Location plays a major role in the success or failure of all types of enterprises. Look at the changes taking place in your own community: Why does a large local supermarket close in your neighborhood? Why does a large discount chain (box store) open in town? Why does a manufacturer move its operations from New York to Mexico? from California to Utah? or from Alabama to Taiwan? Why did your favorite pizza shop move from the north side of town to the south side? One principal part of the answer is *location*!

Business activities spanning wide geographic areas demand intelligent business decisions based on location. Organizational decisions about operational locations require maintaining records by those locations. You don't have to be a marketing research analyst to figure out why skis sell better in Colorado or New York than they do in Florida or Arizona or why in-line skates sell better in urban locations than in rural locations. However, not all needed information regarding location is so obvious when organizations consider expanding their markets. For example: Why are production costs higher in one location than another? Is the climate of a location important to sales? What about the average age of the populations or their literacy and income levels? Good management decisions are based on reliable information, and operational records collected and stored by location help provide it.

Now let's explore how geography (location) relates to your study of geographic records storage. You have already studied alphabetic storage by name and by subject. In this chapter, you will learn a third alphabetic storage method—by location. **Geographic records management** is a method of storing and retrieving records in alphabetic order by location of an individual, an organization, or a project.

Examples of businesses that may store records by the geographic method include the following:

1. Multinational companies with plants, divisions, and customers outside the boundaries of the United States.

Companies with customers outside the United States might use geographic records management.

2. E-commerce businesses that need information about customer locations and target sales areas.
3. The petroleum industry, mining companies, government offices, and other organizations that store maps and other related location- and land-oriented records.
4. Businesses that have many branches (possibly sales offices) at different geographic locations within the U.S. and have a high volume of intracompany correspondence.
5. Insurance companies, franchised operations, banks, and investment firms that are licensed to operate in specific states and whose records are kept according to those states.
6. Mail-order houses and publishers with business conducted through the United States mail and customers' records referenced first by geographic location or by a number (ZIP Code or Account No.) representing a specific location or region.
7. Companies that direct their advertising promotions to specific geographic areas such as the West Coast, East Coast, Southern States, or Northern States.
8. Utility companies (electricity, gas, telephone, water) whose customers are listed by ZIP Code, street name, and address.
9. Real estate agencies that list their properties by areas such as foreign countries, divisions of countries or cities, groupings of subdivision names, or streets within a metropolitan area.
10. Government agencies with records stored according to geographic areas, such as state, county, township, or other locales, depending upon the scope of the governmental function.

Who uses geographic records storage?

ADVANTAGES AND DISADVANTAGES OF GEOGRAPHIC RECORDS STORAGE

Like any records system, geographic records management has advantages and disadvantages; however, when information requests are by location, records need to be stored by location. In these situations, the advantages outweigh the disadvantages. This section describes advantages and disadvantages of geographic records management.

Advantages

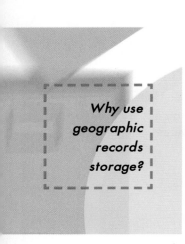

Why use geographic records storage?

Geographic storage provides reference to information specific to certain geographic areas for making decisions about those locations. For example, measuring the space required to store records created in various geographic areas is one means for comparison of business activity by location. An analysis of those records can be used constructively to note (1) areas with the most complaints; (2) aggressive selling effort or the lack of selling effort; (3) areas that need special attention to personnel, production, shipping costs, and the like; or (4) where territories need to be combined, separated, or subdivided. If territories need adjustments, geographic file guides and folders are easily rearranged. Each geographic area in storage is a unit or a group, and the shift of groups of records is easily accomplished by moving an entire group from one file location to another.

Disadvantages

One disadvantage of the geographic method is the complexity of the guide and folder arrangements that may be required in some large systems. For example, a geographic arrangement takes more time to establish than an alphabetic name or subject file when the nature of the organization requires many subdivisions. Storing and retrieving records can be more time-consuming, too, because reference must be made first to an area (such as a state), then to a location within that area (such as a city), and finally to a correspondent's name and address.

Another disadvantage is the need for an alphabetic index of all correspondents' names and addresses. If the location of a correspondent is not known, an alphabetic index must be referenced to learn the location before a record can be filed or retrieved from the geographic file. Like the subject and numeric storage methods, geographic storage may require two operations to store and retrieve a record—a check of the index for the correct file location and then the actual search of the file. These disadvantages become insignificant, however, for business operations requiring important data by geographic location.

GEOGRAPHIC RECORDS STORAGE ARRANGEMENTS

The geographic arrangement of records in an office depends on the following:

1. The type of business.
2. The way reference is made to records (i.e., by state, by ZIP Code, by geographic region, by country).
3. The geographic areas related to records.

The geographic arrangement can be as simple as a file of city streets or countries of the world. More complex systems include subdivisions and are arranged in order from *major* to *minor* geographic units; for example, (1) country name, (2) state name or state equivalent (provinces, for example), (3) city name, and (4) correspondent's name. In general, the filing segment in geographic records storage includes geographic filing units first, followed by the correspondent's name. If geographic areas are subdivided by subject such as Accounts Receivable, Sales, or Purchasing, the subject area would be considered second and then the correspondent's name. Subdivisions by subject may be appropriate for centralized records in a company that maintains extensive business operations through branch offices in different locations. The location of the branch office could be subdivided by operational functions and then by correspondent names. Most likely, such centralization of records would be through centralized electronic records accessed in various company sites through an intranet.

Two basic arrangements are commonly used in geographic storage: (1) the dictionary arrangement and (2) the encyclopedic arrangement. You studied the dictionary and encyclopedic arrangements in Chapter 7, Subject Records Management. Your familiarity with these two arrangements will add to your understanding of the discussion and illustrations that follow.

What are the two geographic storage arrangements?

Dictionary Storage Arrangement

The **dictionary arrangement** for geographic records is an arrangement of records in alphabetic order (A–Z). Use the dictionary arrangement when filing *single* geographic units such as all streets, all cities, all states, or all countries. Two guide plans are possible: the lettered guide plan or the location name guide plan.

What are two commonly used guide plans?

Lettered Guide Plan

A **lettered guide plan** is an arrangement of geographic records with primary guides labeled with alphabetic letters. The lettered guide plan can be used in any geographic arrangement. For a large volume of records stored geographically, alphabetic guides cut storage and retrieval time by guiding the eye quickly to the correct alphabetic section of storage.

Figure 9–1 shows a dictionary arrangement of records by country in a lettered guide plan. The primary guides are one-fifth cut lettered guides arranged in a straight line in the first file drawer position (from left to right). The general country folders are third-cut folders arranged in a straight line in the third folder tab position (far right) in the file drawer. As you can see, a lettered guide plan may be excessive in a file consisting of only a few, diverse names.

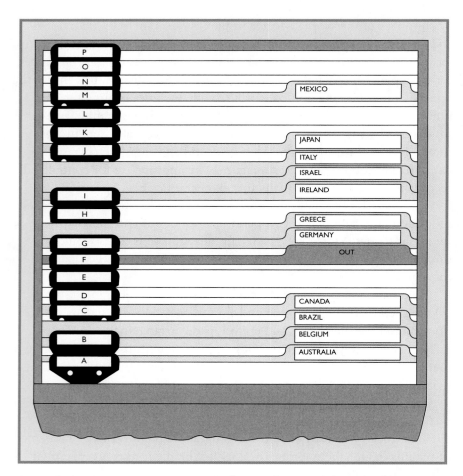

Figure 9–1 Dictionary Arrangement of Records, Lettered Guide Plan

Location Name Guide Plan

A **location name guide plan** is an arrangement of geographic records with primary guides labeled with location names. When location names are few but diverse, use the location name guide plan.

Figure 9–2 shows a location name guide plan in a dictionary arrangement of foreign country names. The primary guides are one-fifth cut country name guides arranged in a straight line in the file drawer first position. The general country folders are one-third cut folders arranged in a straight line in the file drawer with a third-position tab location (far right side). Figures 9–1 and 9–2 show the different guide plans in a dictionary arrangement of identical records.

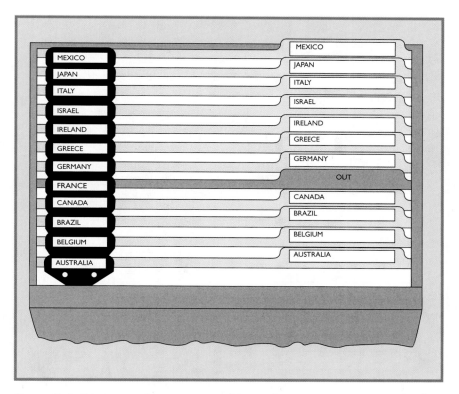

Figure 9–2 Dictionary Arrangement of Records, Location Name Guide Plan

Encyclopedic Storage Arrangement

The **encyclopedic arrangement** is the alphabetic arrangement of major geographic divisions plus one or more geographic *subdivisions* also arranged in alphabetic order. Similar to the dictionary storage arrangement, the encyclopedic arrangement makes use of either a lettered guide plan or a location name guide plan. Guides in a storage system provide sufficient guidance to speed the storage and retrieval of records. Guides should not dominate a storage area and become an efficiency barrier. Although lettered guides with closed captions require more thought when filing (i.e., A–D, E–H, I–P), they provide a means of using fewer lettered guides.

Figures 9–3 and 9–4 (see page 228) illustrate geographic records storage in an encyclopedic arrangement. Compare the guide plans used for these identical records: Figure 9–3 uses a lettered guide plan and Figure 9–4 uses a location name guide plan. The major geographic units in the illustrations are state names; the subdivisions are city names. Refer to the illustrations as you study the following detailed explanations of the file arrangements, the guide plans, and the folder contents.

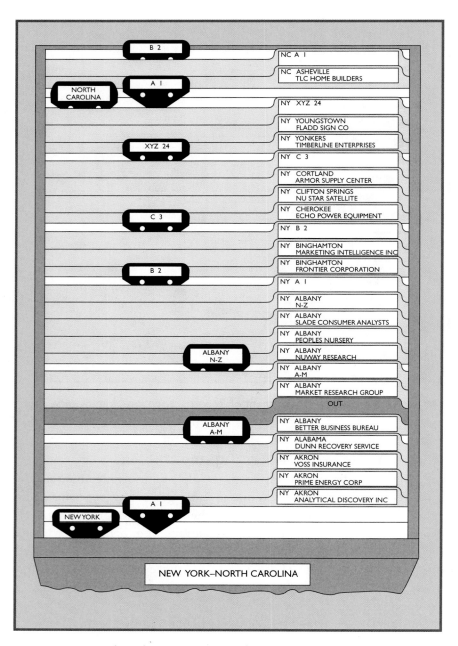

Figure 9–3 Encyclopedic Arrangement of Records, Lettered Guide Plan

Lettered Guide Plan

Figure 9–3 shows part of a drawer of New York and North Carolina records stored by the lettered guide plan. Refer to Figure 9–3 as you study the following arrangement description:

1. In first position in the drawer are fifth-cut, primary guides for the state names NEW YORK and NORTH CAROLINA, the largest geographic division in this storage plan.

2. In second position are the secondary guides. The secondary guides are fifth-cut alphabetic guides that divide the states into alphabetic sections. Each guide indicates the alphabetic section within which records with city names beginning with that letter are stored. The guide tabs are numbered consecutively so that they will be kept in correct order.

3. In third position are special guides. Special city guides indicate cities with a high volume of records (NY ALBANY). A–M and N–Z provide a separation of correspondents' *names* in the NY ALBANY city section. These guides are fifth-cut.

4. In fourth position as your eye moves left to right across the contents of the file are the folders. Folders are one-third cut, third-position tab folders arranged in a straight line at the right of the file drawer. Notice the three kinds of folders used in this file arrangement: general alphabetic state folders, special city folders, and individual folders.

   a. Each secondary guide is accompanied by a corresponding general alphabetic city folder, which is placed at the end of that alphabetic section. The folder has the same caption as that of the secondary guide. Each general alphabetic folder contains records from correspondents located in cities with names beginning with the letter of the alphabet on the folder. For instance, the general A 1 folder might contain correspondence from organizations and individuals in New York cities such as Adams, Akron, Alabama, and Amsterdam but not from Albany because that city has its own special city folders.

   b. The special city folders accompany the special city guides (NY ALBANY A–M and NY ALBANY N–Z).

   c. Individual folders for correspondents are arranged alphabetically by city and then by correspondents' names. The label caption for individual folders includes the name of the correspondent's state and city on the first line. The correspondent's name is on the second line.

5. Also in fourth position in the drawer are OUT guides. The OUT guides are third-cut, third-position guides and mark the location of a borrowed folder.

What kinds of folders are needed?

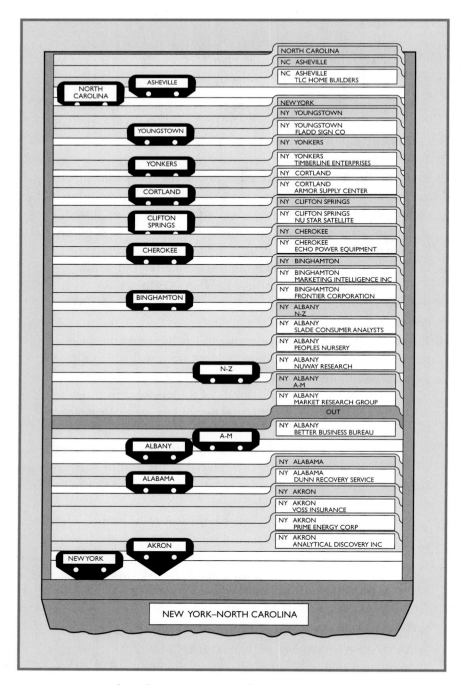

Figure 9–4 Encyclopedic Arrangement of Records, Location Name Guide Plan

Location Name Guide Plan

Probably the most frequently found location name guide plan arrangement is one that uses state names as the first filing segment (or country names for international operations). Figure 9–4 shows part of a drawer of

New York and North Carolina records stored by the location name guide plan. Refer to Figure 9–4 as you study the following arrangement description:

1. In first position in the drawer are primary guides for state names NEW YORK and NORTH CAROLINA. The guides are one-fifth cut, first-position guides.

2. In second position are city guides. AKRON is the first city guide after the NEW YORK state guide. Because the city guides stay in the drawer in their correct positions, they do not need to include the name of the state. The guides are one-fifth cut, second-position guides.

3. In third position are special lettered guides A–M and N–Z. These special guides show an alphabetic division of correspondents' names in the city of ALBANY section. Special guides speed the location of active or high-volume records. The guides are one-fifth cut, third-position guides.

How are special guides used?

4. In fourth position in the drawer are all folders. *General* folders are shaded in the illustration to distinguish them from *individual* folders. The folders are one-third cut, third-position folders. Notice that a general city folder bearing the same caption as the city guide comes at the end of the folders behind each guide.

   a. The general state folder for NEW YORK is at the end of the NEW YORK section. File correspondence from New York in this general state folder when no general folder for that city is in the file. Arrange the records alphabetically in the general state folder by city name first, followed by the correspondent's name. If correspondent's names are identical, use the street name and house number to determine correct order. Store all records from the same correspondent in chronologic order with the most recent record in front.

   b. A general city folder is used for every city guide used in the file drawer. Place the general city folder at the end of the city subdivision. ALBANY has two general city folders, one for correspondents' names beginning with A to M and a second general city folder for correspondents' names beginning with N to Z. Store all records in general city folders alphabetically by correspondent's name. Arrange records from the same correspondent with the most recent record in front. When records begin to accumulate for one correspondent, say five or more, consider opening an individual folder for that correspondent.

   c. Individual folders for correspondents are arranged alphabetically by name within their state and city sections. The folder label captions include the state and city locations as well as the correspondents' names. Because folders will be removed from the file, the comprehensive caption helps to prevent misfiles when borrowed records are returned to storage. Arrange records in individual folders with the most recent record in front. Be sure to store all records in folders with the top of the document at the left of the folder.

5. Also in fourth position in the file drawer are one-third cut OUT guides, which show the location of borrowed records.

GEOGRAPHIC RECORDS STORAGE INDEXES

You are already familiar with indexes because you studied the use of alphabetic and master indexes in Chapter 7, Subject Records Management, and alphabetic indexes and accession logs in Chapter 8, Numeric Records Management. Because geographic records are arranged first by location and then by company or individual names, the correspondent's location must be known before a record can be located. If the location of a correspondent is not known, the file user must use an alphabetic index.

Alphabetic Index

The alphabetic index lists all correspondents in geographic storage. This index can be a computer database index, a printed list, or a card file. However the index is maintained, the index must be easy to update and keep current. Names will be added and deleted, and names and addresses will change. Information in the index should include the correspondent's name and full address. Figure 9–5 is a database alphabetic index for geographic records storage. The correspondents' names are in alphabetic order in column one. The state, city, and street locations are shown in the remaining columns. All correspondents are listed in the index, including correspondents whose records are stored in general city and state folders. If the information for this index is stored in a database, users can access an individual name on the screen without looking for the name on a printed list. Even with the capability to check electronic indexes, a printed copy of the index should be available.

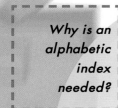

Why is an alphabetic index needed?

Master Index

A master index is a complete listing of all filing segments in the filing system. Figure 9–6 on page 232 is a database master index. States were sorted first, then the city names, and finally the correspondents' names. The master index shows at a glance the geographic units covered in the filing system and is especially useful to new file users. A printed copy of the index is kept in the front of the file drawer or another readily accessible location. If the alphabetic index is prepared with database

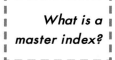

What is a master index?

INDEXED NAME	STATE	CITY	BLDG	STREET	SEE ALSO
ANALYTICAL DISCOVERY INC	NY	AKRON	4873	CENTER ST	
ARMOR SUPPLY CENTER	NY	CORTLAND	1601	FOURTH ST	
BETTER BUSINESS BUREAU	NC	ASHEVILLE	389	MAIN ST	NY ALBANY
BETTER BUSINESS BUREAU	NY	ALBANY	150	ROWAN ST	NC ASHEVILLE
COMPUTER MAGIC	NY	GENESEO	38	MAIN ST	
DUNN RECOVERY SERVICE	NY	ALABAMA	60	JACKSON RD	
ECHO POWER EQUIPMENT	NY	CHEROKEE	174	MILITARY RD	
FLADD SIGN CO	NY	YOUNGSTOWN	30	CUMMINGS ST	
FRONTIER CORPORATION	NY	BINGHAMTON	20	SHUMAN BLVD	
KERRY COMPANY THE	NY	ALBANY	204	DELAWARE AVE	
LUCKY STORES INC	NY	BINGHAMTON	145	ROSEMARY ST	
MARKET RESEARCH GROUP	NY	ALBANY	4055	MOTOR AVE	
MARKETING INTELLIGENCE INC	NY	BATH	451	DUNBAR RD	
NU STAR SATELLITE	NY	CLIFTON SPRINGS	11	MAIN ST	
NUWAY RESEARCH	NY	ALBANY	44	BROADWAY	
PEOPLES NURSERY	NY	ALBANY	727	SECOND ST	
PRIME ENERGY CORP	NY	AKRON	2470	MILES RD	
SLADE CONSUMER ANALYSTS	NY	ALBANY	58	SYLVAN AVE	
TIMBERLINE ENTERPRISES	NY	YONKERS	3034	WALL ST	
TLC HOME BUILDERS	NC	ASHEVILLE	20	RIVER DR	
VOSS INSURANCE	NY	AKRON	1422	EUCLID AVE	

Figure 9–5 Database Alphabetic Index for Geographic Records Storage

software and names are kept updated, queries can be created for viewing or printing an updated alphabetic or master index at any time; or an individual record can be viewed or printed. Other software packages that allow re-sorting and moving of columns can also produce a master index.

GEOGRAPHIC RECORDS STORAGE AND RETRIEVAL PROCEDURES

Supplies used in the geographic method are similar to those used in other storage methods. These supplies consist of guides, folders, OUT indicators, and an alphabetic index. You may want to review the section on filing supplies in Chapter 5 before continuing with the discussion of storage and retrieval procedures.

The same basic steps for storing records in alphabetic, subject, and numeric methods (inspecting, indexing, coding, cross-referencing,

STATE	CITY	INDEXED NAME	BLDG	STREET
NC	ASHEVILLE	BETTER BUSINESS BUREAU	389	MAIN ST
NC	ASHEVILLE	TLC HOME BUILDERS	20	RIVER DR
NY	AKRON	ANALYTICAL DISCOVERY INC	4873	CENTER ST
NY	AKRON	PRIME ENERGY CORP	2470	MILES RD
NY	AKRON	VOSS INSURANCE	1422	EUCLID AVE
NY	ALABAMA	DUNN RECOVERY SERVICE	60	JACKSON RD
NY	ALBANY	BETTER BUSINESS BUREAU	150	ROWAN ST
NY	ALBANY	KERRY COMPANY THE	204	DELAWARE AVE
NY	ALBANY	MARKET RESEARCH GROUP	4055	MOTOR AVE
NY	ALBANY	NUWAY RESEARCH	44	BROADWAY
NY	ALBANY	PEOPLES NURSERY	727	SECOND ST
NY	ALBANY	SLADE CONSUMER ANALYSTS	58	SYLVAN AVE
NY	BATH	MARKETING INTELLIGENCE INC	451	DUNBAR RD
NY	BINGHAMTON	FRONTIER CORPORATION	20	SHUMAN BLVD
NY	BINGHAMTON	LUCKY STORES INC	145	ROSEMARY ST
NY	CHEROKEE	ECHO POWER EQUIPMENT	174	MILITARY RD
NY	CLIFTON SPRINGS	NU STAR SATELLITE	11	MAIN ST
NY	CORTLAND	ARMOR SUPPLY CENTER	1601	FOURTH ST
NY	GENESEO	COMPUTER MAGIC	38	MAIN ST
NY	YONKERS	TIMBERLINE ENTERPRISES	3034	WALL ST
NY	YOUNGSTOWN	FLADD SIGN CO	30	CUMMINGS ST

Figure 9–6 Master Index for Geographic Storage

sorting, and storing) are also followed in the geographic method. Minor differences are explained in the following paragraphs. Retrieval procedures (requisitioning, charging out, and following up) are also basically the same.

Inspecting and Indexing

Check to see that the record has been released for storage (inspect) and scan the letter for content to determine its proper place in storage (index). In Figure 9–7 the handwritten letters JK indicate that the letter is released for storage.

Coding

Code the document for geographic storage by marking the correspondents' *location* (address) first. Code by circling the filing segment (see Figure 9–7 Raleigh, NC). Write numbers above or below the filing segment to show the order of indexing and alphabetizing units. Then code the name of the correspondent by underlining the name, placing diagonals between the units, and numbering the succeeding units. Figure 9–7 shows a letter coded for the geographic storage method.

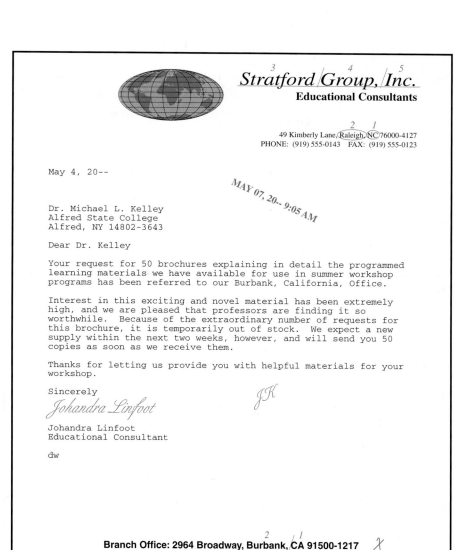

Figure 9–7 Letter Coded for Geographic Method

After coding documents, consult the alphabetic index to see if the correspondent is currently in the system. If not, add the new correspondent's name and address to the index.

Cross-Referencing

Cross-referencing is as necessary in the geographic storage method as it is in the alphabetic storage method. In Chapters 2 and 3, personal and business names are listed that may require cross-references. In this chapter, additional cross-references may be needed for (1) names of organizations having more than one address and (2) organizations located at one address and doing business under other names at other locations.

What names require cross-references?

In the geographic storage method, insert cross-references in both the alphabetic index and the storage file. In the alphabetic index, prepare an entry for every name by which a correspondent may be known or by which records may be requested. For the letter shown in Figure 9–7, a cross-reference shows a branch office located in another city—two locations where a filer might look for a record from the Stratford Group, Inc. (see Figure 9–8). Figure 9–9 shows a cross-reference entry in a database record.

In the file, three types of cross-references can be used: (1) cross-reference sheets that are stored in folders to refer the filer to specific records, (2) cross-reference guides that are placed in storage as permanent

CROSS-REFERENCE SHEET

Name or Subject
CA/Burbank
Stratford/Group, / Inc
2964 Broadway

Date of Record
May 4, 20 - -

Regarding
Programmed learning materials for summer workshop

SEE

Name or Subject
NC Raleigh
Stratford Group, Inc
49 Kimberly Lanec

Date Filed ___ *5/7/20 - -* ___ By ___ *JK* ___

Figure 9–8 Cross-Reference Sheet for Geographic Method

CUSTOMERS

INDEXED NAME	BETTER BUSINESS BUREAU
NAME	BETTER BUSINESS BUREAU
BLDG	150
STREET	ROWAN ST
CITY	ALBANY
STATE	NY
ZIP CODE	12201-1560
SEE ALSO	NC ASHEVILLE
DATE	09/09/2001

Record: ◄ ◄ 5 ► ►► ►✱ of 21

Figure 9–9 Cross-Reference in a Database Record

cross-references, and (3) SEE ALSO cross-reference notations on sheets or on folder tabs. Each of these cross-references is explained next.

A **cross-reference sheet** is a sheet placed in an alternate location in the file that directs the filer to a specific record stored in a different location other than where the filer is searching. The cross-reference sheet in Figure 9–8 is made for the branch office indicated on the letter shown in Figure 9–7. The original letter is stored in the N section of geographic storage (NORTH CAROLINA), but the cross-reference sheet is stored in the C section (CALIFORNIA).

A **cross-reference guide** is a special guide that serves as a permanent marker in storage indicating that all records pertaining to a correspondent are stored elsewhere. For example, the cross-reference guide in Figure 9–10 shows that all records for Lockwood, Inc., are stored under the home office location in Ann Arbor, MI, not the branch office location in St. Clair Shores, MI. The words *Ann Arbor* must be written on each record when it is coded. The cross-reference guide is stored according to the location on the top line of its caption in alphabetic order with other geographically labeled guides and folders.

A **SEE ALSO cross-reference** is a notation on a folder tab or cross-reference sheet that directs the filer to multiple locations for related

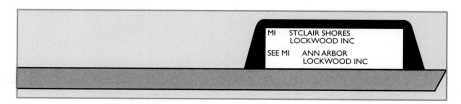

MI	STCLAIR SHORES
	LOCKWOOD INC
SEE MI	ANN ARBOR
	LOCKWOOD INC

Figure 9–10 Cross-Reference Guide for Geographic Method

How are
SEE ALSO
references
prepared?

information. If a company has two addresses and records are stored under both addresses, two SEE ALSO cross-references would be used. For example, if Windsor Publishing Co., Inc., conducts business in Houston, TX, and also in Milan, Italy, the references would indicate that information for this company can be found in two storage locations. If these SEE ALSO cross-references are sheets of paper, they are kept as the first items in their respective folders so that they will not be overlooked (see Figure 9–11). Instead of being written on separate cross-reference sheets, this SEE ALSO information may be keyed on the tabs of the two folders for the Windsor Publishing Co., Inc. (see Figure 9–12).

CROSS-REFERENCE SHEET

Name or Subject
TX/Houston
Windsor/Publishing/Co., /Inc.
1313 North Sixth Street

Date of Record

Regarding

SEE ALSO

Name or Subject
TX Wichita Falls
Windsor Publishing Co., Inc.
2264 Evanston Avenue

Date Filed   11/4/20--   By   JK

Figure 9–11a **Cross-Reference Sheet for SEE ALSO References**

CROSS-REFERENCE SHEET

Name or Subject

TX/Wichita/Falls

Windsor/Publishing/Co., /Inc.

2264 Evanston Avenue

Date of Record

_____

_____

_____

Regarding

_____

_____

_____

_____

SEE ALSO

Name or Subject

TX Houston

Windsor Publishing Co., Inc.

1313 North Sixth Street

Date Filed _____*11/4/20 --*_____ By _____*JK*_____

Figure 9–11b **Cross-Reference Sheet for SEE ALSO References**

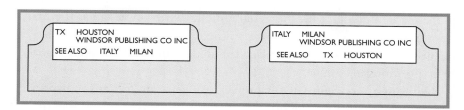

Figure 9–12 **SEE ALSO References on Folder Tabs**

Sorting

Sort records alphabetically by location. Sort first by the largest geographic unit such as country or state name; then sort by the first subdivision such as state equivalent or city; finally sort by the names of the
correspondents, in alphabetic order.

Storing

Individual correspondents' folders, special city folders, alphabetic subdivisions of cities with their corresponding general folders, general folders
for alphabetic grouping of cities, and general state or regional folders may
be part of a geographic records storage arrangement. Therefore, placing a
record in the wrong folder is easy to do. Because of the complexity of a
geographic arrangement, be extremely careful when storing.

Lettered Guide Plan

Assuming that the arrangement is by state and city, look for the primary
state guide. Then use the lettered guides to locate the alphabetic state
section within which the city name falls. After finding that section, look
for an individual correspondent's folder. If you find one, store the record
in that folder in chronological order with the most recent record on top.

If an individual folder for the correspondent is *not* in the file, look for
a general city folder. If a general city folder is in the file, store the record
according to the correspondent's name in the same manner as in an
alphabetic arrangement. If a general city folder is *not* in the file, store the
record in the general alphabetic folder within which the city name falls.
Again, arrange the city names according to the rules for alphabetic
indexing.

Within a city, arrange the names of correspondents alphabetically;
group the records of one correspondent with the most recent date on
top. If identically named correspondents reside in one city, follow the
rules for filing identical names (see Chapters 2 and 3 for review).

When enough correspondence has accumulated to warrant making a
separate folder for a specific city, a specific geographic section, or an individual correspondent, remove the records from the general folder and
prepare a new folder with the geographic location on its tab as the first
item of information. Then prepare a similarly labeled guide, if one is
needed, for the folder. Finally, place the folder and guide in their alphabetic positions in storage.

Although requirements for preparing a separate folder for a specific
geographic location vary, a good rule of thumb is this: When five or
more records accumulate that pertain to one specific geographic location (such as a state, city, or a region), prepare a separate folder for that
location.

Location Name Guide Plan

Again, assuming that the arrangement is by state and city, find the primary state guide and look for the correct city name on a secondary guide. If a city guide is present, search for an individual correspondent's folder. If one exists, store the record in the folder according to date.

If an individual folder is *not* in the file, store the record in the correct general city folder according to the geographic location of the correspondent and then by name, in alphabetic order with the other records within the folder. If more than one record is stored for a correspondent, arrange the records chronologically with the most recent date on top.

If a general city folder is *not* in the file, place the record in the general state folder, first according to the alphabetic order of the city name and then by correspondent's name and street address (if necessary), according to the rules for alphabetic indexing.

Retrieving

Retrieving a record from a geographic file involves these five steps:

1. Asking for the record (requisition).
2. Checking the alphabetic index to determine the location of the record.
3. Removing the record from the files.
4. Completing charge-out documentation for the record.
5. Following up to see that the record is returned to storage within a specified time.

> *What are the retrieval procedures?*

Requisition

Requests for a record stored by geographic arrangement may identify it by location or by correspondent's name. If the request is made by location, finding the record should be simple. If the request is made by name, however, refer to the alphabetic index or a computer database to locate the address used to store the record.

Charge-Out

After you have located and retrieved the record, charge it out in the same manner that you charge out records from any other storage method. Be sure to insert an OUT indicator at the storage position of the record. A Charge-Out field can be added in a records database and shown in the alphabetic index.

Follow-Up

The follow-up procedures used to secure the return of borrowed records are the same for the geographic method as those used with any other storage method. Use a tickler file or another reminder system to be sure that records are returned to storage at designated times and to remind yourself of records that need to be brought to someone's attention in the future. If OUT information is recorded in a database table, this information can be sorted by date and used as a tickler file.

IMPLICATIONS OF E-COMMERCE FOR GEOGRAPHIC RECORDS

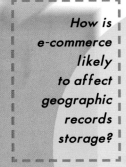

How is e-commerce likely to affect geographic records storage?

Because e-commerce offers businesses opportunities to compete globally for new customers, the number of businesses establishing a positive, on-line presence is growing rapidly. The growing use of the Internet can be expected to continue for years to come, as wireless technology and portable devices that connect with the Internet are likely to become as common as the telephone. As businesses use the Internet effectively to reach out to new locations and market their goods and services worldwide, they will likely store and evaluate records by these new locations as well.

SUMMARY

Geographic records management, grouping and storing records by location, is expected to become increasingly important as more businesses, small and large, expand operations to world markets. The Internet and advances in communication technology have boosted a global economy. Multinational companies, government offices, petroleum industries, financial companies, mail-order houses, publishers, utilities, and real estate agencies are examples of organizations that are likely to use geographic records management.

Geographic records storage requires a more complex system of guides and folders than other types of records storage, and storing and retrieving records can be more time-consuming. However, companies that need information by location to make good business decisions are likely to choose geographic records management.

Two basic arrangements are commonly used in geographic storage: the dictionary arrangement and the encyclopedic arrangement. The arrangement used depends on whether subdivisions of the geographic units are necessary. Either the lettered guide plan or the location name guide plan can be used. Whether the files contain a small number of diverse names or a large number of similar names will likely determine the guide plan.

Because geographic records are arranged first by location and then by company or individual names, the correspondent's location must be known before a record can be located. When correspondence is stored by the geographic method, an alphabetic index is essential. A master index, which shows at a glance the geographic units covered in the filing system, is also helpful and is especially useful to new file users.

Except for indexing and coding, the storage and retrieval procedures for geographic records storage are similar to those used for other storage methods. Indexing and coding require looking first at the location of the document and then at the name, the document subject, or project title being stored. Cross-references should be placed in both the alphabetic index and the storage file.

A greater use of geographic records storage is expected as more organizations use the Internet's capability to expand in domestic and global markets and as wireless, portable devices that connect to the Internet become commonplace.

IMPORTANT TERMS

cross-reference sheet
cross-reference guide
dictionary arrangement
encyclopedic arrangement

geographic records management
lettered guide plan
location name guide plan
SEE ALSO cross-reference

REVIEW AND DISCUSSION

1. How has the developing global economy created a greater need for geographic records storage? (Obj. 1)

2. Name three kinds of businesses that are likely to use the geographic method of storage. (Obj. 2)

3. What are the advantages and disadvantages of the geographic storage method? (Obj. 3)

4. Explain how the dictionary and encyclopedic arrangements of geographic records differ. (Obj.4)

5. Explain the difference between the lettered guide plan and the location name guide plan. (Obj. 5)

6. Describe the arrangement of guides and folders in an encyclopedic arrangement of a geographic file using the lettered guide plan. The geographic units covered in the arrangement are state names and city names. (Obj. 6)

7. In your description of guides and folders in your answer to question 6, did you include general STATE folders? Explain why you did or did not include them. (Obj. 6)

8. Explain how an alphabetic index is used in geographic records storage. (Obj. 7)

9. Explain how indexing and coding for the geographic method are different from indexing and coding for the alphabetic method of records storage. (Obj. 8)

10. List three types of cross-references used in the geographic method and state where they are placed or stored in the filing system. (Obj. 9)

11. Explain the effect e-commerce is likely to have on geographic records storage in the future. (Obj. 10)

APPLICATIONS (APP)

Critical
Thinking

APP 9-1. Selecting the Most Efficient Geographic
Arrangement (Objs. 4, 5, and 6)

For each of the following scenarios, identify the most efficient geographic arrangements and explain the reasons for your choices. Identification of this arrangement should include as many of the following elements as appropriate: major and minor geographic units, encyclopedic or dictionary arrangement, lettered guide plan or location name guide plan.

1. A local pizza parlor keeps a database of delivery records by customer ZIP Code, street address, and name.

2. The home office of a large food processing/packing plant is located in Iowa; however, the company maintains correspondence and records to branch offices in three regions of the United States—Western, Northeast, and South Central—as well as in Japan, Canada, and England.

3. A newspaper publisher in Scranton, PA, maintains a file of *all* streets in the city. The street name file identifies paper carriers who distribute home delivery to those locations. The newspaper also has mail subscribers in the states of Pennsylvania, New York, Ohio, and West Virginia.

4. A garment manufacturer maintains records by its operations in ten cities. City locations include the following:

United States	Canada
Los Angeles, CA	Montreal, Quebec
Philadelphia, PA	Calgary, Alberta
Detroit, MI	London, Ontario

Central America	South America
Managua, Nicaragua	Cuernavaca, Morelos, Mexico
León, Nicaragua	Zamora, Michoacan, Mexico

Data Disk

APP 9-2. Geographic Indexes (Objs. 8 and 9)

1. Open the *Access* database file, APP 9–2.mdb, from the data disk. Open the APP 9–2 table. Three records from the list below have been entered as examples. Enter the remaining records into the database. The BLDG field is a number field; do not add leading zeros. For names with more than one address, enter each record separately and enter cross-reference information in the SEE ALSO field. (This information may seem unnecessary when all records are viewed. When an individual record or a subset of the records is viewed, however, the SEE ALSO field alerts users that the same name is filed in another location.) Use all caps for all fields and enter punctuation only in the NAME field. Sort the table in ascending order by the INDEXED NAME field.

2. Create a query named Alphabetic Index to include the INDEXED NAME, STATE, CITY, BLDG, STREET, and SEE ALSO fields. Design the query to sort by INDEXED NAME, then by STATE, then by CITY, and then by STREET fields. (Do not sort the BLDG or SEE ALSO fields.) Print the query table.

3. Create a query named MASTER INDEX to include the STATE, CITY, INDEXED NAME, BLDG, STREET, and SEE ALSO fields. Design the query to sort by STATE, then by CITY, then by INDEXED NAME, and then by STREET fields. Print the query table.

Records:

a. John Powers Electronics
   24 Delaware Ave.
   Rochester, NY 14623-2944

b. Indian River Community
   College
   3209 Virginia Ave.
   Fort Pierce, FL 34982-3209

c. Computer Land, Inc.
   30 Shepherd Rd.
   Springfield, IL 62708-0101

d. Portland Cement Co.
   12000 Lakeville Rd.
   Portland, OR 97219-4233

e. Wilkes Tree Farm
   400 Stanton Christiana Rd.
   Newark, DE 19713-0401

f. Ms. Beverly C. Monroe
   1000 Gordon Rd.
   Rochester, NY 14623-1089

g. Electric City, Inc.
   3201 Southwest Traffic Way
   Kansas City, MO 64111-3201

h. Abba D Plumbing
   901 S. National Ave.
   Springfield, MO 65804-0910

i. Penn Valley Community
   College
   3300 Southwest Traffic Way
   Kansas City, MO 64111-3300

j. Cerre Ceramic Studios
   7250 State Ave.
   Kansas City, KS 66112-7255

k. Toby Leese Tack Shop
   175 University Ave.
   Newark, NJ 07102-1175

l. John Powers Electronics
   10 State St.
   Rochester, NY 14623-2944

m. City Office Supplies
   4281 Drake St.
   Rochester, MI 48306-0698

n. Armstrong State College
   11935 Abercorn St.
   Savannah, GA 31419-1092

o. Pioneer Center Furniture
   560 Westport Rd.
   Kansas City, MO 64111-0568

p. Amy's Sports Center
   874 Dillingham Blvd.
   Honolulu, HI 96817-8743

q. Genesis Cinema
   1325 Lynch St.
   Jackson, MS 39203-1325

r. Computer Magic
   84 Center St.
   Springfield, MA 01101-2028

s. Computer Magic
   24 Fourth Ave.
   New York, NY 10018-4826

t. The Computer Store
   2847 14th St.
   New York, NY 10018-2032

APPLYING THE RULES

Job 12, Geographic Filing.

PART 4

RECORDS MANAGEMENT TECHNOLOGY

10 Electronic Records

11 Image Records

Part 4 provides comprehensive coverage of electronic and image records. Optical disks are presented in depth in Chapter 10 as electronic image records. Micrographics technology is discussed in Chapter 11. All phases of the micrographics process—filming, processing, producing, and reading/viewing are discussed. Software programs used in electronic and image records are discussed as well.

CHAPTER 10

ELECTRONIC RECORDS

LEARNING OBJECTIVES

1. Define *electronic record* and identify uses of electronic records.
2. Define and describe types of magnetic and optical media.
3. Discuss the systems concept as it relates to electronic records systems.
4. Describe indexing and retrieving electronic records.
5. Discuss electronic records issues related to records retention—duplicate records, media compatibility and stability, access, and electronic mail.
6. Describe types of storage equipment for active and inactive electronic records.
7. Discuss electronic records retention.
8. Explain the need for electronic records system and network security.
9. Discuss the need for records and information management software for electronic records.
10. Describe three emerging technologies.

USE OF ELECTRONIC RECORDS

Why is paper usage increasing?

Paper records have been the most widely used records media for decades. Because of the number of paper records stored in workplaces and off-site storage facilities, paper will be the primary records media for some time. Paper usage is increasing, mainly because of increased use of photocopiers, fax machines, and high-quality printers. Word processing and spreadsheet software programs also have contributed to the use of paper because users can make changes or corrections and print a new copy much more quickly than when this type of work was done with a typewriter. However, in some companies or in some departments, electronic records are the primary records media. An **electronic record** is a record stored on electronic storage media that can be readily accessed or changed. An electronic record is often referred to as a *machine-readable record*—digitized and coded information that, to be understood, must be translated by a computer or other type of equipment.

Although computers are more commonly associated with creation, storage, and processing of electronic records, other machines can produce and maintain electronic records as well. For example, voice dictation machines, telephone answering machines, and other audiotape recorders; video recorders and playback devices; medical instruments used for diagnostic testing and imaging; and scientific instruments used for various geographic imaging applications create and store electronic records.

Electronic records may contain quantitative data, text, images, or sound that originate as an electronic signal. **Data** are groups of characters that represent a specific value or condition. Data that have been given value through analysis, interpretation, or compilation into a meaningful form is **information**. Information is electronically encoded for storage and processing by computer, audio equipment, video devices, or other machines. A memorandum created with word processing software and stored as a computer file is an electronic record. A printed copy of that memorandum is not an electronic record. A computer database index of a subject filing system is an electronic record. A computer-generated copy of the subject index printed on paper or microfiche is not an electronic record.

Improvements in computer equipment and software are the main reason for the growth of electronic records usage. The number of video equipment installations, audio recorders, and scientific and medical instruments has similarly increased. Accounting, payroll, and other financial areas were the earliest computerized applications. Human resources data, inventory management, and physical property records are also stored electronically. Other electronic records applications include student records maintained by schools and colleges; experimental data maintained by research laboratories; medical records maintained by hospitals and clinics; construction project drawings and site plans.[1]

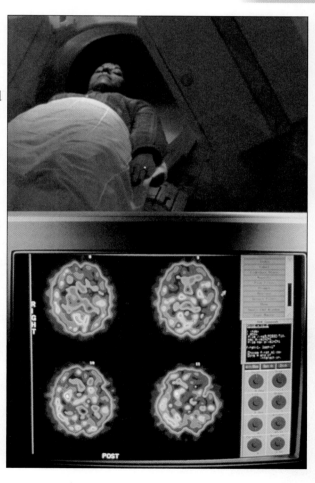

Modern medical equipment provides electronic records of patient data.

What do electronic records contain?

[1]William Saffady, *Managing Electronic Records*, 2d ed. Prairie Village, KS: ARMA International, 1998.

The computing environment has evolved from large mainframe computer installations, to microcomputers or personal computers (PCs), to network centers. A **network** is a group of computers connected to each other by communication lines to share information and resources. A **local area network (LAN)** is a data communication network intended to allow several computers, connected through one computer within a limited geographic area, to share data and software. Computers or workstations connected by a LAN are usually within the same building or within one mile of each other. A **wide area network (WAN)** is a high-speed data transmission network that links mainframe computers, personal computers, and other equipment located in geographic places more than one mile apart, allowing user groups to share computer data and software. The Internet is a wide area network. A **storage area network (SAN)** is a high-speed network that provides fast, reliable access among computers and independent storage devices. A SAN carries only traffic between servers and storage devices; it does not carry e-mail or other applications.

Managing records in electronic form requires cooperation and understanding between records and information managers and information technology/information systems managers. Records and information management and information technology/information systems areas are converging as digital media blur the distinctions among visual, print, audio, and multimedia records.[2]

TYPES OF ELECTRONIC MEDIA

What media is electronic media?

Electronic media include both magnetic media and optical media. Optical media are also electronic image media. (Image media are discussed in Chapter 11.) Magnetic recording has been the primary computer storage technology since the 1950s. It is also the most widely used technology for video and audio recordings. Magnetic media can store and retrieve a document faster than other storage media. Because the moving parts of magnetic media are subject to failure, backups are regularly scheduled. When erased or damaged, data can be restored from backups.

Magnetic Media

Magnetic media are a variety of magnetically coated materials used by computers for data storage; e.g., cartridge, cassette, floppy disk, hard disk, magnetic tape, etc. Magnetic cartridges and cassettes may be incorporated into a variety of applications. Microcomputer users are familiar with hard

[2]Sue Myburgh, "The Convergence of Information Technology & Information Management," *The Information Management Journal* Vol. 34, No. 2 (April 2000), pp. 4–16.

and floppy disks. Larger computer installations are more likely to use magnetic tape, which has been the preferred secondary storage medium for decades. *Secondary storage* is used when data are migrated or moved from on-line storage to off-line or off-site storage. On-line electronic records are on media housed on magnetic or optical disk drives within a computer system, also known as *primary storage*. Electronic records stored off-line are on media located apart from the computer device on which they will be retrieved and processed.

A magnetic disk is a platter created from a material, such as aluminum, coated with a magnetizable recording material. The recording surface is divided into rings or tracks, and an electronic read/write head is used for recording and playback. A computer sends instructions to a magnetic disk drive, which positions the read/write head above a track while the rotating platter brings the selected disk segment under the head. Information is usually recorded linearly within each track.

Magnetic disks may be rigid (hard disks) or flexible (floppy disks). A **hard disk** is a thin, rigid metal platter covered with a substance that holds data in the form of magnetized spots. A hard disk is usually called a *hard drive* because the storage device and the recording medium are considered as one unit. Hard drive storage capacity is measured in megabytes (MB) (one thousand characters) or gigabytes (GB) (one thousand megabytes or 1,000 million characters). Compression software that removes blank spaces between words, in boxed material, and in graphical material can conserve disk space in such a way that more data can be stored on a disk. Decompression software can restore the data to useable form for viewing or processing.

Several small hard drives can supply mainframe-class storage capabilities when configured in an array. A computer's operating system treats multiple drives in a hard disk array as a single unit for recording and retrieval. Arrays of multiple 3.5-inch hard drives are often found in **redundant array of independent disks (RAID)** configurations. RAID is a computer storage system consisting of over 100 hard disk drives contained in a single cabinet that send data simultaneously to a computer over parallel paths. Magnetic tape drives may also be configured into RAIDS. A RAID system is reliable because another disk drive will take over if a drive fails. RAID devices are connected to computers over SANs, and these devices may be linked together to store large numbers of documents. Devices with 3.5-inch hard drives are much less expensive to purchase, install, operate, repair, and replace than larger capacity drives; they require less floor space; and they consume less power.

When fixed magnetic disks become full, they must be replaced with higher capacity drives or additional hard drives must be purchased. Some electronic records must be deleted or transferred to magnetic tapes or other media for off-line storage, which will free space for

> *Why are data compressed?*

new information. Using hard drives with removable media has several advantages:

Why are removable media needed?

- Hard drives can support a large number of disks and, therefore, provide unlimited storage capacity.
- Removable media can be stored in locked cabinets, vaults, or other secure locations to prevent unauthorized access.
- Removable disks can be used in other computer systems with compatible drives.
- Removable disks can be used to back up conventional hard drives and to restore electronic records if a hard drive fails.
- Removable hard disks can be used with an identical device if a removable hard drive fails.

A **floppy disk**, or *diskette*, is a piece of round plastic that stores data and records by electromagnetic charges. This flat disk (housed in a paper or plastic enclosure) has a magnetic coating that magnetically stores data. Diskettes are the most widely used removable magnetic disks in microcomputer installations. As of this writing, the more commonly used floppy disk is the 3.5-inch disk, which stores 1.44MB of data. Zip™ drives, internal or external, use flexible media encased in plastic cartridges, and are used for backing up computer files. They are often used to store files containing graphics because of their large storage capacity. (See Figure 10–1.) These drives are proprietary and do not accept disks manufactured by other companies. Zip cartridges are 3.5 inches, but they are thicker than conventional 3.5-inch floppy disks. Current storage capacities include 100MB and 250MB disks. These disks are used to back up entire microcomputer system files as well as data files. Other superfloppy disks with similar large storage capacities are available for microcomputers and can be used in a standard 3.5-inch floppy drive.

Figure 10–1 **Zip Drive and Disk**

Magnetic tape is a long strip of polyester film coated with magnetizable recording material, capable of storing information in the form of electromagnetic signals. Magnetic tape drives were the primary media for secondary storage devices in early computer installations. However, to access information on a selected portion of tape, the tape drive must pass through all preceding information because information is recorded sequentially. Magnetic tapes became the most widely used media for off-line data storage and backup protection as higher capacity magnetic disks became available. Tape reels that measure 10.5 inches in diameter and contain 2,400 feet of tape are the most widely used. Information is recorded and read by a peripheral device connected to a computer that is called a *reel-to-reel tape drive*, a *half-inch tape drive*, or a *nine-track tape drive*.

Digital audiotape (DAT) is a type of magnetic tape originally developed for audio recording only, but it is primarily used currently for data backup, archiving, and audio recording. DAT cartridges measure 3 inches by 2 inches by 0.4 inch, may contain 60- or 90-meter tape, and may have a storage capacity of 1.3GB or 2GB. Data compression will almost double the amount of storage capacity for a single cartridge. See Figure 10–2.

Why are magnetic media used for backup?

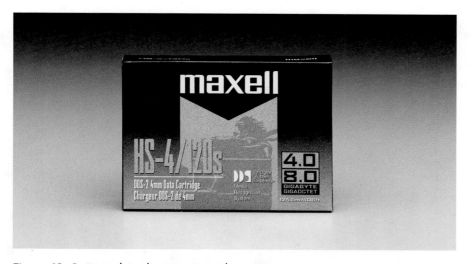

Figure 10–2 Digital Audiotape Cartridges

Voice dictation systems, voice mail systems, telephone answering machines, and other audio recording devices used in offices use magnetic tape cassettes. A **magnetic tape cassette** is a storage device consisting of two plastic spools of magnetic tape, a supply spool and a take-up spool, contained in a plastic case—in cassette or microcassette configurations. The "standard size" or C-type cassettes are usually identified by a code that indicates their recording time in minutes. C-90 cassettes provide 90 minutes of double-sided recording time, or 45 minutes per side.

Microcassettes are designed for voice use in portable dictation equipment or desktop audio recording devices. Other types of magnetic tape cassettes are designed for recording music.

Videotape is a magnetic tape on which visual images are electronically recorded, with or without sound. Most video recorders use the VHS format, which has two versions: Super-VHS (S-VHS) and VHS-Compact (VHS-C). S-VHS cassettes contain higher grade recording materials and produce high-quality images. VHS-C cassettes are smaller and are used in camcorders. Eight-millimeter videocassettes are used primarily in camcorder applications, especially the very compact, lightweight camcorders. Eight-millimeter tape lengths are identified by a code that indicates recording time in minutes—from fifteen minutes to two hours for each cassette.

Other magnetic media or computer tapes widely used for data archiving, backup protection, and distribution of information and software include nine-track magnetic tape, 34XX data cartridges, 3590 data cartridges, digital linear tape (DLT), and quarter-inch cartridges (QIC). These formats vary by width and length of magnetic tape. Their use is determined by the application. High-density DLT reduces time and the number of tapes required for backups. The DLT equipment shown in Figure 10–3 connects by a LAN or SAN to computers and provides automated backup storage.

Figure 10–3 Digital Linear Tape Equipment

Optical Media

Optical media include optical disks, magneto-optical disks, computer output to laser disk, compact disks, digital videodisks, and optical cards and tape. An **optical disk** is a high-density storage medium where digitally encoded information is written and read by means of a laser. It is a high-capacity storage medium for microcomputers or large mainframe computers. An optical disk is platter-shaped and coated with optical recording material. Optical disks are available in write-once and rewritable media. Write-once-read-many is known as *WORM* technology. Rewritable media options are preferred over WORM or read-only media. Read/write optical disks are removable media that are usually encased in a plastic cartridge that protects the surface during loading, removal, and other handling. Single- or double-sided recording is possible on read/write optical disks. Most optical disk drives, however, are single-sided devices that require disks to be removed and turned over to record on the other side.

Which optical media are preferred?

A **magneto–optical (MO) disk** is a rewritable optical disk. Previously recorded segments may be deleted or overwritten with new information. Information is recorded and read by laser, but it is stored magnetically. These disks are reliable and can store large amounts of data, especially when placed into a jukebox. A **jukebox** is a storage device that holds optical disks or tapes and has one or more drives that provide automatic on-line access to the information. A jukebox, also known as an *autochanger*, can store multiterabytes. (One terabyte is one trillion characters.) Successive versions of large databases or documents and multimedia files can be stored on the same magneto-optical disk. The term *multimedia* means information that includes two or more data types: text, graphics, animation, video, or sound. Interactivity of the user with the software is a computer multimedia characteristic. By clicking a button, touching a screen, or selecting a key on a keyboard, the user determines what part of the software program is activated.

Which optical disks are rewritable?

What is a jukebox?

Optical disks—write-once and rewritable—are categorized by size. Optical disks are available in 2.5-inch, 3.5-inch, 4.75-inch, 5.25-inch, 12-inch, and 14-inch sizes. The large-format 12- and 14-inch disks are usually seen only in mainframe and minicomputer installations. These disks store from 12 to 25GB of data. The 5.25-inch and smaller optical disks are intended for use in microcomputers and network servers and can store multigigabytes of data. A 5.25-inch magneto-optical disk drive and cartridge are shown in Figure 10–4 on page 254.

Another form of long-term or archival computer storage that integrates the imaging of paper documents with electronic records is **computer output to laser disk (COLD)**. COLD is a technique for the transfer of computer-generated output to optical disk so that it can be viewed or printed without using the original program. COLD combines the capabilities of scanning paper documents created on another system and linking them to COLD documents (computer-created records saved by laser to optical disks). At a point in the life cycle of data when it is ready to be migrated from primary storage, it can be downloaded onto optical media used in a COLD system for nearline or off-line storage.

What are COLD documents?

Figure 10–4 5.25-inch Magneto-optical Disk Drive and Cartridge

Nearline data is available on a secondary storage device where it can be retrieved rapidly but slower than from on-line computer storage. COLD technology is subject to obsolescence and, therefore, provides a medium-term solution. COLD systems have a reliable retention period of five to ten years.

COLD technology uses an optical disk jukebox with a controller and a server. Each disk can store more than 200,000 pages. Software management for optical drives and jukeboxes is available for microcomputer and minicomputer environments. COLD technology provides fully automated search and retrieval capability with selected records displayed on a screen or printed to paper copy. COLD records distributed through networks permit shared access to databases with rapid retrieval from various work sites.

A **compact disk–read-only memory (CD-ROM)** disk is a high-density digital disk storage medium that can be read only. It is a magneto-optical disk that cannot be written on. **Compact disk–recordable (CD-R)** and **compact disk–rewritable (CD-RW)** disks are read/write optical disks. CD-R products are write-once, and CD-RW disks are erasable. CDs provide safe and reliable media that can store images for long periods of time, sometimes up to 100 years. CDs store databases, documents, directories, publications, and archival records that do not need alteration. CDs do not require special hardware or software to retrieve information; however, the storage capacity is limited. A standard CD can hold from 12,000 to 15,000 documents. Because CDs can be stored in a jukebox that can hold as many as 500 CDs, a larger number of documents can be stored on a large number of CDs.

Full-motion video requires huge amounts of storage space. One solution to the high-storage capacity needed for multimedia is the digital videodisk. A **digital videodisk** or **digital versatile disk (DVD)** is a read-only optical storage medium that stores approximately 130 minutes of full-motion video. These disks offer the same storage capacity as a magneto-optical disk and provide reliable long-term storage. With continued decline in the cost of DVD recorders, DVD use will likely increase; it may replace magneto-optical disks in the future.

An **optical card** is a small electronic device about the size of a credit card that contains electronic memory and possibly an imbedded integrated circuit. It is a compact storage media for microcomputers that can hold approximately 4.2MB of data. This card is also known as an *optical memory card,* an *optical digital data card*, and a *smart card*. (See Figure 10–5.) Optical cards are coated on one side with a reflective strip of optical recording material and are available in read-only and read/write versions. They are used to store patient medical records and digital cash and to generate computer network identifications for security purposes. Although optical cards are portable, reader/writer equipment availability is limited, which prevents wide adoption.

What can be stored on a smart card?

Figure 10–5 Smart Card and Smart Card Reader

Optical tape is available, but it is not widely used. Similar to magnetic tape, optical tape is a ribbon of tape that is coated with an optical recording material. A large 12-inch tape reel can store massive quantities of data and is useful for storing scientific data. One reel of optical tape can store as much as 5,500 nine-track magnetic tapes. Optical tapes could be used to consolidate a significant number of magnetic tapes stored in large tape libraries and conserve space.

SYSTEMS CONCEPT

What is an automatic records system?

Computers have given records and information managers and other information specialists a broader—and clearer—view of organizations and how their parts work together. The ability of computer technology to create, process, store, retrieve, and distribute information to all divisions or departments in an organization helps managers and workers in all departments relate to the total organization and to see the relationships among departments. An **automatic records system** is any system that applies computer technology to any or all records management tasks such as the creation, collection, processing, maintenance, retrieval, use, storage, dissemination, and disposition of records.

A **system** is a regularly interacting or interdependent group of items forming a unified whole. In records management, the primary concerns are records and information management systems. Within a system, various groupings of interrelated components that accomplish one phase of a task are referred to as a **subsystem**. For example, *records storage* is a *subsystem* of a *records and information management system*, as described in Chapter 1. Each lower level of a system is called a *subsystem*. Other records management subsystems include records creation, distribution, usage, and disposition. You will recognize these subsystems as the phases of the records life cycle. All systems have phases or subsystems necessary to complete the system task.

Systems achieve tasks through input, process, output, control, and feedback. In a computer system, an operation begins with information entered (input) into the system. **Input** is the data entered into a computer, and it can also mean to enter data into a computer system. In order to use the data, the computer must *process* it or change it. Software provides instructions for organizing the data to produce the desired product or result (output). **Output** is the machine-readable or human-readable data produced by a computer. Various system *controls* are applied to set and maintain certain standards for processing that computer system operators use to improve output. People control the preparation and input of data into a computer; maintain reasonable turnaround schedules for delivering output; and protect the stored information. Software controls the computer's operation. Communication based on evaluation of output against quality and quantity standards is *feedback*. Feedback is information that helps evaluate the effectiveness of the process or any step in the process. Computer systems software, as well as other software programs, displays feedback messages on a computer screen when errors occur. Computers can also be programmed to exchange messages with other devices connected to the computer; e.g., the computer screen displays a message that the printer is not ready when a file is sent to print if the printer has not been turned on or if it is out of paper. Two main system components relating to electronic records systems—data input and data output—are discussed next.

Data Input

Data (groups of characters that represent a specific value or condition) provide the building blocks of information. A computer has the capacity to sort, compute, analyze, interpret, compile, and categorize data to create information. A software program determines the processing steps to be completed by a computer.

> *How does data become information?*

Computer data entry most often is done through a computer keyboard; however, other input devices such as scanners, bar codes, optical character recognition (OCR), fax machines, modems, light pens, and various handheld devices are also used. Remember that hard disks, floppy disks, and other removable disks are also input devices. With voice-recognition software and a microphone, individuals who do not have full use of their hands may enter data by dictating letters, memos, messages, or other documents into a computer or by speaking commands to a computer.

A **scanner** is a device that converts an image (text, graphic, or photograph) of a document into electronic form for processing and storage. A scanner passes light over a document or object and converts it to dark and light dots that become digital code. Scanners may be handheld devices that are passed over an item to be entered or desktop models that scan a document from a flat surface. A desktop scanner is shown in Figure 10–6 on page 258. A desktop document scanner used in records and information management applications must have an automatic document feeder, which will allow a stack of paper to be placed into a tray and automatically brought into the scanner one page at a time. Scanners that do not have an automatic document feeder are designed for graphics and require each page to be manually placed onto the scanner. Most scanners can handle 8.5 inches by 11 inches and smaller paper. Some can handle 11 inches by 17 inches, and a few can handle E-size engineering drawings that are 34 inches by 44 inches.

> *How does a scanner enter data?*

Figure 10–6 Desktop Document Scanner

Another type of scanned input uses bar codes for computer data entry. *Bar code* is a coding system consisting of vertical lines or bars set in a predetermined pattern that, when read by an optical reader, can be converted into machine-readable language. In records management, bar codes are used for tracking locations of files or boxes of records. With bar code software, users can print labels from a computer or from a dedicated bar code printer. Bar code stickers (labels) are placed on each document or on the first page of a multipage document that is scanned into a computer. With appropriate software, scanned documents can be separated and assigned to folders much faster than can be done manually. Information assigned to the bar codes can be used for indexing, tracking, and retrieval. Bar codes are also used to check out items in libraries, to record items shipped and received, and to record items stocked on shelves in supermarkets. Bar codes are used with the prices or inventory numbers on products in a supermarket or department store. The Universal Product Code (UPC) used for bar coding has from 13 to 21 bars. Each bar can be on (present) or off (absent). A **bar code reader** is a photoelectric scanner that translates bar code symbols into digital forms so that they can be read by a computer.

Optical character recognition (OCR) is machine reading of printed or written characters through the use of light-sensitive materials or devices. A device, such as a wand, is used to read special preprinted characters and to convert them into digital form for computer data entry. A department store associate uses OCR scanning to enter prices from a product. OCR technology is often used in organizations that process a large number of forms. A form template (pattern) can be set up in a

What is a bar code?

How does OCR enter data?

computer. Regions or areas/fields on the forms can be assigned to fields on the template. The OCR equipment and software can automatically populate the fields in the template and automatically index and sort information in those fields. For example, a customer name, invoice number, shipping date, or any other information that can be found in a standard location on an invoice form can be extracted from an invoice and assigned as an index to that page. The form is then ready for lookup and retrieval in one scan-OCR-index step. Manual data entry is reduced and forms processing is automated.

Modems (MOdulator/DEModulator) provide another means of inputting data. A **modem** is a device that converts digital data from a computer to an analog signal that can be transmitted over an ordinary telephone line. A modem is an electronic board placed inside a computer microprocessor (internal modem) or an external device placed on a desk and connected to the microprocessor or central processing unit. Communication software used with modems translates the digital computer code from the sending computer into analog signals used for telephone line transmission and then back into digital code for the receiving computer. Internet connections are made via a modem. An individual home user will usually have only one modem. An Internet service provider has many modems to serve the number of computers connected to the Internet service. Wherever a traveling executive conducts business, a cellular modem handles business transactions such as entering purchase orders, reviewing customer records, or reading electronic mail.

What device will connect a computer to the Internet?

Another means of sending and receiving written messages over telephone lines and satellite relays is the facsimile machine, more commonly referred to as a "fax." A **facsimile (fax) machine** is a device that transmits an exact reproduction of an image to another location electronically. A desktop fax machine scans an image and converts it into digital code enabling transmission to another fax machine or to a computer with a fax modem and fax software. A fax modem and fax software may be installed as part of a computer system to simulate a fax machine's input and output.

Other computer input devices include a mouse; trackball; light pen; touch screen; and pen-controlled, handheld computers. A **mouse** is a hand-driven input device used to select and point on a computer screen by moving the device on a flat surface. A **trackball** is a ball mounted, usually in a computer console, so as to be partially exposed and is rotated to control the movement of a cursor on a display screen. A mouse or trackball can also be used to create or edit text and graphic records. A **light pen** is used for writing or sketching on a display screen. As the pen reacts to the light from the screen, the image written or sketched is digitized by the computer for processing, storing, and printing. A touch screen is a sensitized computer display screen that receives input from the touch of a finger. Touch screens are typically menu driven and easy to

How is a PDA used?

use. Some bookstores have touch screen stations that allow customers to search for books by author, title, or subject. Another example is an automatic teller machine that customers may use to make cash deposits or withdrawals. A **personal digital assistant (PDA)** is a handheld computer controlled by a pen similar to a stylus. PDAs process handwritten commands and messages. You can write or draw on the screen and store the pen input "as is" for signatures or convert the handwriting to digitized data. You can also select items from a menu that will direct the PDA to perform functions or record your choices. Palm™ handheld devices (www.palm.com) have four standard software applications—an address book, a date book, a memo pad, and a to do list—that are used with a stylus. However, numerous additional applications are available to enhance the usefulness of the devices. Some devices provide digital voice memo capability, Internet connections and e-mail, or a CD containing an expense-tracking application. Palm operating system (Palm OS®) and other software enable data transfer between Palm units and a computer, which provides automatic backup of databases. Bar code scanning and a keyboard are also available. A Palm V handheld is shown in Figure 10–7.

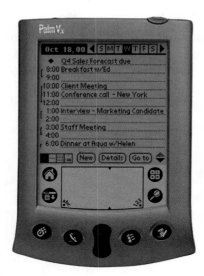

Figure 10–7 Palm™ V Handheld Device

Customers and vendors may use electronic data interchange (EDI) to enter information directly into data files maintained by each other's computers. **Electronic data interchange (EDI)** is the computer-to-computer transmission of records in standardized, computer-readable format. It is a communication procedure between two companies that allows the exchange of standardized documents (most commonly invoices or purchase orders) through computers. If the two companies have compatible systems, the computers communicate with each other through a connection. For example, Company A sends a purchase order to Company B by EDI. When Company B ships the order to Company A, an invoice is created and sent to Company A, again through EDI. Company A can then pay Company B by transferring electronic funds via EDI. *E-business* is a term applied to business transactions conducted over the Internet. *Business-to-Business*, or *B2B*, refers to transactions between two companies over the Internet. The previous example of Companies A and B using EDI to issue a purchase order and an invoice is a B2B transaction.

Data Output

After a computer processes data, the information may be presented in printed form, displayed on a video monitor, or saved to a storage device. *Output* is the machine-readable or human-readable data produced by a computer. Output devices include computer secondary storage devices such as floppy disks, removable disks, and magnetic tapes; paper copies produced with printers; visual displays on a video screen or monitor; or digital voice recordings. Modems and faxes are output as well as input devices. Electronic communication from computer to computer, as well as high-volume records such as customer files, are likely to be printed in paper form (hard copy) only when required for a specific purpose. A **hard copy** is a printed copy of a record that can be read without use of mechanical assistance.

> *What is a hard copy?*

Electronic records are particularly system dependent because they contain machine-readable, digitally encoded information derived from electronic signals. Electronic storage media and the records on them are designed for recording and reading by specific devices and software. Records created using word processing and spreadsheet software can be processed only by the same type of software. In some cases, these records may be converted to the format of another word processing or spreadsheet software program. However, such conversion software often is not available in offices. Therefore, records and information managers must understand the characteristics and capabilities of systems that create and store machine-readable information. The ability to retrieve and use electronic records in the future depends on technological advances, which promote product obsolescence and discontinuations. This issue is discussed in the next section.

ELECTRONIC RECORDS ISSUES

As the use of electronic records has made electronic media a primary records storage media, storage and retrieval of those records has presented new concerns. Indexing electronic records is just as important as indexing manual records and for the same reason—to locate and retrieve records or information. For electronic records, retrieval is a records retention issue. Information redundancy, media compatibility and stability, and access are also related to records retention.

Indexing

The value of records increases when users are assured that they can be retrieved when needed, especially electronic records. Indexing provides the means to locate, group, retrieve, and manage documents. Having well-indexed records reduces financial and legal risks, improves standards compliance, and enhances productivity. Unless a good quality indexing system is built into a document or records and information management computing application, the system will fail to perform one of its primary purposes—locating and retrieving the document-based information. Indexing should not be taken lightly. Indexing involves planning and making decisions such as what to index and which index terms to use.

Why are records indexed?

In paper-based storage systems, indexing involves units and sometimes subjects. Indexing computer-based records is similar in that *units* become *fields* and *subjects* become *keywords*. Index fields can be used to categorize documents, to track creation or retention dates, or to enter subject matter. As in a paper-based system, indexing electronic records is essential for finding and retrieving the *right* information.

Indexing a computer record is the mental process of deciding the name or code by which it will be stored and retrieved. Coding the record is entering the record identifier code or filename for storage. Electronic files, particularly those files on floppy disks, are often carelessly identified with abbreviations as filenames that only the record creator could interpret. PROJONESCO illustrates a filename that means nothing to anyone other than the person creating it. Storing a description of the record with the filename aids retrieval.

How is a computer record indexed?

Full-text indexing provided by OCR-capable software eliminates the need for someone to read and manually index documents using keywords. OCR software "reads" a scanned document or page and indexes every word to track its location. Consequently, documents can be found using any word or phrase in them.

Paper records are located by looking into a particular file cabinet, into a certain drawer, and into a specific file folder. An electronic storage system should be able to re-create this same type of hierarchical system through multiple levels of nested folders or directories and subdirectories as described in Chapter 4. A well-designed electronic records system makes retrieval easy.

Retrieval

Electronic information is stored on a network hard disk, a user's local hard disk, an optical disk, or a diskette. These files must be identified so that they can be easily retrieved, used, and dispositioned. Consequently, users need to identify the categories and subcategories to which the electronic information belongs. They also need to create matching directories and subdirectories on their computers where the information will be stored. Consistency in naming directories, subdirectories, and files is necessary for locating computer records. An index or log of directories, subdirectories, and filename categories should be kept up-to-date and accessible to employees creating and storing electronic records. Assume that the filename illustrated in the previous paragraph stands for *Jones Co. proposal*. This file could be in a directory called PROPOSALS with a subdirectory called JONES CO. The filename could be the specific project with the Jones Co. (SUNSETMALL). The index or log would show all subdirectory names under the main directory, PROPOSALS, and would give the uniform file extensions for files in that directory. Operating system software, such as *Microsoft Windows*, automatically maintains a directory and filename index of files.

Computer storage peripherals, such as removable hard disk drives, floppy disk drives, and optical disk drives, are often represented by labeled icons on a computer's desktop. Storage peripherals and their fixed or removable media are computer-based equivalents of file cabinets. When a storage device is selected, usually with a mouse, a directory of the device's recording medium is displayed. The root directory is displayed first and provides an overview of the contents. The root directory typically contains subdirectories that are identified by folder icons.

Large magnetic tape libraries use similar indexing and retrieval methods; however, files stored on large magnetic tape reels may be indexed by batches or groups of files. For example, one tape may be labeled *accounts receivable records 1998—2000*. An on-line index for off-line records speeds retrieval considerably. Software can identify the location of a tape and guide a robotic arm to retrieve the tape in a tape library.

Floppy disks, microcassettes, tape disk cartridges, compact disks, optical disks, videodisks, or other removable secondary storage devices must be clearly labeled. Labels should show the following information: (1) department, unit, or organization that created the records; (2) name of the records series; (3) inclusive dates, numeric series, or other identifying information; (4) type of computer on which the records were created; and (5) name and version of the software used to create the records. In centralized data processing facilities, much more information may be required on media labels. This information may include: (1) a complete listing of files contained on the medium; (2) manufacturing date for the medium; (3) security precautions and access restrictions; (4) type of copy—working or storage—discussed later in this chapter; and (5) any special attributes of the medium. All this information will not fit onto small labels. Consequently, label contents may be limited to brief identifiers with more complete information recorded manually into a logbook.

> *What should be on a floppy disk label?*

A **data warehouse** is a collection of data designed to support management decision making. Data warehouses contain data that present a clear picture of business conditions at a single point in time. A data warehouse includes systems to extract data from operating systems and a warehouse database system that provides flexible access to the data. *Data warehousing*, or *data mining* as it is sometimes called, generally refers to combining many different databases across an entire organization. Records can be assembled from various applications, platforms (operating systems), and storage devices into formats for presentations to management for decision making or other business purposes. For example, executives may retrieve and assemble electronic records from several departments that will help them assess the profitability of their organization.

Duplicate Records

How are duplicate records created?

In many organizations, users may be able to access the same information in machine-readable and human-readable formats. Storing duplicate copies of the same information is called *information redundancy*. Word processing documents may be created on a computer and revised and edited through several versions before a final document is produced. These versions may be retained to provide a history of development of the document. Each version may be printed for review and corrections. The computer files may also be backed up for protection and retention. Consequently, one document may be available in several versions and formats, which means redundant information and redundant recordkeeping. Records and information management is affected by space needs—file cabinet, floor space, and media space for electronic records. During the discovery phase of a lawsuit, electronic records, paper records, and microfilm records may be subject to review by opposing parties. Paper records may be routinely purged and destroyed, but electronic records may not be subject to the same controls. Records retention schedules and policies must apply to electronic records as well.

Media Compatibility and Stability

If you have worked with computers for a number of years, you have probably witnessed changes in electronic storage media. For example, new microcomputers no longer have a 5.25-inch floppy drive, only a 3.5-inch floppy drive. Records on 5.25-inch disks that are in long-term storage may not be recoverable unless an organization has also stored an older working computer that has a compatible drive and software. Software also can become obsolete, be discontinued, or an organization can change the software used across the organization. **Media compatibility** refers to how well the media and the equipment needed to access information stored on the media work together. Records created in an obsolete or discontinued software program may no longer be accessible.

New software programs that provide backward compatibility with older versions help overcome some software upgrade problems. Current media may not be compatible with future equipment or software. Operating systems may also change, which will prevent access and retrieval. A *Windows* operating system may be replaced by a *Linux* operating system or a newer operating system. Records and information managers must look toward the future when selecting storage media and equipment.

Media stability refers to the length of time the media will maintain its original quality so that it can continue to be used. The useful life of paper and photographic media is longer than the retention periods for the information stored in these formats. The useful life of electronic media depends on the number of times the media is accessed. The stable life expectancy of electronic records is often shorter than the required retention period for the information stored on the media. Magnetic and optical media should be inspected regularly. Samples may be inspected in large storage collections. Inspection should include a visual inspection as well as retrieval and playback of the information. Diskettes may be refreshed by using defragmentation or disk scanning software. Magnetic tapes should undergo a slow unwind/rewind cycle (called *retensioning*) to obtain an evenly tensioned tape before they are stored to extend their useful life. Other electronic records can be recopied onto new media at predetermined intervals to extend their lives for the required retention period. Periodic recopying is known as *renewing* the media. Copying can also be used to transfer information from deteriorating or obsolete media. Digitally coded information can be copied an indefinite number of times without degrading the quality. However, video and audio recordings based on analog signals lose image and/or sound quality with copying. Recopying makes managing electronic records difficult and requires a future commitment of labor and resources with no certainty that the technology needed to recopy records onto new media will be available. **Migration** is the process of moving data from one electronic system to another, usually in upgrading hardware or software, without having to undergo a major conversion or re-inputting of data. Electronic records should be inspected and migrated regularly.

> Why do records need to be migrated?

Access

Users can access paper records by going to storage areas and retrieving them. Paper can be removed from cabinets and other storage containers for reference or taken to another work area for use (checked out). Electronic records, however, may be stored in remote locations where users cannot see the records or know what type of media is used. Remote workstations connected by a network or intranet allow many users to access data at the same time. Organizations connected to the Internet may allow access by customers and employees to forms and other information. Customers may complete forms on-line and submit them to the organization much faster than by conventional means. Internet or intranet access also provides the opportunity for creating new records such as on-line forms. These new records must be incorporated into the records and information management system and retention periods assigned. Freedom of access also raises safety and security concerns, which are discussed later in this chapter.

Electronic Mail (E-mail)

When does e-mail become a record?

E-mail messages transmitted through an organization's e-mail system are usually considered the organization's property and, therefore, are subject to management under the organization's records and information management system.[3] E-mail and Internet use is monitored in many organizations. If e-mail messages contain information about programs, policies, decisions, and important transactions; document oral conversations or meetings during which policy was discussed or formulated; or document planning, discussion, or transaction of other business, they may have ongoing value. Consequently, records retention policies may apply. Users decide whether a message is a record or a nonrecord, based on the information in the message, and file it in appropriate directories and subdirectories. An e-mail system may provide a way to arrange messages into folders, but it is not a records system. E-mail messages must be transferred to a proper recordkeeping system for long-term storage.

When e-mail messages are part of an organization's records system—paper or electronic—users may transfer e-mail to a subdirectory (folder) on a local hard drive, network drive, diskette, or other electronic storage medium. If records and information management software is used to manage and identify information, then appropriate metadata must be entered into the records management system when the message is placed into it. **Metadata** is data about data. Metadata describes how, when, and by whom a particular set of data was collected, and how the data is formatted. Metadata is essential for understanding information stored in data warehouses.

Because e-mail messages can be subject to discovery in a lawsuit, a clear and enforced e-mail policy is necessary. The policy should be established and implemented by senior executives who make clear the intent to enforce the policy. The policy needs to address e-mail content to assure that derogatory and negative remarks of any nature will not be tolerated. The policy needs also to address retention. A commonly used retention period is thirty days after the recipient has read a message. After that time, all messages are automatically purged from the system. If the content of an e-mail message requires longer retention, employees must

---

[3]ARMA International, *Guideline for Managing E-mail*. Prairie Village, KS: ARMA International, 2000.

migrate the document (message) from the e-mail system to archival storage on another medium. They may print the message and store it in a paper records system or save it to a floppy disk. E-mail should be backed up to tape for disaster recovery purposes (discussed in Chapter 12); however, thirty days is the recommended retention period for these messages as well.

ELECTRONIC RECORDS STORAGE AND RETENTION

As discussed in Chapter 6 and earlier in this chapter, electronic records must be included on an organization's records retention schedule and destroyed according to the schedule. Records and information managers have long recognized the importance of records retention for visible records media such as paper and microfilm. The same controls need to be applied to electronic records as well.

Active Records Storage

Data is a valuable organizational resource, and users want and need to have access to that data from many locations, sometimes in different time zones. Consequently, storage systems that provide necessary access are vital to many organizations. For effective storage management of electronic media, storage copies need to be differentiated from working copies. Working copies are intended for ongoing information processing and reference requirements. Storage copies are created to satisfy retention requirements. The most active or working copies of electronic records are usually stored where they can be quickly accessed. That location may be inside a computer on a hard drive or on floppy disks, CDs, or optical disks that are stored nearby. Diskettes may be stored in desktop containers or media pages that may be inserted into three-ring binders or folders. CDs may be stored in desktop storage boxes or towers or media pages. Optical disk cartridges may also be stored in towers. Diskette and CD storage containers are shown in Figure 10–8 on page 268.

Where are the most active records stored?

Inactive Records Storage and Archives

When records are transferred to inactive files or archives, systematic storage according to standard filing procedures apply. Storage copies, sometimes called *master copies*, of electronic records are usually recorded onto removable magnetic or optical media. These copies often contain inactive records that have been transferred from hard drives, and they are seldom referenced. Use of storage copies may be limited to making additional working copies if existing working copies are damaged. These copies also are used to recover and restore information if a system failure

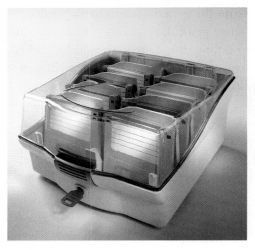

Figure 10–8 **Diskette and CD Storage**

Where are inactive records stored?

or other disaster occurs. The long-term quality of magnetic storage media has not been determined. Because magnetic records can be damaged by extreme temperature or proximity to magnetic charges, vital records should be on a more permanent medium for archival storage.

Although optical disks have a predicted life expectancy of approximately 100 years, retrieving records from optical disk storage requires computer equipment and software. Computer equipment and software can become obsolete, which affects retrieval of records created on that hardware and software. Newer versions of some software and hardware accept earlier versions and save the records in the new version. However, media format or size may change, which will make locating the specific type of disk drive difficult. For these reasons, microfilm remains a popular medium for long-term storage of vital records. Microfilm and other archival storage media and equipment are discussed in Chapter 11.

Many media formats and equipment have been replaced or become obsolete; however, older media will often be located when a records inventory is conducted. Maintaining a current inventory of electronic records helps records and information managers develop effective retention schedules for those records. They are also better able to make data migration decisions—which records need to be migrated and to what media they need to be migrated. State-of-the-art technology is sometimes state-of-the-art for a short time.

Retention

As you learned earlier in this chapter, electronic records may be stored on-line, nearline, or off-line. Retention periods apply to each storage location. On-line retention reflects the length of time the data should remain on primary storage devices, usually magnetic disks. The on-line retention period may be a few days, weeks, or months, but rarely more than a year. Nearline retention reflects the length of time data needs to remain on-site but off-line in secondary storage devices, usually optical media. Nearline retention also is usually a short period of time, a few months or a year or so. Off-line retention reflects the length of time the data needs to be off-line, usually off-site, and usually on magnetic tapes. Retention periods should be assigned according to the records series stored on the tapes. A total retention period, required for most records retention schedules, reflects the length of time the data should remain in computer-processible form. After that time has expired, all data should be purged from all storage devices supporting the system.[4]

Disposition

If electronic information is in directories and subdirectories, a software file manager can sort the files by date and identify records due for disposition (retain or destroy). To dispose of information on a magnetic disk, the file(s) must be deleted from the disk, and the space the files occupied must be overwritten to make recovering the information almost impossible. When users delete files, the space is marked for re-use, but the information is not physically removed or erased from a disk. With the help of commonly used utility programs, a user may restore deleted files that have not been overwritten. Defragmentation and disk scanning software can overwrite areas of a hard disk or diskette that are no longer being used.

Electronic files on magnetic tape that are ready for disposition must be marked for deletion, and the space overwritten. Usually, all files must be restored to a hard disk, the marked files deleted, and the remaining files written to the tape. After all files have been written to the tape, the restored files must be deleted from the hard disk. Defragmentation or disk scanning software should be used to overwrite the disk.

All CD-ROM files must be restored to a hard drive, the selected files deleted from the hard disk, and the remaining files written onto a new CD-ROM. CD-R and CD-RW disks also must be restored to a hard drive, the selected files deleted, and remaining files rewritten on the same disks. The same process should be applied to optical disks when records must be destroyed. CD-ROMs must be destroyed because they use WORM technology—write once read many.[5] Shredding is a preferred method of destroying CDs and optical disks.

[4]David O. Stephens and Roderick C. Wallace, *Electronic Records Retention: An Introduction.* Prairie Village, KS: ARMA International, 1997, pp. 15–16.

[5]Alan S. Zaben, "Managing Electronic Records," *Technologies for Managing Information* Vol. 3, No. 2 (March 1998), pp. 24–25.

ELECTRONIC RECORDS SYSTEM AND NETWORK SECURITY

Safeguarding records against intentional or unintentional destruction or damage and protecting records confidentiality is known as *records protection*. Protecting records, regardless of their media, and their proper use and control are essential. Computer records systems connected by a LAN or a WAN are vulnerable to outside intruders through Internet access. Safety and security of electronic records are discussed in this section.

Records Safety

Records safety refers to protecting records from physical hazards existing in an office environment. The following procedures apply to controlling and protecting records from physical hazards:

Adopt protective measures for hardware, software, and media. These measures include using surge protectors to protect computer equipment from changes (surges) in electrical voltage and affixing locks to areas containing computer files and equipment to protect against misuse or theft. Optical and magnetic media should not be stored in direct sunlight, placed near radiators, or exposed to heat sources. CD-R media that are not housed in cartridges may be damaged by exposure to light. They should be stored in containers that are stored in closed cabinets. High humidity, extreme heat or cold, exposure to light, electro-magnetic sources, dust, smoke, and various storage conditions can damage electronic records; therefore, controlling temperature and humidity and other storage conditions helps protect these records. Dust and other contaminants can infiltrate high-density media housings and render portions of recorded information unreadable. Air conditioning is usually required to control temperature and humidity and to remove pollutants. Media storage areas should be cleaned regularly.

Adequate preparation for and protection from natural disasters, such as floods, fires, and earthquakes, should be provided. Protection from natural disasters involves advance planning to select a second equipment site for emergency operation and for making duplicate copies of vital records for the alternate location. See Chapter 12 for more on disaster preparation and recovery.

Convert records stored on magnetic media to hard copy, optical disks, or microforms for long-term storage. As discussed previously, the life expectancy of magnetic records may be limited, depending on storage conditions. Therefore, careful attention must be made to environmental conditions for long-term storage of magnetic tapes. Vital records should not be on magnetic media for long-term storage.

Protect against loss of files. Establish a policy of backing up computer files and storing the copies in fireproof cabinets or in an off-site location.

Duplicate electronic records made from backup copies can be done quickly and inexpensively. Backing up records is good insurance that records will be available when needed.

Take measures to prevent computer viruses. A **virus** is a computer program that replicates itself into other programs that are shared among systems with the intention of causing damage. When computer users can access electronic records from remote locations, the opportunity for the introduction of viruses increases. Viruses transmitted over the Internet and through electronic mail can be particularly destructive. Safety measures involve (a) using virus detecting software programs regularly; (b) making backup copies of new software programs on floppy disks before installing them onto a computer (new software on CDs cannot be copied without a CD-R drive); and (c) making daily backup copies of data entered. Always checking for viruses on data disks from outside sources helps eliminate data damage from viruses. Users need to update virus detection software regularly from the detection software company's Web site.

Why are files backed up?

How can computer viruses be prevented?

Records Security

Records security refers to protecting records from unauthorized access. Electronic transmission and distribution of records require special security precautions. With wide use of the Internet to conduct business, organizations take careful measures to provide records security and protection from unauthorized access to the information stored on electronic media. Generally accepted safety measures include the following practices:

Implementing a security policy to ensure safe, reliable operation of the records system. Such a policy is based on a detailed study of equipment used, records functions performed, information contained in the principal records, employees having access to the records, and current security devices.

Conducting security checks and, when necessary, bonding personnel who use hardware and software in the system. The electronic records security policy should include close supervision of records work plus holding employees personally accountable for the proper maintenance of company equipment and information.

Providing deterrents to crime. Some firms have a security warning programmed into their computers for display onto terminal screens. An effective method of controlling access to a computer room is a card reader/combination lock system into which employees must insert their access cards and key in a personal code before the door will open. Other security systems scan and save the scan of each person's eyes, which is matched each time the same person tries to enter a secure area. Voice prints are also used in a similar manner. Networks that facilitate remote access allow the possibility of unauthorized intrusion. A **firewall** is a combination hardware and software buffer that many organizations place between their internal networks and the Internet. A firewall allows only specific kinds of messages from the Internet to flow in and out of the internal network. This limitation protects the internal network from intruders or hackers who might try to use the Internet to break into these systems.

Protecting data stored on disks or tapes. To protect data against unauthorized use, safeguards such as passwords, digital signatures, encryption, or call-back may be used.

How is a password used?

Is an e-signature legal?

- A **password** is a string of characters known to the computer system and a user, who must specify it to gain access to the system. It may be a special word, code, or symbol that is required to access a computer system. Passwords are not sufficient protection because they can be stolen or guessed. You should not use a real word or variation of your name, date of birth, or a word that might logically be guessed. The best password is a mix of letters, numbers, and punctuation marks in a random sequence of at least eight characters.

- A **digital signature**, or *e-signature,* consists of a string of characters and numbers added as a code on electronic documents being transmitted by computer. The receiving computer's special software performs a mathematical operation on the character string to verify its validity. The Electronics Signature in Global and National Commerce Act, passed in 2000, sets national standards for electronic signatures and records and gives them the same legal validity as written contracts and documents. The law provides that no contract, signature, or record shall be denied legally binding status just because it is in electronic form. A contract must still be in a format capable of being retained and accurately reproduced.

- **Encryption** is a method of scrambling data in a predetermined manner at the sending point to protect confidential records. The destination computer decodes the data. Encryption is the process of converting meaningful information into a numeric code that is only understood by the intended recipient of the information. The receiving computer and Internet browser understand the mathematical formulas that turn the information into numeric code and back again into meaningful information. Encryption may be Domestic Grade or International Grade. *International-Grade encryption*, also called *40-bit encryption,* uses billions of possible keys to secure information. *Domestic-Grade encryption*, also called *128-bit encryption,* uses thousands of times more key combinations than International-Grade encryption. As the Internet has become a major vehicle for commercial, proprietary, or sensitive information transmission, the perceived need for encryption or other security measures has risen accordingly.

With encryption, organizations can use EDI to transmit highly sensitive information.

- A **call-back system** is a records protection procedure requiring an individual requesting data from a computer system to hang up after making a telephone request and wait for the computer to call back. In call-back systems, telephone numbers are checked by the computer before information is released to the requesting party to be sure that only authorized persons have access to the requested information.

Transmitting confidential information by fax is equivalent to posting the document on a bulletin board because desktop faxes commonly have multiple users. A fax machine dedicated for confidential material only and located in a less open area or calling ahead to alert the message receiver to watch for a fax provide some security. As mentioned previously, e-mail messages may be obtained as evidence in lawsuits. Damaging evidence can often be found in messages that senders or receivers thought were deleted. Because the main computer makes daily backups of all files, including electronic mail, copies of messages sent and deleted may still be in the backup file. In addition, software programs often make several copies of files and place them in different addresses. Computer experts may be able to recover these files. Security issues stemming from unsuspected file copies call for the following measures: (1) Implement an organization-wide e-mail policy that requires regular purging of files that are no longer active nor needed for future operations or historical records. (2) Follow established e-mail policy and do not put anything into an e-mail message that you would not want repeated or used in court. (3) Protect your password, and always log off (sign off) the system properly so that no one else can create, change, or damage records on your computer.

Why are faxes not secure?

ELECTRONIC RECORDS MANAGEMENT SOFTWARE

Using software to manage electronic records provides much needed control. Because most of these records are not visible, superior management tools are needed. The control of records through computer software increases rapid access to records and reduces the number of misplaced records. Records and information management (RIM) software packages or customized software developed for an organization can be used to maintain records location files, charge-out files, and retention and destruction records. Software programs may be single-function programs that manage only one aspect of the records management area such as off-site

Why is RIM software used?

records storage. Other software options include integrated packages that address the total records management of an organization and modular programs that have separate modules for each records system function. Selection of appropriate software should be determined by several factors:

1. Complexity of the software and amount of training required for employee proficiency.
2. Well-written training manuals that accompany the software.
3. Reliability and experience of the vendor.
4. Initial cost and future costs of the software and installation.
5. Maintenance, backup, and support services offered.

Hierarchical storage management (HSM) is a data storage management strategy in which HSM software is used to separate active and inactive computer data by migrating files between primary and secondary storage media. The most active files remain on-line; less frequently accessed data are migrated to nearline optical storage media or off-line to magnetic tapes. Although HSM offers effective data storage management, it cannot replace a records retention schedule. Software cannot make decisions concerning whether and when to destroy records according to organizational policy. Migrating data does not destroy anything. HSM must be integrated with records retention and disposition policies.

Software programs that provide research capability for users to collect information on applicable laws and regulations that apply to specific records series is extremely important for records and information managers. These programs are often referred to as *retention software. Retention 5.0* by Zasio Enterprises (www.zasio.com) is retention software designed to operate in multimedia environments—imaging, electronic document management, and other records management systems. This program can be installed in addition to a RIM software program that provides document tracking and management of active and inactive storage or on-site and off-site storage, including multiple locations.

For organizations engaged in e-business transactions, records and information software must index and classify records automatically, assign appropriate retention schedule information, store the records, and notify the appropriate person automatically when retention periods expire.[6]

EMERGING TECHNOLOGIES

As the cycles of technology developments become even faster, emerging digital technologies will also grow more rapidly. As a result of the growth in digital technologies, the volume of digital data will gradually overtake

---

[6]Don M. Avedon, "RIM in the E-business Model," *Infopro* Vol. 2, No. 2 (June 2000), pp. 34–38.

the volume of hard-copy records. Three promising developments will increase computer storage capacities—holography, nano-CDs, and electronic paper/ink. Intelligent agents may perform some tasks that humans now perform.

Intelligent agents, sometimes called *smart assistants*, are software applications that follow programmed instructions and learn independently about information they are directed to gather. An intelligent agent can anticipate the need for information, automate a complex process, take independent action to improve a process, and communicate with other agents to collaborate on tasks and share information. Intelligent agents are classified into four types: retrieval agents, watcher agents, helper agents, and shopper agents. Retrieval agents, often referred to as pull agents, seek out and report on specific information. Watcher agents, frequently referred to as push agents, look for a specific event. When the event has occurred, the program notifies the user of the event and reports information the event has generated. Helper agents are maintenance or diagnostic programs that help fine-tune application systems. Shopper agents seeks items the user wants and links the user to the provider of those items. They learn from experience and make searches in reaction to what the user accepts or rejects. Intelligent agents can contribute to digital records management by traveling through an organization's networks to identify records for which disposition decisions are due—remain in storage, archive, or destroy.

Holograms are not only anticounterfeit devices on credit cards and paper currency, but they are also devices that store data. They can store data through the interaction of light waves on special materials. Holographic images are three dimensional and, therefore, information can be stored in layers inside a hologram. Magnetic and optical disks store data sequentially in alphabetic or numeric order. Holographic data is read by tilting the angle of the beam of light (a laser beam) used to read it. With continued improvements in storage capacity and retrieval capabilities, holograms may be available for wide-spread use in five to ten years.[7]

Nano designates a billionth of something. Researchers are working on technology to store information on silicon disks the size of small coins. The data is recorded in tiny pits in grooves on the disks. The data bits are ten nanometers (billionths of a meter). A silicon needle reads the information. The storage capacity of a *nano-CD* is 50GB; a current CD has a capacity of 650MB. A nano-CD could hold more hours of video than a current CD or hundreds of magnetic resonance images (MRIs) for medical purposes. A rewritable nano-CD, which has yet to be developed, will be needed for some storage applications.

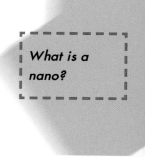

What is a nano?

---

[7]Alan A. Andolsen, "Managing Digital Information: The Emerging Technologies," *The Information Management Journal* Vol. 33, No. 2 (April 1999), pp. 8–15.

Electronic paper/ink are paper-like products that can display digital information, text, and graphics. Electronic paper/ink is composed of tiny plastic balls that are specially treated to retain a specific electrical charge, a transparent silicone-based binding material, and oil, which allows the balls to rotate. Each half of each ball is usually colored white or black, and each half carries a different electrical charge. When the balls are exposed to an exterior charge, they rotate so that only one side of the balls is visible, which creates an image. The patterns of the balls can be programmed to display text or graphics. With additional research and experimentation, full-color images will be possible. The first applications are expected to be billboards or retail signs that can be programmed for text and graphics and revised, edited, or changed without removing them. Electronic books with pages that can be created, updated, or erased by electronic signals transmitted through electrodes connected to a chip in the spine of the book may be storage devices of interest to records and information managers in the future.

SUMMARY

Contrary to some predictions, paper records have not become obsolete, and their use continues to increase. However, the use of electronic records also increases daily. Although computers are the main source of electronic records, voice technologies, audio and video recorders, and medical and scientific equipment also create and store electronic records. Magnetic media and optical media are electronic records. Magnetic media include magnetic cartridges and cassettes, hard and floppy disks, and magnetic tape. Optical media include read-only and rewritable optical disks; computer output to laser disk; read-only, recordable, and rewritable compact disks; digital videodisks; and optical cards and tape.

With an automatic records system, records and information managers can apply computer technology to some or all records management tasks. Important elements in a records and information management system are input and output. Scanners, bar codes, OCR devices, modems, faxes, mice, trackballs, light pens, PDAs, and EDI technology provide records input into an automatic records management system. Output devices include diskettes, removable disks, and magnetic tapes. Hard copies made from printers, visual displays on video screens or monitors, and digital voice recordings are also forms of output.

As in paper-based records systems, indexing is vital for retrieving electronic records. Duplicate records, media compatibility and stability, access, and e-mail are important issues that affect retention of electronic records.

The most active electronic records are stored near the user in easily accessed equipment or on a hard drive inside a computer. Inactive electronic records are stored on-site in a separate location, off-site, or in archives. Because of equipment obsolescence and upgrades, retrieving electronic records created on software and hardware several years ago may be difficult, expensive, or impossible. Consequently, electronic data must be migrated to magnetic tape or other media for long-term storage.

Records safety and security are crucial to preserving electronic records and protecting them from unauthorized access. Various forms of protections are used to prevent electrical surges, misuse, theft, temperature and humidity damage, and damage caused by natural disasters. Records are migrated for long-term storage, backed up, and protected by antivirus software. Security policies and procedures, passwords, digital signatures, encryption, and call-back can prevent unauthorized access and damage to electronic records.

Because most electronic records are not visible, using records and information management software enhances storage and retrieval of those records in active, inactive, on-site, and off-site storage facilities. Hierarchical storage management facilitates active and inactive storage by separating active and inactive records and migrating files between primary and secondary storage media. Future technologies that may be used in records management include intelligent agents, holograms, nano-CDs, and electronic paper and ink.

IMPORTANT TERMS

automatic records system

bar code reader

call-back system

compact disk-read-only memory (CD-ROM)

compact disk–recordable (CD-R)

compact disk–rewritable (CD-RW)

computer output to laser disk (COLD)

data

data warehouse

digital audiotape (DAT)

digital signature

digital videodisk (DVD)

electronic data interchange (EDI)

electronic record

encryption

facsimile (fax) machine

firewall

floppy disk

hard copy

hard disk

hierarchical storage management (HSM)

information

input

jukebox

light pen

local area network (LAN)

magnetic media

magnetic tape

magnetic tape cassette

magneto-optical (MO) disk

media compatibility

media stability

metadata

migration

modem

mouse

nearline

network

optical card

optical character recognition (OCR)

optical disk

output

password

personal digital assistant (PDA)

redundant array of independent disks (RAID)

scanner

storage area network (SAN)

subsystem

system

trackball

videotape

virus

wide area network (WAN)

REVIEW AND DISCUSSION

1. Name three uses of electronic records. (Obj. 1)

2. Define and describe various magnetic media. (Obj. 2)

3. Define and describe various optical media. (Obj. 2)

4. Discuss the systems concept applied to an electronic records system. (Obj. 3)

5. Give examples of three input and three output devices. (Obj. 3)

6. Describe how electronic records are indexed and retrieved. (Obj. 4)

7. Discuss how duplicate records, media compatibility and stability, access, and electronic mail create records retention problems. (Obj. 5)

8. What equipment is used for storing active and inactive electronic records? (Obj. 6)

9. What records retention factors affect long-term storage of electronic records? (Obj. 7)

10. What steps can an organization's managers take to provide electronic records system and network security? Discuss safety and security measures. (Obj. 8)

11. What are the benefits of using RIM software for managing electronic records? (Obj. 9)

12. Name three technologies that may be used in records and information management in the future. (Obj. 10)

APPLICATIONS (APP)

APP 10-1. Issues Affecting Long-term Electronic Records Retention (Objs. 4-8)

Collaborate

Critical Thinking

You are an employee in an organization that recently organized its electronic records and installed records and information management software. Your assignment is to identify and prepare a list of issues that will affect access, retrieval, and long-term retention of the electronic records. These listed items should relate to one or more of the following: hardware, software, and/or procedures for records management. Work with another student in your class to prepare this list.

Critical Thinking

APP 10-2. E-mail Records (Obj. 5)

E-mail messages may be considered records or nonrecords depending on their content and ongoing value to the company.

1. Read the description of each e-mail message below to determine whether the e-mail message should be considered a record.

2. Create a directory system for storing the e-mail files considered records. For all messages considered records, create a meaningful filename for the record and indicate the directory where the record will be stored. Assume that your operating system allows the use of long filenames.

Message Date	Contents
a. 9/3/--	Message from a coworker indicating that a 9 a.m. meeting time next Tuesday is convenient for her.
b. 9/3/--	Message from your supervisor describing new procedures for handling purchase orders.
c. 9/3/--	Message from the vice president of Human Resources describing a new sick leave policy to affect all employees.
d. 9/4/--	Message from a coworker wishing you a happy birthday.
e. 9/4/--	Message from a coworker providing routing instruction for a report you are preparing.
f. 9/4/--	Message from a vendor, Jacobsen, Inc., listing details of an important contract that is being negotiated.
g. 9/4/--	Message from an outside contractor, Morrison Co., giving an estimate for completing a project.

h. 9/5/--   Message from a coworker who is having trouble accessing files on the LAN and wonders if you are having the same problem.

i. 9/5/--   Message to Jacobsen, Inc., with questions regarding the contract under negotiation.

j. 9/5/--   Message from the Accounting Department's administrative assistant summarizing decisions made at a department meeting and listing action items.

k. 9/5/--   Message to Beck and Wallace, Inc., requesting they bid on a project and providing the relevant details.

l. 9/5/--   Message from your supervisor indicating that she will be out of the office next Wednesday.

C H A P T E R   1 1

IMAGE RECORDS

LEARNING OBJECTIVES

1. Identify uses for image records in organizations.
2. Define and describe four types of microforms.
3. Discuss four factors related to microfilm quality.
4. Discuss microfilming procedures.
5. Define and describe microfilming equipment.
6. Discuss microfilm processing and duplicating equipment and commercial imaging services.
7. Describe microform storage, retrieval, and storage environments.
8. Identify and describe integrated image systems.
9. Discuss records retention for image records.
10. Explain how software can be used in image records systems.

USE OF IMAGE RECORDS

Records or documents may be stored in paper, photographic, or electronic formats. Documents composed of vellum or mylar, such as engineering drawings and presentation materials, are also paper formats. Conventional photographic negatives and medical X-rays are photographic documents. Microforms are photographic document storage media. **Microforms** is the collective term for all micro-images such as microfilm, microfiche, aperture card, microfilm jacket, microfilm roll, or microfilm strip. Microfilm records are created by photographing records to reduce their size to miniature images on film (microimages). An **image record** is a digital or photographic representation of a record on any medium such as microfilm or optical disk. Optical disks, discussed in Chapter 10, are electronic image media.

The high storage capacity and durability of optical disks allow the capture of text as well as graphic, photographic, and animation images for viewing on a computer screen. A scanner, along with special software, converts paper records into digital form for computer usage. Technology for scanning records, creating electronic forms, and digitizing handwritten forms has encouraged the conversion of paper records into electronic or

What is an image record?

microfilm records. Electronic document formats include digitized images generated by document scanners and character-coded data or text produced by word processing software, e-mail systems, or other computer programs. Each format (paper, photographic, and electronic) has distinctive attributes that can satisfy specific life-cycle and records retention requirements. However, no format is superior in every circumstance.

Micrographics technology offers significant advantages for both active and inactive phases of the records life cycle.[1] **Micrographics** is the technology by which recorded information can be quickly reduced to a microform, stored conveniently, and then easily retrieved for reference and use. Micrographics technology miniaturizes recorded information. Microforms offer compact storage for active and inactive phases of the records life cycle. Because space is an important business resource, reducing storage space requirements is often the main reason for implementing micrographics technology. Equipment costs to produce microform records are the major implementation costs for these records systems. For long-term storage, equipment costs may be offset by savings in storage cost and retrieval efficiency.

Micrographics applications may be found in financial services companies, insurance companies, manufacturing companies, service industries, healthcare providers, government agencies, and libraries. Banks, savings and loan associations, credit card issuers, credit unions, investment firms, and finance companies use micrographics technology to benefit their information-intensive operations. Microfilming bank checks for compact storage was one of the earliest applications.

Health, life, property, and casualty insurers require convenient access to and appropriate retention of policy files, claims documents, and other recorded information. New documents can be added regularly to microfilm jackets to simplify handling of policy and agent files. Insurance companies also use microforms for storing and retrieving accounting and human resources records.

Micrographics applications in manufacturing companies include engineering drawings, technical reports, product specifications and formulations, parts lists, standard operating procedures, test results, repair manuals, supplier records, and contract files. Micrographics is also useful for manufacturing companies and other organizations seeking ISO 9000 certification. ISO 9000 is a standard developed by the International Organization for Standardization. To be ISO-compliant, an organization must develop effective systems and procedures to create, store, retrieve, and manage quality system documents resulting from product design, development, manufacturing, inspection, testing, installation, and servicing. A micrographics system provides backup protection of quality

[1]William Saffady, *Micrographics: Technology for the 21st Century.* Prairie Village, KS: ARMA International, 2000.

documents and reduces storage space for the very large number of records produced by a quality control program.

Micrographics applications in utility companies typically include accounting records, customer service documents, contracts, facilities drawings, maps and site plans, inspection and repair reports, technical specifications, project files, standard operating procedures, and environmental impact statements. Airlines and package and freight delivery companies use micrographics systems to store bills of lading, cargo manifests, shipping labels, delivery receipts, and other shipping-related documents. Law offices in which complex litigation requires production of thousands or millions of pages of evidence and documentation use micrographics or electronic imaging technology. Public accounting firms store client records on micrographic media.

Hospitals, clinics, health maintenance organizations, and physicians' offices have recordkeeping requirements determined by legal, regulatory, and reference considerations. Their micrographics applications include medical records and patient histories; diagnostic and treatment notes; laboratory reports; and X-rays. Hospitals and other medical facilities also use electronic records to improve access to patient records. Multiple departments can share treatment information and test results, while reducing the risk of misplacing or losing files.

Micrographics systems are installed in all U.S. government branches and in most agencies within the branches, in the U.S. military, in state governments, and in local governments. The federal government retains citizen and taxpayer information. The military maintains records on its personnel, engineering drawings, and weapons systems. State and local governments maintain birth, death, marriage, and adoption records; building permits, mortgages, and other property-related records; law-enforcement records; and so on. Law enforcement agencies also have found electronic imaging beneficial for sharing mug shots, incident reports, and investigative reports. Public schools and colleges retain applications and admission files, registration information, transcripts, attendance and disciplinary records, other student records, and administrative records on micrographics systems. Small colleges and universities find electronic imaging beneficial to faculty and students. Numerous people can share records simultaneously from different locations.

Libraries maintain research and historical information, rare books, and manuscripts on micrographics systems. Some libraries operate their own microfilming departments; others use service bureaus to create microforms from books and other documents in their collections. Most libraries purchase microforms from micropublishers who produce microforms for sale. Reference books, legal abstracts, government reports, newspapers, magazines, and scholarly journals are available as micropublications. Many libraries purchase these microforms to save space and to avoid having to bind periodical issues at the end of each volume year.

Chapter 11 addresses types of microforms, how microfilm is created and processed, storage and retrieval equipment, and integrated imaging systems. Microfilm records and types of microforms are discussed next.

MICROFILM RECORDS

Microfilm is a photographic reproduction of a document greatly reduced in size from the original on fine grain, high-resolution film that requires a reader for viewing. Because the photographic image is greatly reduced in size, it is called a *microimage*, and it cannot be read without magnification. The miniaturized image of a document is called a *microrecord*. *Microfilming* is the process of photographing documents to reduce their size.

Types of Microforms

All microforms originate from roll microfilm. Microforms can be produced from paper documents, called *source documents*, or from computer-generated information. The most common microforms are roll film (open reels and cartridges) and unitized or flat microforms (microfiche, microfilm jackets, and aperture cards). These flat forms contain one unit of information such as one report or one document. Because roll film can hold a large number of images, unrelated documents may be stored on one roll. Therefore, microfilm on reels or cartridges are nonunitized microforms. The main advantage of using microforms is that they provide compact storage and, therefore, reduce storage space requirements.

What are source documents?

Roll Microfilm

Roll film is the most inexpensive and most widely used microform. Microfilm on reels is usually the least expensive microform to create from a collection of source documents. A typical 100-foot roll of microfilm can hold more than 2,000 images. These images may be either positive (black characters on a clear background) or negative (white characters on a black background). Positive images on roll film are similar to black images on a clear transparency for overhead projection. Negative images resemble photographic negatives that accompany a set of developed photographs after the film is processed. Microfilm is available in widths of 16mm (millimeter), 35mm, and 105mm. Microfilm in 16mm width is preferred for documents measuring up to 11 by 17. A l00-foot roll of 16mm can hold approximately 2,500 pages of letter-size documents reduced 24x—about one file cabinet drawer. The 215-foot length of film can hold more than twice the number of images as a 100-foot roll, but it does not cost twice as much. Microfiche is created on 105mm microfilm.

How wide is microfilm?

Microfilm in 35mm width is primarily used for engineering drawings. Commercial micropublishers that specialize in scholarly documents also use 35mm. Libraries, archives, historical agencies, and cultural organizations use it for preservation microfilming. Individual frames cut from 35mm microfilm may be inserted into aperture cards. Strips of 16mm or 35mm film may be inserted into microfilm jackets. Processed 16mm and 35mm rolls may be formatted as open-reel film, which uses a separate take-up reel in a microfilm reader. Processed 16mm microfilm is often inserted into self-threading cartridges. A cartridge is an enclosed reel that also requires a separate take-up reel in a microfilm reader. The plastic casing around a cartridge permits automatic film threading into a reader and protects the film. Cartridges are widely used in computer-assisted retrieval systems in which a computer database is used to index documents stored on 16mm microfilm. A microfilm reel and cartridges are shown in Figure 11–1.

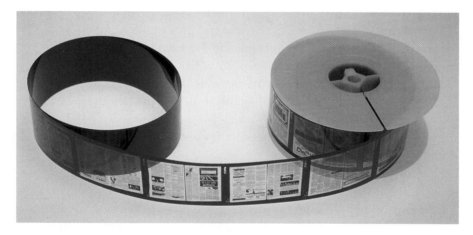

Figure 11–1a **Microfilm Reels**

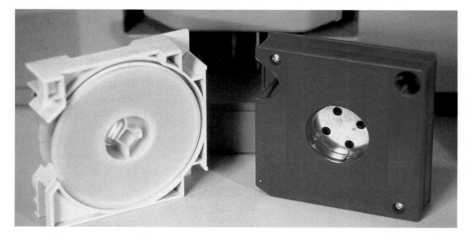

Figure 11–1b **Microfilm Cartridges**

Large volumes of information can be stored on microfilm in a small amount of space at low cost. Roll film is typically used to photograph inactive records. Records are usually photographed and captured on film in a sequential order and must be located sequentially for retrieval, which slows the retrieval process. To locate a specific record on a roll of microfilm, you must fast forward through the film to the record you are seeking. Records stored in a random sequence on roll film need an automated index system that uses computer technology to locate the roll containing the information needed for retrieval and use.

Records requiring frequent changes usually are not stored on roll film. Changes can be made by cutting out old information and splicing in new film. However, such changes in the film are expensive and may weaken the film as well as make it inadmissible as legal evidence in a court of law.

Microfiche

Microfiche, usually shortened to *fiche* and pronounced "feesh," is a microform in the shape of a rectangular sheet having one or more microimages arranged in a grid pattern with a heading area across the top (see Figure 11–2). The human-readable heading strip, called a *header*, does not require magnification. Microfilm in 105mm width is usually cut into 148 mm lengths to create microfiche, usually measuring 6″ by 4″. Fiche is a unitized microform because it contains *one unit* of information such as one accounting report.

Fiche permits direct access to any record without having to advance a roll of film to the appropriate location. Images are arranged in a grid of uniform rows and columns on microfiche. Rows are identified by letters of the alphabet, and columns are identified by numbers. A particular frame or microimage can be identified by grid coordinates such as B-5, meaning row B, column 5. A fixed amount of space is allotted to each film frame. Source documents or computer-generated information must be reduced to fit into the available space. An area at the top of each fiche is reserved for human-readable title information. Adhesive heading strips with human-readable title information can also be affixed to the top row of microfiche.

The maximum number of images contained on one fiche depends on the amount of reduction. Microfiche formats are identified by numeric designations that indicate the reduction used and the number of images each fiche contains. For microfiche produced from source documents, 24/98 is the most widely used format. At a 24x reduction, 98 original images can be stored on one microfiche, arranged in a grid of seven rows and fourteen columns. Records are commonly arranged on microfiche by filming documents in a continuous series by rows. Because users can read the title (header) at the top, fiche can easily be stored and retrieved manually. The index is usually in the lower right corner of a microfiche.

> What kinds of records are microfilmed on roll film?

> What is another name for microfiche?

> How many images can be stored on a 24x microfiche?

Figure 11–2 **Microfiche**

Microfiche is most often used in computer-output microfilm (COM) applications in which computer-generated reports go directly to microfiche. (COM is discussed later in this chapter.) Fiche is also used for business records and library materials.

Microfiche can be quickly and easily duplicated for distribution or security. It can be mailed easily and economically, and it can be produced in colors that closely resemble the colors on the original records. Color fiche can be viewed longer without eyestrain than can black and white pictures. The main disadvantage of using microfiche is cost. Creating microfiche can cost more than creating microfilm. Microfiche cameras are more expensive. Because of their size, fiche can easily be misplaced or stolen. Color-coded headers, corner cuts, or edge notches reduce misfiles.

Microfilm Jackets

A **microfilm jacket** is a flat, transparent, plastic carrier with single or multiple film channels made to hold single or multiple film strips. A jacket has one or more sleeves or channels for inserting strips of 16mm or 35mm microfilm—cut from roll film (see Figure 11–3 on page 288). Usually, camera-original microfilm rolls are duplicated, and the copies are cut into strips for insertion into jackets. Original rolls are retained as storage copies for retention or security purposes. The most commonly used microfilm jacket format is 6″ by 4″ with 4 channels holding 12 images each. Strips of film in a jacket are protected and are easily organized into units of information similar to microfiche. Jacketed film may be duplicated without removing it from the jacket. In addition, new microfilm may be inserted into a jacket for quickly updating information. A header identifying the jacketed strips can easily be affixed at the top of the microform for easy storage and retrieval, similar to microfiche. Jackets are useful for keeping together related records such as personnel and

What is the purpose of microfilm jackets?

Figure 11–3 Microfilm Jacket

medical records, correspondence, legal, customer, and policyholder files. Jacketed records can easily be purged and destroyed in accordance with records retention schedules. However, their compact size makes them easily misplaced or stolen. Color-coded headers, corner cuts, and edge notching can reduce misfiles.

Aperture Cards

An **aperture card** is an electronic data processing card ($7^3/_8''$ by $3^1/_4''$) with a rectangular hole (aperture) specifically designed as a carrier for a film image or images. Aperture cards are used primarily for holding engineering drawings or blueprints on 35mm film. Very large documents may be microfilmed in segments that are held on several cards.

Aperture cards for storing 16mm film may hold up to eight images. Four letter-size (8.5″ by 11″) pages can fit within the aperture when reduced at 16x; up to eight pages, reduced at 24x, will fit. Each aperture card provides space for human-legible information that identifies and describes the microfilmed documents. This information may be handwritten, typed, or computer printed. The front and back of an aperture card can be custom printed for special application requirements. Cards are available in various colors and with color striping for indexing and retrieval. A record is easily updated by removing an obsolete card and inserting a new one. Interfiling new cards or replacing cards within a file of cards can be accomplished quickly. Aperture cards can also be easily stolen or misplaced. Color-coded headers, corner cuts, and edge notching can reduce misfiles. Backup copies in 35mm rolls or duplicate cards provide the best protection against loss. Figure 11–4 shows an aperture card.

Figure 11–4 **Aperture Card**

Large businesses and government agencies use aperture cards to store maps and other drawings, X-rays, and business records. The principal disadvantage of using aperture cards is cost. The expense of purchasing card supplies, mounting the images, and storing fewer images on each aperture card makes the cost of these cards higher than for other microforms. Filing space requirements for aperture cards may be at least five times greater than records maintained on roll film.

What kinds of records are placed on aperture cards?

Microfilm Size

Although unexposed microfilm lengths vary from 50 feet to more than 1,000 feet, 100-foot and 215-foot lengths are the most commonly used. Microfilm width is measured in millimeters (mm). The three most commonly used widths are 16mm, 35mm, and 105mm. The narrowest film (16mm) is most frequently used for filming small documents such as checks, and standard- and legal-size records. Larger records, such as newspapers, maps, and engineering drawings, require 35mm microfilm. Microfiche generally is filmed using 105mm microfilm.

What microfilm size is generally used for microfiche?

Microfilm Quality

A microfilm copy of a record is no better than the original document. Blurred copies do not microfilm well. Colors on original documents may not microfilm. Defects on an original document may be magnified on the microrecord. Special procedures, equipment, and specific types of film are required to maintain a high level of microrecord quality. Four factors relate to quality in the microfilming process: (1) resolution, (2) density, (3) reduction ratio, and (4) magnification ratio. After inspecting the quality of the microimage using these factors with established standards of acceptability, the original record is usually destroyed. The purpose of using microforms is to transfer paper documents to a dependable media that can be stored for long periods of time in a small amount of space—not to create a long-term duplicate records system.

Resolution

Resolution is a measure of the sharpness or fine detail of an image. Good resolution requires high-quality film and a camera with a good lens. High resolution means that a microimage is clear and easily readable when magnified on a reader with a viewing screen and a light source or when printed from the reader.

What must be done to assure good resolution?

Density

Density is the degree of optical opacity of a material that determines the amount of light that will pass through it or reflect from it. A **densitometer** is a device used to measure the contrast between the dark and light areas of microfilm. A high-quality microimage has a wide variation in the dark and light areas of the microfilm. *Line density* indicates the opacity of characters, lines, or other information in a microimage. *Background density* refers to the opacity of noninformation areas. The higher the contrast, the easier the images are to read. If too little difference exists between line and background densities, microimages may look faded. If background density is too high, fine lines may widen, and interline spaces may fill in. Uniform densities are important for microforms used in automated duplicators, enlarger/printers, and scanners. Contrast sharpness depends on the quality of the source document as well as the proper lighting during filming.

What device measures contrast on microfilm?

Reduction Ratio

The **reduction ratio** is the relationship between the dimensions of the original or master and the corresponding dimensions of the photographed image. The ratio also is a measure of the number of times a dimension of a document is reduced when photographed. For example, a reduction ratio expressed as 1:24 (or 24x) means that the image is 1/24th the size of the original record, both horizontally and vertically. Reduction ratios range from 5x to 2400x, with 24x being the most commonly used reduction. Higher reduction ratios result in smaller images; consequently, a greater number of images can be photographed on one square inch of microfilm. For example, 8,100 regular-size bank checks can be photographed on 100 feet of microfilm at 24x reduction; 16,600 checks, at 50x. Banks use microfilm in 2,000-foot lengths. For easy retrieval, however, the film is cut into 100-foot or 215-foot lengths after developing.

What is meant by "the higher the reduction ratio, the smaller the images"?

Magnification Ratio

A microimage must be enlarged or magnified for reading. Magnification is the opposite of reduction. It measures the relationship between a given linear dimension of an enlarged microimage as displayed on a screen or printed on paper and the corresponding dimensions of the microimage itself. Magnification is expressed as 24x, 48x, and so on. Magnification can also be expressed as a ratio—1:24, 1:48, and so on. The **magnification ratio**, also called the *enlargement ratio*, is a method of describing the relationship between the size of an image and the original record when viewed on a microfilm reader screen. For example, a one-inch square microrecord that is magnified ten times (10x) appears in its enlarged form as ten square inches. An image filmed at 24x reduction must be magnified at 24x to produce an original-size copy.

How is magnification expressed?

MICROFILMING PROCEDURES AND EQUIPMENT

An **image system** is a combination of procedures and equipment that form an efficient unit for creating and using records in microform or electronic images. Figure 11–5 on page 292 identifies records procedures used in the three stages of an image records system: preparation, processing, and use of records. The procedures and equipment used in an image system are described in the next section.

Document Preparation

Preparing source documents for microfilming is one of the most time-consuming and labor-intensive aspects of microfilming. Document preparation is entirely manual work necessary for preparing documents and placing them into proper sequence for filming. Correspondence and other documents must be removed from file cabinets or other containers and folders and stacked neatly in correct sequence. Documents must be checked carefully; all paper clips and staples removed; torn pages mended; and attachments to records, such as envelopes, routing slips, and notes, removed. Source documents are usually prepared for microfilming in batches so that an entire 100- or 215-foot roll can be filmed at one time.

How are documents prepared for imaging?

Indexing Procedures

Recording information to serve as a location directory for microforms or electronic records is referred to as *indexing.* An index attaches identification data, called an *address,* to microrecords or electronic records. In micrographics technology, the term *index* refers to a list of microrecords on roll film, microfiche, microfilm jackets, or aperture cards.

Microrecord indexing may be prepared manually during filming or after filming. An index may be handwritten, typed, or created in a

What is the purpose of indexing?

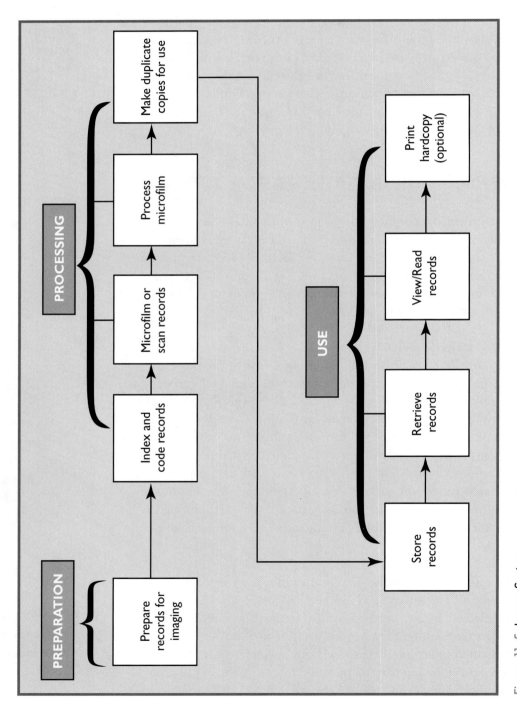

Figure 11–5 Image System

computer. To index manually during filming, a computer operator stationed adjacent to a microfilm camera assigns identifiers during filming. To index microrecords after filming, an operator places a roll of microfilm into a reader, views each image, and assigns an identifier by keying the identifier and sequential number of the microimage into a computer. Commonly used methods of indexing roll microfilm include flash target indexing, sequential frame numbering, blip coding, and bar coding. These four methods as well as methods of indexing unitized or flat microforms are discussed in the following paragraphs and illustrated in Figure 11–6. Carefully selected indexing methods facilitate retrieval of microimages, which is discussed later in this chapter.

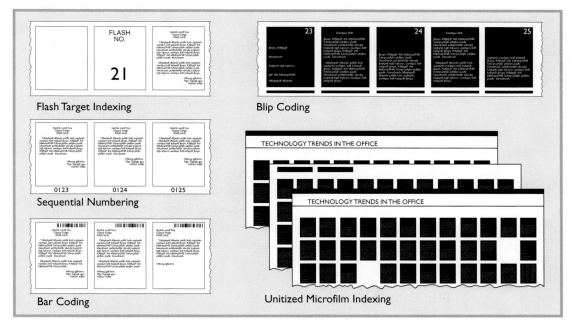

Figure 11–6 **Methods of Indexing Microrecords**

Flash Target Indexing

An often-used method of indexing and retrieving microfilmed records uses specially prepared pages and blank frames to identify and separate groups of related source documents during microfilming. The specially prepared pages, called *flash targets*, are inserted between source documents during preparation. The targets precede and describe the microimages that follow them. Each 100-foot length of 16mm or 35mm microfilm is divided into sections or groups of records similar to the way guides separate sections in a file drawer. The flash targets are human-readable and typed, handwritten, or computer-printed using large characters. These targets are visible when browsing microimages in readers, reader/printers,

How does flash indexing help locate records?

or reader/scanners. Blank frames precede the targets to alert the user to an upcoming target. Similar human-readable targets may be used to identify images recorded on microfiche or microfilm jackets. Containers for storing processed microfilm should be marked to show the section position and contents of each section on the film. When flash targets are used in preparing computer-output microfiche, an index of contents may be placed in the last frame.

Sequential Frame Numbering

Sequential frame numbering is an indexing technique for manual retrieval of microimages. Sequential numbers are assigned to each frame within a 16mm microfilm reel, 16mm microfilm cartridge, or 35mm microfilm reel. A two-part number identifies the roll and frame address of each microimage. For example, the number 15-7890 identifies a micro-image recorded on reel or cartridge number 15 at frame number 7890. The next image would be numbered 15-7891.

Some microfilm cameras will record an incrementing number with each frame as successive documents are microfilmed. The number may appear in the top or bottom of the frame. Individual pages can also be numbered by hand or with an automated stamping device before they are microfilmed. After filming, the document description, roll number, and sequential number are keyed into a computer database for an index. However, an index may also be handwritten or typed. To locate and retrieve a document, the operator consults the index for the roll and frame address to locate the microform. Then, the correct roll is inserted into a reader, reader/printer, or reader/scanner, and the film is advanced to the document frame number.

Blip Coding

A **blip code** is an optical mark, usually rectangular, that has been recorded on microfilm, appearing below an image, used for counting images or frames automatically. Three different sizes of blips may be used for subdividing documents. Blip coding is compatible with an automated system for indexing and retrieving microrecords from 16mm roll film that is inserted into self-threading cartridges. Blips are opaque, uniformly spaced marks that are usually placed below microimages; however, they may be placed in other locations. They permit accurate frame counting by specially designed retrieval devices. Blip coding is an automated variation of sequential frame numbering.

Some cameras can record blips in both top and bottom edges of each film frame. Other cameras can record blips in two or three different sizes. To retrieve a document, the user consults an external index to find the roll and frame address or number and keys this information into a calculator-style keypad on the retrieval device. When the frame address of the desired microimage is located, the cartridge containing the image is mounted into a microfilm reader, reader/printer, or reader/scanner that has blip-counting capability. This device advances the film, counts the blips at high speed, and stops when the requested image number is found.

Bar Coding

Bar codes help automate the indexing for scanned or microfilmed documents. Bar code stickers, as described in Chapter 10, may be affixed to documents before they are scanned or microfilmed. If the identifiers are sequential numbers, bar code stickers can be computer-generated in order and printed on adhesive tape or printed with a bar code printer. Bar codes are also used to identify storage areas for archived records and as a method of indexing optical disk images.

How are bar codes used?

Unitized Microform Indexing

Unitized or flat microforms may be indexed in various ways. Microfiche, jackets, and aperture cards can be indexed by adding a title (header) at the top of the microform. This header may be created by the camera or added manually. The header usually includes the name of the document and microrecord sequence number. A bar code may also be affixed to the header. Microfiche and jackets may have a color band on the header for color coding. A color code represents a batch of records or an entire file and identifies a particular type of record. Color coding helps filers locate misfiled records quickly.

Microfilming Equipment

Records may be captured on microfilm through use of special equipment. Both manual filming equipment and computerized equipment for imaging are described in this section.

Rotary Camera

For filming large-volume records, such as checks and invoices, a rotary camera may be used. It is the least expensive records filming camera. A **rotary camera** is a microfilm camera that uses rotating belts to carry documents through the camera and makes images on 16mm film at a speed of over 500 documents a minute. The rotary camera shown in Figure 11–7 on page 296 can index, feed, film, endorse, and stack up to 500 check-size documents per minute.

What documents are filmed with a planetary camera?

Planetary Camera

A **planetary camera** is a microfilm camera that uses 35mm microfilm to film large engineering drawings, hardbound books, and other large documents. These documents are placed on a plane (flat) surface for filming. This camera is slower than the rotary camera because documents

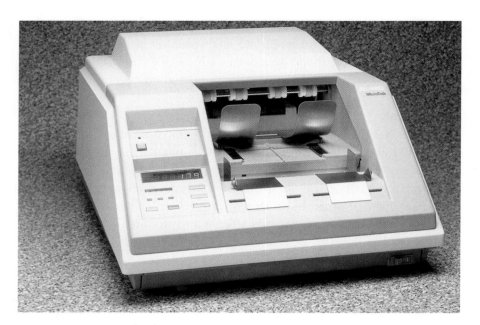

Figure 11–7 Rotary Check Camera

remain stationary during filming and are photographed one by one. Because of the greater time involvement, filming with a planetary camera is more expensive but produces higher quality images than a rotary camera. The planetary camera shown in Figure 11–8 is a compact desktop camera that can apply 3 levels of blips and has 12-digit numbering capability.

Step-and-Repeat Camera

A **step-and-repeat camera** is a microfilm camera that produces a series of separate images, usually in orderly rows and columns. It uses 16mm and 35mm microfilm to produce microfiche. This camera films images directly onto a 4-inch film width, which when cut into 6-inch lengths, produces a standard 6" by 4" master microfiche. In systems requiring frequent changes in the records—as in maintaining inventory records—an *updatable microfiche camera* (a modification of the step-and-repeat camera) is available. With such a camera, additional images can be added to a microfiche at any time if unexposed space exists on the fiche. Also, the camera can alter existing images by overprinting such words as VOID and PAID.

When is a step-and-repeat camera used?

Aperture Card Camera

An **aperture card camera** is a microfilm camera that records miniaturized images of engineering drawings or other large source documents onto 35mm film frames that are premounted into tabulating-size cards. The cards, called *camera cards*, contain unexposed film that the camera uses to photograph a drawing or other source document. Aperture card

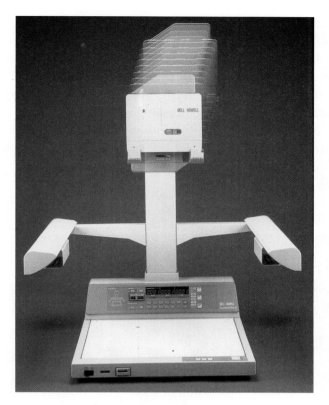

Figure 11–8 Planetary Camera

cameras are similar to planetary cameras except that they are camera-processors. They help alleviate time-consuming tasks of manual cutting and mounting individual images onto aperture cards. A source document is placed face-up onto a flat copyboard, and the aperture card camera takes a picture of it. After exposure, a camera card passes through a processing chamber and is delivered, fully developed, in about one minute. If a security copy is needed, the source document may be filmed twice or a duplicate aperture card can be produced from the camera card.

Filmer/Scanner

A **filmer/scanner**, sometimes called a *camera/scanner* or *scanner/filmer*, is a microfilm camera that can also operate as a scanner. Some records and information management applications rely on electronic document imaging for rapid retrieval, but microfilm is preferred for long-term retention and storage. With a filmer/scanner, source documents are microfilmed and digitized in one operation. Microfilm images can be scanned at the same time they are filmed. This dual process updates the electronic image file as it produces microfilm rolls for legal, archival, or historic purposes. A filmer/scanner can operate as a microfilm camera only or a scanner only, depending on the application. Rotary filmer/scanners that produce 16mm

> *How does a filmer/ scanner work?*

microfilm are the most commonly used type, although planetary filmer/scanners are available. Most filmer/scanners are heavy-duty devices designed for high-volume operations in large imaging projects, centralized document conversion operations, or commercial service bureaus. The Canon rotary filmer/scanner shown in Figure 11–9 allows filming in analog format for microfilm, digital scanning for magnetic media, or completing both operations simultaneously. It can accommodate document sizes from checks up to 11" by 17" documents and feed up to 90 letter-size documents per minute for filming/scanning. Electronic images provide immediate access; the microfilm provides a record for long-term retention.

Figure 11–9 **Filmer/Scanner**

Microfilm Processing and Duplicating Equipment

After records are microfilmed, the film is processed. A **microfilm processor** is a mechanical device that applies heat and chemical treatments to make microimages visible for display, printing, or other purposes. Most processors do not require a darkroom and can operate in daylight; the exposed film is protected by a cover on the processor in which the film is placed or by a canister placed over the exposed film outside the processor. An organization may purchase processing equipment or use commercial service bureaus for microfilm processing.

Duplicating Equipment

Microform duplication is the production of a single copy or multiple microform copies from a master microform, which may be a 16mm or 35mm microfilm roll, a microfiche, a microfilm jacket, or an aperture card. A master microform may be a camera-original microform produced directly from source documents or a copy that is one or more generations removed from the original microform. The term *generation* is used to indicate the relationship of a copy to the original source document. Camera-original microforms are first-generation microforms. Copies made from camera-original microforms are second-generation microforms. Copies of those copies are third-generation microforms, and so on. The master microform is the storage copy, and it is not circulated for use. Duplicates are used as working copies. Working copies may be distributed for use or serve as intermediate copies from which more copies will be produced. A duplicate may also be made by simultaneously exposing two rolls of film in the film unit of the camera.

Contact printing is the most frequently used method of making multiple copies. It is a process that makes a duplicate copy of microfilm by placing the emulsion side of the developed original film in contact with the emulsion side of the copy film and directing a light beam through the original image to the copy. Developing the copy film then produces a duplicate. Microfilms used for microform duplication are also referred to as *print films* or *copy films*. These films include silver gelatin, diazo, and vesicular microfilms. The decision of which film to use is based on the type of application in which it will be used, polarity of the film, and the stability characteristics of the copies. Polarity refers to the relationship between dark and light areas of a source document or microimage. Media stability is important for long-term retention requirements of microfilm records.

Production-type duplicators are designed for high-volume operations in centralized microfilming facilities, microfilm service bureaus, or micropublishers. Desktop duplicators are designed for low-volume operations in which on-demand copies of microfiche, microfilm jackets, or aperture cards are required. Most microform duplicators produce copies in the same format as the master.

Production Equipment

After 16mm roll microfilm is processed and duplicated, it may be inserted into cartridges. Newer style cartridges are simple enclosures for a reel of film. Manual or motorized loaders may be used for inserting film into older style cartridges. A microfilm roll must be removed from a reel and inserted into a cartridge. Leaders and trailers must be spliced onto the film to help it load into microfilm readers, reader/printers, or reader/scanners. A *jacket viewer/scanner*, sometimes called a *viewer/filler* or a *reader/filler*, is a reader-like device used to identify microimages for insertion into microfilm jackets. Magnified images are displayed onto a screen for examination and selection. When the last image to be inserted is displayed, the operator pushes a button or presses a lever that activates a

What does generation mean?

How is a microfilm jacket produced?

knife. The knife cuts the film and pushes it into the sleeve. The process is repeated until all jacket sleeves or channels are filled. Aperture card mounters operate in a similar manner.

Commercial Imaging Services

Commercial service bureaus provide an alternative to in-house microfilming and processing. Equipment costs to produce microform records or optical disk records represent the major implementation costs for these records. Instead of purchasing specialized equipment for microfilming or scanning records to electronic format, organizations may use commercial services. A microfilm service bureau may offer microfilming, processing, duplicating, inspecting and testing, cartridge loading and labeling, and producing microfilm jackets and aperture cards.

What advantages do commercial imaging services offer?

Small and mid-size companies may use service bureaus as part of their records and information management systems to avoid purchasing expensive equipment. Limited physical facilities and/or lack of specialized staff sometimes make outsourcing the best choice for producing microfilm or capturing images to optical disks. Micrographics service bureaus are often used for microform scanning and related services to integrating micrographics and electronic document imaging technologies. Commercial records storage centers often are used to store the master copies of vital records. Service bureaus may be selected for their reputation for good service, technical expertise to perform designated tasks, short turn-around time, safety (security) of storage facilities, efficiency in records retrieval, and reasonable cost of their services.

MICROFORM STORAGE AND RETRIEVAL

Microform storage copies are intended for retention purposes, and t hey are seldom referenced. Working copies are prepared for reference and use. Both storage and working copies should be stored in the vertical, upright position to prevent warping. They should not be stacked horizontally or subjected to pressure or weight. Storage equipment specifically designed for microforms is available for each type of microform used as working copies. Drawer cabinets for microform reels (16mm or 35mm film) and cartridges have high storage capacities but require relatively little floor space. Microfilm reels are stored in boxes whether they are stored on shelves or in drawer cabinets partitioned to fit the boxes. Cartridges may be stored in carousels with partitioned shelves or in small workstation storage units. Figure 11–10 shows an example of a roll film storage cabinet.

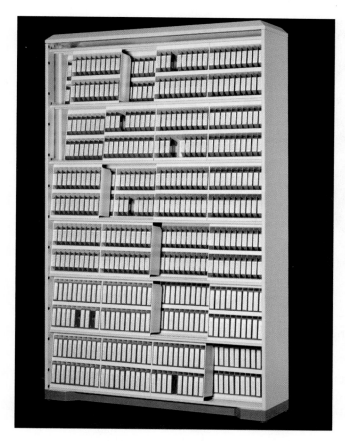

Figure 11–10 Roll Film Storage

Flat microforms may also be stored in drawer cabinets. Groups of related microfiche, microfilm jackets, or aperture cards can be separated by tabbed dividers within drawers, similar to guides in a paper records file. Tray files may be open or closed; microforms are inserted upright into tray files. Tray files are convenient for desktop storage, but they can also be stored on shelves or in cabinets for reference when needed. Microform storage panels contain pockets for inserting microfiche or, sometimes, microfilm jackets. Multiple panels can be placed into ring binders or mounted onto desk stands or carousels. Figure 11–11 on page 302 shows a workstation tray for storing microfiche records.

Microfilm Storage Environment

Because working copies are used, they are subjected to dust, skin oils, fingerprints, liquid spills, contamination by foreign materials, and exposure to excessive light and temperatures. Microfiche may be folded or torn. Microfilm in jackets or aperture cards may become separated from their carriers. Microfilm cartridges can crack. All microforms may be damaged by readers or display devices, printing equipment, duplicators, scanners,

> *What kinds of storage units are used for microfilm?*

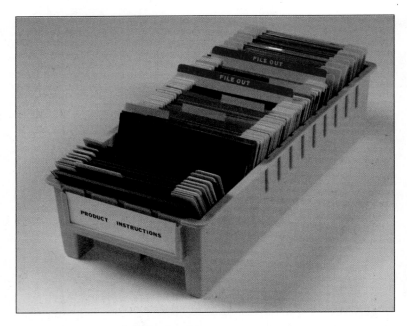

Figure 11–11 Microfiche Storage

or storage equipment. Records and information managers must ensure that established procedures are followed for the protection of microfilm records. Recommended procedures include:

Why do microrecords need controlled temperature and humidity?

- Eating, drinking, and smoking should be prohibited in all microform work areas.
- Work areas, storage containers, readers, reader/printers, duplicators, and scanners should be kept clean when using working copies.
- Storage copies must have physical and chemical properties suitable for long-term retention. Because of unique chemical properties of microfilm, special precautions must be taken to control the storage environment, especially temperature and humidity. Microrecords that have a long-term retention period should be stored under controlled conditions that include a maximum temperature of 70 degrees Fahrenheit and relative humidity less than 50 percent. Maintaining a constant temperature between 50 and 70 degrees Fahrenheit and humidity between 20 and 40 percent is important; the change in a 24-hour period should never be greater than 10 degrees in temperature or 5 percent humidity.
- Microfilm maintained for medium-term retention periods (at least ten years) requires less stringent environmental conditions. The maximum temperature cannot exceed 77 degrees Fahrenheit, although 70 degrees is preferable. Relative humidity for medium-term storage may range from 20 to 50 percent, and variations must not exceed 10 percent a day.

- Microform storage copies should be stored in a fire-resistant room or vault. All storage equipment must be noncombustible and noncorrosive. To provide further protection from fire, storage copies that contain valuable information (vital records) can be stored in insulated cabinets within fire-resistant storage areas. For maximum protection, duplicate copies of vital microforms may be stored in another location that has the same storage conditions for the retention period.
- Because microimages can be damaged by light, storage copies should be kept in dark enclosures. If possible, film should be stored in closed containers such as drawer cabinets or shelving units with doors. If open shelving or storage racks are used, then boxes or other closed containers should be used.
- Air in the storage room should be carefully controlled by an air-conditioning or air-filtration system that will remove abrasive particles and gaseous impurities that can harm the film.
- Film reels, storage boxes, and paper enclosures or attachments to microfilm should be acid free. Acids and other contaminants can cause destructive chemical reactions on film.
- Deteriorating microforms should be removed from storage areas immediately. Duplicate replacement copies should be made as soon as deterioration is noticed. Replacement copies of items obtained from micropublishers must be purchased.
- Microfilm records require the same kinds of safety and security protection as other types of records. Access should be limited to authorized users. Procedures must be in place to safeguard storage or master copies against damage or loss.

Retrieval and Viewing Equipment

Microforms are duplicated so that one or more working copies are created for viewing, printing, or scanning. Performing any of these three activities requires special equipment. However, before microimages on microforms can be viewed, printed, or scanned, they must be removed from their storage containers. For manual location of microforms on reels and cartridges, extra equipment is not required. Human-readable headers on flat microforms make retrieval easy. No special equipment is required for manual retrieval of microfiche or jackets. Computer hardware and software may be used to locate and/or retrieve microforms as well as electronic records. Microforms may be stored onto and retrieved from a microfilm drive, also called an *M drive*, in a personal computer. Images are displayed onto a computer screen.

Five types of display devices for microforms are available: readers, viewers, projectors, reader/printers, and reader/scanners. Readers, viewers, and scanners are display-only devices. Readers are the most important display devices, and they have the broadest application. A

microform reader is an optical device for viewing a projected and enlarged microimage. The image is displayed on a screen for reading. A reader's optical system contains a lens, mirrors, and a lamp that provides artificial light. Microform readers may be single-purpose or multipurpose devices. A *single-purpose reader* accepts only one type of microform. A *multipurpose reader* accepts more than one type of microform, but not all microforms. Some readers can accommodate interchangeable carriers that will allow different types of microforms to be used. A *stationary reader* provides a large screen for viewing and a wide choice of optional features such as a hood to reduce glare.

A **microform viewer**, sometimes called a *portable reader*, is a hand-held magnifier for microfiche, microfilm jackets, or aperture cards. Viewers usually weigh less than ten pounds and can be powered by a dry cell battery or by an automobile battery using a cigarette lighter/power port. A microform is inserted into a slot and manually positioned for viewing. Viewers are suitable for brief reference and are often used by field engineers, surveyors, and equipment maintenance personnel at construction sites or in vehicles.

A **microform projector** is a device that magnifies microimages for display on a wall or wall-mounted screen. Microform projectors are readers without a screen that allow microforms to be used as group presentation aids. A projector may be used at an engineering project meeting to display site surveys, construction plans, or other drawings. A projector also may be used in classrooms to display newspaper pages or various library materials.

A **reader/printer** is a microform reader with the added capability of reproducing an enlarged microimage in hard copy. The desired microimage is located, displayed, focused, and aligned for printing. Hard copies generally range in size from 8.5″ by 11″ to as large as 18″ by 24″. When larger sizes are desired, an *enlarger/printer* must be used. Reader/printers are the most widely installed type of microform printing equipment (see Figure 11–12). They may be single-purpose or multipurpose devices, depending on types of microforms they will accept. A *universal reader/ printer* uses interchangeable carriers for roll and flat microforms.

A **reader/scanner**, or *digital microimage workstation*, is a microform reader that combines the capabilities of a reader and an image digitizer. It produces electronic document images from magnified microimages. Microimages are located, displayed, focused, and positioned for scanning. Some readers automatically rotate and center microimages. If it is connected to a laser printer, a reader/scanner becomes a digital reader/printer. Digitized magnified microimages are transmitted to a laser printer for printing a hard copy. Reader/scanners can also digitize microimages for input into electronic imaging systems for distribution over networks. These images may be sent as attachments to e-mail messages, used for

> **What equipment is needed for manual microform retrieval and use?**

> **What equipment is used to make hard copies of microforms?**

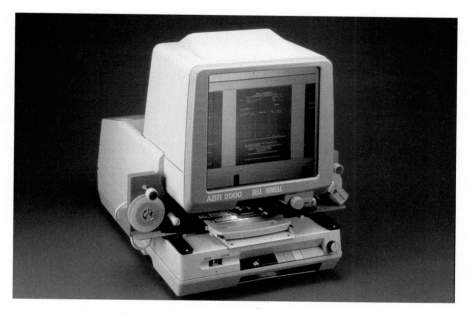

Figure 11–12 Microfilm Reader/Printer

optical character recognition, used for input into desktop publishing programs, or used for other purposes. A reader/scanner can also be equipped with a fax modem for transmitting faxes of digitized images.

Microform readers, viewers, projectors, reader/printers, and reader/scanners are stand-alone display devices. A **microfilm drive**, or *M drive*, is a computer peripheral device that retrieves and digitizes microimages for display on a personal computer to which it is connected. M drives operate much like magnetic tape drives, floppy disk drives, and other storage peripherals that use removable media. They accept 16mm microfilm cartridges that are manually loaded into a microfilm drive connected on-line to a personal computer. The computer instructs the drive, which advances the microfilm to the desired frame. The drive scans the retrieved microimage and displays it onto the computer screen. The digitized image can be printed, transferred to other storage media, input into an electronic imaging system, processed by OCR programs, or distributed electronically via fax, or e-mail. Typical scanning time is less than five seconds per microimage.

> *What is an M drive?*

INTEGRATED IMAGE SYSTEMS

Combining computer hardware and software with imaging technology increases efficiency in the creation and retrieval of microrecords while maintaining the long-term storage benefit of using microrecords. Micrographics has not been replaced by computer technology. Instead,

> *What are the advantages of using integrated imaging systems?*

microfilm integrated with electronic imaging and computer indexing and retrieval provides stable, archival storage media with rapid access to records. Integrated image systems include computer-assisted retrieval, computer-output microform, computer-input microform, and computer output to laser disk.

Computer-Assisted Retrieval (CAR)

Manual retrieval methods perform effectively when records or documents are requested by a single number or another identifier. Computer-assisted retrieval systems are designed for complex records and information management situations in which records or documents are requested by multiple identifiers. **Computer-assisted retrieval (CAR) systems** combine the document storage capabilities of micrographics with the indexing and retrieval capabilities of a computer database. A CAR system includes micrographics and computer subsystems. Each subsystem creates and maintains a database. The micrographics database is a collection of document images on 16mm microfilm cartridges or other microforms. The computer database contains an index of all records stored in microform, usually on a hard drive. The computer database also contains one record for each document in the micrographics database. Database records are organized into fields that correspond to index categories based on application characteristics and user requirements.

Using CAR, incoming paper records may be microfilmed in random sequence because records may be stored and retrieved randomly by a computer through an index. During filming, each paper record is assigned a sequential location number (address) that corresponds to the location of the microfilmed image. Next, the microrecord address and keyword descriptors, such as record title or subject, dates, amounts, and document numbers, are entered into a computer. This information becomes the computer index to the microfilmed records. The computer compares the keywords/numbers entered with the corresponding record keywords and numbers in the index to find the desired records. When a match of identifiers is made, the records found are listed on the computer screen. The user can then decide which, if any, microimages to access.

CAR systems may be off-line or on-line. In an *off-line CAR system*, microrecords are stored in standard storage equipment according to the location code index stored in a computer. To retrieve a microrecord, the user enters the appropriate record identification information into a computer. Next, the computer searches its memory for the location code of the microrecord. When the record is located, the location number (page and frame numbers of microfiche, for example) or the frame number and cartridge or roll number of the microfilm record are displayed on the screen. With this information, the user manually retrieves the microform containing the desired record from the file for use in a reader.

In an *on-line CAR system*, microrecords retrieval is connected directly to a computer. To retrieve a requested record, the operator keys record identification information into a computer. The computer searches its on-line index and directs its micrographic retrieval device to locate and display the internally stored microimage on the screen, or if desired, prints the record.

What is an on-line CAR system?

Computer-Output Microform (COM)

Computer-output microform (COM), also called computer-output microfilm, is computer output converted directly into microform without paper printout as an intermediary. The term also refers to the equipment that produces the microform or the process as a whole. Computer-created microforms can be processed faster and more economically than microforms created by the traditional microfilming process. With the use of a tape-to-film photographic device called a *recorder*, computer records on magnetic tape are converted into a microimage on roll film or microfiche. Less than four ounces of microfiche can store the equivalent of sixty pounds of hard copy. By eliminating the need for hard copy output, COM reduces cost and space storage requirements.

How does COM reduce hard copy computer output?

COM may be *on-line*; that is, a COM recorder photographs records directly from a computer. With on-line COM systems, a computer interacts with a COM recorder just as it would with a printer. Microfilming with a COM recorder not directly connected to a computer is an *off-line* operation. The computer generates a magnetic tape that contains all the data to be put onto microfilm. This tape serves as input to a COM recorder that creates microfilm.

COM recorders are expensive, and a high volume of microform production is required to justify the expense. Consequently, many organizations use commercial COM service bureaus. Service bureaus can allow an organization to implement COM at a reasonable cost. Some COM service bureaus offer substantial discounts to attract high-volume users.

Computer-Input Microform (CIM)

A computer can be used with records already on microfilm. **Computer-input microform (CIM)** is computer input taken directly from microform by scanning and character recognition. CIM also refers to the system of software and hardware that makes possible this method of transferring data to disk. COM and CIM may be combined into one system to exchange both input and output between the computer and the microimage system.

How does a CIM system work?

Computer-based document imaging has emerged as a means of managing paper-based information such as billing records, policy files, customer correspondence, legal contracts, and vital records not readily converted to database storage. Paper documents are captured on microfilm, and locations of these film images are maintained in a database. Digitized images created from microfilm may be viewed at special workstations or on networked workstation microcomputers using image display software. During the microfilming process, bar code or optical character recognition (OCR) can provide automatic image indexing.

Computer Output to Laser Disk (COLD)

Another form of long-term computer storage discussed in Chapter 10 that integrates the imaging of paper documents with electronic records is *computer output to laser disk* (COLD). COLD combines the capabilities of scanning paper documents created on another system and linking them to COLD documents (computer-created records saved by laser to optical disks). This combination of digital image scanning of paper documents, optical disk storage, and search capabilities of database software facilitates development of a computerized records storage and retrieval system for both active and long-term records.

Software management of optical drives and jukeboxes are available for microcomputer and minicomputer environments.

COLD technology includes fully automated search and retrieval capability with selected records displayed on a screen or printed to paper copy. Distribution of COLD records through networks permits shared access to a database with rapid retrieval from various worksites.

What are the benefits of using a COLD system?

Hybrid Imaging Systems

A **hybrid imaging system** is a system that contains mixed components of other systems. A hybrid system integrates microfilm-based images with electronic image processing technologies. A hybrid system includes devices that can scan microfilm; computers that can display the scanned images; and software or hardware that can process the images, compress them, and manipulate them to allow users to move them around a network efficiently. Optional components include fax capabilities, laser printers, and networks that can transmit images across local- or wide-area networks or to mass storage devices—magnetic or optical.

A hybrid system operates in the same manner as a microfilm-retrievable system up to the point at which a scan is complete. When a records request is received, the system operator locates the image or images on microfilm, retrieves the film image, and projects the image onto a device. However, instead of printing a hard copy of the image, the image is digitized and transmitted to a microcomputer for further processing.

After an image is transmitted to a microcomputer, it can be manipulated and printed on a local or network laser printer. The image can be sent through an e-mail system or faxed to the user. Additionally, the image can be routed to a character recognition device for conversion to textual data or to a magnetic or optical storage device. With digital

How does a hybrid imaging system work?

imaging, a computer can deliver information where it is needed, when it is needed, and in the form in which it is needed. A digital image also can be incorporated into word processing software for editing and for removing confidential information before it is delivered to a user.

A primary advantage of using a hybrid system is that stored images can be delivered using a system already in place in many organizations— e-mail. For example, a user can e-mail a request for a certain document from the microfilm storage center. Personnel in the center can retrieve the document image, scan it, compress it (remove redundant spaces), attach it to the e-mail reply message, and send it back across the system. All the user needs is software to decompress (restore to original format) the image for viewing, printing, or faxing. The ability to distribute information, to incorporate it into other processes, and to integrate it with software provides the cost justification for hybrid systems.[2]

> *What are the benefits of using a hybrid imaging system?*

IMAGE RECORDS RETENTION

The life span of microfilm is as long as the life span of paper records. In a carefully controlled environment, microfilm records can be protected and preserved for decades with estimates extending to hundreds of years. This durability strengthens the practicality of microfilm storage. Optical disks, including CD/DVD, have useful life spans ranging from 10 to 100 years (depending on the brand, storage, and use conditions). However, to ensure protection of microfilm or electronic records, records and information managers do not circulate the master copy of electronic, microfilm, or microform records. A *master* is the original microfilm, microform, or optical disk. Copies made for everyday use or for loan are duplicates of the master. Many records and information managers establish a policy of transferring optical disk records to new disks every ten years. The process of making new copies of the master record is called *remastering*, and it is one means of extending the life span of electronic records.

Records kept for three years or less may be kept as paper records or on magnetic or optical disk storage. Records kept from 7 to 15 years should be considered for optical disk storage or microfilming. These records can be kept accessible and stored in less space. In many states, microfilm is approved for archival storage and may be used to store official state archive records; optical disks often are not.

> *What is a microform master?*

Vital and archival records are often kept on microfilm because of its established durability. Microfilm records remain in original text format, just reduced in size; reading the text requires only projection

---

[2]Dan Kehoe, "Hybrid Imaging Systems: The Reincarnation of Microfilm," in *Proceedings of the ARMA International 40th Annual Conference, Nashville, TN, October 22-25, 1995,* (Prairie Village, KS: ARMA International, 1995), 149-160.

and magnification. This standardized format of microfilm protects records from technological obsolescence that could occur over long periods of time with electronic records. In addition, long-standing federal law permits acceptance of microfilmed records as legal documents, admissible as evidence in a court of law.

IMAGE RECORDS SOFTWARE

Several software vendors offer various types of software that facilitate storage, retrieval, and use of microimages. Some software can be used with any personal computer, others require a dedicated workstation. In any case, users may view and manipulate documents stored on 16mm roll microfilm. Users request images from a central retrieval area, then display and manage their processed requests as desktop images. Request processing may be enhanced when images can be accumulated from different rolls into a single folder. (Remember the electronic document hierarchy of directories, subdirectories, and folders?) Software can also be used to maintain the most active files in a variety of magnetic storage devices, including stand-alone drives and automated disk libraries. Digital readers and scanners use software to digitize microforms for electronic viewing, storing, and printing.

How can RIM software be used with image records?

Records and information management software, discussed in earlier chapters, has the capability to track and manage image records in the same manner as it tracks and manages paper or electronic documents. Records centers or records and information management departments usually have one software program that performs all necessary functions for the records system. A software program may allow users to build a microfilm storage unit on a computer screen and assign numbers or bar codes to microfilm boxes. Indexes for microfilm records may be stored on-line as part of the indexing function. Less work is involved with charging out microimage records because microforms are copied for use.

SUMMARY

Microfilm and optical disks are used extensively for storage of long-term records. Integrating systems of computer technology with microfilm systems has enhanced the efficiency of creating and retrieving microfilm records. Optical disk storage, with a predicted long-term life and high storage capacity, has enabled organizations to computerize both long-term and active records for rapid creation, retrieval, and transmission to multiple workstations. Both microfilm and optical disk storage represent considerable space savings for records storage as well as durable, dependable records systems.

Miniaturized images of documents on roll film, microfiche, microfilm jackets, or aperture cards are called microforms. Records managers need an understanding of equipment and processes for creating high-quality microfilm images and storing microforms in a safe and secure environment.

Microfilm lengths range from 50 feet to over 1,000 feet. Microfilm is available in 16mm, 35mm, and 105mm widths. Factors that indicate quality of microfilm are resolution, density, reduction ratio, and magnification ratio.

Imaging involves various steps throughout document preparation, processing, and use. Special equipment and procedures must be in place to ensure that documents are properly prepared for processing, appropriate camera equipment or scanners are used, records are stored in protected environments, and the documents can be rapidly retrieved and viewed.

A microfilm records system, combined with the use of computer hardware and software, is an integrated imaging system. Automated records systems have not replaced micrographics; however, the use of computer-assisted retrieval (CAR), computer-output microform (COM), computer-input microform (CIM), computer output to laser disk (COLD), and hybrid imaging systems have made records and information management systems more responsive to organizational needs.

COLD technology is a dependable alternative to microforms. With predicted long-term storage durability, optical disks are replacing microforms in many businesses. However, microfilm records will not likely disappear. Enlarging and viewing microforms is less dependent on specific technology and, therefore, less subject to technical obsolescence. However, large organizations that need rapid creation, storage, retrieval, and transmission of records are implementing COLD technology.

Hybrid imaging systems combine microfilm and scanning technology with computerized records systems. Records are kept on microfilm, retrieved, digitized, and transmitted to a microcomputer for processing, printing, or sending to another site through e-mail or fax.

IMPORTANT TERMS

aperture card

aperture card camera

blip code

computer-assisted retrieval (CAR) systems

computer-input microform (CIM)

computer-output microform (COM)

contact printing

densitometer

density

filmer/scanner

hybrid imaging system

image record

image system

magnification ratio

microfiche

microfilm

microfilm drive

microfilm jacket

microfilm processor

microform projector

microform reader

microform viewer

microforms

micrographics

planetary camera

reader/printer

reader/scanner

reduction ratio

resolution

rotary camera

step-and-repeat camera

REVIEW AND DISCUSSION

1. Give examples of the use of image records in three different types of organizations. (Obj. 1)

2. Describe and compare four types of microforms: roll film, microfiche, microfilm jacket, and aperture card. (Obj. 2)

3. Describe four factors related to processing that affect microfilm quality. (Obj. 3)

4. Discuss document preparation and indexing procedures. (Obj. 4)

5. Define and describe four types of microfilm cameras. (Obj. 5)

6. Discuss microfilm processing and duplicating equipment and commercial imaging services. (Obj. 6)

7. Describe storage equipment for storage and working copies of microforms. (Obj. 7)

8. Describe the proper storage environment for image records. (Obj. 7)

9. Describe retrieval and viewing equipment for image records. (Obj. 7)

10. Identify and describe four integrated imaging systems. (Obj. 8)

11. Discuss records retention periods for image records, especially vital records. (Obj. 9)

12. Explain how records management software can be used in image records systems. (Obj. 10)

APPLICATIONS (APP)

APP 11-1.   Microform Questionnaire (Objs. 2, 3, and 7)

Relate what you have studied about image records systems to their actual use by surveying businesses in your local community. Team with a partner in your class to determine how microfilm, microfiche, and aperture cards are used in various businesses and organizations. To complete this survey:

1. Use a telephone directory and/or your knowledge of the community to compile a list of businesses, organizations, or governmental agencies that are likely users of microrecords.

2. Prepare a questionnaire to identify which microforms are used, how microforms are used, how microforms are produced, how microforms are stored, how microrecords are retrieved, and what types of equipment are used for preparation, storage, and retrieval.

3. Prepare a cover letter to send with the questionnaire explaining this class project and its relevance to the study in your class. Be sure to ask for cooperation from businesses and organizations on your list.

4. Design a database for entering responses to the questionnaire into a computer. Design a report format for summarizing the survey results.

APP 11-2.   Determine the Image Media or System (Objs. 2 and 8)

Determine the appropriate image media or media system to use in each of the following applications.

1. Extensive use of computer records that are microfilmed for use and long-term storage.

2. Engineering drawings, maps, and X-rays.

3. Inactive records.

4. Need to share access to a database from various worksites.

5. Medical records often updated.

6. Need to use microfilmed records in a computer.

7. Need to consolidate library materials to save space.

8. Want to use computer database index to retrieve microimages.

9. Want to scan microfilm images into a computer to distribute documents by fax or e-mail.

10. Human resources records often updated.

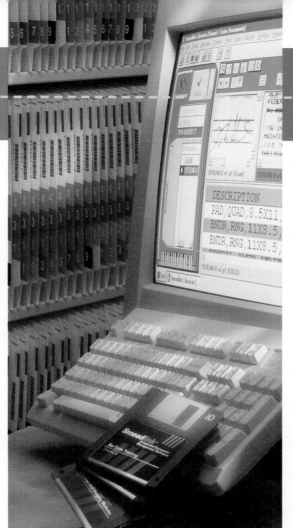

RECORDS CONTROL

12 Controlling the Records and Information Management Program

Part 5 provides a review of components of a comprehensive records and information management program presented in preceding chapters. The emphasis is on controlling the program. Topics of discussion include standards, control tools, and types of controls used to evaluate a records system. Practical procedures for controlling records creation related to correspondence, record copying, and forms are covered, along with disaster prevention and recovery issues.

CHAPTER 12

CONTROLLING THE RECORDS AND INFORMATION MANAGEMENT PROGRAM

LEARNING OBJECTIVES

1. Define *control* as a management function.
2. Identify the elements of a records and information management program.
3. Explain how the records management manual, knowledge management activities, ISO 9000 guidelines, a records inventory, records retention schedules, records audits, and a disaster recovery plan function as tools in controlling a records and information management program.
4. Describe the roles of efficiency, cost, and performance controls in controlling a records and information management program.
5. Identify major costs of operating records and information management programs and ways to control these costs.
6. List the objectives of a forms control program.
7. List guidelines for constructing a well-designed form.
8. Identify principal costs involved in producing correspondence and suggest methods of reducing such costs.
9. Explain how to control copymaking costs.
10. Describe and discuss electronic document management systems.

RECORDS AND INFORMATION MANAGEMENT ELEMENTS

A comprehensive records and information management (RIM) program includes responsibilities for paper, magnetic, and electronic records storage; micrographics technology; forms management; reports management; disaster prevention and recovery; knowledge management; ISO 9000 records; and sometimes information technology/information systems (IT/IS). The records management function often falls within the IT area. See Appendix A for an organization chart for the records management function.

Knowledge Management

If an organization recognizes that it is a part of the knowledge economy and that it employs knowledge workers, it may be engaged in knowledge management activities to make effective use of its knowledge resources. *Knowledge management* is an interdisciplinary field that is concerned with systematic, effective management and utilization of an organization's knowledge resources. It encompasses creation, storage, retrieval, and distribution of an organization's knowledge—similar to records and information management.

A knowledge resource may be explicit knowledge or tacit knowledge. *Explicit knowledge* is contained in documents, databases, e-mail, or other records. *Tacit knowledge* is acquired through observation, practice, and imitation. It relies on experience, judgment, and intuition and is exhibited through employee skills or "know-how."[1] Employee knowledge, skills, and experience are valuable resources that, with proper management, can be fully utilized. The first step in managing knowledge is to conduct a knowledge inventory to determine what knowledge, skills, and experience employees have and where they are located. Once that information is collected, organized, and stored in a knowledge database, employees can be used in areas where their knowledge, skills, and experience are needed. Sometimes a department or office borrows an employee from another department for a short period of time to perform specialized duties.

What is knowledge management?

ISO 9000 Guidelines

If an organization is engaged in international sales and marketing of its products, it is probably involved in ISO 9000 activities. *ISO 9000* is an international standard for organizing and documenting processes and procedures used to establish a quality system, developed by the International Organization for Standardization (ISO). Its purpose is to improve the quality of products and services while increasing productivity and reducing costs. ISO 9000 guidelines specify the types of procedures and documentation that a company must develop, the records or evidence it must create, and the training and measurement it must conduct if it is to do business with other ISO 9000 registered organizations. Organizations registered with ISO 9000 build and maintain a system of excellence that staff, clients, and users can depend on and trust.[2]

What is ISO 9000?

---

[1]William Saffady, *Knowledge Management: A Manager's Briefing*, Prairie Village, KS: ARMA International, 1998, p. 4.

[2]Wendy Duff and Sue McKemmish, "Metadata & ISO 9000 Compliance," *The Information Management Journal* Vol. 34, No. 1 (January 2000), p. 11.

To establish and organize a comprehensive RIM program, the records and information manager and the IT manager should work together to assure the completion of the following steps:[3]

1. Conduct a records inventory.
2. Determine which records systems should be electronic; develop policies for managing the electronic system.
3. Develop and implement a legally valid records retention schedule for all records media.
4. Establish a vital records protection plan.
5. Develop systems for managing active records.
6. Implement electronic imaging wherever possible and appropriate.
7. Develop systems for managing inactive records.
8. Assure that historical data is properly archived.
9. Implement RIM software for organization-wide records and information management.

With such broad responsibilities, a records and information manager must implement controls for the records system. A **control** is a device or mechanism used to regulate or guide the operation of a system. It literally means to check or verify by comparison with a *standard*. **Standards** are a complete and well-defined set of published rules pertaining to a certain subject. A standard is a measure or yardstick by which the performance of a system or program is rated. In records and information management, controlling is an important management function in which managers measure how well their program objectives have been met. With this information, they can make any necessary adjustments.

Organizations that develop standards for record and information management areas, such as micrographics and other technologies, include the Association of Records Managers and Administrators (ARMA International; www.arma.org), the Association of Information and Image Management (AIIM; www.aiim.org), the International Organization for Standardization (ISO), and the American National Standards Institute (ANSI; www.ansi.org). ANSI publishes numerous standards for size and quality of microfilm, microfilm cameras, microfilm processors, microfilm viewing equipment, and other micrographics equipment. ARMA published a competency standard for RIM professionals in 2000. This standard lists basic competencies and knowledge required for records and information management job descriptions. The purpose of publishing this standard is to provide guidelines for coursework provided by educational institutions and private training organizations. A draft of an international RIM standard developed by representatives from Australia, Canada, China, France, Germany, Netherlands, Poland, the United Kingdom, and the

What is a standard?

---

[3]Mark Langemo, "Records Management Software," *OfficeSystems 99*, October, 1999, p. 23.

United States has been released for review by ISO members. When the draft is approved, it will be published as a standard. This chapter is about measuring—or evaluating—a records and information management program.

Control Elements

Organizing the essential elements of a records and information management program may or may not be a records and information manager's direct responsibility. For example, some records and information managers' responsibilities begin with the *storage* phase of a record rather than the *creation* stage of a record's cycle. Nonetheless, a complete records and information management program should provide the following essential elements:

1. *Systematic control* over creating, handling, processing, filing, storing, retrieving and disposing of *all media* containing business information; i.e., paper media, magnetic media, optical media, microforms, audiotapes, and videotapes.
2. *Adequate evidence (records) of all business activity* needed to document accurately and protect legally the interests of an organization, including its shareholders, its employees, and its clients.
3. *Uniform policies and procedures* for identifying, storing, and retaining every type of records medium used. Records need to be classified and indexed so that they can be identified and retrieved quickly and accurately.
4. *Systematic and accurate distribution of and access to* records used in day-to-day operations while still controlling access to confidential information.
5. *Protection for all records* from accidental loss and disaster; a disaster recovery plan, which protects vital and historical records and those records needed for business continuity.
6. *A records appraisal process* that results in a records retention program developed after consulting program users, corporate attorneys, and auditors to be sure that user needs and legal requirements are met.
7. *Cost, efficiency, and performance controls* to evaluate personnel, space use, equipment needs, and procedures. Such controls result in reduced labor costs, space requirements, and number of lost and misfiled records while increasing response time to requested information.
8. *Training and education* to assure that all users are familiar with the program and are made aware of any program changes.

Control Tools

When developing RIM programs, records and information managers develop policies and standards for operating the programs. All main elements in a records system are involved with control.

> **What does a complete records and information management program provide?**

What are
some records
control tools?

What is a
records
management
manual?

To achieve control, records and information managers use tools that are defined and described in a records management manual. These tools include the records inventory, records retention schedule, records audit, and disaster recovery plan.

Records Management Manual

The most important control reference for a records management staff is the **records management manual.** This manual contains all information necessary to manage the records and information management program in an organization, e.g., policy statement, records retention schedules, procedures, vital records procedures, records inventory, etc. Especially useful in conducting the records audit, this manual is the official handbook of approved policies and procedures for operating the records and information management program. Responsibility for various phases of the program, standard operating procedures, and aids for training employees are included in the manual. Some organizations may also include information about their knowledge management and ISO 9000 activities. The contents of a typical records management manual are as follows:

Main Sections	Section Contents
1. Records and information program overview	Definition, goals, policies, and personnel responsibilities, records retention schedules, disaster recovery plan
2. Classification systems	Records classifications, alphabetic index, subject records classification codes, retention and disposition codes
3. Creation criteria and storage procedures for: a. paper records b. image records c. electronic records	*What* to store and when; preparing records for storage; classifying and coding; preparing cross-references; sorting records; storing records; restricting access to records; retrieval suggestions; charge-out system and follow-up; folders and storage container maintenance
4. Records retention schedules	Short-term and long-term retention periods; separate retention schedules for specific departments
5. Storage locations	Department sites, central sites, off-site locations
6. Annual program evaluation	Purposes and requirements of each program evaluation

7. Records disposition	Disposition functions; implementing records retention schedules; packing records and labeling boxes; transferring records; retrieving inactive records from storage; destroying records in inactive storage
8. Disaster recovery plan	Plan steps; contact persons; emergency procedures
9. Records management manual	General policies and procedures; records and information manual distribution, maintenance, and use; records retention schedules; administrative responsibilities

Records Inventory

Before a records and information manager can decide what records to retain, a records inventory must be taken. A records inventory is a survey that provides a detailed listing of an organization's records. The inventory includes quantity, type, function, location, and frequency of use of the records surveyed. Chapter 6 explains the records inventory and the benefits that can be achieved from such a survey.

Records Retention Schedule

A basic records control tool is the records retention schedule, a listing of an organization's records along with the stated length of time the records must be kept. The records retention schedule is illustrated and discussed in Chapter 6.

Records Retention Schedule Development. After records inventory surveys completed by each department in an organization are collected, a tentative records retention schedule is prepared. Members of each department, members of the legal staff, and others involved with regulatory requirements review the schedule and verify suggested retention periods. When all parties agree, the records retention schedule is finalized. If the information technology department maintains a separate retention schedule for electronic records, appropriate laws and regulations are used to assign appropriate retention periods.

Records Retention Schedule Implementation. To assure that all organization members are aware of and adhere to records retention schedules, they are distributed to each department along with detailed instructions for their use. Special meetings may be held to explain further if necessary.

Records Audit

A **records audit** is a periodic inspection to verify that an operation is in compliance with a records management program. From the audit, managers hope to find ways of improving the program's performance. Large organizations may use their own trained staff to undertake such an audit, or they may hire outside consultants (usually having more objectivity and expertise) for this purpose. Small firms often use outside auditors because they usually do not have a qualified records auditor on staff.

A records audit provides three kinds of information about a records and information management program:

What does a records audit provide?

1. *Information about current operations.* This information includes how well the objectives are being achieved; whether written policies and procedures are available and followed by all personnel; whether policies and procedures actually reflect the way documents are processed; and the scope of records and information management activities and any problems associated with them.
2. *Analysis of the current system and its needs.* This analysis includes the layout of files; effectiveness and validity of policies and procedures; qualifications of the staff; uses of available equipment; active and inactive storage systems; costs of operating the system versus projected costs; and security measures for preserving and protecting records.
3. *Recommended solutions for improving the RIM program.* These solutions also include cost estimates for implementing the recommendations.

Software is also used to provide audit trails for tracking document usage and, consequently, staff productivity. A system administrator can monitor electronic image and electronic records usage by determining who has been viewing which documents, where, and when. Monitoring sensitive case documents that need to be kept secure, tracking staff productivity, and tracking search activity among public records can be done using audit logs generated by the software.

Disaster Recovery Plan

Also referred to as *contingency plan*, a **disaster recovery plan** is a written and approved course of action to take when disaster strikes, ensuring an organization's ability to respond to an interruption in services by restoring critical business functions. The plan also details how records will be handled prior to and during a disaster and after in the recovery stage. Procedures for the immediate resumption of business operations after a disaster are included as well. How an organization prepares for a disruption to its business determines how well, or if, it survives. Flooding is the most common cause of business interruptions, followed by equipment outage, power outage, fire or explosion, earthquake, hurricane, and building outage resulting from construction or from environmental problems.

Why is a disaster recovery plan necessary?

A disaster recovery plan ensures that an organization can restore critical business functions after a disaster occurs.

Some records and information managers differentiate emergencies from disasters. An **emergency** is an unplanned adverse event that requires organization personnel to initiate activities to secure operations or protect assets from harm.[4] An emergency could be a broken water pipe, bomb threat, severe storm, or other events that require action but not always significant effort to control. Emergencies do not usually result in major losses. A **disaster** is an emergency event that results in conditions that require resources beyond the organization's abilities. Disasters may include a fire, flood, or a tornado that causes major damage to one or more facilities. A disaster may be limited to one building or business, or it can be community-wide. Disasters result in significant financial loss.

Hurricanes, earthquakes, and the well-publicized bombings in major cities and in federal office buildings have alerted all businesses to the critical importance of a disaster recovery plan. Such a plan needs to identify procedures for four phases: prevention, preparedness, response, and recovery. The prevention phase outlines activities or measures to reduce the probability of loss if an emergency occurs. Preparedness means that an organization's resources are positioned before an emergency occurs. Preparedness activities include developing and updating the plan, testing emergency systems, training employees, stocking emergency supplies, arranging for recovery vendors, and establishing *hot sites* (locations where a complete computer operation is set up and ready). Responding to an emergency event means activating resources necessary to protect the organization from loss. These activities occur before, during, or directly after an emergency and include contacting the response team, notifying appropriate authorities, securing facilities, notifying RIM recovery vendors. Recovery activities are associated with restoring resources or

[4]Virginia A. Jones and Kris E. Keyes, *Emergency Management for Records & Information Programs*, Prairie Village, KS: ARMA International, 1997.

operation following an emergency or disaster. These activities include dehumidifying records, restoring data onto computers, and returning vital records from off-site storage.[5]

A disaster recovery plan is the basis for:

1. Identifying preventive measures against records and information loss.
2. Initiating a company-wide response to disasters that threaten records and information.
3. Identifying response personnel and their roles.
4. Estimating cost of and various types and lengths of business disruptions.
5. Providing off-site storage for vital records and backup computer data storage.
6. Designating alternative sites for mission-critical tasks including computer-related operations.
7. Establishing recovery procedures for damaged records and information.
8. Establishing recovery priorities.
9. Identifying sources of supplies, equipment, and services for recovery and restoration of damaged records and media.
10. Testing the plan through mock disasters and making appropriate changes.

Records can be lost and/or damaged when necessary precautions are not taken to protect them. Small precautions are taken routinely to protect electronic data such as controlling extremes in temperature and humidity, backing up high-value data, installing antivirus programs that detect and remove computer viruses, installing surge protectors to minimize damage caused by electrical variances, and removing magnetic items from around hard drives and floppy disks. Discussions in Chapters 10 and 11 include procedures for (1) controlling and protecting records from physical hazards existing in an office environment, (2) controlling environmental conditions necessary to ensure safe storage of all records, and (3) protecting records from unauthorized access.

The test of a sound disaster recovery plan—and any other precautionary procedures and safety measures taken to protect records and business operations—is one that allows business activity to resume within a few days after a disaster. Such a plan includes *not only* a recovery of records *but also* a recovery of the worksite, essential equipment, and the work force.

Efficiency, Cost, and Performance Controls

Three specific types of ongoing controls are efficiency controls, cost controls, and performance controls. When these controls are applied to people, storage space, storage equipment, and routine procedures, they become key elements that make a records and information management program function effectively. All three controls are based on the **cost-benefit ratio**—a comparison to determine that *every cost (input) results in*

---

[5]Ibid.

an equal or greater benefit (output). When applied, the cost-benefit ratio gives guidance and purpose to the process of efficiency, cost, and performance controls.

Efficiency Control

An **efficiency control** is a method for evaluating the ability to produce a desired effect with a minimum expenditure of time, energy, and space. When efficiency controls are applied to storage and electronic equipment, many possibilities surface for delivering faster data output, documents, and paper records while conserving time, energy, and space.

Efficiency controls also include measuring filers' speed and accuracy and developing standards from such measurements. Practical standards for storing and retrieving records are developed by answering three important questions: (1) How much time is required to store a record from the time such storage is authorized? (2) How much time is required to retrieve a record from storage? and (3) What is the expected turnaround time—the amount of time required to find and deliver a record to a requester after a request for a record has been made? Time standards depend on whether a task is performed manually or electronically. Also, times may vary among organizations because of types of records stored, storage facilities and equipment selected, and filers' skills. The three questions can be directly related to published standards for manual storage and retrieval systems, such as those outlined in Figure 12–1, that large

> *What are two efficiency controls?*

TASK	TIME UNIT (h = hour; m = minute)
Manual Systems	
Code typical one-page letter	200/h
Key folder labels	100/h
Sort invoices into 3-digit numeric sequence	1,500/h
Sort coded letters	250/h
Place records into subject file	150/h
Place vouchers into numeric file	250/h
Retrieve record from color-coded file	2.5/m
Retrieve correspondence and prepare charge-out records	70/h
Electronic Systems	
Store and retrieve files: Depends on *access time* (microseconds of time required for a specific computer to store and retrieve data).	

Figure 12–1 Records Storage and Retrieval Standards

firms and standards associations have developed. Efficiency controls have value and include not only *efficiency standards* but also *efficiency ratios*.

Efficiency Standards. Because providing needed information is the main function of any records and information program, the most important test of any records system is the speed with which stored information can be located. Efficiency standards used to measure filers' ability to locate information include:

1. The number of misfiles, usually about 3 percent of the total number of records filed.
2. The number of "can't find" records, which should be under 1 percent.
3. The time required to find a record, which should never exceed 2 to 3 minutes.

At least once a year, an office or records and information manager should check the efficiency of a records and information program. In addition to the three efficiency standards mentioned previously, other measures to check include: (1) the number of records retrieved compared to the total cubic feet of stored records, (2) the number of records received (in number of records or in cubic feet of space occupied), (3) the amount of space being used for records compared to the total square feet of floor space, (4) the amount of unused space available, (5) how often records are requested from the files, (6) how much equipment is (or is not) being used, and (7) how many records have been destroyed or transferred from active to inactive storage.

Efficiency Ratios. An **efficiency ratio** is a standard for measuring the efficiency of various aspects of records systems. Ratios provide records and information managers with a quantifiable means of measuring efficiency, progress or decline in efficiency, and the ability to establish an efficiency or to compare their organization's efficiency against another's. The most useful ratios relate to: (1) the **activity ratio,** (2) the **accuracy ratio,** and (3) the **retrieval efficiency ratio.** These ratios are explained in Figure 12–2.

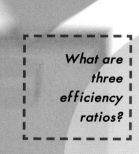

What are three efficiency ratios?

Cost Control

Managing the volume of paper records, as pointed out in Chapters 1 and 6, carries with it tremendous costs. These costs include salaries, space, equipment, and supplies.

Labor costs represent the largest percentage of total records and information management costs, and the greatest potential for controlling costs is by controlling human resources costs. This cost factor includes managerial, supervisory, and operating personnel salaries along with employee benefits such as retirement plans, social security contributions, and health insurance. Reducing long-term labor costs by installing automated systems should not be overlooked. Although electronic media

TYPE OF RATIO	HOW RATIO IS CALCULATED
1. **Activity ratio** (measures the frequency of records use)	$$\frac{\text{Number of records requested}}{\text{Number of records filed}}$$ Example: 500 records requested; 5,000 records filed or a 10% activity ratio. (When the ratio is below 5%, all records in the file that fall below 5% should be transferred to inactive storage or destroyed.)
2. **Accuracy ratio** (measures the ability of filers to find requested records)	$$\frac{\text{Number of records found}}{\text{Number of records requested}}$$ Example: 5,950 records found, 6,000 records requested, or a 99.17% accuracy ratio. (When the ratio falls below 97%, the records system needs immediate attention.)
3. **Retrieval efficiency ratio** (measures the speed with which records are found and verifies how filers spend their time)	$$\frac{\text{Time to locate records}}{\text{Number of records retrieved}}$$ Example: A ratio of 75% (retrieving 80 records in 60 minutes) suggests an efficient records system and a productive filer, depending on the type of files and filing conditions.

Figure 12–2 Efficiency Ratios for a Records System

costs are declining, storage and management costs are increasing. A clearly defined records retention policy prevents an organization from retaining unnecessary data.

Records systems studies point out many opportunities for identifying and reducing costs. The steps commonly taken to reduce costs include:

1. *Identify elements in the four main cost categories—salaries, space, equipment, and supplies.*
2. *Assign cost figures to the elements in the records system.* These elements include hourly rates for all records personnel, costs of equipment, and cost of the space that equipment occupies. Thus, the costs of maintaining typical files (such as five-drawer vertical cabinet files) can be computed and used in cost-reduction studies.

How are records costs controlled?

3. *Compare labor costs for storing and retrieving records in-house and using off-site or commercial storage facilities.* For example, applying the cost-benefit ratio to using a commercial records center. Evaluate the cost of picking up records, storing records, using a pick list to retrieve records, delivering records to the company, and destroying records. Include costs incurred by emergency records requests and fast delivery.

Costs of equipment, space, salaries, and supplies can be controlled by (1) eliminating unnecessary records, (2) carefully supervising the use of equipment and supplies, and (3) selecting equipment and media that require smaller amounts of space and less time to operate. Implement performance standards to reduce labor costs. Employee performance can then be measured against these standards.

Performance Control

The attitudes that each records employee brings to the job affect performance standards. In addition to the efficiency and cost controls discussed earlier, each of the following aspects of human behavior needs to be understood and controlled:

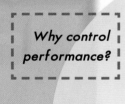

Why control performance?

1. Poor attendance—frequent tardiness and absences.
2. Excessive need for overtime work.
3. Numbers and patterns of errors in the work of each employee.
4. Slow response to work assignments.
5. Low morale and lack of interest in the work assigned.
6. Lack of concern for, or inability to follow, budget limits.
7. Repeated failure to meet performance standards.

Supervisors should discuss these performance problems with their employees. By working together in this way, solutions can be developed for increasing productivity in the records system.

CONTROLLING RECORDS CREATION

How does paper selection affect cost?

Ideally, the records and information manager is involved with records from their creation to their destruction. Unfortunately, this situation does not always occur. If it did, a records and information manager's involvement with records creation would begin by controlling paper selection. A cost-conscious records and information manager realizes that various documents require different paper qualities. Whether the document is one- or two-sided, whether the document is for internal or external use, or whether the document contains graphics and requires sharp details—all these requirements affect paper selection and ultimately the total cost of operating a records and information management program.

To control records creation beyond paper selection, the records and information manager must influence those who are responsible for creating and using the records; namely, the records originators, records receivers, and the administrative staff that distribute and manage the records. Records originators need to be reminded that the most expensive cost in a record's cycle is incurred at its creation stage and be urged to exercise restraint at this time. Also, records receivers and administrative staff need to distinguish between records required for documentation from those that may be destroyed. The easiest way to control records costs is to reduce the number of records that enter the system by destroying those records that are *not* needed and controlling only those that are needed for business or historical purposes. The importance of controlling correspondence, extra copies, and forms is addressed in this section.

Correspondence Control

Correspondence may be two types of records—external messages written to and from persons or organizations outside an organization and internal messages or memos transmitted among departments within the firm. Fax messages and Internet messages sent and received may be either internal or external messages. For example, e-mail and fax messages may be sent to a branch office or to an outside company. The total system of producing correspondence includes composing the message (dictating, handwriting, or composing at a keyboard), transcribing or formatting into final copy, and transmitting or mailing the correspondence.

Labor costs of dictating and transcribing correspondence comprise a major portion of correspondence costs. As salaries increase, the cost of producing a letter increases as well. Yet, computer and electronic equipment costs for e-mail and fax communications also need to be considered relative to the need to move information more rapidly.

In correspondence systems, specific costs related to the production of letters and reports include salary and time of dictator, salary and time of assistant taking dictation and transcribing the correspondence, nonproductive labor (waiting time, interruptions, etc.), fixed costs (rent, taxes, overhead including supervision, and employee benefits), materials costs (stationery, etc.), and mailing costs (postage, gathering, sealing, stamping, and sorting). Labor time represents the greatest percentage of total costs. Because correspondence accounts for such a large portion of all stored documents, creation, distribution, use, and storage costs require close examination and evaluation. Originators can exercise restraint in their use of correspondence by seeking alternative, less expensive means of communicating such as a telephone call or e-mail. Originators can also dictate and create correspondence using speech-recognition programs, thus eliminating the cost of transcription. The only alternative to controlling correspondence is to ensure that such documents are being produced, distributed, and stored by the most economical and efficient means.

> *How are correspondence costs controlled?*

Many automatic features of word processing software save valuable time for office staff. Using form letters saves the time of dictators, or word originators. Commonly used paragraphs, letterheads, special letter parts, special forms, and a variety of text data and graphics can be indexed and stored in computer word processing files and retrieved as needed. The user selects paragraphs (usually from a binder containing copies of these printed letter parts) to include in a letter or memo or an entire letter/memo. The computer operator compiles the paragraphs into the letter/memo and prints it for signature.

Controlling correspondence includes evaluating the tasks of creating, distributing, using, storing, and eventually disposing of correspondence and then looking for the most economical ways of accomplishing these tasks. However, the ultimate goal of controlling correspondence is to reduce the number of records that must be stored and maintained.

Copy Control

Why control copymaking costs?

Computers and photocopiers produce records by the millions, many of which are unnecessary and add to storage expenses. To control copy-making costs, records and information managers are conscious of this overriding point: *Every cost originated should result in an equal or greater benefit*—the cost-benefit ratio mentioned earlier. In other words, when the benefits realized are divided by the cost, the result should be 1 or greater. Records employees, therefore, need to identify all costs of creating and copying records (personnel, equipment, supplies, space, and so on) already mentioned. In addition, they should uncover hidden costs, including the costs of ordering supplies, filing equipment for records storage, and mailing.

Easily implemented ways to control copymaking costs include: (1) select the most suitable—and least expensive—methods and supplies; (2) use only one or two copier models to reduce maintenance costs; (3) calculate per-copy costs regularly; and (4) charge all copymaking costs to the department involved (called *chargeback*). Even tighter controls over copiers are possible by requiring employees to obtain approval from a supervisor before making copies and by installing copiers that require a key or access card to unlock and use them. Such a copier may also record the job number, the number of copies made, and a reference for charging the copy costs to the using department. These copiers can then regularly process usage reports.

A photocopier creates more copies with greater speed than any other office machine. Because producing extra copies of documents and reports can easily become standard practice in an office, photocopying is an important part of the total control process.

Forms Control

A **form** is a fixed arrangement of predetermined spaces designed for entering and extracting prescribed information on a paper or electronic document. (See Figure 12–3.) A records and information manager's responsibilities include controlling business forms. In large organizations that use many forms, this responsibility may be delegated to a forms manager and staff who are part of the records and information management program. See Appendix A for more about forms management positions.

A form contains two types of data: (1) **constant data**—data that are preprinted on a form. Constant data (such as the word "date" and the phrase "Pay to the order of" on a bank check) do not require rewriting each time the form is filled in; and (2) **variable data**—data that change each time a form is filled in. Examples of variable data on a bank check are the filled–in date, the payee's name, the amount of money, and the signature.

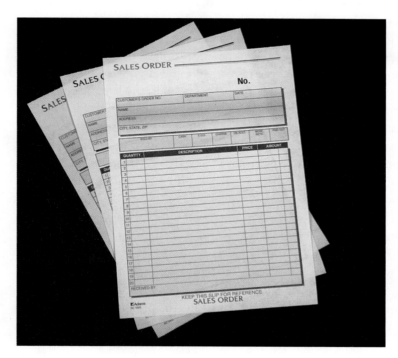

Figure 12–3 Printed Forms

Forms Control Goals

Large firms use thousands of forms for recording information. To ensure that these forms are efficiently and economically used, these firms develop company-wide (also called *enterprise-wide*) programs to control all phases of forms work. Typical goals of forms control programs are to:

> **Why control business forms?**

1. *Determine the number and use of forms.* This step occurs as a part of a records inventory.

2. *Eliminate unnecessary forms.* This goal includes: (a) eliminating forms that overlap or duplicate each other by combining them, (b) eliminating forms that collect unused information, and (3) eliminating forms no longer needed.
3. *Standardize form size, paper quality, and design features such as company logos and form numbers.* Standardization results in lower form costs because one type and size of paper can be used.
4. *Ensure efficient forms design.* Apply sound design principles.
5. *Establish efficient, economical procedures for printing, storing, and distributing forms.* These procedures should include an inventory control program to allow sufficient time to revise forms before reordering them.

Types of Forms

Forms are produced in several types of construction and are used for many different purposes. *Single-copy forms,* called "cut sheets," such as telephone message forms, are used within one department for its own needs. *Multicopy forms,* called "unit sets" or "snap sets," such as a four-copy purchase order, are used to transmit information outside the creating department. These preassembled sets of forms are perforated for easy removal of each copy. *Continuous forms* with punched holes in the left and right margins are used in computer printers for high-volume usage. (See Figure 12–4.) In automated records systems, *electronic forms,* created by special forms design software, appear on terminal screens for data input from a keyboard. Unlike paper forms, electronic forms are not printed and stocked. Instead, they are designed, filled in on-line, and either transmitted to another workstation or printed.

Forms Design

When designing a business form, the designer must understand: (1) how the form will be used; (2) the types of items to be filled in and their sequence; (3) the size, color, and weight of paper stock to be used; and (4) the amount of space needed for each "fill-in."

What determines a well-designed form?

The main objectives in forms design are to make the form efficient to fill in (whether manually or electronically), efficient to read and understand, and *efficient to store and retrieve.* These objectives can be met by applying the design guidelines shown in Figure 12–5 on page 334. Study carefully the application of each guideline that appears in the right column.

Although forms design should be left to experts, forms design books and computer software allow computer operators to design professional-quality forms.[6] Application software programs that have forms templates (patterns) can be used to design commonly used

[6]Marvin Jacobs and Linda I. Studer, *Forms Design II: The Course for Paper and Electronic Forms.* Prairie Village, KS: ARMA International, 1991. This text provides step-by-step instructions for designing professional, efficient paper and electronic forms.

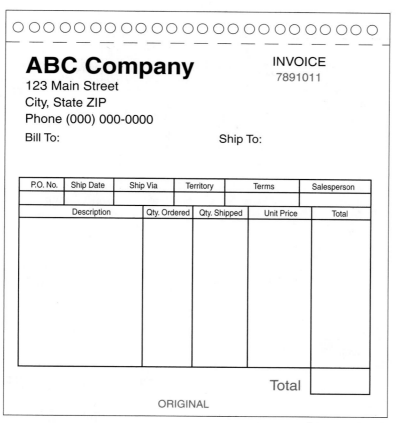

Snap-out Form

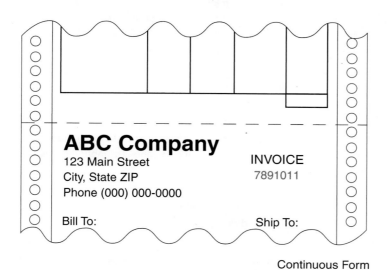

Continuous Form

Figure 12–4 Snap-out and Continuous Forms

GUIDELINES	APPLICATIONS
1. Design forms with users in mind.	• Use a different color for each department receiving its own copy of the form. Use heavy card stock for forms to be used outdoors or subject to large-volume indoor use.
2. Keep the design simple by eliminating excessive graphic features such as borders and drawings and unnecessary or unlawful information.	• Don't ask for both age and date of birth even when this information must be obtained. • Don't request information that may be personal or used for illegal purposes (religion, ethnicity, etc.). • Don't use horizontal ruled lines when the fill-in is to be typewritten or printed by computer.
3. Give each form a name that designates its function and a number that shows its sequence within the creating department. Include revision date with the form number.	• Name: Sales Invoice (not Sales Invoice Form) • Number: S-15(05/00)—to identify the 15th form in the Sales Department revised 05/00.
4. Use standard paper stock size and standard typefaces.	• Use card/paper sizes that may be cut from standard 17″ × 22″ mill-size stock without waste. Standard paper sizes, such as 5″ by 3″, 6″ by 4″, 8″ by 5″, and 8.5″ by 11″, are economical to buy, use, and store. • Use sans-serif typeface for captions and serif for text.
5. Arrange items on the form in the same order in which data will be filled in or extracted from the form.	• Use same order of data on purchase orders as used on purchase requisitions. • Arrange items in the normal reading pattern of left to right and top to bottom.
6. Preprint constant data to keep fill-in (variable data) to a minimum and allow fill-in to stand out clearly.	• Use black ink for scanning and microfilming. • Use print size smaller than elite spacing (10 pt.) on a typewriter or printer to draw the reader's attention to the fill-in.
7. Adapt spacing to the method of fill-in (handwritten or machine) to allow sufficient space. (Computer software controls spacing on computer forms.)	• Allow a minimum of one inch for every five characters for handwriting. Allow double vertical spacing (1/3″) for typewriting or machine fill-in.

8. Use check boxes to minimize fill-ins and save time.	• Poor design: Married? <u>yes</u> Gender? <u>male</u>
	• Good design: Marital Status Gender
	          ☑ Single ☐ Widowed ☑ Female
	          ☐ Married ☐ Divorced ☐ Male

9. Locate instructions for filling in the form where they are easily read. Locate filing or routing information properly to speed retrieval of the form.	• Place instructions for filling in the form at the top. • Place distribution and filing information on the bottom of the form.
10. Use the box design style rather than caption-on-the-line style or caption-under-the-line style for constant data.	• Poor design: Name _____ Address _____ • Good design: | Name | Address |
11. Key captions in all caps; key text in upper- and lowercase.	• Key instructions that appear in several lines or paragraphs in lowercase and initial caps.

Figure 12–5 Forms Design Guidelines

forms. The forms templates (patterns) typically include a purchase order, invoice, cost estimate, job application, different letter and memo styles, etc. Some software programs allow drawing horizontal and vertical lines, shading, and other graphic features when designing forms. Figure 12–6 shows an invoice template found in *Microsoft Excel*.

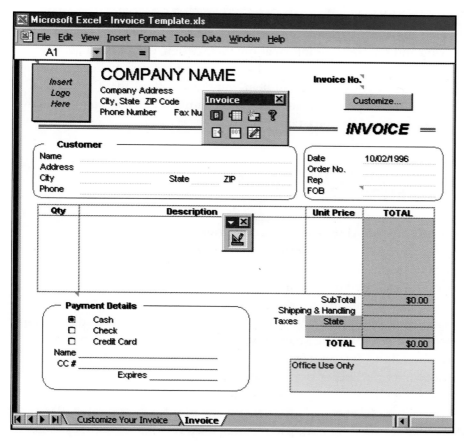

Figure 12–6 *Microsoft Excel* Invoice Template

Forms Costs

The cost of paper and ink to print the forms often attract the most attention in trying to control the cost of business forms. Actually, the cost of *using* forms, estimated to be as high as forty times the physical cost, is the place to look for cost savings. Such costs include users' fill-in time; processing costs; and costs of acquiring, storing, retrieving, and distributing the forms. Each cost is mainly related to various types of labor.

How are forms costs controlled?

Purchasing Forms

New forms may be purchased from office supply stores. Examples of such forms are statements or invoices, telephone message forms, purchase requisitions, and sales receipts. Buying standard forms is less expensive than custom-designed forms as long as a standard form meets the needs of the office. As you have already seen, some word processing programs and special forms software provide the necessary tools for producing professional-looking forms that can be tailored to individual needs.

Standardized forms are used in large numbers because they are capable of handling large quantities of information in the least amount of time, effort, and space. As forms continue to be an efficient way of gathering and transmitting information, their design, use, cost, and storage will require managerial approval and periodic evaluation. Forms management features of software can help, and organizations that make use of RIM software programs are sure to have a more efficient and productive forms management program.

ELECTRONIC DOCUMENT MANAGEMENT SYSTEMS

What is EDMS?

An **electronic document management system (EDMS)**, also referred to as a *document management system (DMS)*, is a management control system used to regulate the creation, use, and maintenance of electronically created documents. This system links paper, image, and electronic documents into one flexible and expandable document management system. EDM systems allow for a gradual conversion from paper to electronic and image records storage to integrate all information media. Digital images, raw data, facsimile transmission, e-mail, sound or video clips, and paper records can be linked through a single indexing and retrieval application. Color-coded labels may be prepared with file names, bar codes, and color codes on adhesive labels as needed. Bar code technology used on both paper and imaged documents allows all records to be indexed, tracked, and retrieved through a single user application.

Simultaneous, remote access to scanned documents by multiple users is possible through the scanning and network features of some systems. Records can be indexed, stored, retrieved, printed, or faxed by all authorized users on a network. Fax messages are captured, stored, routed, or refaxed, eliminating the need for hard copies. Once retention and destruction parameters are defined, users can maintain electronic and hard copy records in compliance with retention schedules. Bar coding technology and remote scanners provide automatic charge-out and follow-up of all hard copy records. Electronic documents can be stored on optical as well as electronic media, and raw data can be automatically and instantly located via searches on computer output to laser disk (COLD).

Electronic document management (EDM) applies to several technologies that are frequently combined to provide for storage, retrieval, and other management of an organization's document-based information. The important technologies include document management, full-text retrieval, electronic document imaging, film-based imaging, and workflow systems.

Document management systems provide for managing documents created on desktop computer systems by helping to organize production of electronic documents and providing access and distribution over networks at workgroup and organization levels. Full-text retrieval systems enable users to retrieve textual documents based on words, phrases, or concepts contained in the documents that may be stored in a text database or other document storage. Electronic document imaging systems convert paper-based documents to digital format for storage on optical media. Film-based imaging systems provide capture of documents and data on microfilm and microfiche. Workflow systems provide automation of work processes and scheduling, controlling, and routing electronic documents and other work items around an organization. Workflow systems are usually directed to transaction-type work where large volumes of paper-based, usually manual, transactions take place. EDMS systems are used in international organizations and other organizations that incorporate global technologies.[7]

SUMMARY

To control a records and information management program, understand the essential aspects of a records and information program and the management function of controlling. Tools for controlling a records and information management program include a records management manual, knowledge management activities, ISO 9000 guidelines, a records inventory, records retention schedules, records audits, and a disaster recovery plan. To provide information quickly and at the lowest possible cost, apply efficiency, cost, and performance controls to records and information management personnel, space requirements, equipment, and procedures.

Controlling records creation is an important part of the overall control process because more records are stored on paper than any other storage medium. Give careful attention in the control process to correspondence and business forms because they comprise a large part of paper records storage. Seek ways to minimize the costs of creating, distributing, and storing these kinds of records. Copies not only produce excessive records, they sometimes contribute unnecessarily to a

Continued

[7]David O. Stephens, "The Globalization of Information Technology in Multinational Corporations," *The Information Management Journal* Vol. 33, No. 3 (July 1999), 66-71.

paper storage problem and therefore need control as well. Electronic document management systems link paper, image, and electronic documents and provide access to multiple users in various work locations.

The guidelines discussed in this chapter are intended to acquaint you with the many aspects involved in controlling a records and information management program and are offered as a basis from which to grow. Your success as an office worker will depend on your ability to manage records well. To contribute in this regard, you need to know all you can about filing methods and filing procedures. Study the chapters in this text on the technology that has reduced the amount of paper records that must be stored. Know as much as you can about new storage equipment, supplies, and technology so that you can make a difference in the office where you will work. Ways and means to improve productivity, cut personnel requirements, save space, reduce equipment and supply costs, and reduce or eliminate lost or misfiled documents will be important objectives for all office workers in the years ahead.

IMPORTANT TERMS

accuracy ratio

activity ratio

constant data

control

cost-benefit ratio

disaster

disaster recovery plan

efficiency control

efficiency ratio

electronic document management
  system (EDMS)

emergency

form

records audit

records management manual

retrieval efficiency ratio

standards

variable data

REVIEW AND DISCUSSION

1. Define *control* as a management function. (Obj. 1)

2. List three elements of a comprehensive records and information management program. (Obj. 2)

3. List five control tools commonly used in a records and information management program. Explain their functions. (Obj. 3)

4. Describe efficiency, cost, and performance controls and explain how each assist in controlling a records and information management program. (Obj. 4)

5. What do the three efficiency ratios (activity, accuracy, and records retrieval) measure? How is each ratio computed? (Obj. 4)

6. What are the major costs involved in operating records and information management programs? How can these costs be controlled? (Obj. 5)

7. Identify the major costs involved in producing correspondence. How can such costs be reduced? (Obj. 8)

8. Give suggestions for holding copymaking costs in line. (Obj. 9)

9. List three objectives of a forms control program. (Obj. 6)

10. Why is forms control important in achieving control in a records and information management program? How have computers affected forms design? (Obj. 7)

11. List at least three guidelines to follow when constructing a well-designed form. (Obj.7)

12. How do electronic document management systems facilitate records and information management? (Obj. 10)

APPLICATIONS (APP)

Critical Thinking

APP 12-1. Designing a New Video Rental Application Form (Objs. 8 and 9)

You work part-time for Cinema Video Central (CVC), a local video rental store. Your manager asked you to design a form to gather information from customers who rent movies, music videos, and games. The information gathered will be keyed into a computer database *in the following order*:

(1) Account number; (2) customer name, address, and telephone number; (3) date of the application; (4) movie video preference; i.e., science fiction, romance, western, classic, drama, psychodrama, adventure; (5) whether customer rents music videos and games; (6) a signature line preceded by "I agree to all CVC video rental terms and conditions."; and (7) a short application approval line for the manager's initials (Approved _____).

The manager designed the following form and asks you to improve it if you can. Apply the forms design guidelines presented in this chapter to design a better form that will meet the needs of the video store. Be sure to include in your form all needed data for input into the store's computer database. Be prepared to defend any changes you make to the old form.

Customer Name _____ Acct. No. _____

Customer Address _____

Telephone No. _____ Date _____

_____

List your movie video preferences: science fiction, romance, western, classic, drama, adventure, psychodrama.

_____

Do you rent Music Videos?: _____ Yes _____ No

Do you rent Games?: _____ Yes _____ No

I agree to all CVC video rental terms and conditions.

_____
Signature   Approved _____

Critical Thinking

APP 12-2.   Improving Control in a Records System (Objs. 4-9)

You are assistant office manager in a law office of three attorneys. During the past month, you have carefully observed your records operations, noting especially the following typical conditions:

1. Each of three keyboarding specialists uses a different style of letter when keying correspondence.

2. Resorting an alphabetized client file of 500 cards into numeric order by ZIP Code required five hours.

3. Over a one-week period, 20 of the last 75 records requested could not be found quickly or were not found at all.

4. Two of the 25 four-drawer file cabinets have not been accessed for records retrieval during the past two weeks.

5. One of three office personal computers went down, and no data could be accessed for five days.

6. Each of six office employees designs his or her own forms and orders them from outside firms.

7. Each employee has free access to the office copier at all times.

8. The most common problems found when examining the files were these:
   a. Few guides were used in file drawers.
   b. Different folder cuts in a variety of positions were used with some handwritten captions.
   c. Some label captions were handwritten and hidden from view; caption positions on labels varied with each person preparing them.
   d. Many folders were overcrowded (some contained five inches of filed records).

   Analyze these problem areas cited. What specific control problems do you see? What can be done in this office to eliminate, or, at least, to improve these conditions? Key a report answering these questions.

APPENDICES

APPENDIX A

RECORDS MANAGEMENT CAREER OPPORTUNITIES AND JOB DESCRIPTIONS

When you were introduced to the field of records management in Chapter 1, you were briefly exposed to the three job levels and job titles in the records management field. At this point, whether it be for supplemental reading following Chapter 1, or for additional information as you complete the last chapter, a more in-depth look at career opportunities in records management and related areas is in order.

Appendix A offers (1) a concise overview of the growth of the information profession of which records management is a part, (2) a discussion of career opportunities and job descriptions at the various job levels in records management, and (3) a look at professional development programs to enhance advancement in the records management field. Special attention is given to jobs and related career opportunities that will allow students who are entering the world of office work to advance in their profession.

THE GROWTH OF INFORMATION PROFESSIONS

By following the daily news reports on the world economy, you find that one point, among all others, stands out: *The United States is rapidly moving from a production-based economy to a service-based economy.* As such, businesses and industries are, for example, becoming less involved with producing steel and its many by-products and more involved with computers and related information services that computers make possible. Additionally, all organizations are looking at managing information to gain a strategic advantage in the industries in which they compete. Even government agencies are trying to find the best way to deliver information to the public.

With this new focus in mind, you should ask yourself several questions about the career you are considering. They are:

1. What effects are the rapid changes in the United States and world economies and information technology having on the records management field?

2. What specific jobs in records management and allied fields are being created (or maintained) in the new service- and information-oriented economy?
3. Which jobs are changing significantly or being eliminated?
4. How can you keep up-to-date on career opportunities in records management to take advantage of opportunities as they occur?

As you seek answers to such questions, keep in mind that in a service-oriented world, *information is a* (and in most cases, *the*) *key resource.* To be successful, all organizations, workers, and citizens in general must accept this viewpoint. Further, they recognize that for information to be used repeatedly, it must be recorded. Time and time again as you worked your way through this textbook, you were reminded of the vital role that records play in operating business organizations.

Records and their relationship to information systems are briefly discussed next. (Even though some of these concepts have been discussed in one or more of the twelve chapters in this textbook, they are discussed here in the context of careers so you can understand the relationship of such careers to the business firm and the world economy of which it is a part.)

Records and Information Management

Many new information technologies are rapidly being employed in the operation of businesses. Consider how important computers, microimage systems, telecommunications, and many other hardware and software systems are to the operation of a business. These technologies impact not only your access to vast amounts of information, but also the speed and accuracy with which you can retrieve that information. (Notice, for example, the almost universal presence of computers, computer terminals, and printers in offices of all sizes.)

Because of the importance of information to large and small firms, a new concept of information management has emerged. **Records and information management (RIM)** is dedicated to establishing company-wide controls over the staff, equipment, and services that generate and maintain information. This term places emphasis on the role of information in the records management field. These controls include the traditional records management responsibilities for creating, processing, storing, retrieving, and using information. Because technology is interwoven into all aspects of businesses today, RIM must be concerned not only with the necessary paper records systems but also with the growing number of technological developments being applied to handle a firm's information needs. Information is an expensive and vital resource that must be represented at the top levels of management. For this reason, many forward-looking firms have created the position of **chief information officer (CIO),** a high-level position where the person is responsible for all the information needs of the entire organization. Such an approach recognizes the importance of information as a vital resource that will help support and achieve organizational goals. With the expanded processing and use of information, many new jobs in information-related fields have been created. Thus, records management as a part of RIM continues its rapid growth as the need for information increases.

Records Management—A Growing Area

A few years ago, records management was known as the efficient storage and retrieval of paper records. With the passage of time, the increase in the amount of information, and the advancements in technology, however, organizations are growing larger and more complex. As a result, the records management field has expanded to include many diversified areas dealing with information resource management. Examples of such areas include:

- Forms and reports management (electronic and paper forms).
- Correspondence management.
- Records center operations.
- Records and information retention.
- Vital records.
- Archival records preservation.
- Integrated technology records applications.
- Workflow analysis as it pertains to information management.
- Understanding of the business world's dependence on timely and accurate information in the global community.

When more records are produced, more jobs are opened to qualified people. As discussed in this section, job opportunities in records management exist in many new, as well as in many long-term, work environments.

The Small Business Environment

Small businesses require generalists—employees who can handle a variety of office tasks. Take the administrative assistant as an example. The typical administrative assistant in a small firm composes responses to routine correspondence, screens telephone calls, makes appointments, handles travel arrangements, and *maintains filing and information systems*. Therefore, if you expect to work for a small business, you will be the "files specialist" responsible for paper and automated records along with your other duties. For example, additional duties may include making computer backups and setting up and maintaining electronic indexes and databases.

The Large Business Environment

Large firms have more specialization. Within departments, administrative assistants and general support personnel such as records clerks may be responsible for all records activities. If a firm has a formal records management program, these responsibilities may be centralized under a records manager with a specialized staff. In addition to supervisory duties, a records manager will, among other things, establish procedures, initiate long-range planning, and develop budgets. The nature of such specialized staff positions is discussed later.

The Professional Office Environment

In an increasingly specialized economy, many professional offices require management of their specialized records (see Figure A–1). Brief examples of such office settings are discussed next.

Figure A–1 Staff Members Generating Specialized Records at a Meeting

Law Office Jobs. Large law firms—some with hundreds of attorneys on their staff—employ records personnel at the three levels (managerial, supervisory, and operating). All three levels require an understanding of general records management principles and practices. Further, such staff members must have specialized knowledge of how attorneys think and work and of the unique characteristics of classifying and storing legal records.

Medical Office Jobs. One- and two-physician offices still dominate the medical field, although the number of multiple-physician clinics is increasing. With an increasing number of medical facilities consolidating, recordkeeping requirements have multiplied. The relationship of records to the health insurance field also creates many new records jobs. Patient charts are used not only for histories, diagnoses, treatment, and research, but also as information needed for insurance claims and bill collections. Other typical records include discharge summaries, operative and pathology reports, X-rays, and health-insurance correspondence. A knowledge of medical terminology, medical diagnosis codes, and records functions is especially important to the individual handling records in the health field.

Other Professional Office Jobs. In other professional offices, such as the government offices at the city, county, state, and federal levels and offices primarily responsible for technical computer processing, special records job opportunities exist. Records personnel in city and county government offices keep track of registrations, licenses, social services cases, taxes, and citizen protection. At the federal and state levels, these same types of records are maintained with additional information—and additional records—required at each succeeding level. In all four levels of government, more and more records are computerized and many are microfilmed. Centralized records management positions are available in most state and federal offices, which provide a longer career path for students to consider. Information on such career opportunities is available from the administrative services or archives division in each state capital and from each main office responsible for administering federal agencies.

Regardless of the type of business or industry, the information worker needs to learn and understand all aspects of the business and how the information flows through the organization. Just as important is to be able to recognize how the management of information impacts or impedes the organization's effectiveness.

Students with career interests that combine the computer and records management must understand basic computer concepts, especially how automated records are created, stored, and retrieved. At the same time, they should know the fundamentals of records control as outlined in this textbook. Armed with such information, students can gain entry-level positions in large organizations in which the computer tracks records through the records life cycle and provides appropriate reports about the records' uses as needed. Similar information on careers in the library records field can be obtained from the American Library Association (ALA), 50 East Huron Street, Chicago, IL 60611 or online at www.ala.org.

RECORDS MANAGEMENT CAREER OPPORTUNITIES AND JOB DESCRIPTIONS

The three job levels and position titles typically found in records management are shown in Figure A–2. By advancing from the operating level to the supervisory level and finally to the managerial level over a period

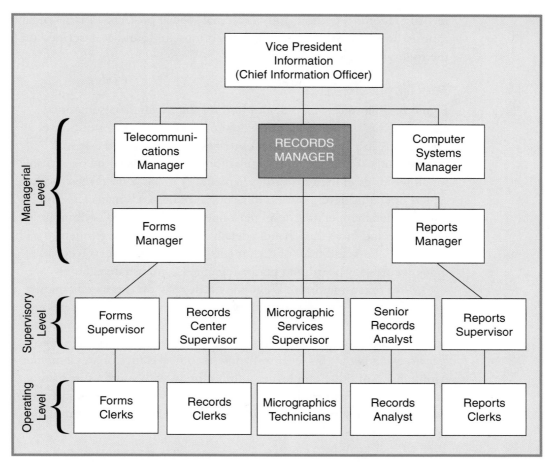

Figure A–2 Records Management Organization Chart

of time, a career path for the employee is provided. Thus, a **career path** outlines a typical route of advancement for workers on the job. Knowing that opportunity for advancement is available motivates workers toward more effective performance; at the same time, a career path stimulates the interest of students seeking opportunities for professional growth and advancement.

In this section, job descriptions for common records positions shown in Figure A–2 are discussed, and job opportunities including career paths for each of the job levels are explored. However, primary attention is given to the operating level because this level is where you will likely enter the work force. If you choose not to pursue a higher educational level, you may find that advancement opportunities are limited.

Operating Level

At the *operating level*, as shown in Figure A–2, workers are generally responsible for routine filing and retrieving tasks and assisting with vital records, records retention, and occasional special projects. In large organizations, however, other more specialized jobs are found as described on the following pages.

Job Opportunities

Figure A–3 illustrates a job description for the *records clerk* (sometimes called a *records and information clerk*), the most common operating-level position. (A **job description** summarizes the content and essential requirements of a specific job. Similar job descriptions would be available for all positions in the records department.) A *records center clerk* is another typical operating-level position in a centralized records management program. Generally, operating-level personnel must be able to communicate well orally and in writing, handle details (such as working frequently with names, numbers, and titles of documents), handle and process records, index records, keyboard, and perform general administrative duties.

Other operating duties assigned will depend on the specific nature of the work to be done, the education and work experience background of the worker, and the records needs of the organization. For example, some organizations provide *forms clerks, reports clerks, records analysts,* and *micrographic technicians* at this level to handle technical duties of an elementary nature. Each of these employees works closely with supervisors having the same special work interests. Figure A–4 provides detailed information on the key duties and job qualifications for each of these common operating-level positions.

Career Path

Employees at this work level have the opportunity for advancement as shown in Figure A–2. Keep in mind that the lowest rung on the career ladder is especially important, for it provides the most basic job information needed to understand the total records system. Workers with the motivation to advance up the ranks usually appreciate most their operating-level experience after their promotion to higher levels of work. Workers with highest levels of education, but without work experience at the operating level, may possess certain limitations that restrict their full understanding of records management programs.

Supervisory Level

Supervisory-level personnel oversee the work of operating-level workers and are responsible for other administrative duties as well. Supervisors must work with budgets; select, motivate, train, and evaluate workers; establish and meet deadlines; and delegate responsibilities. These duties require the ability to write instructional materials and procedures, to give and follow up on instructions, and to plan and organize work efficiently.

JOB TITLE: Records Clerk   Job Code: 482.10

Date: March 1, 20--

Duties
1. Sort and classify documents and other materials for filing.
2. File materials.
3. Retrieve material from files.
4. Maintain charge-out system for records removed from files.
5. Assist in accession, reference, and disposal activities of the department/records center.
6. Assist with vital records.
7. Maintain logs and indexes to provide status of information.
8. Follow up on materials charged out to users.
9. Set up new file categories.
10. Perform other administrative duties as assigned by supervisor.

Job Requirements
1. Ability to maintain pleasant working relationships with all levels of personnel.
2. Strong oral and written communication skills.
3. Ability to analyze data for answers to questions concerning stored information.
4. Mechanical aptitude that allows efficient and effective operation of office equipment, including keyboard data-entry equipment (computer and typewriter).
5. Ability to handle confidential information.

Education/Work Experience
This is an entry-level position requiring:
1. High school diploma or equivalent; or demonstrated skill to perform the job.

   or

2. Work experience as records clerk, office trainee, or clerk-typist in lieu of high school graduation.

Career Path
Advancement to Records Center Supervisor

Figure A–3 Job Description for Records Clerk

Job Title	Duties	Personal Characteristics	Education/Work Experience	Advance to
Forms Clerk	Analyze forms requirements; design forms; revise existing forms; maintain forms; control records	Ability to analyze data; provide answers to questions; work well with all levels of personnel; be accurate in working with detailed information	High school diploma; some experience in working with records preferred	Forms Analysis (if job is available); Forms Supervisor
Micrographics Technician/Clerk	Prepare documents for microfilming; operate microfilming equipment; develop and maintain index and retrieval aids	Ability to work well with people; have mechanical aptitude; understand office procedures	High school diploma or equivalent; technical training in microfilming; two years' business experience required; records experience preferred	Micrographic Services Supervisor
Reports Clerk	Review firm's reports; design report formats; assist forms and records clerks	Ability to work well with people; good writing skills; creativity; self-motivation	High school diploma; some experience in working with records and reports	Reports Analyst (if job is available); Reports Supervisor
Records Analyst	Assess current records systems; define and coordinate changes in retention and workflow	Ability to analyze entire workflow of a process; train users; and understand the purpose of the business	Associates degree; two years' business experience, ideally with records management exposure	Senior Records Analyst

Figure A–4 Job Duties, Personal Characteristics, and Education/Work Experience Required of Four Common Operating-Level Records Personnel

Job Opportunities

Supervisory positions in records management will only be found in large organizations with records management programs because such organizations can afford work specialization. As shown in Figure A–2, supervisory positions include *forms supervisor, records center supervisor, micrographic services supervisor, senior records analyst, and reports supervisor.* In a small business organization, one person fulfills all these duties. Figure A–5 shows a job description for records center supervisor, the most common position at this work level. Figure A–6 outlines key duties and job qualifications for other common supervisory personnel in records management programs. Note that the work of such supervisors requires some college-level education or from three to five years of closely related work experience. Many times this work experience is obtained as the worker advances from operating levels to supervisory levels of work within a business. Such workers, by the time of promotion, know their organizations well and usually can become more productive much sooner than persons hired from outside the organization.

Career Path

The typical promotion route for supervisors in business, industry, and government is to advance to manager. This same principle applies to supervisors in records management programs. In Figure A–2, the career path for each of the supervisors discussed earlier is identified by those positions appearing immediately above on the organization chart.

Managerial Level

The records management program is directed by a *records manager* (sometimes called a *records administrator*), a middle management position. As a rule, both a college degree and considerable work experience with records systems are required for this top position; however, motivated persons can occasionally move up through the "experience" ranks to such a position without a degree. A job description for a records manager is provided in Figure A–7. It shows responsibilities for (1) many administrative duties (organizing resources, recruiting and hiring staff, motivating and evaluating staff, and establishing effective systems), (2) many technical areas (micro-image systems, forms control, and records protection), and (3) a growing body of knowledge of computers and other information technology.

Very large firms may also have other managerial-level personnel reporting to the records manager. These positions include *reports manager* and *forms manager.* Candidates for such positions may "come up through the ranks." That is, they advance from one or more lower levels in the program; or they may be hired from outside the organization. Typical duties and job qualifications for these managers are shown in Figure A–8.

JOB TITLE: Records Center Supervisor   Job Code: 1482.00

Date: March 1, 20--

Duties

1. Supervise the work of the other supervisory personnel and of the operating-level staff.
2. Arrange for pickup and transportation of records.
3. Coordinate the creation, receipt, storage, retrieval, and disposition of records.
4. Develop procedures for controlling all aspects of the record life cycle (from creation through disposition).
5. Coordinate the transfer of records from active to inactive storage.
6. Select, train, supervise, and evaluate staff.
7. Make salary recommendations for records personnel.
8. Plan, schedule, and assign work tasks.
9. Recommend budget for the areas of assigned responsibility.
10. Perform other supervisory-level duties as requested by the records manager.

Job Requirements

1. Strong oral and written communication skills.
2. Ability to supervise effectively and coordinate the use of resources assigned to the program.
3. Ability to plan and organize work, to motivate personnel, and to make sound decisions regarding work assignments.
4. Ability to recognize, analyze, and solve problems.
5. Thorough knowledge of records management principles and practices.

Education/Work Experience

1. Minimum of two years of college, or equivalent level of related work experience.
2. Knowledge of automated records systems principles and practices.

Career Path

1. Records Manager or Records Administrator
2. Other staff positions

Figure A–5 Job Description for Records Center Supervisor

Job Title	Duties	Personal Characteristics	Education/Work Experience	Advance to
Forms Supervisor	Supervise work of forms clerks; analyze forms and coordinate forms control program; provide forms assistance to departments; select, train, and evaluate forms clerks	Ability to work well with and motivate people; good communication skills; broad background in manual and automated forms control practices	Minimum of two years of college; at least five years' experience in business and in records systems work	Forms Manager or Assistant Records Manager
Micrographics Services Supervisor	Plan, organize, and coordinate microimage systems program; select, train, and evaluate staff; work closely with department heads and other records supervisors	Ability to work well with and motivate people; good communication skills; organizational and analytical skills; mechanical aptitude to maintain equipment	High school diploma plus two years' micrographics work experience and four years of related work experience	Records Analyst (if available) or Assistant Records Manager
Reports Supervisor	Supervise work of reports clerks; analyze reports and coordinate reports control program; select, train, and evaluate reports clerks	Ability to work well with and motivate people; maintain confidentiality of data; good writer, planner, and creative reports organizer	Minimum of two years of college; at least five years' experience in business and in records systems work	Reports Manager or Assistant Records Manager
Senior Records Analyst	Develop and implement manual or automated active records systems; train incoming analysts	Ability to work well with and motivate people; good analysis and communication skills; solid understanding of records and company's workflow	Minimum of two years of college; at least three years' experience in business and records systems work	Assistant Records Manager

Figure A–6 Job Duties, Personal Characteristics, and Education/Work Experience Required of Four Common Supervisory-Level Records Personnel

JOB TITLE: Records Manager   Job Code: 2482.01

Date: March 1, 20--

Duties

1. Report, as instructed, to Vice President, Information (Chief Information Officer).
2. Establish company-wide policies and procedures for creating, classifying, storing, retrieving, and disposing of company records.
3. Assist department to plan, develop, improve, and modernize records availability and to maximize service to records users.
4. Coordinate the preparation of records management manuals.
5. Consult on the selection and implementation of automated storage and retrieval systems.
6. Coordinate the use of microimage systems throughout the organization.
7. Select methods for safeguarding records.
8. Coordinate the supervision and evaluation of all records, personnel, equipment, and procedures with supervisors.
9. Report regularly to top management to justify, publicize, and support the records management program.
10. Plan and develop a budget and cost control system for the records management program.

Job Requirements

1. Excellent oral and written communication skills.
2. Strong organizational, planning, and evaluation skills.
3. Ability to lead and motivate people and to work effectively with all levels of personnel in the organization.
4. Professional appearance as evidenced by active participation in professional organizations and up-to-date knowledge of information technology.
5. Excellent overall knowledge of records management and its relationship to information resource management.

Education/Work Experience

1. College degree, with MBA degree and five years' experience in records management preferred. Must demonstrate that coursework has been completed in computer systems, business law, and human relations and must have a working knowledge of automated records systems.
2. Work experience may, in some cases, be substituted for college coursework.

Career Path

1. Vice President, Information Services (Administrative Services)
2. Vice President, Information Resources

Figure A–7 Job Description for a Records Manager

Job Title	Duties	Personal Characteristics	Education/Work Experience	Advance to
Forms Manager	Plan, organize, and implement a forms control program throughout the firm; evaluate the work of forms supervisor; select forms staff	Ability to work well with and motivate people; excellent communication skills; understanding of manual and automated forms system; good problem solver	College degree and five years' experience in forms work	Assistant Records Manager (if available); Records Manager
Reports Manager	Plan, organize, and implement a reports control program throughout the firm; evaluate the work of reports supervisor; select reports staff	Excellent communication skills; high level of creativity in designing and analyzing reports in the organization; ability to work well with people	College degree and five years' experience in reports work	Assistant Records Manager (if available); Records Manager

Figure A–8 Job Duties, Personal Characteristics, and Education/Work Experience Required of Two Common Managerial-Level Records Personnel

(In some progressive firms with strong information services orientation, records and information analysts, as well as an assistant records manager, may also be provided at this same work level.) Depending on the breadth of experience and education, a successful records manager may advance to a higher level of information systems, such as director of administrative services or chief information officer.

Students interested in learning more about such positions should complete more advanced courses in records management and correspond with ARMA, 4200 Somerset Drive, Suite 215, Prairie Village, KS 66208; www.arma.org.

PROFESSIONAL DEVELOPMENT IN RECORDS MANAGEMENT

A wise business executive once said to a college student, "Once you graduate from school, your real education begins." This statement simply means that each new "hire" must learn all phases of the new job; and once experience on that job is gained, the worker must maintain a continuous program of learning through self-development courses as well as participation in the programs offered—some voluntary, some required— by the employer. Further, this self-development should continue throughout the employee's career. Several types of professional development approaches are available.

Taking Professional Development Courses

At the operating level, the records manager, supervisor, or someone in the organization's human resources or training department may teach in-house courses focused on information systems. Courses in forms design, reports management, and records automation may be offered free to an employee on the job as a means of increasing the employee's skill level. With such skills the employee will find the doors will open to better work performance and more advanced opportunities. Outside professional groups such as ARMA, the American Management Association, or consultants with expertise in areas related to the firm's records program offer similar programs. Educational institutions such as a local university or community college offer credit and noncredit courses, often at night, that not only add to the employee's skills level, but also help the employee to accumulate credit toward a college degree. With a degree, a records management employee may be eligible for positions in management sooner than without a degree.

Participating in Professional Organizations

Many forward-looking employees seeking to advance in the business world belong to professional organizations in their fields. These professional organizations are a network of peers with similar business concerns and solutions and can provide educational opportunities as well.

However, membership alone is not enough. You must take an active part; that is, participate on a continuing basis in such organizations to get the maximum benefit from them. Such organizations provide you with the opportunity to:

- Meet professional-minded persons in positions similar to yours.
- Exchange ideas on making your records system more efficient.
- Become acquainted with performance standards recommended by the organization.
- Become aware of, and participate in, the research conducted to improve your records systems operations.
- Keep up-to-date on management thinking and technology affecting the records management field.

Professional organizations of special interest to records personnel include (1) the Association of Records Managers and Administrators, Inc. (ARMA International), for general records management coverage; (2) the Association for Information and Image Management (AIIM), which specializes in microimage and optical disk technology; and (3) the National Association of Government Archives and Records Administrators (NAGARA), for records personnel in the government. Organizations having closely related interests are the Association for Systems Management (ASM), the Society of American Archivists (SAA), the American Library Association (ALA), the American Health Information Management Association (AHIMA), and the National Business Forms Association (NBFA). Information on these professional organizations is available in city, college, and university libraries.

Of all these organizations, ARMA is the most active and most relevant to business records management. Its membership continues to grow in numbers and its importance to the records management profession continues to increase. Typical of ARMA's professional developments are the guidelines for various filing methods discussed in this textbook, job description guidelines for the various records management positions, and the certification program discussed next. ARMA also sponsors technical publications, a series of seminars, and an annual conference. Locate the ARMA chapter nearest you and attend one of more of its meetings. Guests—as prospective members—are always welcome! As a student, you are eligible to join ARMA at a special student membership rate.

Becoming Professionally Certified

Certification programs are designed to test and verify that candidates successfully meeting the program's requirements have the qualifications for managerial work in the area. Having a certification also demonstrates to potential employers that a candidate has specialized expertise that other candidates do not possess. Typically, such certification is attained when a member passes qualifying examinations that test the knowledge, skill, and other relevant information pertaining to the professional field.

The Institute of Certified Records Managers (ICRM) administers the certification program in records management. The CRM examination consists of the following six parts:

1. Management principles and the records and information management program.
2. Records creation and use.
3. Filing systems, storage, and retrieval.
4. Records appraisal, retention, protection, and disposition.
5. Facilities, supplies, and technology.
6. Case studies.

Parts 1–5 of the CRM exam can be taken in any order, but all five parts must be successfully passed before the candidate is able to sit for Part 6. The first five parts can be taken in any sequence and each part can be re-taken separately, but all six parts must be passed within five years for the individual to be CRM-certified. Candidates for certification must have a minimum of three years' full-time or equivalent professional experience in records management in at least three of the areas covered in the CRM examination. In addition, the candidate must have been awarded a bachelor's degree from an accredited institution before certification can be achieved. In some cases, the ICRM permits the substitution of additional qualifying experience for some of the required education. By meeting these educational, experience, and test requirements, the candidate is given the designation Certified Records Manager, which indicates a high degree of professionalism and competence in records management.

To promote a similar degree of competence in the medical records profession, the American Health Information Management Association (AHIMA) conducts annual qualification examinations to credential medical personnel as Registered Records Administrators (RRA) and Accredited Records Technicians (ART). Information on education programs, certification examinations, and career opportunities in the medical records field is available from AHIMA, 919 North Michigan Avenue, Suite 1400, Chicago, IL 60611-1683.

Other records-related associations also offer certification programs. ASM, mentioned earlier, sponsors the *Certified Systems Profession* (CSP) program covering systems environments, project management, systems analysis, systems design and implementation, and systems tools and technology. The NBFA sponsors the *Certified Forms Consultant* (CFC) program, which covers such topics as business forms production and materials, forms design, construction and control, business systems and procedures, products, and processing and handling equipment. Several computer-based certification programs such as the *Certified Document Imaging Architect* (CDIA) program developed by the Computing Technology Industry Association (CompTIA) are also available.

Professional-minded persons proudly display their certification, which sends a strong message to the business public. CRMs, for example, have met high professional standards and are recognized internationally by their profession. Such attainment leads not only to professional advancement, but also to respect from their subordinates, peers, and superiors on the job.

SOME FINAL THOUGHTS ABOUT A CAREER IN RECORDS MANAGEMENT

Career choices that affect your future are some of the most important decisions you will ever make. Make your decision carefully after considerable study and thought, but in the process avoid letting the growing number of professional associations and detailed information about careers confuse you!

As you prepare for full-time employment (or if you are now employed full time or part time and are seeking other employment), keep in mind these final thoughts about a career in records management:

1. *Information processing is now our biggest industry nationally*, and records—in whatever form—are storehouses of information.
2. *The persons in control of records are actually controllers of information*; and that means power, for using information leads to knowledge, and knowledge leads to power in society as well as in the workplace. More important, however, is that your career should lead to personal satisfaction. Visit one or more records installations in your area and talk to persons with experience in the field before making your career decision.
3. *The days of full-time, often monotonous, manual filing operations are numbered*. In their place will be greater numbers of automated records systems that are integrated with the information systems by which the organization is managed. The "bottom line" then, is that in records management you can become a member of the information systems team and, along with it, enjoy a rewarding and even exciting career. Students with majors in liberal arts, library science, and other non-business fields can find satisfying positions in records management.
4. *Keep up-to-date*. Information on career opportunities as well as new developments in the field can be found on ARMA's Web site: www.arma.org, in the *Dictionary of Occupational Titles*, and in the

Occupational Outlook Handbook. The other professional associations cited earlier also publish valuable periodicals that contain similar information about the field of records management. Copies of such publications are commonly found in college, university, and city libraries.

As always, the final decision is up to you, keeping in mind your interests and your aspirations. Regardless of whether you are employed full time in records management, you will still be using records to a significant degree in whatever field you enter. Good luck to you in making your career decision!

IMPORTANT TERMS

career path
chief information officer (CIO)
job description

records and information
management (RIM)

CARD AND SPECIAL RECORDS

Two types of records are emphasized in this textbook: (1) *paper records* and (2) *nonpaper records* such as image records and electronic records. You will learn that businesses also frequently use a large number of other records. In Appendix B, card and special records that you will use in your personal and professional lives are discussed.

CARD RECORDS

If you were to look behind the records environment in today's businesses, you would find that although computers are becoming commonplace in the work environment, companies continue to store information on cards for internal and external uses. (The definition of card record and a discussion of its advantages and disadvantages are presented in Chapter 2.) Because card records are smaller in size than correspondence, they are usually stored in special noncorrespondence filing equipment.

In this section, card records are described in three ways: (1) by physical characteristics, (2) by use, and (3) by the filing equipment in which they are stored.

Physical Characteristics

Paper companies manufacture card records in standard sizes to fit commonly used storage equipment. The most common card sizes are 5″ by 3″, 6″ by 4″, 8″ by 5″, and 9″ by 6″, with the horizontal measurement of the card listed first.

Cards may be blank or have horizontal and/or vertical rulings such as those used in accounting journals, sales department quotation forms, and patient medical histories. Cards may also be single thickness, folded, or hinged to provide additional sides for recording information. Other cards that are designed as special records are discussed later in this appendix.

Use

A card that contains information used for reference only is called an **index record.** Index records found in most offices contain the following kinds of information:

1. Names and addresses of customers, clients, patients, or students.
2. Names and addresses of suppliers or vendors.
3. Employee or membership lists.
4. Most frequently used telephone numbers.
5. Inventory of locations of furniture and equipment within an organization.
6. Prospective customer lists.
7. Subscription lists.

For example, you could consult an alphabetic card file of names and addresses of customers to answer such questions as: What is the mailing address of Knutson Insurance Company? What is the telephone number of the O'Keefe and Jameson accounting firm? and What is the customer number of Krenlot Temporary Services?

A second type of record classified by use is the posted record. A **posted record**, sometimes called a *secondary record*, contains information that is continually updated. Information on the record is added to, deleted, or changed in some other way to reflect the current status. New information is posted on the card record either by hand or by machine. Examples of posted records include:

- Inventory and stock control cards.
- Medical and dental record cards.
- Department ledger cards.
- Payroll cards.
- Membership files.
- Credit and collection cards.

Filing Equipment

The type of filing equipment used determines how card records are filed. Many card records are filed *vertically*; that is, on edge or in an upright position. A collection of such records is called a **vertical card file**, or a *vertical file*. (See Figure B–1 for an example of a vertical card file.) A second way to file cards is to store such records *horizontally* in an overlapping arrangement. When the cards overlap, one important line of information for each record—usually the bottom margin—is visible when the tray in which the card is held is pulled out from the file cabinet. For this reason, a collection of these records is called a **visible card file**, or a *visible file*. Figure B–2 shows a visible card file with one record tray pulled out. Users can retrieve information or make an entry without removing a card. Many visible records systems also use one-line strips of card stock. The information on the strips may identify a customer/student name, address, telephone number, or some other readily used item of information.

Information on the visible margin of a card summarizes the detailed information entered on the other areas of the card. In an office equipment inventory file, for example, the visible margin of a card may show "ergo-body-fit chairs," while the remaining areas of the card show a history of the receipts and withdrawals of such chairs from inventory over a period of time.

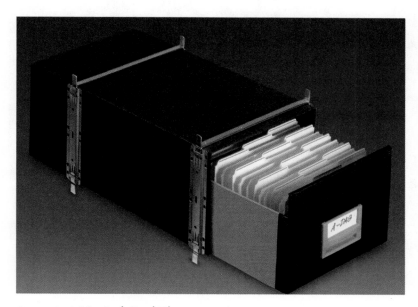

Figure B–1 **Vertical Card File**

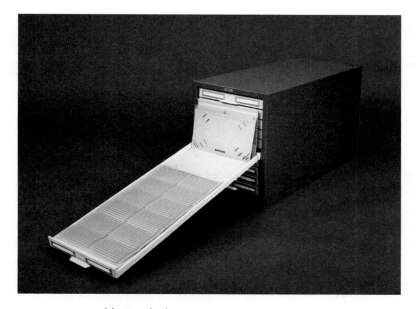

Figure B–2 **Visible Card File**

A third type of equipment used to store card records is **rotary (wheel) equipment**. In rotary equipment, card records are attached to a frame that rotates on an axis like a wheel. Figure B–3 illustrates a small, compact workstation unit. Larger rotary card files are available, as discussed later in this appendix.

Figure B–3 **Rotary Card File**

EQUIPMENT AND SUPPLIES FOR CARD FILES

The equipment and supplies required for card record files depend solely on the type of filing equipment—vertical, visible, or rotary—used. The equipment and supplies used in each type of card record file are discussed in this section.

Vertical Card Files

Remember that records are stored *on end* in vertical card files, as compared with the type of storage used in visible systems. Card records stored in rotary wheel files appear in a modified version of both vertical and horizontal files. The most important special equipment and supplies for vertical card files are explained here.

Equipment

Cards may be filed vertically in two types of filing equipment: (1) manual equipment that includes drawers housed in cabinets, boxes, trays, and rotating wheel equipment; and (2) motorized or power-driven equipment.

Drawer Cabinets. Perhaps the most widely used housing for vertical card records is the *drawer cabinet*, which has drawers similar to, but smaller than, correspondence file cabinet drawers. Filed records rest on their longest edge in these files; that is, the 8″ edge of an 8″ by 5″ card rests on the bottom of the drawer. When card records are used in conjunction with other types of records, such as correspondence, a file cabinet that provides drawers for vertical card record storage and other drawers that accommodate business forms or correspondence may be used. Such cabinets may contain from two to six or more drawers.

Boxes. Boxes of heavy cardboard or high-impact, durable plastic are sometimes used to store card records, which are most often found in 5″ by 3″, 6″ by 4″, and 8″ by 5″ card sizes. Box files are commonly used for home and small-office record storage (See Figure B–4).

Figure B–4 **Box File**

Trays. Card records may be stored on portable trays. Individual trays or a set of multiple trays may be placed side by side on shelves. Individual portable trays may be removed from the multiple group of trays for use at the workstation, for storage in a desk drawer, or for distribution of trays to various departments in the firm. By mixing card and tray sizes, a variety of card records may be stored in a mechanized unit.

Supplies

Folders are not required in vertical card files. Cards are filed upright and separated by guides into the desired sections. Guides and signals are the main supplies used in vertical card files.

Guides. Guides used in vertical card files are much the same as those used in correspondence files, varying only in size. Guides are available for cards filed in drawer cabinets, boxes, trays, and rotary files. In vertical card files, the guide tabs are visible, protruding above the cards to help the filer store and retrieve cards quickly and efficiently. The most important consideration in selecting guides is durability, which in turn depends on the type and weight of the guide material. Although guides are made from various materials, bristol board or pressboard is usually used for guides in vertical card record files. The thickness of the guide stock is referred to in terms of points, a point being 1/1000 of an inch. The greater the number of points, the thicker and more durable the paper or guide.

Vinyl guides in bright colors are also available for vertical and rotary files. Vinyl guides are washable and will not warp, crack, or become dog-eared from extensive use—problems that may develop if paper-based guides, such as bristol board or pressboard products, are used.

Signals. A **signal** is a special marker used for drawing immediate attention to a specific record. Two types of signals are used in vertical card files to convey to the filer special information about the cards. Special add-on or clip-on markers of movable transparent or opaque materials may be attached to the top of selected cards. In other cases, a distinctive color is placed on the signal, on the tab, or on the cards themselves. Different colors may be used to show different types of information on the marked cards.

Visible Records Files

The kinds of equipment and supplies used for visible records depend on the following factors: (1) the requirements of the organization as reflected by the number of cards or strips to be filed; (2) the importance of their location to their use; (3) whether the files must be portable; (4) the frequency of use; and (5) whether the visible records are to be used for reference or for posting purposes.

Equipment

The main types of visible equipment are (1) visible card files and (2) reference visible files. Each type of equipment is discussed in this section.

Visible Card Files. A number of different forms of visible card files, often called *posting visible files*, are available. The most frequently used visible equipment is the cabinet with shallow drawers or trays, each one labeled to show the contents. Each drawer contains a number of overlapping cards held horizontally by hangers or hinges or in slots called *pocket holders*. Figure B–5a shows such equipment with drawers that can be pulled out and down but that remain attached to the cabinet by a hinge. Both sides of most visible cards may be used.

By raising the set of cards preceding a card that requires posting, the filer can quickly post the desired information on the card without removing it from the storage container. Note that Figure B–5b shows an example of the contents of the visible margin on such a card. In this case, the name identifies a piece of office equipment and its stock number.

Cards are inserted into the holders so that one or two lines of each card are visible. Pocket holders are slotted to accommodate cards of various sizes. Some holders have transparent edge protectors, and others have the complete pocket made of transparent material. This see-through covering protects the edge or the entire card from wear, tear, moisture, and dirt.

When portability of cards is a necessity, the volume of cards to be filed is small, or when many employees need to post simultaneously, hinged pocket books may be used instead of other storage methods. These card books may have fastenings at the top of the cards for ease in posting, or the cards may be snapped in and out at any point. Loose-leaf books with removable panels of cards provide portability and contain much data in a small space. Contents of the book are labeled on the back binding or spine.

Racks and cabinets are used to house card books in an upright position. A cabinet may revolve so that several persons can reference information.

Figure B–5a **Visible Records Cabinet**

INVENTORY RECORD

Amount Received	Date Received	Location	Amount Used/Requested	Date Used/Requested	Balance on Hand
25	11-18-1999	*Aisle 10*	10	12-10-1998	15
10	11-15-2000	*Aisle 10*	0		25

H1770
Ergo-Body-Fit Chairs

Location: SH203
Aisle 2

Figure B–5b Contents of a Visible Margin on a Card

Reference Visible Files. If only one line or a few lines of information are needed for reference purposes, *reference visible files* are used. Information is placed on narrow strips of card stock that are inserted into holders attached to panels, trays, or frames. Figure B–6 shows one-line strips of information on panels attached to a revolving center post.

Supplies

Visible records housed in horizontal trays do not need guides. When the trays are pushed into their cabinets, labels on the front of the trays indicate the range of the tray contents. Thus, the only guides used for visible records are those found in vertical equipment with strip file panels such as that shown in Figure B–6. Guide tabs at the sides of the panel are the primary dividers that indicate the range of the names on each panel.

Figure B–6 Visible Strip File Desk Stand

Visible card files also use signals or markers that call attention to some specific condition or content of a card. Signals (also called *flags*) that may be used with visible equipment include colored card stock, special printed edges that may be cut in various ways, and removable metal or plastic tabs of various colors and shapes. (See the signals shown on the record in Figure B–7).

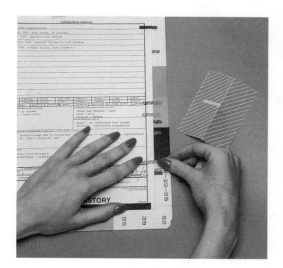

Figure B–7 Signals (Flags) Used to Call Attention to Specific Record Contents

Rotary (Wheel) Files

Two types of rotary files are used for storing card records: (1) manual rotary files and (2) motorized rotary files. Each is discussed in this section.

Manual Rotary Files

Manual rotary files provide an arrangement in which card records are attached directly to the equipment frame. Guides are snapped into place over a center rod, and the cards are kept within bounds by the outer rims of the wheel. Wheel files are shown in the compact rotary card file in Figure B–3 on page 366. The entire file is rotated by hand to locate the desired record.

Larger versions of manual rotary files, called *rotary file cabinets*, rotate horizontally around a hub as shown in Figure B–8. Several persons can access records at the same time when a rotary cabinet is placed between workstations. Fewer misfilings occur because fatigue, discomfort, and poor visibility (often found when using drawer cabinets) are reduced. Also, records need not be duplicated because one set of records can serve several departments; and sliding covers with locks are available on some models to provide security. Rotary files use the same kinds of vertical file supplies (cards, guides, signals) that have been specially designed for the equipment in which they will be stored. Additionally, records kept in such files require less floor space than would be needed to house the same number of records in drawer cabinets.

Figure B–8 Multitiered Rotary File with Shelf for Cards

Motorized Rotary Files

Motorized or *power-driven rotary files* provide shallow trays on movable shelves for storing card records. Because the shelves are powered by an electric motor, any shelf can be brought to the front of the machine by pressing one or more of a series of buttons mounted on a control panel. Figure B–9 illustrates such a motorized unit with trays of cards appearing in a horizontal side–by–side arrangement. The trays can be removed from the shelves, or the operator may reference the card records without removing any trays from the unit.

Figure B–9 Motorized Card Record Storage Unit

SPECIAL RECORDS

Special records are records of unconventional size, shape, or weight commonly used in business and professional offices. Such records often cause difficulty for the filer who does not have an effective procedure for storing these items so that they can be found quickly and also preserved for later use. Therefore, efficient storage procedures for each type of special record are needed and are discussed in the first part of this section. The second part briefly reviews storage and retrieval procedures for special records.

METHODS OF STORING SPECIAL RECORDS

Many of the special records discussed in this section are created because of the advances made in office technology. Automated offices produce large volumes of computer output that require special types of files, and imaging technology has created its own types of special records. Electronic and image records are discussed in Chapters 10 and 11, respectively.

Some records are considered *special* because they differ in size, shape, and construction from the regular office records and are stored in specialized equipment. How these records are stored is determined by the nature of the information, especially the manner by which the information is retrieved.

Accounting Records

Noncomputerized offices in small firms continue to use large numbers of records that are prepared by hand or by relatively simple machines. Records, such as cash receipts, journals, and ledgers, that store administrative information about the accounting system are vital to the survival of a small organization.

A **voucher** is an accounting record used to confirm that a business transaction has occurred. Vouchers are usually larger than checks but smaller than correspondence and are stored alphabetically or numerically in equipment the size of the vouchers. For example, 8″ by 5″ vouchers would be stored in drawers of a corresponding size near the user's workstation.

Drawings

Highly specialized departments in large organizations create and use a wide variety of nonstandard records. For example, art and advertising departments store posters, art prints, tracings, and other types of graphic art. Also, engineering departments commonly use blueprints, charts, maps, and other types of drawings, some of which are very large and bulky. Maps and engineering drawings are often rolled and stored in pigeonholes for convenience. However, this practice is not recommended because rolled records are difficult to use after they have been rolled for any length of time.

For storing large flat items, two alternatives are recommended: (1) placing the records in flat shallow drawers in cabinets made for this purpose, or (2) hanging the items vertically using hooks or clamps. Figure B–10 shows a type of flat-file cabinet commonly used for storing bulky records. The labels on the drawers can show the range of the contents, arranged either by alphabet or number.

Legal Documents

Records maintained in legal offices are on $8^{1}/_{2}$″ by 14″ paper. Legal-size paper is widely used for abstracts, affidavits, certificates of incorporation, contracts, insurance policies, leases, and mortgages. In addition to the use of legal-size vertical file cabinets, legal-size records may be stored in document boxes on open shelves. Numbers are assigned to the boxes, and an alphabetic index and an accession log are required as discussed in Chapter 8. These boxes are labeled appropriately to show their contents.

Figure B–10 Large Records Flat-File Cabinet

Magnetic Records

Many offices store information on a variety of magnetic media such as computer disks, CD-ROMs, laser disks, optical disks, data cartridges, data cassettes, videotape cassettes, and audio cassettes. Thorough coverage of these electronic records is presented in Chapter 10. Magnetic media may be labeled by subject, by originator, or by date. The contents of computer disks are usually identified by a label affixed to the flat plastic casing around the disk. Audio cassettes are usually labeled on their flat, broad surface as well as on the spine of the plastic container in which the cassette is stored. Videotape cassettes, data cartridges, and data cassettes usually have a label affixed to the spine of the outer casing of the media. CD-ROMs, laser disks, and optical disks are typically labeled on the spine of the container in which the media is placed in preparation for storage.

Storage equipment for magnetic media consists of drawers or files made of durable plastic or metal that protects the records from dust and moisture (see Figures B–11a and B–11b on page 376). Sturdy dividers or guides (usually plastic) hold the media in a position for reading the identifying content labels easily. A label attached to an outer surface of a container identifies the content of the magnetic media within the container. Special precautions should be taken to ensure that whatever storage method is used, these items are kept away from magnetic fields and static build-up that could have an adverse effect on the media.

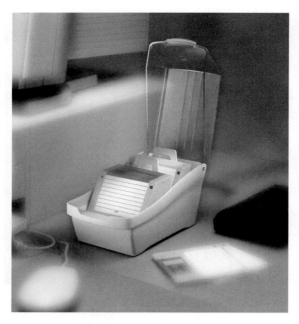

Figure B–11a Computer Disk Storage Unit

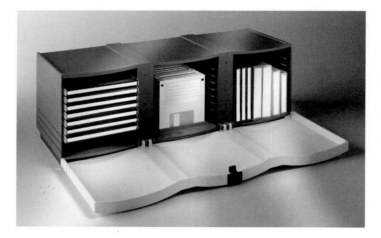

Figure B–11b Multimedia Storage Unit

Photographic Records

Cameras are used to photograph many types of records, some of which are highly specialized. However, only the most common photographic records are discussed here.

Films and Filmstrips

Motion-picture films are commonly placed in canisters that are stored vertically in open wire racks. The canisters may be stored alphabetically by subject or film title or numerically by film number. When a numeric storage system is used, an alphabetic index is required for reference to titles or subjects, and an accession log is necessary for assigning numbers.

Usually, filmstrips are placed in canisters and kept in cabinets with shallow drawers that have compartments formed by adjustable or fixed dividers. The top of a filmstrip container is labeled by subject, alphabetic title, or filmstrip number. Each drawer is labeled to show the range of its contents.

Slides

Slides are usually stored in boxes with compartments, or in ring binders. Rotary slide trays that fit on a projector may store in sequence all slides relating to one subject, with the tray being labeled to indicate the subject. Numbered slots in drawers in which slides may be stored correspond to numbers written on the slides.

Published Materials

The most common methods of storing published materials such as books, catalogs, periodicals, and pamphlets are discussed briefly in this section.

Books

To save office space and still provide convenient access, books should be stored in bookcases or on other types of shelves. Books may be arranged alphabetically by book titles, alphabetically by the names of their authors, or numerically by the decimal method. As a rule, books are labeled on the back binding or spine. Frequently used reference books such as dictionaries and reference manuals are kept at the workstations where they are used. Charge-out procedures, similar to the procedures used for other types of records discussed in Chapter 6, should be developed to ensure proper control over these important and expensive records.

Catalogs

Catalogs are best housed on shelves or in bookcases. A procedure that has proved effective for storing a large number of catalogs is to place the catalogs in alphabetic order by the names of the firms issuing the catalogs. Then prepare a separate subject index listing the names of all firms issuing catalogs on each specific subject. A small number of catalogs may be stored in folders by subject as shown in Figures 7–2a and 7–2b, pages 169 and 170.

Due to high mailing and printing costs, catalog supplements rather than entirely new catalogs may be sent to users. These supplements often contain only a few pages and are, therefore, quite flimsy; file folders are used for storage to provide the needed rigidity. When this practice is used, the folders are labeled according to the storage system used and stored next to the respective catalogs. When a new catalog is received, the old catalog is destroyed. Many vendors now provide on-line catalogs in addition to or instead of print catalogs.

Periodicals

Periodicals are magazines or other publications that are issued at regular recurring intervals. Current issues of magazines are usually kept in stacks and arranged in chronological order by date of publication, with the most recent issue on top. The stacks on the shelves are usually in alphabetic order by magazine name. Sturdy fiberboard or durable plastic boxes with open backs may also be used to house current issues to keep them from becoming worn and dusty (see Figure B–12). Some publishers sell boxes with the names of their magazines already printed on them, in which case only date information needs to be added to the label on the back of a box. These boxes are stored chronologically by date of publication.

Figure B–12 **Periodical File**

Pamphlets

Because they lack rigidity, pamphlets are stored in folders according to subject. The pamphlet folders are stored in alphabetic order by subject as well.

PROCEDURES FOR STORING AND RETRIEVING CARD AND SPECIAL RECORDS

Steps required to store and retrieve special records are the same steps needed to store and retrieve other manually processed records. However, special records have certain unusual features that more traditional records do not possess. These special features affect the procedures for storage and retrieval. In this section, an abbreviated discussion of storage and retrieval procedures is presented.

Inspecting

Inspecting special records requires much more time than does the inspection of paper records because the filer must check to see whether the record is in good condition and complete. Also, such a record should be inspected to be sure that it is clean, properly encased (if a protective cover is required), and that the record bears a cross-reference to its source if it is a partial copy or excerpt of an original.

Indexing

The indexing step requires carrying out the same procedures that are used to index and classify paper records. The filer analyzes the contents of the record to determine the filing segment for coding and storing.

Coding

Because of the wide variety of special records, coding procedures will vary. For example, coding could involve affixing a number on a film canister or affixing a label to the back of a book. The purpose of coding, however, is always the same—to facilitate accurate and efficient storage and retrieval.

Cross-Referencing

In some cases, special records do not require cross-references. Such records are unique and can be stored in only one place. If, however, a record is requested by an alternate name, by a subject, or by a number, a cross-reference should be prepared and inserted in the alphabetic index or a subject listing in the usual manner. Chapters 2 and 3 contain detailed information on cross-referencing procedures.

Sorting

If a number of special records of the same type must be stored, a separate sorting procedure will save time when the filer takes the records to the equipment to be stored. For instance, if 15 numbered filmstrip boxes need to be stored, arranging such boxes in their appropriate order on a carrying tray would save the filer time at the storage cabinet.

Storing

Special records should be stored as soon as possible after they are approved for storage. Because they are unusual and often bulky, special records may be unsightly and give a cluttered, inefficient appearance to an office if they are allowed to accumulate over long periods of time. Care must be taken to turn all special records of the same type in the same direction (covers of books facing forward and spines of magazines readable from the same direction, and so on). Because of the varying sizes of special records, as discussed earlier, large records frequently must be stored alongside small records. Thus, the filer needs to be alert to see that the smaller records do not get crushed among the larger ones.

Retrieving

The efficient retrieval of special records requires a charge-out and follow-up system that includes these steps:

1. Require a requisition form to be presented whenever a special record is removed from storage to be used by someone other than the filer.
2. Insert an OUT or IN USE indicator in place of a record removed from storage.

With this information on hand, the office manager or records manager knows where every record can be located, when it was taken from storage, and when it is due to be returned.

SELECTING EQUIPMENT AND SUPPLIES FOR CARD AND SPECIAL RECORDS FILES

Before equipment and supplies can be properly selected for *any* records file, the system in which the records are used, stored, and retrieved must be studied carefully. In such a study the records manager must ask questions such as the following to obtain information needed in decision making:

1. What kind of information is needed, and why is this information stored on cards (or special records)? Is a better type of record form or media available?
2. Who uses these records and how frequently?
3. How are the records used, stored, and retrieved?
4. What number of records is used presently and how many do you anticipate will be used in the future?
5. How many hours a day/month will the equipment be used and what supplies will be used?
6. What type of records protection and security is required?
7. How much space is available for the equipment and supplies?

The same sources of information used for selecting equipment and supplies, in general, can be used for selecting card and special record files.

CURRENT TRENDS IN RECORDS AND INFORMATION MANAGEMENT

In many offices, records that were once kept on cards are now stored on electronic or image media. For example, records such as customer, employee, or membership lists frequently are stored on image media such as computer disks or in dynamic databases because of the ease with which office workers can update and manipulate the record information. The need to key data into the computer more than once has been eliminated through the use of electronic and image media. Several different indexes, as well as mailing labels, can be created using the same inputted data by retrieving and manipulating the data into a useful format that is appropriate for the situation in which it will be used.

Organizations often keep track of their inventory on computer. In a manufacturing company, computers may be strategically placed in the plant or warehouse so that workers can easily access inventory records to determine the availability of a product and where that product is located. Many retail businesses use computers at checkout lanes, which allows inventory to be adjusted automatically as stock numbers are entered as part of a sales transaction.

Parts departments of auto dealerships and appliance stores now receive parts catalogs on microfiche or CD-ROM rather than the bulky catalogs they once received.

Card records that contain frequently called numbers, such as those in a desk rotary file, continue to be used because of ease of use and portability. (They can be used at various workstations without the aid of expensive or cumbersome equipment.) However, electronic and image media will gradually replace card records.

IMPORTANT TERMS

index record
posted record
rotary (wheel) equipment
signal

special records
vertical card file
visible card file
voucher

GLOSSARY

A

accession log – A serial list of numbers assigned to records in a numeric storage system; also called an *accession file* or *numeric file list*.

accuracy ratio – A measure of filers' ability to find requested records.

active record – A record needed to perform current operations. It is subject to frequent use and is usually located near the user. It can be accessed manually or on-line via a computer system. It is used three or more times a month.

activity ratio – A measure of frequency of records use.

alphabetic index – A list of correspondent names or subjects for a numeric file.

alphabetic records management – A systematic method of storing and arranging records according to the letters of the alphabet.

alphanumeric coding – A coding system that combines alphabetic and numeric characters.

aperture card – An electronic data processing card with a rectangular hole specifically designed as a carrier for a film image or images.

aperture card camera – A microfilm camera that records miniaturized images of engineering drawings or other large source documents on 35mm film frames that are premounted into tabulating-size cards.

archive record – A record that has continuing or historical value and is preserved permanently by an organization.

archives – Records created or received and accumulated by a person or organization in the course of the conduct of affairs and preserved because of their historical or continuing value. Also, the building or part of a building where archival materials are located.

ARMA International – A professional association dedicated to providing education, research, and networking opportunities to records and information management professionals.

ASCII – An acronym for the American Standard Code for Information Interchange. The code assigns specific numeric values to the first 128 characters of the 256 possible character combinations.

automatic records system – Any system that applies computer technology to any or all records management tasks such as the creation, collection, processing, maintenance, retrieval, use, storage, dissemination, and disposition of records.

B

bar code reader – A photoelectric scanner that translates bar code symbols into digital forms so that they can be read by a computer.

bellows folder – A folder that has a top flap and sides to enclose records in a case, with creases along its bottom and sides that allow it to expand like an accordion; also called an *expansion folder*.

blip code – An optical mark, usually rectangular, that has been recorded on microfilm, appearing below an image, used for counting images or frames automatically. Three different sizes can be used for subdividing documents.

block numeric coding – A coding system based on the assignment of groups of numbers to represent primary and secondary subjects.

C

call-back system – A records protection procedure requiring an individual requesting data from a computer system to hang up after making a telephone request and wait for the computer to call back.

caption – A title, heading, short explanation, or description of a document or records.

card record – A piece of card stock used for storing information that is referenced often.

career path – A typical route of advancement for workers on the job.

charge-out – A control procedure to establish the current location of a record when it is not in the records center or central file, which can be a manual or automated system.

charge-out and follow-up file – A tickler file that contains requisition forms filed by dates that records are due back in the inactive records center.

charge-out log – A written or electronic form used for recording what record was taken, when it was taken, who took it, the due date, the date it was returned, the date an overdue notice was sent, and if necessary, an extended due date.

chief information officer (CIO) – A high-level position in an organization where the person is responsible for all the information needs of the entire organization.

chronologic storage – Filing records by calendar date in reverse sequence (with the most recent date on top) or forward sequence (with the earliest date on top).

coding – The act of assigning a file designation to records as they are classified. For paper records, the physical marking of a record to indicate the name, number, or subject under which it is to be stored. When coding paper records, place a diagonal between units, underline the key unit, and number each succeeding unit.

color accenting – The consistent use of different colors for different supplies in a storage system—one color for guides, various colors for folders, one color for OUT indicators, and specific colors of labels or stripes on labels.

color coding – Using color as an identifying aid in a filing system.

compact disk–read-only memory (CD-ROM) – A high-density digital disk storage medium that can be read only. It is a magneto-optical disk that cannot be written on.

compact disk-recordable (CD-R) – A high-density digital disk that is a write-once medium.

compact disk-rewritable (CD-RW) – A high-density digital disk that is erasable.

computer output to laser disk (COLD) – A technique for the transfer of computer-generated output to optical disk so that it can be viewed or printed without use of the original program.

computer-assisted retrieval (CAR) systems – Systems that combine the document storage capabilities of micrographics with the indexing and retrieval capabilities of a computer database.

computer-input microform (CIM) – The process whereby computer input can be taken directly from microforms by scanning and character recognition.

computer-output microform (COM) – The process that converts and records data from a computer onto microfilm in human-readable format. Also called *computer-output microfilm.*

consecutive numbering method – A method of numbering records in the order received and arranging them from lowest to highest numbers.

constant data – Data that are preprinted on a form and do not require rewriting each time the form is filled in.

contact printing – A process that makes a duplicate copy of microfilm by placing the emulsion side of the developed original film in contact with the emulsion side of the copy film and directing a light beam through the original image to the copy.

control – To check or verify by comparison with a standard.

cost-benefit ratio – A comparison used to determine that every cost originated (input) results in an equal or greater benefit (output).

cross-reference – A notation in a file or list showing that a record has been stored elsewhere; an entry directing attention to one or more related items.

cross-reference guide – A special guide that serves as a permanent marker in storage indicating that all records pertaining to a particular name are stored in a different location.

cross-reference sheet – A sheet placed in an alternate file location that directs the filer to a specific record stored in a different location.

D

data – Groups of characters that represent a specific value or condition.

data warehouse – A collection of data designed to support management decision making.

database – A collection of related data stored on a computer system that can be manipulated or extracted for use with various applications but managed independently of them. Databases are organized especially for rapid search and retrieval of specific facts or information.

decimal-numeric coding – A method of coding records numerically in units of ten.

density – The degree of optical opacity of material that determines the amount of light that will pass through it or reflect from it.

densitometer – A device used to measure the contrast between the dark and light areas of microfilm.

destruction date file – A tickler file containing copies of forms completed when records are received in a records center.

destruction file – A file that contains information on the actual destruction of inactive records.

destruction notice – A notification (memo, listing, form, etc.) of the scheduled destruction of records.

destruction suspension – A hold placed on the scheduled destruction of records that may be relevant to foreseeable or pending litigation, governmental investigation, audit, or special organizational requirements.

dictionary arrangement – An arrangement of records in alphabetic order (A–Z) by a major subject or geographic division.

digital audiotape (DAT) – A type of magnetic tape used for data backup, archiving, and audio recording.

digital signature – A string of characters and numbers added as a code on electronic documents being transmitted by computer; also called *e-signature*.

digital videodisk (DVD) – A read-only optical storage medium that stores approximately 130 minutes of full-motion video. Also called *digital versatile disk*.

direct access – A system of records management that permits access to the files without reference to an index or other filing aid.

directory – A subdivision of a disk created using the operating system of a computer.

disaster – An emergency event that results in conditions that require resources beyond the organization's abilities. Disasters result in significant financial loss.

disaster recovery plan – A written and approved course of action to take when disaster strikes, ensuring an organization's ability to respond to an interruption in services by restoring critical business functions.

document imaging – An automated system for scanning, storing, retrieving, and managing paper records in an electronic format.

duplex-numeric coding – A coding system using numbers (or sometimes letters) with two or more parts separated by a dash, space, or comma.

E

efficiency control – A method for evaluating the ability to produce a desired effect with a minimum of time, energy, and space.

efficiency ratio – A standard for measuring the efficiency of various aspects of records systems.

electronic data interchange (EDI) – The computer-to-computer transmission of records in a standardized, computer-readable format.

electronic document management system (EDMS) – A management control system used to regulate the creation, use, and maintenance of electronically created documents. This system links paper, image, and electronic documents into one flexible and expandable document management system (DMS).

electronic mail (e-mail) – A system that enables users to compose, transmit, receive, and manage electronic documents and images across networks.

electronic record – Data stored on electronic media that can be readily accessed or changed. A piece of equipment is required to view and read electronic records.

emergency – An unplanned adverse event that requires organization personnel to initiate activities to secure operations or protect assets from harm. Emergencies do not usually result in major losses.

encryption – The process of converting meaningful information into a numeric code that is only understood by the intended recipient of the information; any procedure used in cryptography to prevent unauthorized use.

encyclopedic arrangement – A filing arrangement in which broad main subject titles or geographic divisions are arranged in alphabetic order with subdivisions arranged alphabetically under the title to which they relate.

external record – A record created for use outside a firm. Examples of such records are letters or faxes sent to a customer or client.

F

facsimile (fax) machine – An electronic means for transferring an exact reproduction of an image using telephone lines. The image is scanned by the transmitter and reconstructed at the receiving station.

field – A set of one or more characters treated as a unit of information in a database. The combination of characters forms words, numbers, or a meaningful code. A database element that is part of a record.

filename – A unique name given to a file stored for computer use that must follow the computer's operating system rules.

filing (storage) method – The way records are stored in a container. The four major methods are alphabetic, subject, numeric, and geographic.

filing segment – The name by which a record is stored and requested.

filmer/scanner – A microfilm camera that can also operate as a scanner; sometimes called a *camera/scanner* or *scanner/filmer*.

findability – An indication of how quickly and accurately records can be located.

fine sorting – Arranging records in the exact order of the filing system in which they will be placed.

firewall – A combination hardware and software buffer that many organizations place between their internal networks and the Internet to protect the internal network from outside intrusion.

floppy disk – A flat disk (housed in a paper or plastic enclosure) with magnetic coating that magnetically stores data; also called a *diskette*.

folder – A container used to hold and protect the contents of a file together and separate from other files. Folders are usually made of heavy material such as manila, Kraft, plastic, or pressboard and can have either top or side tabs in varying sizes. Also, a subdivision of a disk created using the operating system of a computer.

follower block – A device at the back of a file drawer that can be moved to allow contraction or expansion of the drawer contents; also called a *compressor*.

follow-up – A system for assuring the timely and proper return of materials charged out from a file.

form – A fixed arrangement of predetermined spaces designed for entering and extracting prescribed information on a paper or electronic document.

G

general folder – A folder for records to and from correspondents with a small volume that does not require an individual folder.

geographic records management – A method of storing and retrieving records in alphabetic order by location of an individual, an organization, or a project.

guide – A rigid divider with a projecting tab to identify a section in a file and to facilitate reference to a particular record location.

H

hard copy – A printed copy of a record that can be read without use of mechanical assistance.

hard disk – A thin, rigid metal platter covered with a substance that holds data in the form of magnetized spots.

hierarchical storage management (HSM) – A data storage management strategy in which HSM software is used to separate active and inactive computer data by migrating files between primary and secondary storage media.

hybrid imaging system – A system that contains mixed components of other systems. It integrates microfilm-based images with electronic image processing technologies.

I

image record – A digital or photographic representation of a record on any medium such as microfilm or optical disk.

image system – A combination of procedures and equipment that forms an efficient unit for creating and using records in microform or electronic images.

important records – Records that assist in performing a firm's business operations and, if destroyed, are replaceable, but only at great cost.

inactive record – A record that does not have to be readily available, but which must be kept for legal, fiscal, or historical purposes; referred to less than fifteen times a year.

inactive records index – An index of all records in the inactive records storage center.

index – A systematic guide that allows access to specific items contained within a larger body of information.

index record – A card record that contains information used for reference only.

indexing – The mental process of determining the filing segment (or name) by which a record is to be stored, or the placing or listing of items in an order that follows a particular system.

indexing order – The order in which units of the filing segment are considered when a record is stored.

indexing rules – Written procedures that describe how the filing segments are ordered.

indexing units – The various words that make up the filing segment.

indirect access – A system of records management that requires the use of an index to locate a record.

individual folder – A folder used to store the records of an individual correspondent with enough records to warrant a separate folder.

information – Data that has been given value through analysis, interpretation, or compilation into a meaningful form.

input – To enter data into a computer system. Also, the data being entered.

inspecting – The first step in the storage procedure, in which a record is checked for its readiness to be filed.

internal record – A record that contains information needed to operate a firm. Such a record may be created inside or outside an organization.

Internet – A worldwide network of computers that allows public access to send, store, and receive electronic information.

J

job description – A summary of the content and essential requirements of a specific job.

jukebox – A storage device that holds optical disks or tapes and has one or more drives that provide automatic

on-line access to the information contained in the device. Also known as an *autochanger*.

K

key unit – The first unit of the filing segment.

knowledge management – The effective management and use of an organization's knowledge resources, including the knowledge and experience of its employees.

L

label – A device that contains the name of the subject or number given to the file folder contents. It may have other pertinent information, be color-coded to denote its place in an overall filing system, or have a bar code.

lateral file cabinet – Storage equipment that is wider than it is deep; records are accessed from the side (horizontally). Files can be arranged front to back or side to side.

leading zero – A zero added to the front of a number so that all numbers align on the right and will be sorted correctly by a computer.

lettered guide plan – An arrangement of geographic records with primary guides labeled with alphabetic letters.

light pen – An input device used for writing or sketching on a display screen.

local area network (LAN) – A data communication network intended to allow several computers, connected through one computer within a geographic area, to share data and software.

location name guide plan – An arrangement of geographic records with primary guides labeled with location names.

M

magnetic media – A variety of magnetically coated materials used by computers for data storage, e.g., card, cartridge, cassette, floppy disk, hard disk, magnetic tape, etc.

magnetic tape – A long strip of polyester film coated with magnetizable recording material, capable of storing information in the form of electromagnetic signals.

magnetic tape cassette – A storage device consisting of two plastic spools of magnetic tape, a supply spool and a take-up spool, contained in a plastic case.

magneto-optical (MO) disk – A rewritable optical disk on which information is recorded and read by laser and stored magnetically.

magnification ratio – A method of describing the relationship between the size of an image and the original record when viewed on a microfilm reader screen. Also called the *enlargement ratio*.

management – The process of using an organization's resources to achieve specific goals through the functions of planning, organizing, leading, and controlling.

master index – A printed alphabetic listing of all subjects in file order.

media compatibility – How well the media and the equipment needed to access information stored on the media work together.

media stability – The length of time the media will maintain its original quality so that it can continue to be used.

metadata – Data about data. Metadata describes how, when, and by whom a particular set of data was collected, and how the data is formatted.

microfiche – A microform in the shape of a rectangular sheet having one or more microimages arranged in a grid pattern with a heading area across the top.

microfilm – A photographic reproduction of a document greatly reduced in size from the original on fine grain, high-resolution film that requires a reader for viewing.

microfilm drive (M drive) – A computer peripheral device that retrieves and digitizes microimages for display on a personal computer to which it is connected.

microfilm jacket – A flat, transparent, plastic carrier with single or multiple film channels made to hold single or multiple film strips.

microfilm processor – A mechanical device that applies heat and chemical treatments to make microimages visible for display, printing, or other purposes.

microform projector – A device that magnifies microimages for display on a wall or wall-mounted screen.

microform reader – An optical device for viewing a projected and enlarged microimage. The image is displayed on a screen for reading.

microform viewer – A hand-held magnifier for microfiche, microfilm jackets, or aperture cards.

microforms – The collective term for all microimages such as microfilm, microfiche, aperture card, microfilm jacket, microfilm roll, or microfilm strip.

micrographics – The technology by which recorded information can be quickly reduced to a microform, stored conveniently, and then easily retrieved for reference and use.

middle-digit storage – A numeric storage method that uses the middle two or three digits of each number as the primary division under which a record is filed.

migration – The process of moving data from one electronic system to another, usually in upgrading hardware and software, without having to undergo a major conversion or re-inputting of data.

mobile aisle system – Rows of shelving used for compact storage, situated on wheel-fitted carriages that travel on tracks and allow one or more aisles to be opened to access the system.

mobile shelving – A series of shelving units that move on tracks attached to the floor for access to files.

modem – A device that converts digital data from a computer to an analog signal that can be transmitted over an ordinary telephone line. The process is reversed at the receiving end.

motorized rotary storage – A unit that rotates shelves in the unit around a central hub to bring the files to the operator.

mouse – A hand-driven device used to select and point on a computer screen by moving the device on a flat surface.

N

name index – A listing of correspondents' names stored in a subject file. Includes the name and address of each correspondent, as well as the subject under which each name is stored.

nearline – A secondary storage device in which data can be retrieved rapidly, but slower than on-line computer storage.

network – A group of computers connected to each other by communication lines to share information and resources.

nonconsecutive numbering – A system of numbers that has blocks of numbers omitted and arranges records in a sequential order that differs from a consecutive order of numbers normally read from left to right.

nonessential records – Records that have no predictable value to the organization after their initial use and should be destroyed after use.

nonrecord – An item that is not usually included within the scope of official records, such as a convenience file, day file, reference materials, drafts, etc. These records are not required to be retained and do not appear on a records retention schedule.

numeric index – A current list of all files by the file numbers. Shows the numbers assigned to subject titles.

numeric records management – A systematic arrangement of records according to numbers.

O

office of record – An office designated to maintain the *record* or *official* copy of a particular record in an organization.

official record – A significant, vital, or important record of continuing value to be protected, managed, and retained according to established retention schedules. It is often, but not necessarily, an original. In law, an official record has the legally recognized and judicially enforceable quality of establishing some fact.

off-site storage – A potentially secure location, remote from the primary location, at which inactive or vital records are stored. Sometimes called *remote storage*.

on-call form – A written request for a record that is out of the file. Also called a *wanted* form.

on-site storage – Storage of inactive (usually) records on the premises of an organization.

one-period transfer method – A method of transferring records from active storage at the end of one period of time, usually once or twice a year, to inactive storage.

operating system – An organized collection of software that controls the overall operations of a computer. It is the link between the computer hardware, the user, and the application software.

optical card – A small electronic device about the size of a credit card that contains electronic memory and possibly an imbedded integrated circuit.

optical character recognition (OCR) – Machine-reading of printed or written characters through the use of light-sensitive materials or devices.

optical disk – A platter-shaped disk coated with optical recording material. A high-density information storage medium where digitally encoded information is both written and read by means of a laser.

OUT folder – A special folder used to replace a complete folder that has been removed from storage.

OUT guide – A special guide used to replace any record that has been removed from storage and to indicate what was taken and by whom.

OUT indicator – A control device that shows the location of borrowed records.

OUT sheet – A form that is inserted in place of a record removed from a folder.

output – The machine-readable or human-readable data produced by a computer.

password – A string of characters known to the computer system and a user, who must specify it to gain access to the system.

periodic transfer method – A method of transferring active records at the end of a stated period, usually one year, to inactive storage.

permanent cross-reference – A guide with a tab in the same position as the tabs on the individual folder and placed in a location that is frequently assumed to be the location of that folder. The caption on the tab of the permanent cross-reference consists of the name by which the cross-reference is filed, the word SEE, and the name by which the correspondence folder may be found.

perpetual transfer method – A method of transferring records continually from active to inactive storage areas whenever they are no longer needed for reference. Records are removed from current files into inactive storage sites on a scheduled basis.

personal digital assistant (PDA) – A handheld computer controlled by a pen similar to a stylus.

pick list – A list containing specific records needed for a given program or project.

planetary camera – A microfilm camera that uses 35mm microfilm to film large engineering drawings, hardbound books, and other large documents.

pocket folder – A folder with partially enclosed sides and more expansion at the bottom than an ordinary folder.

position – The location of the tab across the top or down the side of a guide or folder.

posted record – A record that contains information that is continually updated; also called a *secondary record*.

primary guide – A divider that identifies a main division or section of a file and that always precedes all other material in a section.

query – A database object used to instruct the program to find specific information.

reader/printer – A microform reader with the added capability of reproducing an enlarged microimage in hard copy.

reader/scanner – A microform reader that combines the capabilities of a reader and an image digitizer. It produces electronic document images from magnified microimages. Also called a *digital microimage workstation*.

record – Stored information, regardless of media or characteristics, made or received by an organization, that is evidence of its operations and that has value requiring its retention for a specific period of time. Also, a database element, part of a table, containing all the fields related to one person or topic.

record copy – The official copy of a record that is retained for legal, operational, or historical purposes; sometimes the original.

record life cycle – The life span of a record, as expressed in the five phases of creation, distribution, use, maintenance, and final disposition.

records and information management (RIM) – The company-wide controls over staff, equipment, and services that generate and maintain information. A term that places emphasis on the role of information in the records management field.

records audit – A periodic inspection to verify that an operation is in compliance with the records management program.

records center – A low-cost centralized area for housing and servicing inactive records whose reference rate does not warrant their retention in prime office space.

records center box – A box, usually made of corrugated cardboard, that is designed to hold approximately one cubic foot (12 inches high by 12 inches wide by 12 inches deep) of records, either legal or letter size.

records destruction – The disposal of records of no further value by incineration, maceration, pulping, or shredding. Complete obliteration of a record beyond any possible reconstitution.

records disposition – The final destination of records after they have reached the end of their retention period in active and/or inactive storage; they may be transferred to an archives for retention or be destroyed.

records inventory – A detailed listing that could include the types, locations, dates, volumes, equipment, classification systems, and usage data of an organization's records.

records management – The systematic control of all records from their creation or receipt, through their processing, distribution, organization, storage, and retrieval, to their ultimate disposition.

records management manual – A manual containing all information necessary to manage the records and information program in an organization; e.g., policy statement, records retention schedules, procedures, vital records procedures, records inventories, etc.

records retention program – A program established and maintained to provide retention periods for records in an organization.

records retention schedule – A comprehensive list of records series titles, indicating for each series the length of time it is to be maintained. It may include retention in active office areas, inactive storage areas, and when and if such series may be destroyed or formally transferred to another entity such as an archives for historical purposes.

records series – A group of related records filed and used together as a unit and evaluated as a unit for retention purposes.

records system – A group of interrelated resources—people, equipment and supplies, space, procedures and information—acting together according to a plan to accomplish the goals of the records management program.

records transfer – The act of changing the physical custody of records with or without change of legal title. Relocating records from one storage area to another.

reduction ratio – The relationship between the dimensions of the original or master and the corresponding dimensions of the photographed image.

redundant array of independent disks (RAID) – A computer storage system consisting of over 100 hard disk drives contained in a single cabinet that send data simultaneously to a computer over parallel paths.

reference document – A record that contains information needed to carry on the operations of a firm over long periods of time. Common reference documents are business letters, reports, and interoffice memoranda.

relative index – A dictionary-type listing of all possible words and combinations of words by which records may be requested.

release mark – An agreed-upon mark such as initials or a symbol placed on a record to show that the record is ready for storage.

requisition – A written request for a record or for information from a record.

resolution – A measure of the sharpness or fine detail of an image.

retention period – The length of time that records must be kept according to operational, legal, regulatory, and fiscal requirements.

retrieval – The process of locating and withdrawing a record from a filing system or records center. Also, the action of accessing information from stored data on a computer system.

retrieval efficiency ratio – A measure of the speed with which records are found that verifies how filers spend their time.

rotary camera – A microfilm camera that uses rotating belts to carry documents through the camera and makes images on 16mm film at a speed of over 500 documents a minute.

rotary equipment – Filing equipment in which card records are attached to a frame that rotates on an axis like a wheel. Also called *wheel equipment*.

rough sorting – Arranging records in approximately the same order as the filing system in which they will be placed.

S

scanner – A device that converts an image of a document to electronic form for processing and storage.

score marks – Indented or raised lines or series of marks along the bottom edge of a folder to allow for expansion.

SEE ALSO cross-reference – A notation on folder tabs or sheets of paper that directs the filer to multiple locations for related information.

shelf file – Open-shelving equipment in which records are accessed horizontally from the open side.

signal – A special marker used for drawing immediate attention to a specific record.

sorter – A device used to arrange records into alphabetic or numeric categories and to hold records temporarily prior to storage.

sorting – The arrangement of records in the sequence in which they are to be filed or stored.

special folder – A folder that follows an auxiliary or special guide in an alphabetic arrangement.

special guide – A divider used to lead the eye quickly to a specific place in a file. Also called *auxiliary guide*.

special records – Records of unconventional size, shape, or weight commonly used in business and professional offices.

staggered arrangement – A system that follows a series of several different positions of folder tabs from left to right according to a set pattern.

standards – A complete and well-defined set of published rules pertaining to a certain subject.

step-and-repeat camera – A microfilm camera that produces a series of separate images, usually in orderly rows and columns. It uses 16mm and 35mm microfilm to produce microfiche.

storage – The actual placement of records, according to a plan, into a folder, on a shelf, or in a file drawer, or electronically saving a record to a disk.

storage area network (SAN) – A high-speed network that provides fast, reliable access among computers and independent storage devices.

storage (filing) method – A systematic way of storing records according to an alphabetic, subject, numeric, geographic, or chronologic arrangement.

storage procedures – A series of steps for the orderly arrangement of records as required by a specific storage method or records management system.

storing – The act of placing records into storage containers.

straight-line arrangement – A system that aligns folder tabs in one position; for example, all folder tabs are third position.

subject records management – An alphabetic system of storing and retrieving records by their subject or topic.

subsystem – Groupings of interrelated components that accomplish one phase of a task.

suspension folder – A folder with built-in hooks on each side that hang from parallel metal rails on each side of a file drawer or other storage equipment. Also called *hanging folder*.

system – A regularly interacting or interdependent group of components forming a unified whole.

T

tab – A projection for a caption on a folder or guide that extends above the regular height or beyond the regular width of the folder or guide.

tab cut – The length of the tab expressed as a proportion of the width or height of the folder or guide.

table – A database element containing a group of records related to one subject or topic.

terminal-digit storage – A numeric storage method in which the last two or three digits of each number are used as the primary division under which a record is filed.

tickler file – A date-sequenced file by which matters pending are flagged for attention on the proper date. Also called *suspense file* and *pending file*.

trackball – A ball that is mounted usually in a computer console so as to be partially exposed and is rotated to control the movement of a cursor on a display screen.

transaction document – A record used in a firm's day-to-day operations. Transaction documents consist primarily of business forms such as invoices, requisitions, purchase orders, bank statements, and contracts.

unit record – A record that contains one main item or piece of information.

useful records – Records that are helpful in conducting business operations and may, if destroyed, be replaced at slight cost.

variable data – Data that change each time a form is filled in.

vertical card file – A collection of card records stored on edge or in an upright position; also known as a *vertical file*.

vertical file cabinet – Conventional storage equipment that is deeper than it is wide and has files arranged front to back.

videotape – A magnetic tape on which visual images are electronically recorded, with or without sound.

virus – A computer program that replicates itself into other programs that are shared among systems with the intention of causing damage.

visible card file – A collection of records stored horizontally in an overlapping arrangement in which the bottom margin of each card is visible when the card is held and pulled out from the file cabinet; also known as a *visible file*.

vital records – Records, usually irreplaceable, which are necessary to the continued operation of an organization.

voucher – An accounting record used to confirm that a business transaction has occurred.

wide area network (WAN) – A high-speed data transmission network that links mainframe computers, personal computers, etc., located in geographic places more than one mile apart, allowing user groups to share computer data and software.

World Wide Web – A worldwide hypermedia system (a network of networks containing hyperlinks) that allows browsing in many databases; the multimedia center of the Internet.

INDEX

inspecting, 118-119; in a subject records system, 178; special records, 379

Institute of Certified Records Managers (ICRM), 360

institutions, indexing of, 55

integrated image systems, 305-309

intelligent agents, 275

internal record, 4

Internal Revenue Service Revenue Procedures, 13: Revenue Procedure 81-46 for microfilm records, 13; Revenue Procedure 91-50 for computer-based systems, 13; Revenue Procedure 97-22 for electronic imaging, 13

International Organization for Standardization (ISO), 317, 318

Internet, 10; as reference for government information, 62

inventory, records, 133-138, 321

inventory, records worksheet, illus., 136

ISO (International Organization for Standardization), 317, 318

ISO 9000 guidelines, 317-318

jacket, microfilm, 287-288, illus., 288

job description, 350; records center supervisor, 354; records clerk, 351; records manager, 356

job in records management: illus., 19; managerial level, 353-358; operating level, 349-350; supervisory level, 350-353

jukebox, 253

key unit, 29

knowledge management, 11, 317

labels, 108-111; bar code, on a label, 110; caption, on a label, 108; caption, preprinted, illus., 110; color-coded, illus., 196; container, 108; folder, 109; guide, 108-109, illus., 172; media, illus., 193; subject folder, illus., 173

LAN (local area network), 248

large business environment, information professionals in, 346-347

large records flat file cabinet, illus., 375

laser disk, computer output to, 253, 308

lateral file cabinet, 92, illus., 92

law office jobs, 347

leading zero, 82

legal documents, storing, 374

legal value of records, 6

letter, properly released and coded, illus., 121

lettered guide plan, dictionary storage arrangement of geographic records, 223-224; encyclopedic storage arrangement of geographic records, 227-228

life cycle of records, 14

light pen, 259

local area network (LAN), 248

local government, alphabetic indexing, 60

location name guide plan, dictionary storage arrangement of geographic records, 224-225; encyclopedic storage arrangement of geographic records, 228-230

location of records management in a large organization, 17

log, accession, 196; illus., 197

lost records, 127-128

Lycos infoplease.com, 62

machine-readable record, 246

magnetic media, 248-252

magnetic records, storing, 375

magnetic tape cassette, 251

magneto-optical disk, 253

magneto-optical disk drive and cartridge, illus., 254

magnification ratio, of microfilm image, 291

mail, electronic (e-mail), 9, 266-267; confidentiality of, 273; retention of, 266

management, 2, 14

managerial level, job description, 353, 356-357; personal characteristics and education/work experience required, 357

manual, records management, 320-321

manual tickler file, illus., 125

master, 309

master index, 175; for geographic records storage, 230-231

media: compatibility, 264-265; stability, 265; magnetic, 248-252; optical, 252-256; types of electronic, 248-256

medical office jobs, 347-348

metadata, 266

microfiche, 286-287, illus., 287; storage, illus., 302

microfilm, 284; cartridges, illus., 285; drive (M drive), 305; jackets, 287-288, illus., 288; procedures and equipment, 291-298; processing and duplicating equipment, 298-300; quality of, 289; reader/printer, illus., 305; reels, illus., 285; sizes of, 289

microform projector, 304; reader, 304; viewer, 304

microforms, 281; types of, 284-288; storage and retrieval, 300-305

micrographics, 282; advantages of, 282; examples of uses in business, 282-283; lifespan of, 309

middle-digit storage, 208-210

migration, 265

minor words in business names, alphabetic indexing of, 32

misfiled records, 127-128

mobile aisle system, illus., 94

mobile shelving, 94; side-to-side, illus., 94

modem, 259

modern records, 8

motorized card record storage unit, illus., 373

motorized rotary storage, 95

mouse, 259

multicopy forms, 332

multimedia storage unit, illus., 376

National Business Forms Association (NBFA), 359

nearline, 254

network, 248; local area, 248; wide area, 248

network security, in an electronic records system, 270-273

nonconsecutive numbering methods, 206-210

nonessential record, 5, 138

nonrecord, 134

no-walk carousels, illus., 95

numbered folders, 194

numbered guides, 194

numbers, in business names, indexing of, 53-54

numeric coding systems, 210-212: alphanumeric coding, 212; block numeric coding, 210; decimal-numeric coding, 211; duplex-numeric coding, 211

numeric index, 178

numeric method: alphabetic file, coded correspondence, illus., 201; numbered file, coded correspondence, illus., 200

numeric records management, 190

numeric records storage, consecutive numbering method, 192; nonconsecutive numbering method, 206; overview, 190-191; reasons for using, 191; uses of in business, 191-192

one-fifth cut file folder, illus., 102

one-period transfer method, 150

one-third cut file folder, illus., 102

on-site storage, 147

operating level, career path, 350; job description, 351-352; personal characteristics, education/work experience required, 352

operating system, 83

optical card, 255

optical character recognition (OCR), 258

optical disk, 252

optical media, 252-256

oral records, 3

order, indexing, 30

organization chart, illus., 349

organizations, indexing of, 55

organizing folders and files, 84

OUT folder, 108; illus., 107

OUT guide, 106-107

OUT indicator, 106; disposing of, 144; use of in charge-out procedures, 144; use of in subject records systems, 174

OUT sheet, 108; illus., 107

output, 256, 261

P

pamphlets, storing, 377

paper selection, 328

Paperwork Reduction Act of 1980, 13

particles, indexing of, 52

password, 272

PDA (personal digital assistant), 260

performance control, 324, 328

periodic transfer method, 150

periodical file, illus., 378

periodicals, storing, 378

permanent cross-reference, 122

perpetual transfer method, 149

PHOTO CREDITS

PART 1: THE FIELD OF RECORDS MANAGEMENT
page 1, top center: © Myrleen Ferguson/PhotoEdit
page 1, bottom left: © 2001/PhotoDisc, Inc.

Chapter 1: Records Management in Review
page 4, Fig 1-1a: © Kevin R. Morris/CORBIS
page 4, Fig 1-1b: Photo courtesy of Bell & Howell, Imaging
page 4, Fig 1-1c: SEMCO, Inc.
page 7: © 2001/PhotoDisc, Inc.
page 8, Fig 1-2: © 2001/PhotoDisc, Inc.

PART 2: ALPHABETIC STORAGE AND RETRIEVAL
page 25, top center: © Terry Vine/Tony Stone Images

Chapter 3: Alphabetic Indexing Rules 6-10
page 52: © Hans Peter Merten/Tony Stone Images

Chapter 4: Alphabetic Indexing Rules for Computer
   Applications
page 77: Sourcelight Technologies, Inc.
page 84: © David Young-Wolff/PhotoEdit

Chapter 5: Alphabetic Records Management
page 92, Fig 5-1a: The HON Company
page 92, Fig 5-1b: The HON Company
page 93, Fig 5-1c: The HON Company
page 93, Fig 5-1d: Courtesy of TAB Products Co.
page 94, Fig 5-2a: Adjustable Shelving's White Aisle-Saver
page 94, Fig 5-2b: Adjustable Shelving's White Aisle-Saver
page 95, Fig 5-3a: White Systems, Inc.
page 95, Fig 5-3b: White Systems, Inc.
page 99, Fig. 5-6: Courtesy of Esselte Corporation
page 105, Fig 5-12: Courtesy of Esselte Corporation
page 106, Fig 5-14: The HON Company
page 107, Fig 5-15a: Courtesy of TAB Products Co.
page 107, Fig 5-15b: Courtesy of TAB Products Co.
page 109, Fig 5-16a: Colorflex
page 109, Fig 5-16b: Colorflex
page 110, Fig 5-17a: Photography by Erik Von
   Fischer/Photonics
page 110, Fig 5-17b: Labels supplied by Engineered Data
   Products, Inc.
page 115, Fig 5-19: Courtesy of Esselte Corporation
page 117, Fig 5-20: Courtesy of TAB Products Co.
page 118, Fig 5-21, both photos: The Smead Manufacturing
   Company

Chapter 6: Records Retention, Retrieval, and Transfer
page 145: White Systems, Inc.
page 149: © Michael Newman/PhotoEdit
page 152, Fig 6-7, both photos: Fellowes Manufacturing
page 156, Fig 6-8: ZASIO Versatile Enterprise. ZASIO. 15
   August 2000. http://www.zasio.com/WhatRMSee.Htm

**PART 3: SUBJECT, NUMERIC, AND GEOGRAPHIC
STORAGE AND RETRIEVAL**
page 161, top center: © Roger Ressmeyer/CORBIS
page 161, bottom left: © First Light/CORBIS

Chapter 7: Subject Records Management
page 173, bottom: The Smead Manufacturing Company

Chapter 8: Numeric Records Management
page 193, Fig 8-1: Courtesy of Dataware® Labels
page 196, Fig 8-3: Courtesy of Ames Safety Envelope Company

Chapter 9: Geographic Records Management
page 221: © Ron Dahlquist/SuperStock

PART 4: RECORDS MANAGEMENT TECHNOLOGY
page 245, top center: © 2001/PhotoDisc, Inc.
page 245, bottom left: © Chigmaroff/Davidson/SuperStock

Chapter 10: Electronic Records
page 247: © Premium Stock/CORBIS
page 250, Fig 10-1: Courtesy of Iomega Corporation
page 251, Fig 10-2: Maxell Corporation of America
page 252, Fig 10-3: Dell Computer Corporation
page 254, Fig 10-4: Pinnacle Micro, Inc.
page 255, Fig 10-5, both photos: Gemplus S.A.
page 258, Fig 10-6: Canon, USA
page 260, Fig 10-7: Palm, Inc.
page 268, Fig 10-8, both photos: Fellowes Manufacturing

Chapter 11: Image Records
page 285, Fig 11-1a: © Bill Aron/PhotoEdit
page 285, Fig 11-1b: Photo courtesy of Bell & Howell,
   Imaging
page 288, Fig 11-3: Photo courtesy of Bell & Howell, Imaging
page 296, Fig 11-7: Photo courtesy of Bell & Howell, Imaging
page 297, Fig 11-8: Photo courtesy of Bell & Howell, Imaging
page 298, Fig 11-9: Canon, USA
page 301, Fig 11-10: Microfilm storage products – Russ Bassett
   Media Storage Solutions
page 302, Fig 11-11: Courtesy of Luxor Corporation
page 305, Fig 11-12: Photo courtesy of Bell & Howell,
   Imaging

PART 5: RECORDS CONTROL
page 315, top center: The Smead Manufacturing Company
page 315, bottom left: © 2001/PhotoDisc, Inc.

Chapter 12: Controlling the Records and Information
   Management Program
page 323: © Deborah Davis/PhotoEdit
page 331, Fig 12-3: Adams Business Forms Inc.

APPENDICES
Appendix A: Records Management Career Opportunities and
   Job Descriptions
page 347, Fig A-1: © Bill Bachmann/PhotoEdit

Appendix B: Card and Special Records
page 365, Fig B-1: Fellowes Manufacturing
page 365, Fig B-2: Kardex Systems, Inc.
page 367, Fig B-4: Photography by Erik Von
   Fischer/Photonics
page 369, Fig B-5a: Kardex Systems, Inc.
page 371, Fig B-6: Kardex Systems, Inc.
page 371, Fig B-7: Courtesy of Ames Safety Envelope
   Company
page 372, Fig B-8: Datum Filing Systems, Inc.
page 373, Fig B-9: Kardex Systems, Inc.
page 375, Fig B-10: Safco Products Company
page 376, Fig B-11a: Fellowes Manufacturing
page 376, Fig B-11b: Fellowes Manufacturing
page 378, Fig B-12: Fellowes Manufacturing